Race Harmony and Black Progress

Jack Woofter and the Interracial Cooperation Movement

Mark Ellis

INDIANA UNIVERSITY PRESS
Bloomington and Indianapolis

This book is a publication of

Indiana University Press
Office of Scholarly Publishing
Herman B Wells Library 350
1320 East 10th Street
Bloomington, Indiana 47405 USA

iupress.indiana.edu

Telephone orders   800-842-6796
Fax orders   812-855-7931

Library of Congress Cataloging-in-Publication Data

Ellis, Mark, [date]-
    Race harmony and black progress : Jack Woofter and the interracial
cooperation movement / Mark Ellis.
        pages cm
    Includes bibliographical references and index.
    ISBN 978-0-253-01059-9 (cl : alk. paper) — ISBN 978-0-253-01066-7
(eb) 1. Woofter, Thomas Jackson, 1893-1972. 2. Alexander, Will Winton,
1884-1956. 3. Jones, Thomas Jesse, 1873-1950. 4. Odum, Howard
Washington, 1884-1954. 5. Commission on Interracial Cooperation.
6. Southern States—Race relations—History—20th century. 7. African
Americans—Southern States—Social conditions—20th century.
8. Sociologists—United States—Biography. I. Title.
    E185.98.W66E55 2013
    301.092—dc23
    [B]
                                                        2013019196

1 2 3 4 5 18 17 16 15 14 13

In Memory of
  Josephine Ellis
  and
  Kathleen Ellis

Contents

Acknowledgments

MY INTEREST IN T. J. Woofter Jr. began when I came across his defense of the record of African American soldiers in World War I. He served as an officer in the AEF HQ under Pershing and was certain that derogatory comments made about the Ninety-second Division during and after the war were false. All I knew then was that he was a white southern sociologist whose work was widely referenced, especially in relation to black migration and farm problems during the Great Depression. I was unaware of his work for the Phelps-Stokes Fund, the Commission on Interracial Cooperation, or the Institute for Research in Social Science, or his association with key figures in the wider interracial cooperation movement and the antilynching campaign. As I examined the range of his activities and publications, it became clear that his work between 1910 and 1930 combined key elements of the Social Gospel, southern liberalism, and the engagement of the social sciences with the race problem. In his energetic yet diffident manner, Jack Woofter advanced all three phenomena.

Woofter left no collection of papers, so his career before the New Deal has to be constructed largely from the records of organizations that employed him or individuals with whom he worked or corresponded. I am grateful for the essential advice I received from archivists and librarians in many repositories, including the Strathclyde University Library, the Albert and Shirley Small Special Collections Library at the University of Virginia, the Auburn Avenue Research Library on African American Culture and History in Atlanta, the David M. Rubenstein Rare Book and Manuscript Library at Duke University, the Hargrett Rare Book and Manuscript Library at the University of Georgia, the Joyner Library at East Carolina University, the Rockefeller Archive Center at Sleepy Hollow, New York, the Southern Historical Collection of the Wilson Library at the University of North Carolina, the Tuskegee University Archives, the Center for Oral History at Columbia University, the Danville, Virginia, Public Library, the Manuscripts and Archives Division of the New York Public Library, the Schomburg Center for Research in Black Culture of the New York Public Library, the Manuscript Division of the Library of Congress, the National Archives and Records Administration, and the National Personnel Records Center.

I would also like to thank the British Academy for a research grant that has enabled me to pursue aspects of this work further, and the School of Humanities at the University of Strathclyde for assistance toward the cost of reproducing photographs.

Many people helped me with various questions, including Julie O. Kerlin, Clarence T. Maxey, Sally Guy Brown, Lesley Leduc, and Alfred Perkins. For their kindness and hospitality, I am especially grateful to John and Sharon Mackintosh. For their support and advice, I am indebted to my colleagues David Brown and Allan Macinnes, and especially to Richard Finlay, for ensuring that I had the time to begin this project; and also to Tricia Barton and Ann Bartlett for countless favors.

I owe the biggest thanks of all, for their support and inspiration, to my father and to my wife, Sue, and to Tom and Sam.

Abbreviations

AEF HQ	American Expeditionary Force, Headquarters
AGO	Adjutant General's Office
AMEZ	African Methodist Episcopal Zion
ANISS	Association of Negro Industrial Secondary Schools
ASNLH	Association for the Study of Negro Life and History
AUC	Robert W. Woodruff Library, Atlanta University Center, Atlanta, Ga.
CCRR	Commission on the Church and Race Relations
CIC	Commission on Interracial Cooperation.
CND	Council of National Defense
CUCOHC	Columbia University Center for Oral History Collection, New York
DNE	Division of Negro Economics
GEB	General Education Board
GFWC	Georgia Federation of Women's Clubs
GSCRR	Georgia State Committee on Race Relations.
GSIC	Georgia School Improvement Club
HRBML	Hargrett Rare Book and Manuscript Library, University of Georgia, Athens
IRSS	Institute for Research in Social Science
ISRR	Institute of Social and Religious Research
LC	Library of Congress, Manuscript Division, Washington, D.C.
LSRM	Laura Spelman Rockefeller Memorial Collection, Rockefeller Archive Center, Sleepy Hollow, N.Y.
MWL	Mississippi Welfare League
MUGAB	Minutes of University of Georgia Board of Trustees, Hargrett Library, University of Georgia, Athens
NA	National Archives, College Park, Md.
NAACP	National Association for the Advancement of Colored People.

NACW	National Association of Colored Women
NGA	National Governors Association
NPRC	National Personnel Records Center, St. Louis, Mo.
NRC	National Research Council
NUL	National Urban League
OPF	Official Personnel Folder.
PAA	Population Association of America
PSF	Phelps-Stokes Fund Papers, Schomburg Center for Research in Black Culture, New York Public Library
RAC	Rockefeller Archive Center, Sleepy Hollow, N.Y.
RRBML	David M. Rubenstein Rare Book and Manuscript Library at Duke University, Durham, N.C.
RG	Record Group
SC	Schomburg Center for Research in Black Culture, New York Public Library
SHC	Southern Historical Collection, Wilson Library, University of North Carolina, Chapel Hill
SFCWC	Southeastern Federation of Colored Women's Clubs
SPC	Southern Publicity Committee
SSC	Southern Sociological Congress
SSRC	Social Science Research Council
TUA	Tuskegee University Archives, Tuskegee, Ala.
UCSRQ	University Commission on Southern Race Questions
UGA	University of Georgia
UMAL	Special Collections and University Archives, University of Massachusetts Amherst Libraries
UNC	University of North Carolina, Chapel Hill
UNIA	Universal Negro Improvement Association
YMCA	Young Men's Christian Association
YWCA	Young Women's Christian Association

RACE HARMONY AND BLACK PROGRESS

Introduction

Jack Woofter and Southern Research

This book assesses the interracial cooperation movement in the South before the New Deal and focuses on the work of its most important young white activist, the Georgian sociologist Thomas Jackson (Jack) Woofter Jr. (1893–1972). As a field worker, researcher, and organizer, he maintained an unshakable faith in the "effectiveness of cooperation rather than agitation when real results are desired."[1] The extent to which this approach led the interracial cooperation movement to achievements of lasting note has divided both contemporary critics of the Jim Crow system and subsequent analysts.

The three main goals of the interracial cooperation movement—local dialogue between the races, improvements in education, and the reduction of lynching— were most clearly expressed by the Commission on Interracial Cooperation (CIC), founded by white reformers in Atlanta in 1919 with the support of conservative African American leaders. Its staunchest black ally, Robert Russa Moton, the Virginian son of former slaves who succeeded Booker T. Washington as principal of Tuskegee Institute in Alabama, saw the CIC as "the organized conscience of the forward-looking white South . . . [attempting] to purge itself . . . [for] the development of a new national conscience in dealing with the Negro as a free man." He shared the cooperationists' view that change had to be sought at a pace that took account of southern traditions. At the end of the 1920s, he wrote:

> The movement is launched not as an assault from the outside but as a confession from within that all is not as it should be; it is not one section coming to another section espousing the cause of a third party; it is instead the aggrieved parties themselves—the white man and the black man—meeting in peaceful conference, but with utmost candour, first of all to understand one another and then to work out a programme of cooperation up to the point of understanding, leaving to the future the handling of such problems as may still prove too difficult to approach.[2]

In the aftermath of Populism, a loose network of southern white writers and organizers had been inspired by education reformer and social critic Edgar Gardner Murphy to harness the power of "goodwill." Emboldened by the Social Gospel and Progressivism, awakened by black migration and equal rights activism, and alarmed by the racial violence that accompanied World War I, these white liberals rejected, to some extent, New South orthodoxies that had smothered dissent

1

since the restoration of white supremacy. Historians have assessed the contributions of a generation of reformers born between 1875 and 1890, including Will W. Alexander, Jessie Daniel Ames, Lucy Randolph Mason, Howard W. Odum, Julia Peterkin, Willis D. Weatherford, and Aubrey Williams. Lesser lights, such as Lily Hardy Hammond, Louis I. Jaffe, and Gerald W. Johnson, have also been subjects of recent work, but numerous other conscience-stricken southern professionals were highly active in the revival of the interracial cooperation movement, and remain little known or evaluated—industrialists like John J. Eagan, journalists like James Banks Nevin, university professors like Edwin Mims, and social workers like Carrie Parks Johnson.[3] They tended the flame of white liberalism between Murphy's retirement in 1909 and the New Deal, when a new generation of white dissenters emerged, such as Virginia Foster Durr and Howard Kester.

Jack Woofter has been one of the unsung, yet his name is familiar to careful students of America in the first half of the twentieth century from his own publications and countless references to them in the work of American historians, sociologists, economists, demographers, and political scientists. Since the 1920s, hundreds of studies of American race relations, migration, rural development, population change, and social security have cited him as an essential authority. His work spanned several disciplines, was always accessible, and provided subsequent researchers with solid starting points on numerous topics. In a forty-five-year career, beginning in 1913, he led or assisted dozens of philanthropic, academic, and governmental investigations into aspects of social justice, race, region, welfare, rural economics, demography, and statistical methodology, many of which were the first of their kind. Indeed, Woofter has been credited with the first academic pairing of the words "ethnicity" and "race."[4]

The southern reformers who influenced Jack Woofter saw the moral, economic, and cultural advancement of African Americans as an urgent objective—if only for the sake of the South—and one requiring thorough investigation. Calls for more research after 1900 were led by the Mississippi-born historian Samuel Chiles Mitchell, a member of the Southern Education Board and president of the University of South Carolina from 1908 to 1913. Mitchell wanted to see "a scientific habit of investigation as to the facts of [the black American's] progress, coupled with an intelligent interest in his development." He also saw opportunities for the proper integration of the South into the American economy and political system, now that education reform was blossoming and black disfranchisement had "removed the fear of negro domination." His allies included David Crenshaw Barrow, chancellor of the University of Georgia (UGA).[5] As an undergraduate at UGA, Jack Woofter shared his student peers' uncritical belief in the necessity of disfranchisement and racial segregation, but he gradually developed a sense that white people had an obligation to assist black people to overcome the lingering effects of slavery. He disliked the way racism dominated life in Georgia, preventing change, and eventually he took a clear stand against most forms of discrimination.

During the 1910s, Woofter did the spadework for a series of philanthropically funded studies of African American education, labor, and urban conditions. These reports were far from comprehensive, but they broke new ground and offered some of the most robust national data available. War service delayed the completion of his PhD on black migration at Columbia University, but by 1920 Woofter had gained a reputation for well-researched, dispassionate, and timely studies of African American life. During the first half of the 1920s, as a key staff member of the CIC, he immersed himself in the practicalities of fostering southern interracial cooperation and opposing the Klan, before returning to research. In the following decades, his work on migration, urban problems, race relations, and lynching helped to develop a social science critique of white supremacy that would bolster the civil rights movement.

Self-effacing and frequently changing jobs, Jack Woofter is hard to categorize and less well known than his associates, but the quality of his scholarship is widely noted. John H. Stanfield, in a survey of World War I–era sociology, referred to Woofter's "long, profitable career as an influential race scholar" and to the originality of his publications, and judged that he "contributed immensely to the work of the Phelps-Stokes Fund, the Commission on Interracial Cooperation, the University of North Carolina Department of Sociology, and New Deal reform programs."[6] Dewey W. Grantham cited Woofter as a prime example of those "southern white scholars . . . [who] helped develop greater sophistication in the study of race in the South. . . . Few social scientists were associated with a wider array of organizations and research projects concerned with the South than Woofter."[7] The southern geographer Charles S. Aiken ranks Woofter alongside Howard Odum, Arthur Raper, Ralph Bunche, Charles S. Johnson, Hortense Powdermaker, and Rupert Vance, as one of "the revisionist interpreters of the South who created a new professional research literature."[8]

When the federal government began to regard university social science departments as crucibles of public policy, Woofter became a particularly successful example of the talented and industrious scholar who transferred smoothly from academe to Washington, D.C. He claimed to deal in "verified facts, rather than . . . sentimental beliefs or traditional prejudices," and saw many of the South's problems stemming from a tendency at all levels in society to behave and think in ways that relied more on tradition than on reality.[9] A disciple of the Columbia University sociologist Franklin H. Giddings, who encouraged empirical work heavily laced with statistics, Woofter was part of a generation that assumed the task of demonstrating social conditions with numerical precision and a heavy dose of survey analysis. Jennifer Platt, in her history of American sociology, notes Woofter's aptitude as a statistician and argues that the interwar "objectivism" of which he was a part was a response to attacks on social science by religious and conservative groups. White sociologists, in particular, took refuge in what they claimed were "objective truths independent of values," as they presented evidence that intruded on deep-seated prejudices—but only up to a point.[10] Liberals such as Woofter wrote studies that pierced the hide of racism in several places, but they were reluctant to twist the knife by making all the critical judgments and recommendations that the facts invited. This protected them from the fury of anti-black extremists, but it also invited condemnation from black social scientists and publicists who saw the white researcher's habit of accumulating data about inequality without examining its causes and remedies as dishonest and pandering to Jim Crow.

For all his attempts at detachment, Woofter was thoroughly southern—the kind of commentator who, as Daniel Singal put it, "still harbored a sizable remnant of Victorian belief, [and] who remained attached to the South's traditional mythology even as they acted to vitiate it."[11] Woofter eventually rejected the idea that one race was inherently superior, but never lost his belief that white people and black people were at different stages of social and cultural development and that a certain distance would remain between them. In 1925, as research director of the CIC, he wrote, "It is certain that the colored man has some special contribution to make to American life if he only bestirs himself to develop his own peculiar strong points and is aided by the white man to develop these capabilities and find places where they fit into the scheme of American progress." There, in just a few words, Woofter managed to ascribe to African Americans the deficiencies of backwardness, indolence, dependency, and otherness.[12]

At first glance, Woofter's vision seems not far removed from that expressed by Robert Russa Moton, who wrote, "For all that the Negro has accomplished so much to-day, there is a definite limit to his achievements without the practical support and cooperation of the white man. The experience which the latter has already gained and the hold which he has upon the resources and organization of society make it impossible for the Negro to make any considerable advance without his assistance."[13] But the two men approached black uplift from very different perspectives. Moton was being pragmatic, and his long-term objectives were unlimited, whereas Woofter's comment was loaded with liberal presumption, paternalism, and what Stanfield has called "sociocultural evolutionism."[14] It revealed an interracial cooperation movement committed to improving the lives of African Americans, so that they could play an enhanced subaltern role in southern society.

Some of Woofter's research projects attracted controversy, especially among black radicals, but even those with reservations about his work and associations did not doubt his importance. A contemporary critic acknowledged toward the end of Woofter's career that in the field of interracial cooperation he had been "an outstanding leader and technician."[15] White commentators on Woofter's work were almost uniformly complimentary. His senior colleague at the University of North Carolina (UNC), Howard W. Odum, told officials of the Laura Spelman Rockefeller Memorial fund in 1927, "I have never seen anyone with more skill and better judgment in matters of research." This ability was later recognized by the Swedish sociologist Gunnar Myrdal, during the Carnegie Corporation–funded "Study of the Negro in America" that produced *An American Dilemma* (1944). Myrdal drew on several conversations and written exchanges with Woofter, regarding him as a reliable spokesman for southern white liberalism (a strain Myrdal considered "beautiful and dignified"), and a glance through the index of *An American Dilemma* shows Woofter as one of the most cited authors in the final report.[16]

Woofter's relative anonymity has persisted partly because in his varied existences—as an agent of philanthropy, a government-sponsored researcher, a campaigner for interracial cooperation, a university professor, and a civil servant—he always lived in the shadow of a more feted individual. He owed his career to the trust, affection, and resourcefulness of three ebullient fellow Methodists: Thomas Jesse Jones, Will W. Alexander, and Howard Odum. Jones, an outspoken and driven Welsh immigrant, was educational director of the New York–based Phelps-Stokes Fund and trained Woofter as an investigator for northern charities and government agencies between 1913 and 1917, setting him on a path that would separate him ideologically from most white southerners on questions of race and equality. Northern philanthropy not only paid Woofter's salary; it provided his moral and intellectual compass. Alexander, the humane and incisive director of the CIC, turned Woofter into a resilient and composed organizer and activist in the early 1920s during an effective southern campaign against lynching. As a fieldworker trying to assist embattled black farmers, as a lobbyist for state legislation and law enforcement, and as a publicist working with the northern and southern press, Woofter played a major role in articulating southern white opposition to racial violence. Alexander also encouraged Woofter to address the inadequacy of prewar liberal southern analyses through more rigorous studies of race problems. In 1927, Odum added Woofter to the staff of the new Institute for Research in Social Science (IRSS) at UNC. Other Odum protégés, such as Guy B. Johnson, Guion Griffis Johnson, and Arthur Raper, are better remembered at Chapel Hill, but Woofter played a significant part in establishing the institute as the leading center for southern studies. In the 1930s, Alexander and Woofter would be reunited in Washington, where the latter directed research for the Resettlement Administration, the Farm Security Administration, and the Federal Security Agency, undertaking studies that supported the implementation of New Deal farm and relief programs and assisting in the postwar development of the American social security system. Thus, Jack Woofter's work between 1917 and 1950 comprised several important building blocks of twentieth-century American social science research on race, rural conditions, and population.

Southern Goodwill

Between 1910 and 1930, the scattering of liberal middle-class white southerners who campaigned for better education and health-care provision for African Americans, the reduction of violence, and local cooperation between the races were partially successful, principally because their objectives were limited. The advocates of interracial cooperation never mounted an explicit challenge to segregation or disfranchisement, but they exerted a positive influence on the tense racial climate of the South after World War I, when the rising expectations of black people and the racist traditions of the white majority seemed destined to produce uncontrolled strife.

In 1924, the editor of the *Nation* magazine, Ernest Gruening, invited the African American scholar-activist W. E. B. Du Bois to sketch a southern state for the second volume of *These United States*. Du Bois contributed "Georgia: Invisible Empire State," a beautifully executed essay about "the bitter fight between Georgia and civilization." Only one thing gave Du Bois hope that the state with the worst lynching record since 1890 might change: the small group of white people in Atlanta who openly opposed the pervasive racial hatred. He had attended civic league meetings with some of these people in the aftermath of the Atlanta riot of 1906 and found their condescension and refusal to discuss segregation frustrating, but he recognized that now they were taking a risk in speaking out on the subject of race. It was, after all, "fairly easy to be a reformer in New York or Boston or Chicago. . . . But in Atlanta?" Although he doubted whether any white southerners could shed enough of their racist upbringing to challenge radically the injustice around them, he understood why any dissent was so hard:

> Of the spiritual dilemmas that face men today I know of none more baffling than that which faces the conscientious, educated, forward-looking white man of Georgia. On the one hand is natural loyalty to what his fathers believed, to what his friends never question; then his own difficulty in knowing or understanding the black world and his inbred distrust of its ability and real wish; there is his natural faith in his own ability and the ability of his race; there is the subtle and continuous propaganda—gossip, newspapers, books, sermons, and "science"; there is his eager desire to see his section take a proud place in the civilized world. There is his job, his one party, his white primary—his social status so easily lost if he is once dubbed a "nigger lover." Facing all this is lynching, mob murder, ignorance, silly self-praise of people pitifully degenerate in so many cases, exploitation of the poor and weak, and insult, insult, insult heaped on the blacks.[17]

Du Bois had deftly outlined the predicament of white promoters of interracial co-operation and their loose network of regional organizations, community groups, churches, charities, and educational institutions. For a decade after the Atlanta riot, they had gathered in meetings of the Southern Sociological Congress (SSC) and the University Commission on Southern Race Questions (UCSRQ), but inter-racial cooperation remained an essentially leaderless tendency, in which a few hundred committed white people and a smaller number of black supporters mobi-lized opinion and resources at a critical juncture in American history, in the hope of shaping the debate on race relations.[18] In particular, they sought to reduce the levels of hatred and habitual cruelty that allowed the practice of lynching to per-sist. Despite differences of race, class, and religious denomination, the men and women who sustained interracial cooperation shared a faith in the power of good-will and sought a southern solution to southern problems. Stirred by Progressiv-ism and the Social Gospel, they formed a southern alliance to speak out against injustice and clearly thought of themselves as part of a cohesive phenomenon explicitly referred to as a *movement*.[19] In March 1920, Thomas Jesse Jones wrote Robert Russa Moton regarding the "great inter-racial movement," and in Novem-ber 1921 the white president of Atlanta University, Edward T. Ware, confidently assured Jack Woofter, "The movement is certainly one of great promise, and good results are proceeding from it."[20] Historians of the South and racial thought have also characterized it as a movement. At the height of the civil rights protest of the 1960s, George B. Tindall wrote about "a trend toward more thoughtful and sympathetic attitudes among southern whites that began to flower into the inter-racial movement during the years from 1910 to 1919."[21] It was, he wrote, the off-spring "of a union between paternalism and the progressive urge to social justice [, seeking] . . . Negro advancement within the framework of segregation and dis-creet contacts across the veil of separation."[22] In 1990, Ronald C. White rounded off his study of the Social Gospel with a discussion of "the ecumenical interracial movements growing out of World War I."[23]

Several historians have remarked on the striking and far-reaching role that women played in initiating interracial cooperation and propelling reform. This activity originated in the late nineteenth century, predating organizations such as the SSC, the UCSRQ, and the CIC. After 1890, black women from several re-ligious denominations seized opportunities to promote African American com-munity interests and home life, with the consequence that some white women, eager to stabilize race relations and the social order, paid new attention to black women's groups and needs.[24] No scholars have explored this process during the Progressive Era and the 1920s to greater effect than Jacquelyn Dowd Hall, Glenda Gilmore, and Rebecca Montgomery. Hall saw the interactions between black and white women that accompanied the formation of the CIC as coupling "the drive of organized white women for efficacy in the public sphere with the rising militancy of black women."[25] This process began at least a decade earlier and represented a significant crack in the edifice of white supremacy. For example, collaboration between black and white women in the Women's Christian Temperance Union in North Carolina between 1880 and 1900, albeit through separate chapters, fostered a shared female critique of society, and in Virginia reformist interracial cooperation by middle-class women after 1910, under the leadership of Mary-Cooke Munford and Ora B. Stokes, enabled black women to achieve a new prominence and autonomy in education and the delivery of social services, despite (and, to a degree, because of) growing segregation. As Gilmore notes, "white women were overwhelmingly complicitous in shoring up white supremacy in 1898, yet they were at the vanguard of the movement for interracial cooperation by 1920."[26] In her study of Georgia between 1890 and 1930, Montgomery shows in detail how club women incorporated interracial cooperation into their efforts to "transform the 'community of men' into a 'community of families,' transcending the limitations of male-centered localism by replacing white male individualism with the greater social good as a basis for political decision making."[27]

Many of the women who served on the CIC's state committees and county-level committees during the 1920s were veteran campaigners for what Lily Hardy Hammond called the "vigorous development of social conscience in the South."[28] Interracial cooperation work demanded a special courage and belief of women like Hammond, a journalist and first director of the Methodist Women's Bureau of Social Service, and Charlotte Hawkins Brown, an African American teacher. It required conviction on the part of men, too, but the risks of social ostracism for white women and outright intimidation for black women were considerably greater, because of the larger perceived transgressions of white women in seeking interaction with black people and of black women in seeking nonsubservient roles in southern life. Without the efforts of such women at crucial moments, the movement would probably have faltered badly before the mid-1920s; it was their raised voices that ultimately carried moral authority in the CIC's effective campaign against racial violence. Despite this, white men continued to be overrepresented in the upper reaches of the interracial cooperation movement during the 1920s, especially in the central CIC office. These men were unwelcoming toward women activists, because they doubted women's capacity for emotionally taxing work and feared hostile reactions toward white women collaborating with black men.

Some white support for interracial cooperation sprang from concerns about the economic effects of black migration and the damage to the South's reputation caused by lynching, but women were moved mainly by humane considerations and Christian imperatives. As they inquired into African American household conditions and as black women responded in frank terms about their needs, some white women began to question the triptych depicting the black man as rapist, the white man as protector and avenger, and the white woman as vulnerable ward. Moreover, they were shocked by the constant anxiety that black women felt about the threat to their families' physical and economic security posed by white men. Forced, therefore, to confront the most crushing feature of white supremacy—lynching and the attitudes that condoned it—some white women openly rejected the argument that racial discrimination in the South operated fundamentally for their benefit. Hence, the gradual inclusion of white women in the published lists of those who supported the work of the CIC and like-minded organizations, such as the Young Women's Christian Association (YWCA). Montgomery contends that throughout the 1920s liberal reformers retained an "abiding faith in women's ability to effect change for the common good" and that "it would be hard to overemphasize the symbolic importance of women's efforts at interracial cooperation."[29] At the local level, in particular, those efforts were much more than symbolic.

The effects of World War I in this story were profound. In the war's immediate aftermath, against a backdrop of black migration and a summer of rioting in 1919, a clear political opportunity existed for the advancement of interracial cooperation in the South as an expression of the Social Gospel. White liberals seized the opportunity to highlight injustice, developing strategies for promoting racial harmony and black progress and forging networks within southern educational and northern philanthropic circles. The effect was to influence southern discourse about race in ways that steadily reduced the level of violence and challenged the most explicit vehicle for hatred, the Ku Klux Klan. The energy and resources of interracial cooperation were harnessed to a clear agenda by CIC director Will Alexander, but this was not a new impulse; the CIC had its forebears in earlier liberal attempts to debate issues of concern to the South, such as the education and voting rights of the former slaves and rural poverty. In the late nineteenth and early twentieth centuries, dissenting writers such as George Washington Cable, Atticus Greene Haygood, J. L. M. Curry, and Edgar Gardner Murphy, secretary of the Southern Education Board, all of them affected by memories of the Civil War or Reconstruction, challenged Americans to apply Christian teachings not just to their own lives, but to the wider social problems around them. Inspired by Cable, who regarded racial justice as the truest test of American democracy, they called on leaders of white opinion to speak up for the freedmen and condemn violence, but they rarely criticized state governments, preferring to talk about a national responsibility. Following the line taken by Haygood and Curry, Murphy tried to persuade white readers that the future of the United States would be determined by how well it treated its black people. Impressive charitable donations were raised for black education at the turn of the century, but these amounted to only a quarter of the sums the states provided annually from tax revenues to which black people directly contributed relatively little. Black education spending came to be regarded as a fragile and unpopular state subsidy that penalized white families, as Murphy conceded: "The negro has shared this burden, but his vast numbers, his great needs, and his low productive capacity have necessarily reduced the amount which the South could expend upon her white children."[30] He argued in vain that, since the federal government had failed black people, their uplift through education was a national duty. After 1910, other supporters of the interracial cooperation movement called on southern states and school boards to divert resources to black schools, but rarely challenged the argument that gaps in per capita spending on black and white pupils merely reflected the relative wealth of the races.

Ultimately, white liberals effected only small changes in black education because they surrendered to the general belief in segregation and fell back on the hope that a combination of northern aid, black economic progress, and liberal southern expertise would improve the system. Murphy regretted that segregation meant white people never saw the best side of black Americans or appreciated their achievements. In *The Basis of Ascendancy* (1909), his last major work before his death in 1913, he also dismissed white anxieties about race "amalgamation." He called for the vote to be restored to black men and attacked the idea that black progress could happen only at the expense of white progress.[31] But Murphy probably influenced more northern readers than southern readers. Most "Silent South" humanitarian paternalists were so preoccupied with maintaining peace and so convinced of intellectual differences between the races that they gladly embraced the idea of separate industrial education promoted at Hampton and Tuskegee Institutes, and found common ground with northern philanthropists in the premise that black children did not require, and were not suited for, the same schooling as white children.

Liberal professionals in the South, faced with problems of health care, education, temperance, prison reform, child labor, and poverty, were influenced by a strand of the Social Gospel movement that stressed both social reform *and* racial separateness.[32] Finding a "fellowship in the gospel" (Philippians 1:5), they held that active good works embodied Christian duty and furthered the ends of the church better than the perfection of the soul sought by evangelical Protestantism. They were influenced by the northern Congregationalist minister Washington Gladden, an advocate of greater fairness in the treatment of African Americans, who was moved by meeting Du Bois in Atlanta and reading *The Souls of Black Folk* (1903). As the author of *Applied Christianity* (1887) and president of the American Missionary Association between 1901 and 1904, Gladden asserted both the need for radical reform in the South and the existence of distinct racial traits. His followers were thereby encouraged to combine elements of Darwinism with the liberal theology of the Social Gospel, to construct an argument that "backward" groups could progress wherever the "fittest" provided the right opportunities and encouragement.[33] Social gospelers working for better race relations also found meaning in Walter Rauschenbusch's *Christianizing the Social Order*, published in 1912. In the same year, Willis D. Weatherford made the annual conference of the SSC into one of the few settings in which black and white academics and social workers could meet for frank face-to-face discussions, within an emerging program akin to the Social Creed of the Federal Council of Churches.[34]

The Social Gospel in the South influenced the establishment and operation of several educational institutions and charities, but its longer-term contribution lay in enunciating certain principles. Its energy was diminished by the death or retirement of many of its leading figures by the end of World War I, but its legacy to the interracial cooperation movement was the belief that dialogue based on an attitude of goodwill and Christian sisterhood and brotherhood could lead to mutual understanding and harmony without fundamentally altering the political and economic status quo. In the 1920s, Will Alexander and the CIC became effectively the successors of Weatherford and the SSC.

The Historical Location of Interracial Cooperation

Southern white liberalism prior to 1914 has been well studied, and the same is even truer for the period after 1930, but the intervening years have attracted less attention. Historians have implied that the rapid growth of the interracial cooperation movement during World War I and the early 1920s was either an extension of earlier work or the stirrings of a subsequent struggle, but neither has been clearly established. Accomplished doctoral dissertations were written on the CIC in the 1970s and the 1990s, along with several articles, but a reader searching for an extended recent treatment has to settle for passages in broader monographs.[35] A notable example has been Diana Selig's *Americans All*, in which the CIC's work in southern schools is presented as "a paradox: the simultaneous expression of both virulent racism and education for racial cooperation." Selig captures the way in which the CIC's education program attacked intolerance and unkindness, and thereby lowered racial tension in the interwar period, but also avoided any challenge to segregation or the economic and political structures that preserved inequality in the South. Also useful is political scientist Kimberley Johnson's examination of the attempts of southern liberals to "mitigate the worst of Jim Crow while bringing the South into rough alignment with American democratic ideals." She argues that "Jim Crow reform," in which the CIC played a part, allowed liberals to endorse conservative "folkways" while opening debates about the governance of the southern states.[36]

One of the most influential academic critiques of Progressive-era interracial cooperation was issued by George Fredrickson in the first edition of *The Black Image in the White Mind* (1971). Acknowledging that "accommodationist racism . . .

was in part a reaction against the brutality of the extremists," Fredrickson attempted to explain the liberals' motives and how it was that they co-opted conservative African American leaders like Washington and Moton, and, for a time, even radical thinkers like Du Bois and Kelly Miller:

> Dissenting from extreme manifestations of Negrophobia, a group of white moderates took it upon themselves to work for interracial harmony and accommodation. Since they did not usually object to the notion that blacks were inferior or even to the dictum that they remain a separate caste, moderate "liberalism" was seriously flawed and doomed to ineffectuality; it may even strike modern readers as an exercise in hairsplitting to distinguish the moderates from the militant racists with whom they professed to disagree. But in the early twentieth century there did seem to be a substantive difference between their approach and that of the extremists . . . not because the moderates promised full equality but because they appeared to offer certain immediate and tangible benefits which might make the difference between a better future and further oppression.[37]

When a new edition of his book appeared in 1987, Fredrickson admitted that the 1971 edition had "reflected the mood of frustration and pessimism about black-white relations that was particularly strong among those who [like himself] had identified fervently with the civil-rights movement." He considered, looking back, that his pessimism and his "tendency throughout to find white-supremacist warts on white racial 'liberals' of the past were obviously influenced by a sense of the failure of American liberalism that had been exacerbated by the Vietnam war." He allowed that historians should be "more understanding of the inability of past reformers to break out of the bounds set by the culture and ideology of their time."[38]

Much has since been written about liberal southerners who were sufficiently emboldened to criticize aspects of white supremacy during the New Deal era and the late 1940s. Subjects of biographical studies include writers and editors such as Ralph McGill, Hodding Carter II, Virginius Dabney, Jonathan Daniels, Lillian Smith, and William Cash; administrators such as Clark H. Foreman; religious activists such as Howard Kester; and academics such as Arthur F. Raper—all of whom were born around 1900. These individuals and organizations they associated with in the 1930s, such as the Southern Conference for Human Welfare, are presented in the works of John T. Kneebone, Patricia Sullivan, Daniel J. Singal, John Egerton, and others as a vanguard of the civil rights movement. They have been more coolly assessed by writers like Morton Sosna, James C. Cobb, and David Chappell.[39] Clearly, these southern liberals advanced views of their region's history, its place in the Union, and its economic and racial problems that dissented from the consensus broadly prevailing since the 1890s. The Great Depression produced what Ralph McGill called a "mighty surge of discussion, debate, self-examination, confession and release," and some historians have found this fertile terrain.[40]

In contrast, most historians who have considered the work of the CIC *before* the New Deal are critical of what they perceive as the interracial cooperation movement's deep-seated racism, or, at best, irresolution. They point to the failure of white liberals in the 1920s to shed attitudes they were brought up with, and their reluctance to state the true nature of white supremacy or attack its underlying structures. The most common formula characterizes white liberals after World War I as well-intentioned but intellectually dishonest and basically racist do-gooders, who evaded the real issues of segregation and disfranchisement and were of questionable significance. David Chappell, for example, has called the CIC "timid . . . closet dissenters."[41] Kenneth Janken, the biographer of Walter White of the National Association for the Advancement of Colored People (NAACP), also refers to the CIC's basic "timidity." Janken notes that individual "southern liberals who spoke out against lynching displayed courage, of course, and risked being ostracized by their communities . . . [but] they were chained to a past in which 'good Negroes' deferred to the 'better class of whites' and the system of white supremacy was the natural order."[42] Morton Sosna acknowledged the "vitality" of the CIC's opposition to lynching during the 1920s, but regretted that "Will Alexander adopted a moderate stance because he thought the commission could do more to help Southern blacks in this way than it could by challenging Jim Crow head-on." Alexander, according to Sosna, changed the outlook of some southern whites, but worked under "great constraints" imposed by Populism's "bitter heritage of racism and demagoguery." Above all, Sosna argued, the CIC did nothing to advance black civil rights: "In attempting to soften and humanize segregation as it was practiced in the South during the 1920s and 1930s, the Commission in effect sanctioned the idea of the Southern Negro as a second-class citizen."[43] Christopher Waldrep, in his study of extralegal violence, also asserts that the CIC only wanted "to soften and humanize segregation" and that Will Alexander took no action to combat lynching until its apparent resurgence at the start of the 1930s.[44] Paul Harvey, in *Freedom's Coming,* acknowledges "the thin but tough community of liberals, Christian socialists, and radicals [who] revolted against the limitations of Progressive Era notions of reform and uplift [and] explored avenues toward Christian interracialism. The work of churchgoing women paved their way." He presents the CIC as nevertheless ineffectual and possibly harmful to the cause of black progress.[45] The historical sociologist John H. Stanfield has argued that southern support for interracial cooperation was slight, that it revealed little about the South in the interwar period, and that the CIC owed its existence to successful bids for northern money on which it promptly became dependent.[46] Finally, J. Douglas Smith, in *Managing White Supremacy,* argues that "interracial cooperation provided a means to the proper management of white supremacy," which included defending segregation and dissuading blacks from joining radical movements. He adds, "Southern interracial activity in the 1920s and 1930s addressed only the most obvious inequities of Jim Crow—substandard housing, education, recreational facilities, and transportation—but never the causes." A vocal CIC campaign against racial violence in Virginia, led by Louis I. Jaffe, editor of the *Norfolk Virginian-Pilot*, produced a state antilynching law in 1928, but Douglas found the CIC was generally less effective than the NAACP.[47] In some of this historical literature, perhaps, the interracial cooperation movement is being judged against the later achievements of the civil rights movement.

Historians who have presented the work of the CIC in a generally positive light include William A. Link, Dewey W. Grantham, W. Fitzhugh Brundage, Patricia Sullivan, John Egerton, David Fort Godshalk, John T. Kneebone, and Leroy Davis: all have stressed the humanitarianism of the CIC, despite the strong whiff of white supremacy in some of its public statements. Twenty years ago, in *The Paradox of Southern Progressivism*, Link adroitly recounted a shift in liberal thought concerning race around the period of World War I. He saw paternalism "eroded" as a new white perspective emerged, heavily influenced by the war and the changing mood of black people themselves. Although the postwar southern liberal tendency was still wedded to notions of racial difference that sustained inequality, Link argued it had progressed to a position well to the left of the New South liberalism of the 1890s and 1900s. He argued that the CIC, for all its organizational weakness and hesitancy, fostered real interactions between the races and represented a significant new step beyond the paternalistic uplift of black people that previously characterized southern liberalism. He also detected a new depth of heart-searching among the supporters of the CIC and a basic desire to treat black people fairly, and most of the time as equals, if the surrounding culture would only allow it.[48] Grantham argued that the very idea of interracial cooperation and careful investigation of racial problems "represented a departure from the past" and that the movement "had some effect in reversing the trend toward increasing separation between black and white southerners." He concludes, "While its approach was cautious and its reforms largely superficial, the Commission on Interracial Cooperation was nonetheless a bolder and more liberal social experiment than the racial uplift of prewar progressives."[49] Brundage accords particular significance to whites who campaigned against lynching: "Although most shied away from attacking segregation, they had challenged white complacency, urged forward racial reform, and pioneered many of the techniques that would contribute to the ultimate demise of segregation and white supremacy."[50] Sullivan, in *Days of Hope*, is less positive about the CIC's legacy, but recognizes that Will Alexander had little choice but to "proceed cautiously" in the face of "firmly entrenched" attitudes: "Moreover, the CIC was isolated in the America of the 1920s. Its efforts received little recognition or encouragement from the national liberal community and were ignored by both major political parties. The group avoided all discussion of ultimate goals; its primary aim was to move beyond mutual ignorance."[51] Egerton, in *Speak Now against the Day*, notes that the CIC "was hardly a radical force," but admires Alexander's leadership and his construction of "a curious image of liberal activism within the bounds of cautious and proper respectability." Although the CIC condoned existing segregation ordinances and opposed federal legislation to suppress mobs, Egerton sees its supporters as "benign and honorable men and women of high motivation and goodwill."[52] According to Godshalk, the CIC's preoccupation with reducing racial violence led to its "goal of marginalizing radical black voices while simultaneously reining in what many CIC participants viewed as a disorderly class of poor whites." It nevertheless became "a hub for wide-ranging efforts at promoting interracial cooperation and moderate racial reform throughout the South," relieving the isolation of white liberals and promoting liberalism among the young.[53] Kneebone also sees the CIC as effective in communicating with the black and white middle classes, while Davis sees the commission as "radical only in a Southern context" but sincere in wishing to improve the lives of all southerners through racial harmony and improved education.[54]

Other historians have taken a more agnostic line regarding white liberal thought on racial problems in the 1910s and 1920s. Joel Williamson, in *A Rage for Order*, was curious about the support of academics, especially historians and sociologists, for interracial cooperation: "Many of these people were moved by paternalism, by a Southern Christian faith, and by a sensitivity that led to sympathy and action." They pursued truth "through conventional methods of scholarship, and that pursuit led to an appreciation of the racial realities." He remarked that "Academic Liberals tended to group together, and they flowed through certain channels," including Chapel Hill.[55] Jacquelyn Dowd Hall, in *Revolt against Chivalry*, accepted that the CIC's founders "believed themselves to be in the forefront of a significant departure in southern race relations" and that the CIC itself "could be seen as the first thaw in a long winter of repression," but also acknowledged the validity of African American skepticism as to its capacity or desire to pursue fundamental change.[56] Adam Fairclough has noted the achievements of the CIC in education, but concludes, "For all its good works . . . the interracial movement was small, weak, fitful, and beset by internal contradictions." And although it offered a rare chance for "calm, rational discussion," it was dominated by committed segregationists and was regarded with suspicion by blacks.[57] In an essay on Lily Hardy Hammond, Elna C. Green refers to the interracial cooperation movement as "committed to working in the quietest way possible, desiring no fanfare or publicity that might scare away more timid white supporters." She also remarks on the "apparent drift and lethargy of that movement."[58] In a broad study of southern intellectuals and social critics, Daniel Singal argued that academic liberals were obliged to be cautious: "[B]eing a sociologist in the South required a mixture of courage and restraint during this period. . . . Race relations remained a dangerous topic in the South, to the point where its very mention could jeopardize one's employment."[59] The sincerity of the liberal belief that open debate about segregation could wreck the possibility of further cooperation is recognized by Glenda Gilmore in *Defying Dixie,* a sweeping study of social justice movements, wherein the CIC is described as "an indigenous solution designed to prove that Southerners themselves could steer a middle course between racial violence and interracial democracy." Until the 1930s, she argues, the interracial cooperation movement served a purpose by holding back "a deluge of oppression," but it contributed no vision of a reformed South.[60]

Thus, in general, historians have found southern white liberalism in the era of World War I and the 1920s intriguing, but not compelling; some have been puzzled by it, some repelled, and some have skated over it. Few have asserted any close connections or similarities between the interracial cooperation movement and the post-1945 civil rights movement (or even the "long civil rights movement"), and readers will not find that view proposed here. This study examines twenty years of southern interracial cooperation during a period of rapid economic and social change and records the tenacity of a man who epitomized the movement's spirit and shortcomings. Jack Woofter fought what he called "a citizen's fight" against lynching and became a consistently successful scholar, making what were, for the time, essential and original contributions to a wider understanding of modern American society. Deeply influenced by southern history and that of Georgia in particular, he was determined that the region should accept change in the twentieth century. He qualifies as one of Daniel Singal's "Modernists by the Skin of Their Teeth" and deserves a wider appreciation.[61]

1 Jack Woofter
The Education of a Southern Liberal

Born in macon, Georgia, in 1893, Thomas Jackson ("Jack") Woofter Jr. was raised in an atmosphere of New South optimism about public education, economic regeneration, good roads, and the resurgence of the white middle class. An only child, with slight connections to the planter aristocracy in Georgia, he was part of the post-Populist generation that assumed responsibility for the modernization of the region and the consignment to history of feudal features of southern life.

His father, T. J. Woofter Sr., one of eight children of a West Virginian farm family distantly related to Thomas "Stonewall" Jackson, became a schoolteacher at the age of sixteen and was principal of a normal school at twenty-three. After studying law at the University of West Virginia, he crisscrossed the South as a teacher and superintendent until 1893, when he became a mathematics instructor at Mercer University in Macon. In 1897, he moved to Milledgeville, the old state capital about one hundred miles southeast of Atlanta, to teach psychology and philosophy at Georgia Normal and Industrial College. Having completed a PhD by summer study with the American School in Chicago, he joined the University of Georgia (UGA) in Athens in 1903 as a professor of philosophy and education, specializing in rural schools and modern testing methods. He pushed for better funding for black normal schools and the admission of women to UGA, where a colleague described him as "congenial in association and conversation, [but] of rather solemn face"; his students called him "gloomy." He was to play a key role in the academic and physical growth of UGA until the 1920s. An influential president of the Southern Education Council, he sat on the Georgia Board of Education from its creation in 1911 until 1919, a period of extensive reform. He was a Freemason, a Democrat, and a skilled fundraiser, securing money from the Georgia-born Wall Street banker George Foster Peabody and Governor M. Hoke Smith for several new projects. President Theodore Roosevelt commended him for persuading New South universities to undertake social and economic research and train reform-minded public officials.[1] In 1904, he told the chancellor of UGA, "The University must furnish the constructive thinkers and leaders. No greater opportunity for genuine service is now open to the university."[2] And yet, as a Virginian Baptist who owned no land, T. J. Woofter Sr. remained a parvenu in Georgia.

Jack Woofter's sense of his southernness came primarily from his mother's family. He idealized Callender (Callie) Gerdine as "a daughter of slaveholders, whose tender spirit embodied the true soul of the old south, whose sympathy for the weaker race set a high example."[3] The oldest of eight children, she grew up in West Point, Mississippi, where her grandfather had settled with slaves he brought from Oglethorpe County in Georgia. In 1860, the Gerdine family plantation at West Point was valued at $48,000 and held more than eighty slaves.[4] She married T. J. Woofter Sr. when he was the district school superintendent and moved soon afterward to Georgia. Several of her siblings also moved to Georgia, including a sister who married the owner of a large plantation near Milledgeville, where Jack and his cousins played with the children of black tenants. As he later recalled, he also began to discover things about whiteness.

> Not far from my uncle Harvie's plantation a "cracker" whom we shall give the alias of Butch Carmody had a small three-tenant farm. I could tell from the tone and expression of my elders whenever the subject of Butch was mentioned that they would have preferred it if he had settled in some other neighborhood. It was not uncommon in passing his place to hear the howls and whacks which floated down the road as the harness strap was applied to bare, black buttocks.[5]

After her husband's appointment at UGA, Callie Woofter joined the charitable work of the Athens Woman's Club, raising funds for the university's hospital, opened in 1915, and helping to create a circulating library for rural schools.[6] She brought her son up in the Methodist Episcopal Church, South, through which he encountered liberal ideas, the Social Gospel, and networks of reforming women's organizations. In the 1950s, Jack Woofter claimed, "Neither from her nor from any of my other Southern relatives do I recall ever hearing any remarks indicating prejudice or intolerance toward Negroes." That seems highly improbable, but indicates a consciousness that he was raised differently from most other white men in Georgia. The Woofters, he considered, were "for that place and time, a fairly liberal Southern family. . . . As I look back at my early contacts and environment, I see that I was fortunate not to be taught prejudice at an early age."[7] At various points in his life, liberal Methodism would prove morally inspirational and personally advantageous. George Foster Peabody, whose vast banking fortune supported several southern welfare and education programs, befriended the Woofter family and took an interest in Jack's career, as did other Methodist friends, including the philanthropic agent Thomas Jesse Jones, the Georgian sociologist Howard W. Odum, and the outstanding interracial cooperationist Will W. Alexander.

Although Jack Woofter glimpsed rural life during his childhood, his racial outlook was heavily influenced by life in college towns, where overt tensions were rare. He claimed that, as a child, his sense of race as a force in daily life was confined to seeing separate lines of black and white pupils as they walked to school. He had scattered recollections of playing with black children before the age of ten, of fights that broke out among white children if one called another "nigger," of stories about miscegenation, and of his black nurse being permitted to ride with him and his friends in the white people's seats on streetcars ("There was no way around it. We were too young to be unattended and for us to have gone into the Negro section with her would have been unthinkable.").[8] Race, itself, may not have been a prominent factor in his life, but he knew he was a southerner. During his childhood, memories of the Confederacy, the Civil War, and Reconstruction were more strongly preserved in Georgia than in any other southern state, and the sense of American history that young Georgians gained from popular culture and their schoolwork was thoroughly imbued with Lost Cause sentiments. It would have been impossible for Woofter to have remained unaffected by the dominant creed regarding racial difference and the South's lasting sensitivity to outside criticism.[9]

In 1908, when at age fifteen he entered the University of Georgia to study for a BA, the university and Athens itself were undergoing rapid change. For the first hundred years after its foundation in 1801, UGA offered courses in agriculture, the arts, science, and law, but in the 1890s, as pressure built for the renewal of southern education at all levels, Georgia led a regional debate about the purposes of the modern university. Extra state government funding, supplemented by donations from philanthropists led by Peabody, and the introduction of students' fees allowed UGA to become a center for professional training and research on regional problems. The energetic chancellorships of Walter Barnard Hill and David Crenshaw Barrow saw the academic programs and campus transformed, so that by the time Jack Woofter enrolled, his father had become the director (later, dean) of the new Peabody School of Education. Schools of pharmacy and forestry were under construction, and in 1910 the graduate school would open, followed by new schools of business and journalism.[10]

As an undergraduate, Jack Woofter excelled at mathematics, but became more interested in southern social problems and the applications of social science research. Only two elements of his degree dealt with race—an independent investigation in his senior year concerning black benevolent associations and a class taught by Robert Preston Brooks on the economic development of Georgia, in which Woofter and two other students were encouraged to trace the origins of current problems. Brooks epitomized New South academia: the son of a Methodist minister from Milledgeville and one of the first Rhodes scholars at Oxford University in 1904, he gained his PhD at the University of Wisconsin, a hotbed of progressive reformism. His treatment of race and agriculture in classes on Georgia's history strongly influenced Woofter's subsequent work on migration and rural economics. The Brooks version of the Old South presented slavery and cotton as mixed blessings with long-term costs that the post-Bourbon generation struggled to address. Under slavery, according to Brooks, "Negroes were lazy, inefficient, and unintelligent," and his low opinion of post-Reconstruction black labor gave rise to remarks about "the present-day negro's shiftlessness and aversion to work." He hoped to see black Georgians thrive, but warned, "Unless closely supervised, the negro will not work steadily." He saw the minority of prosperous African American farmers as "the hope of the race because they are a standing refutation to the belief held by many persons that the negro is incapable of advancement."[11]

Outside the classroom, Woofter recalled, he and his friends in the Chi Phi fraternity "seldom debated subjects that struck too close to home. We would talk about woman suffrage, the tariff, and the regulation of railroad rates in an abstract manner but never anything about local economic or social conditions."[12] The impact of Progressivism on young, white, middle-class men in the South was limited, and race was a subject too sensitive to be debated properly, especially in the aftermath of the Atlanta race riot of 1906. From the surrounding culture, the teenage Woofter easily absorbed what he called the "Southern ideology of race"—the unshakable certainties: black people were deficient and always would be; white supremacy was inevitable and just; segregation and disfranchisement were necessary; and the South should be allowed to deal with the race problem in the way it knew best. This was the rigid Georgian mindset that W. E. B. Du Bois described as "the grim bars and barriers; subjects that must not be touched, opinions that must not be questioned."[13] Later, when Woofter examined those issues closely and saw their effects firsthand, he would abandon much of what his peers firmly believed.

Along with the "race suicide" theories of mainstream sociologists such as Edward A. Ross, southern white students were exposed to a raft of faux-academic literature on race before World War I. Typical were Thomas Nelson Page's *The Negro: The Southerner's Problem* (1904), William Benjamin Smith's *The Color Line* (1905), and R. W. Shufeldt's *The Negro: A Menace to American Civilization* (1907). Page, a Virginian aristocrat, deplored lynching, but charged black people with being too slow to condemn rape, a crime he claimed was "well-nigh wholly confined to the Negro race" and caused by "the talk of social equality that inflames the ignorant Negro."[14] Smith, who taught mathematics at Tulane University, wrote about the horrors of "amalgamation" and "a nation hopelessly sinking in the mire of Mongrelism." Shocked by the unwillingness of the Columbia University anthropologist Franz Boas to ascribe higher qualities to one race, Smith called on the South to erect "at all times, and at all hazards, and at all sacrifices, an impassable social chasm between Black and White." In order to defend the "'continuous germ-plasma' of the Caucasian Race," he argued, the South should insist on the "absolute denial of social equality to the Negro, no matter what his virtues or abilities or accomplishments."[15] Shufeldt, an army doctor, referred to a "seething mass of black sensual bestiality" and declared "these savage and semi-simian creatures" were almost impossible to educate, control, or reform.[16] As expressions of visceral extremism, such books were little better than Hinton Rowan Helper's egregious compilation, *The Negroes in Negroland* (1868), published forty years earlier. The fact that academic racism also thrived outside the South strengthened the position of southern writers: the Pennsylvanian ethnologist David Garrison Brinton claimed in *Races and Peoples* (1890) that physical differences between Caucasians and Africans proved that the former was at a more advanced stage of development, and the New England-born psychologist G. Stanley Hall claimed in 1905 that the two groups differed more, physically and psychologically, than any two races in history. Less pejorative work, such as that of Boas, was available by 1910, but most American social scientists insisted that white superiority was a fact and that segregation of the races was required for the avoidance of amalgamation and conflict. At the University of Mississippi, the progressive southern teacher Thomas Pearce Bailey welcomed Boas's anthropological investigations as part of further intense study of "the Negro question," but told students including Howard Odum that to suggest blacks were not inferior invited miscegenation.[17] Thus, racist writers stressed the importance of Jim Crow laws, even as they engaged with new social science ideas indicating that race was a worthwhile field of scholarship.[18]

In the cloistered academic community of Athens, Woofter's acceptance of scientific racism was tempered by his introduction to the ideals of interracial cooperation. His undergraduate studies coincided with a growth in northern philanthropic aid for the investigation of southern problems, particularly regarding African American education, health, and commerce. At the first gathering of the Southern Sociological Congress (SSC) in 1912 at Nashville, delegates resolved to establish a University Commission on Southern Race Questions (UCSRQ). Led by James Hardy Dillard, the director of the Anna T. Jeanes Foundation, the UCSRQ represented a departure from the dogmatism of university presidents such as Charles Dabney of the University of Tennessee, Edwin Alderman of the University of Virginia, and Walter Barnard Hill of the University of Georgia, who believed the race problem would be solved by strict segregation and industrial education. The all-white middle-ranking membership of the UCSRQ would attempt to engage southern college students and faculty in ways that encouraged the spread of southern liberalism.[19]

In 1912, aged nineteen, Woofter graduated in a BA class of thirty-three students and embarked immediately on research on African American life.[20] In doing so, he signed up with the interracial cooperation movement, beginning a connection with the Phelps-Stokes Fund that assisted his career until the 1930s. The fund was

Jack Woofter, aged nineteen in 1912, the year he graduated from
the University of Georgia. *Pandora* (UGA Yearbook), 25 (1912): 39.

a recent addition to the ranks of northern philanthropy, stemming from a bequest
in 1909 by New York heiress Caroline Phelps Stokes for housing improvements in
the city and the education of African Americans, American Indians, "needy and
deserving white students," and native people in colonial Africa. The trustees recognized "cooperation between racial and national groups as a fundamental element in human progress . . . [and encouraged] all movements that make for the
development of mutual sympathy and cooperation for the general good." Historian Eric S. Yellin suggests this "Christian civilizationism" was intended to help
black people overcome the supposed legacy of African cultural and moral backwardness. The Phelps-Stokes Fund was also part of a wider philanthropic effort
after 1890 to compensate for the failure of state governments to create opportunity in deprived cities and regions of the United States.[21]

The fund's first major donations were $12,500 apiece to the University of Georgia and the University of Virginia for annual $500 fellowships in the departments of sociology, economics, history, or education, "to enable southern youth of broad sympathies to make a scientific study of the Negro and his adjustment to American civilization." Next, the Phelps-Stokes Fund gave $2,500 to help the Jeanes Foundation deploy black supervising teachers in southern counties, one of the most efficient programs devised by the northern charities. In June 1912, after the UGA board "favorably recommended" the dean of education's son for a research award, Chancellor Barrow invited Jack Woofter to become the first Phelps-Stokes fellow. Barrow assured Anson Phelps Stokes, chairman of the Phelps-Stokes trustees and secretary of Yale University, that the younger Woofter was an "interested student of the negro question" and that his work would "have value."[22] In the long term, Barrow was right, and sociologist John H. Stanfield has commented that sponsoring Woofter as the first Phelps-Stokes fellow was "the program's greatest accomplishment," launching a notable career in interracial cooperation, higher education, and federal government.[23]

Woofter chose to study the black population of Athens, supervised by Brooks, who was an active member of the UCSRQ. As background, Woofter read other social surveys, including W. E. B. Du Bois's microscopic studies of contrasting African American communities in the 7th Ward of Philadelphia in 1896 and Farmville, Virginia, in 1898. (Du Bois, himself, had been influenced by Charles Booth's *Life and Labour of the People in London* [1889–1903].) Woofter also read several Atlanta University publications initiated by Du Bois on other aspects of black life and would later acknowledge the "pioneer" nature of Du Bois's scholarship.[24]

Woofter presented his preliminary findings at the second meeting of the UCSRQ in December 1912, a heady experience for a young researcher. His audience included Dillard, Joel E. Spingarn of the National Association for the Advancement of Colored People (NAACP), and the heads or representatives of ten large southern universities. Sitting through the sessions of the UCSRQ, as a succession of eminent scholars pronounced on African American needs and white people's duties, and the central role of the universities in delivering enlightenment and progress, Woofter must have sensed an opportunity to serve. The following spring, he attended the second conference of the SSC in Atlanta, a pivotal moment in the interracial cooperation movement. Audiences of up to three thousand black and white people were drawn to the proceedings, which were dominated by racial issues. Only white speakers gave papers, but, according to one participant, Luther Lee Bernard of the University of Florida, the frankness and goodwill exhibited in the panel discussions and audience contributions surprised members of both races—"there for the first time the southern white man and the Negro met on an equal plane, intellectually, for the discussion of their common problems."[25] Here,

Woofter also met the educational director of the Phelps-Stokes Fund, Thomas Jesse Jones, who would dominate his life for the next four years and permanently shape his thinking on race.

Brooks had suggested a dissertation using secondary data and a survey of local opinion on the black community, but Woofter chose a more thorough approach.[26] He spent February, March, and April 1913 visiting over a thousand dwellings (91 percent of the homes in the dispersed black districts of Athens), interviewing members of 1,224 families regarding household size, income and expenditure, and home ownership. He also gathered data on "schools, churches, lodges, and domestic service."[27] The resulting sixty-page report was crammed with information, but his interpretations were those of a privileged young man at ease with many assumptions of the southern white middle class. *The Negroes of Athens, Georgia,* reads as if Woofter was trying to impress his parents and their neighbors on Cloverhurst Avenue, rather than a wider audience that might have included black readers. He wrote from the perspective of a frustrated paternalist, keen to expose the dire accommodation of black families, yet chiding them for the persistence of bad conditions. It was a detailed account of local black life, but his blinkers prevented him from seeing that racial discrimination was the fundamental problem. According to Woofter, black Athenians led relatively easy lives, encountering more educational and industrial opportunity and less prejudice than blacks elsewhere. He presented the black community as a burden and his solution—increased cooperation between the better sort among both races—assumed that no black voice would be heard in city government, itself. And yet, merely by proposing greater cooperation and dialogue for the purpose of uplifting the black residents of Athens, he was departing from the racist orthodoxy in Georgia that held most black people to be irredeemably feckless.

Segregation in Athens, as in many southern cities, produced several overcrowded black residential pockets, rather than exclusive occupation of large areas by one or other race, as in the North. It was a hilltop town, Woofter noted: "The white or most valuable properties follow the ridges; the less valuable properties, following the hollows and streams which run through the town, being occupied by negroes." His eyes were opened as he walked these low-lying, disease-ridden roads, lined with primitive sanitation and contaminated wells.[28] He called for urgent improvements, but he seemed concerned less about the health of black residents than about their dangerous proximity to white families. The absence of a sewage system, he complained, was "a menace to the community, especially when the negro communities are as close to white residence quarters as is the case in Athens." Woofter was also convinced that domestic service was linked to the spread of disease: "The evil effects of the negro's way of living get even into the white home, where food is cooked by servants from unclean surroundings, and children are cared for by nurses whose bodies and minds are contaminated by the evil conditions under which they live."[29]

Regarding education, he considered the public and private schools for black children were insufficient and unsuitable. Black teachers were resourceful (he congratulated one teacher on the "way she adapts the studies and exercises to the smarter mulattoes and also to the duller blacks"), but he thought they needed white expert advice—the sort of comment welcomed by the Phelps-Stokes trustees.[30] He made conventional remarks about the emotionality of black worship and noted rising membership in fraternal orders, attributing this to the appeal of their insurance schemes and secret lodge rituals. He also reported that skilled blacks were being pushed out of trades such as building and barbering by white migrant and immigrant labor and complained that it was hard for white families to hire clean, competent, and honest domestic servants.[31]

He drew, for effect, on data showing that workers in Germany spent most of their income on food, whereas "[t]he negro's standard of life is so low that he is able to spend the bulk of his earnings not on the necessities of life, but on pleasure and recreation." In essence, he claimed that blacks preferred to live in squalor on a very basic diet supplemented by food obtained from their employers, while squandering their money on alcohol and trinkets. They ought to want something better out of life, he complained—"an increase in self-respect, a desire to have an attractive home, clean surroundings, substantial furniture, wholesome food, and educated children"—and they could be led in this direction by their churches and schools, with the support of well-intentioned white people: "Negroes are highly responsive to suggestions emanating from whites whom they consider really concerned in their welfare. The dominant race of the South has not only too long neglected its duty towards the negro, but has been blind to its own self-interest in bettering the conditions under which the weaker race lives."[32]

Woofter's analysis was naïve, predictable, almost juvenile stuff, reflecting the narrowness of his experience—as he later admitted, referring to "the immaturity of my observations." His fact-gathering had been thorough, but it was not methodical, and while his later reputation would be gained as a social scientist, this was not so much a work of sociology as a progressive social survey.[33] He had acquired a mass of basic information from black residents, but neglected to record their opinions and failed to consider the impact of segregation, class, crime, law enforcement, politics, or the press, and largely ignored the black experience outside Athens. He seemed unaware, for example, that black landownership was already common in Clarke County: the 1910 census recorded 210 white and 198 black landowning farmers—a near-parity inconceivable in the 1880s (although white farms were typically bigger and poor black tenants outnumbered poor whites). Woofter's study also contained no fundamental insights, such as Du Bois's attribution of the frailties of Philadelphia's black community to its marginalization by the white population. Black readers, therefore, found parts of *The Negroes of Athens, Georgia* distasteful. The historian Carter G. Woodson was thinking mainly of Woofter when he scoffed at the Phelps-Stokes fellowships: "Scholars . . . have not looked favorably upon the all but undergraduate type of dissertations produced by these students."[34] Woofter's analytical apparatus and moral horizon would widen enormously after he left Athens, but he always sounded as though he were writing for a white audience, and this was one reason why he was heavily criticized toward the end of the 1920s. The constant "otherness" of the black presence in Woofter's writing meant he never achieved, if he ever sought, a racially objective tone of address, although he was fully aware of his black readership.

For all that, *The Negroes of Athens, Georgia,* showed Woofter's capacity for energetic research and his faith in the black middle class; it was an attempt to promote reform and was very much in tune with liberal white discourse within the interracial cooperation movement before World War I. Moreover, his fieldwork made him confront extreme poverty in his hometown and strengthened his personal commitment to the Social Gospel; it gave him experiences that few middle-class white southerners shared and, while it was no epiphany, it sparked a lifelong interest in the improvement of race relations.[35]

Above all, racial research forced Jack Woofter to choose between conformity and transgression. For all the relative douceness of Athens, liberal attitudes toward race problems were unusual, and Woofter realized that he was out of step with his white peers. The Phelps-Stokes fellowship gave him what he called "my first taste of the feeling of isolation which came to a Southerner . . . who was a moderate on questions of race." He was taken aback to find that advocating interracial cooperation and some small local reforms represented a radical stance. When he was over sixty years old, his "one lasting impression" of the fellowship at UGA was the chilling recognition that engaging with the black community was frowned upon and that he was cutting himself adrift from most of the white citizenry of Athens.

> Not that I was then a flaming liberal. I was simply doing something which, to the people of my home community, was unprecedented. They were all most polite and non-committal, because I was working under the sponsorship of the University, but no one showed any interest in discussing what I was doing beyond the exercise of a mild curiosity. I did sense, however, some lifting of eyebrows behind my back.

Now he knew something of the loneliness of the white southerner who sought the amelioration of black life: "A nonconformist on race was likely to be looked on as a renegade or 'nigger lover' in the community and I can imagine that one who also lacked the full sympathy of his family would have been courting melancholia."[36] Absorbed in his research project, he worked alone in intellectual and social isolation, so that meeting the southern reformers of the UCSRQ and the SSC must have spurred feelings of relief and collegiality. Woofter's work on Athens was "nonconformist" only insofar as it said that white people should take more of an interest in the African American community, but this was sufficient to raise local suspicion. His parents' support proved crucial, but other white liberals were less fortunate, especially the white women who worked for better race relations. For example, the Commission on Interracial Cooperation's leader in South Carolina, Clelia McGowan, who organized the first interracial meeting in Florence and set up a local committee in Charleston, despaired, "In my own case, all my family are opposed to it, which is a very real and constant trial. I had expected criticism and severe judgment from outsiders."[37]

Some African American observers in the South recognized the vulnerability of any white person who raised questions about the status or treatment of the black population. Robert Russa Moton, who succeeded Booker T. Washington as principal of Tuskegee Institute, knew how hard it could be for whites with "sensitive consciences" to openly protest against racial discrimination. He suspected they feared the kind of reaction that scalawags faced after the Civil War: "This dread of what his neighbour may think more than anything else appears to paralyze the white man in America when it comes to public dealings with the Negro. This is true from the lowest circles to the highest, from the weakest to the strongest."[38]

The dogma of southern antiblack thought in the Progressive Era was so rigid that any imagined deviation was likely to be denigrated, as the reactionary stances of Georgian politicians such as Tom Watson and Hoke Smith amply demonstrated. To some extent, the disapproval directed at the interracial cooperation movement was an expression of southern nationalism; it flowed from the tendency to regard any attempts to draw attention to the South's problems as the perpetuation of northern lies. As David Carlton and Peter Coclanis have noted, "a persistent sense of grievance led most whites to identify any internal criticism with treason, and to force even the mildest dissenters into silence or exile." Consequently, as John Egerton remarked, "it took a special kind of courage—or madness—to speak and act against such overwhelming force."[39]

Jack Woofter knew about the backlash he was courting, and his persistence certainly showed courage. During the early years of the Progressive Era, the few southern whites bold enough to question the morality of denying black people civil rights drew ferocious responses on a number of occasions. The cases of three academics, one in Georgia and two in North Carolina, might have given Woofter pause for thought. In 1902, Andrew Sledd, an ordained Methodist and son-in-law of Bishop Warren A. Candler, was hounded out of his classics position at Emory College by protests led by the writer and suffragist Rebecca Felton. Sledd had stated in the *Atlantic Monthly* that lynching was simply "brutal murder" and should be punished as such; that, despite "the essential inferiority of the negro," a black citizen had human feelings and "inalienable rights," and that white people in the South should "give him fair and favorable conditions, and suffer him to work out, unhampered, his destiny among us." His article was partly inspired by the mutilation and burning of Sam Hose in 1899 at Newnan, in Coweta County, after special trains were run for spectators. Sledd understood that his "manifestly just view seems both disloyal and absurd" to most white southerners, which was confirmed when his effigy was burned at Covington, near the Emory campus, but he succeeded in generating debate about lynching.[40] The following year, John Spencer Bassett, a Methodist historian at Trinity College, near Durham, wrote in the *South Atlantic Quarterly* that racial strife was caused by needless fears concerning miscegenation and that whites should welcome black progress in "the spirit of conciliation." He advocated "the adoption of these children of Africa into our American life. In spite of our race feeling, of which this writer has his share, they will win equality at some time. We cannot remove them, we cannot kill them, we cannot prevent them from advancing in civilization. They are now very weak; some day they will be stronger." Booker T. Washington, he added almost incidentally, was "all in all the greatest man, save General Lee, born in the South in a hundred years; but he is not a typical Negro." For weeks afterward, partly because he took a swipe at "political editors," he was attacked in the white press, especially by Josephus Daniels, owner of the *Raleigh News and Courier,* which led the call for disfranchisement of African Americans in North Carolina. Bassett survived this test, but left for Smith College in 1906 in search of "a peaceful atmosphere."[41] In 1909, at the 12th Conference for Education in the South in Atlanta, Charles Lee Coon, a former superintendent of African American normal schools in North Carolina, criticized unequal educational provision for black children. In a speech on "Public Taxation and the Negro School," described by the *Bulletin of Atlanta University* as "frank and courageous," he demonstrated that in North Carolina, Virginia, and Georgia, far from being a burden on white taxpayers, black people were paying more in taxes than their states were spending on black children's education. How could it be right, he asked, that only 14 percent of the $32 million allocated annually by southern states to public education was spent on black children, who represented 40 percent of the enrolment? Coon opened up an issue that was still controversial when Jack Woofter grappled with it in the late 1920s. In a subsequent address to the Negro State Teachers Association, Coon poured scorn on "that species of the white race who would doom any other race to mental slavery." He outlined a blueprint for the interracial cooperation movement by calling on black people to "interest the white people in your schools. . . . Then get your churches, lodges, and societies to help. . . . We must see to it that we interest the local communities, white and black."[42] The apparent subversiveness

of Sledd, Bassett, and Coon lay not only in suggesting, as white men, that southern economic and social problems sprang from flaws in the white mind, but also,
as Mark K. Bauman has argued, in airing their complaints in forums where they
could be heard or read by northerners.[43]

The charge by these white men that the South was treating black people in
an uncivilized and irrational manner provoked a furious reaction that merely
proved their point. And yet they had never hinted that white people should consider blacks their social and political equals—merely that the law should be color-
blind. Sledd and Bassett, in particular, went to some lengths to make clear the
limits of their dissent. In his original article, Sledd stated baldly that the African American population's "inferiority is radical and inherent." He added, "It is
not necessary, nor desired, that the negro should be the social equal of the white
man. . . . Freedom does not, indeed, imply social, intellectual, or moral equality;
but its very essence is the equality of the fundamental rights of human creatures
before God and the law."[44] Similarly, Bassett assured the president of Trinity College that, although black progress was inevitable, "this does not mean, nor did I
intend that it should mean, that there will be social mingling of the races."[45] In
the view of Kelly Miller, the African American dean of arts and social sciences at
Howard University, the contortions of these representatives of George Washington Cable's "silent South" sprang from a caste system in which the "ethical and
political foundations of social order are ruthlessly overborne by the fiat of a silly
phrase"—social equality. The presence of white liberals in the South was, Miller
thought, "the only hopeful rift that we can see in the dark and lowering cloud . . . ,
[but] they have become tongue-tied, and are as completely divested of freedom,
either of action or utterance, as the poor Negro who bears the brunt of it all."
Liberals might question some of the consequences of white supremacy, but when
they also declared their rejection of "social equality," they were actually bolster-
ing the caste system that they purported to criticize, since the system itself rested
so heavily on the specter of "amalgamation." As it was, they were barely permitted to speak at all. As Miller put it, "If liberal-minded Southern white men, like
George W. Cable, or John Spencer Bassett, or Andrew Sledd, though still yield-
ing allegiance to the prevailing social dogma, dare lift their voice, even in faintest whisper, in protest against the evil perpetrated in its name, they are forthwith
lashed into silence by popular fury and scorn."[46] This backlash was also evident
to young white liberals like Jack Woofter.

One genuinely radical figure, who was prepared to speak out in terms that
virtually none of his fellow white liberals dared repeat, was the Rev. Henry Stiles
Bradley, the Methodist pastor of Trinity Church in Atlanta. A native Georgian,
Bradley had been a professor of biology and vice president at Emory College and
was known for his controversial views on evolution and admiration for Booker T.

Washington. In July 1905, he reacted to a mass lynching at Watkinsville, in Oconee County, the birthplace of Bishop Haygood, by preaching that, in effect, white supremacy was unchristian:

> The negro in the south has never had a fair chance, socially, politically or commercially. . . . The social caste that has grown up among us has led many of us to believe that somehow because we happened, without any choice or merit of our own, to be born with a white skin the Lord loves us better and thinks a little more of us than he does anybody with a darker skin. But I want to say to you that the man who does not admit and live up to the fraternity of the negro—yes, the fraternity, that is the word—whatever else he may be is not a Christian. I am not afraid of race equality, and I'll tell you my opinion of the man who is. It is this, that his social status must be very, very insecure that he should be so infinitely solicitous about safeguarding it.[47]

Booker T. Washington called this "one of the bravest and most encouraging sermons that I have ever read."[48]

The Oconee County ordinary (the probate court judge who effectively governed the county), John C. Johnson, offered a different view. In a two-thousand-word diatribe in the *Atlanta Constitution,* he claimed to speak for the white citizens of Watkinsville by condoning the lynchings and denouncing Bradley's "social equality doctrines" and his "cruel, premeditated" assault on "the fixed order of things in the south."

> The God of the universe made the white man white, and the black man black, and until he sees fit to change the colors, no self-respecting southern man will meet the negro on a level. It is . . . impossible for the black man to respect race equality in the south. . . . One race or the other must be master here. . . . In the south the negro has the fairest chance to earn an honest living of any section of the country. There is no people on earth who know him quite as well as the southern man; and no people who are more disposed to give him a 'square deal,' so long as he occupies the station that God created him to occupy, and none more ready to administer a rebuke when he aspires to social equality. . . . There is no place in southern Methodism for a follower of Darwin and his theories of evolution and there can never be a place for a preacher of social equality. Brand him a renegade. Dismiss him. We demand it in the name of every unprotected white woman in Georgia and throughout the south. His damnable doctrines would place a black claw at the throat of every helpless woman in the south.

Finally, Johnson questioned Bradley's own racial heritage and accused him of falling "prostrate at the feet of all Yankeedom for applause."[49] Two months later, the Methodist Episcopal Church, South, announced that Bradley would exchange places with a minister in St. Louis, Missouri, but not before he was tried for heresy by the North Georgia Conference. He was acquitted, but four years later he abandoned Methodism and became a Congregationalist minister in Massachusetts.[50]

Such episodes laid open southern white Methodism's struggle with race as a moral problem and a missionary challenge. What were the duties, Methodists asked, of the "white brother in Christ" toward his "black brother in Christ"? Since segregation was apparently inviolable, how could the South justly accommodate the black population? Or, as the *Christian Advocate,* a Nashville Methodist publication, asked in 1908, "How can races different in all essentials as much as human beings can differ best live together?"[51] Despite a sheltered upbringing in Athens, it is unlikely that Jack Woofter would have been unaware of Sledd, Bassett, Coon, or Bradley and the extreme reactions that unorthodox views on race could provoke. As he completed his Phelps-Stokes fellowship in 1913, a new furor broke out concerning the president of the University of South Carolina, Samuel Chiles Mitchell, a trustee of the Negro Rural School Fund of the Jeanes Foundation, who was forced out by Governor Coleman Blease for supporting extra funding for a black college.[52]

The interracial cooperationist movement that Woofter now joined represented a minority position in southern white community action, and yet he devoted himself to the examination of racial issues and their implications for the South for the next twenty years, and this remained an important theme in the rest of his life. On several occasions before the New Deal, he could have turned away to do other work, but, as he told the avuncular Anson Phelps Stokes in June 1913, "My work under the Phelps-Stokes Fellowship this year has probably marked the turning point in my life, and I hope that in succeeding years the fellowship, of which I was the first beneficiary, will mean as much inspiration to other students at the University of Georgia."[53] The fellowship was certainly a turning point, leading directly to his engagement by the Phelps-Stokes Fund as an educational researcher for the next three years.

After 1900, there was an upsurge in theoretical and philanthropic enthusiasm for the practical training offered at Hampton Institute in Virginia and its offshoot, Tuskegee Institute in Alabama, where the respective principals, Hollis B. Frissell, a white northern missionary, and Booker T. Washington, a former slave, became standard-bearers of agricultural and industrial education for African American youth. Washington and Frissell, who died in 1915 and 1917, respectively, won wide support for a social philosophy that implicitly endorsed the subordination of black people for the foreseeable future as they encouraged efforts to replicate the Hampton-Tuskegee model. Just as New South educationists, such as T. J. Woofter Sr. and UGA chancellors Walter Hill and David Barrow, embraced the Hampton instructional model, its economic virtues were extolled by northern philanthropists such as merchants Robert C. Ogden and Julius Rosenwald, entrepreneurs Andrew Carnegie, John D. Rockefeller Jr., and George Eastman, and railroad magnates William H. Baldwin Jr., and Arthur Curtiss James. Although these men agreed on the need for higher education in the arts and sciences for exceptionally talented African Americans, they saw no legitimate alternative to practical schooling in the techniques of industry, agriculture, and domestic science for the great majority. In committing vast sums of money, they stressed the national and regional economic benefits of a suitably educated, cheap, nonunionized workforce and the benefits to black people themselves of a training that would allow them to prosper gradually and separately in the South—their supposed "natural environment." In a period of mass immigration, there were also some who argued that a better-educated southern black workforce could block the incursion into the region of thousands of non-Protestant foreigners. Undoubtedly, northern philanthropy was an expression of what Ralph Ellison later called "the Negro's strongest weapon in pressing his claims: his hold upon the moral consciousness of Northern whites." The millionaires' funds were channeled through bodies with overlapping personnel and programs, such as the Southern Education Board, the General Education Board, the Anna T. Jeanes Foundation, the John F. Slater Fund, and, latterly, the Phelps-Stokes Fund, the Julius Rosenwald Fund, the Laura Spelman Rockefeller Memorial, and the Social Science Research Council.[54] As historian Adam Fairclough has observed, "The fact that the men who administered these foundations constituted an interlocking directorate, sitting on each other's boards, magnified their influence."[55]

Black educators generally welcomed northern donations, but Kelly Miller spoke for many when he wondered whether, at least in terms of higher education, the time had come for blacks to help themselves: "The white race, through philanthropy, has done much; but its vicarious task culminated when it developed the first generation of educated [black] men and women. They must do the rest. The philanthropists spoke for us when our tongues were tied. They pleaded our cause when we were speechless; but now our faculties have been unloosed."[56] The challenge black teachers faced was enormous. African American schools suffered the hostility of white taxpayers and the indifference of state governments; they also lacked endowments, occupied shabby buildings, and competed for charitable handouts that were spread too thinly. In 1915, in the whole of the South, there were only sixty-four public secondary schools for black children, mostly found in the larger cities of the border states.[57]

The "new leaders of southern thought"—as William Baldwin called white professionals and businessmen who supported universal education for both races—were convinced that only northern philanthropy could inject quickly the necessary funds to transform black education. However, the political realities were not lost on the northern charities. Noting the unwillingness to increase taxes for black schools, they understood that many southerners would be equally uneasy about enlarged black educational provision funded by northern millionaires. As historian Walter A. Jackson has put it, "Foundation officials realized that the combination of Yankee meddling, Rockefeller money, and Negro education made them a vulnerable target for Dixie demagogues."[58] Indeed, northern charities were criticized by conservatives, fearful that enhanced black education would generate economic and political turmoil. To minimize the appearance of outside interference, the philanthropic funds handed over their central operations and fieldwork to southern agents, such as James Hardy Dillard, who controlled the Jeanes and Slater Funds, and Jackson Davis, who worked for the General Education Board and, later, the Carnegie Fund. They argued that citizenship training and industrial education would deliver peaceful progress, but critics retorted that a well-educated black population would reject menial work, compete with white labor, and seek restoration of the vote and other rights. In the first decade of the twentieth century, before southern black families began to migrate northward in vast numbers, such views were common: a Virginian journal, the *Farmville Herald*, stated, "When they learn to spell dog and cat they throw away the hoe"; the owner of a small farm in North Carolina complained in 1900, "We are tired of educating negroes to 'sass' us"; and a sawmill owner in the same state reckoned "the uneducated negro [is] the best we have for drudgery."[59] Some southern white labor leaders were equally hostile to additional expenditure on black education—Alabama labor spokesman Henry C. West ran for public office declaring, "This is a white man's country. I am opposed to negro education, because it is an established fact that an 'educated negro' is as a rule a worthless imp."[60]

In his last years, Booker T. Washington was preoccupied with fighting such attitudes. He traveled a thousand miles on a two-week tour of Louisiana in 1915, speaking to vast outdoor audiences on education and the spirit of interracial cooperation. He crafted two equally utilitarian lectures—one for black listeners and one for whites. To black audiences, he said:

> After you receive your education, your conduct will be closely watched by white people and by black people. Remember you are on trial. Education teaches men to love labor. It does not make of a man a dude or a fool. It makes him a useful citizen. Education makes you love the community in which you live. It makes you love your race and honor your father and mother. Education is meant to make a person modest; simple in language, polite; and love God.
>
> Don't be ashamed to work. With all your education just be an ordinary, useful human being. Be of real service to somebody. Remember that an educated man is simple, honest, humble. Don't advertise your troubles over-much.

To white audiences he said:

> You have in your mind a vivid picture of a so-called educated Negro that you saw twenty-five or thirty years ago—a Negro who was different from everybody else in the community. This educated Negro wore, perhaps, red socks, a gay necktie, patent-leather shoes, a silk hat, carried a walking stick, smoked a big cigar, and talked a language which nobody else understood—and which he himself did not quite understand.

Negroes have passed through their "silly" period. They now know how to use their education. It will pay southern planters to give Negroes good rural schools and good homes. Many good Negro farmers are leaving the plantations and moving into a town to secure better school accommodations for their children. If you give Negroes training in scientific farming, manual arts, cooking and sewing, you will be repaid.

It is better to spend money to educate Negroes than to take care of criminals.[61]

It was an appealing exegesis of his Atlanta Compromise address twenty years before: black southerners should go to school, improve themselves without openly aspiring, and head back to the field, workshop, or laundry; whites, in turn, should permit and pay for better black education in the knowledge that the outcome would be a docile, dependable workforce. Not all black people agreed—in the NAACP's *Crisis* magazine, Victor P. Thomas, a New Orleans civil servant and part-time journalist, observed that people leading modest rural lives were still subjected to "malice, abuse, unjust treatment, overbearing conduct, false accusation, summary punishment, lynching, confiscation or usurpation of property, [and] expulsion from the community for trivial offenses. . . . Mr. Washington forgot to tell his white audience that thirteen Negroes were lynched in Louisiana last year alone and not a single person punished for these mob murders."[62]

Although Washington's social message was widely accepted in the South, the vast funding gap in education remained. As the newest of the large charities working in this field after 1910, the Phelps-Stokes Fund sought to reassure wealthy northern neo-abolitionists that their money was well spent and that African Americans were capable of rapid progress, given the right kind of training and support. At the end of 1912, encouraged by Frissell, Washington, Dillard, and the evangelist of interracial cooperation, Edgar Gardner Murphy, the Phelps-Stokes trustees committed themselves to a large-scale survey of black education in the South. The project was a response to concerns about the quality and usefulness of the six hundred private schools that had sprung up in the South (and a further two dozen in the North) to serve black parents who wanted better schooling for their children than that provided by the local public schools. The private schools—mostly elementary, with a scattering of high schools and colleges—catered for only 4 percent of southern black children, but they absorbed large amounts of philanthropic money and recruited some of the best-trained black teachers. Frissell and Washington were convinced that many of the private schools were worthless; the latter claimed that in "many so-called industrial schools . . . the work is a mere sham" and that few institutions calling themselves colleges or universities merited such titles. Since these schools could not charge high fees, their principals went cap-in-hand to charities to cover the costs of salaries, books, and buildings. Washington maintained that many of them knew so little about education that they tarnished the reputations of Hampton and Tuskegee. This prejudged an ongoing investigation into higher education in the South by a black agent of the Slater Fund, William T. B. Williams, who found twenty-two black colleges worthy of the name in 1912, but only 11 percent of their students were taking college-grade classes.[63]

The Phelps-Stokes trustees agreed to appoint an agent at a salary of $3,500 to carry out a comprehensive survey and asked their secretary, Anson Phelps Stokes, to find the best person. He narrowed the field to two white northerners, Booker T. Washington's adviser and ghostwriter, Robert Ezra Park, and the former Hampton Institute teacher, Thomas Jesse Jones. Washington insisted that Park was "by far the best qualified white man in any part of the country to have charge of this work," having "a wider vision of the whole Southern field than is true of Dr. Jones," who was just "a professional statistician." He added that Park had "the knack of meeting all classes of people in a way to get from them valuable information and at the same time not offend them," implying (with reason) that Jones lacked this skill. Dillard and Frissell recommended Jones, leaving Anson Phelps Stokes to interview both candidates.[64]

From the outset, Phelps Stokes was clearly inclined toward Jones, later described by Jack Woofter as a "fiery little Welshman." Citing Jones's immigrant origins, Phelps Stokes detected in him "a certain intellectual detachment from the problem"; he also noted that the Bureau of Education in Washington "would in all probability allow him to continue to occupy his office there, [which] would be an important consideration."[65] Jones was offered the job, leading Park to conclude, "I did not seem to [Phelps Stokes] to represent science. Perhaps also, there was a distrust of the ability of anyone concerned with a Negro school to do scientific work." Park undertook a small survey of black industrial schools across the South in 1913, reviewing the performance of teachers and principals trained at Tuskegee, but his failure to secure the Phelps-Stokes post hastened his decision to accept a job at the University of Chicago, where he would build a stellar career as a professor of sociology.[66]

Jones's appointment as the agent of the Phelps-Stokes Fund gave him a national profile in several strands of educational reform. During the next thirty years, he would be the most controversial white apostle of the Hampton-Tuskegee "uplift" program at home and abroad, shaping policies on the schooling of a whole generation of American minorities and colonial peoples. According to a fellow reformer, Jones's upbringing in a Welsh-speaking family in Ohio gave him "perhaps a racial sympathy for the underdog" and Jack Woofter also believed he "had some first-hand knowledge of the feelings of a member of a minority group." Jones graduated from Marietta College in Ohio, where he met the leading social gospeler, Washington Gladden, the author of *Applied Christianity* (1887), before studying divinity at Columbia University's affiliate, Union Theological Seminary. In 1904, he gained a PhD in sociology at Columbia, with a dissertation on immigrants in New York City, and investigated tuberculosis among African Americans. He was supervised by Franklin H. Giddings, a founder of American sociology, who drew ideas from social science pioneers such as Lester F. Ward, Charles H. Cooley, and John R. Commons. Jones became a lifelong devotee of Giddings (who directed Jack Woofter's doctoral work ten years later), attending the fortnightly meetings of Columbia's F.H.G. Club with Paul and Arthur Kellogg, the editors of the *Survey* magazine, which reported on practical applications of new social science research. Jones also absorbed the "social efficiency" ideas of Edward. A. Ross and David Snedden, who believed the aptitudes of different groups in American society required different kinds of education. He concluded that immigrant groups represented distinct intellectual types, with Anglo-Saxons occupying the highest tier. Jones was appointed to teach social studies at Hampton Institute, where his ideas chimed with those of founder Samuel Chapman Armstrong, a leading proponent of vocational education for former slaves and their children. Jones's citizenship curriculum at Hampton reflected Giddings's belief that African Americans lagged thousands of years behind in the "evolution of races" and that this primarily explained their unequal place in society, although progress could be accelerated by contact with Nordic civilization. Like Booker T. Washington, Jones held that race prejudice would subside as black people became useful citizens through carefully adapted vocational education; meanwhile, it was essential that they accept that their status was a function of cultural evolution, rather than oppression and deliberate injustice.[67] Jones saw the uplift of African Americans as part of the Americanization phenomenon and was convinced that cooperation between different groups was vital: "Americanization does not mean simply adapting foreign groups to an American community life and standards. It means arousing all native born citizens of all races to a new enthusiasm for American ideals of living and of mental development."[68]

In 1910, Jones oversaw the collection of data on African Americans for the federal census and remained in Washington, D.C., to work for the Interior Department's Bureau of Education and Howard University. He chaired the social studies committee of the National Education Association's Commission on the Reorganization of Secondary Education, which reported in 1916. He was also secretary of Dillard's twice-yearly Conference of Educational Boards' Representatives and persuaded U.S. commissioner of education Philander P. Claxton, a Tennessean Progressive, to collaborate with the Phelps-Stokes Fund in its survey of black education. Claxton had been party to the suppression of a national academic ranking exercise on American higher education in 1911–12, but he approved of inspecting black schools, telling an international gathering at Tuskegee in April 1912, "No State can be strong if one-third of its people are weak; no State can count itself rich if one-third of its people must be condemned to poverty. . . . No State can reach the highest degree of power and citizenship until all of its people are able to comprehend the possibilities of citizenship and its duties."[69]

The Phelps-Stokes Fund struck a deal with the Bureau of Education, making Jones the director of the bureau's Division of Racial Groups, with added responsibility for Indian and Mexican education. Most missionary attempts to shape black education after the Civil War had stuttered long before 1910, but Jones was determined to effect change. His massive two-volume report on black education in the South, *Negro Education: A Study of the Private and Higher Schools for Colored People in the United States,* would be published in 1917. The report claimed that hundreds of private schools attempting to fill the gaps in poor state provision were mismanaged, ill-equipped, short of qualified staff, and wedded to an inappropriate classical curriculum.[70] Although the Division of Racial Groups was abolished in 1919, the Jones report played a central role in determining which schools would be supported by northern philanthropy and the kind of vocational black education the states themselves should develop. To Jones's mind, "education must be closely related to the actual life of those who have to be taught. It must take account of their instincts, experiences and interests as distinct from those of people living in quite different conditions. Its aim must be to equip them for the life which they have to live. . . . Further, education must take account of the life not only of the individual but of the community."[71] The implication that the curriculum should shrink infuriated black critics such as W. E. B. Du Bois and Carter G. Woodson, who saw Jones as an unqualified meddler, but Jones could point to important African American allies, such as Robert Russa Moton, who said in 1912 when he was at Hampton, "We must not be misled by high-sounding phrases as to the kind of education the race should receive, but we should remember that the education of a people should be conditioned upon their capacity, social environment, and the probable life which they will lead in the immediate future."[72]

As a result of his Phelps-Stokes fellowship at UGA, Jack Woofter was chosen in 1913 to be one of Jones's assistants, giving him permanent membership in the interracial cooperation movement and his first sense of the potential for the practical application of the social sciences. He absorbed Jones's ideas and attitudes, which seemed to offer objective explanations for things that disquieted Woofter about southern race relations. Jones had enormous energy and self-confidence, academic credentials, and impressive Progressive connections; he became a role model and father figure to Woofter—someone to whom the latter turned for advice for the next twenty years. Jones, in turn, saw Woofter as a bright young southerner who could help him lead an enlightened generation toward a Christian, rational solution to the race problem.

2 Thomas Jesse Jones and *Negro Education*

Education reform was the most freely debated aspect of southern race relations after 1910, but most educationists, philanthropists, and state officials concurred on the need to enhance cheap, practical, segregated schooling for black children. Michael Dennis, among others, has argued that the expansion of industrial education meshed with the models favored by progressive educators and politicians in the South for reasons of racial control and regional economic rehabilitation.[1] From 1913 to 1916, Jack Woofter was to become centrally involved in an intensive examination of black education that was so loaded with cultural, pedagogical, and economic prescription that northern black activists denounced its authors, including Woofter, as purveyors of an unwarranted vocational curriculum designed to create a dependent laboring caste.

Through his father's work as dean of education at the University of Georgia, Jack Woofter was familiar with arguments surrounding rural education reform in the South and the persistent inability of local, state, and private bodies to fulfill properly the responsibilities they assumed after 1900. He was aware that black schools generally offered a more basic education than white schools, and he probably attributed this to differences in the intellectual capacities of black students and the generally lower educational attainment of their teachers. Until he ventured into the meanest homes in Athens as a graduate student, he had little understanding of the scale and stultifying effects of black poverty, or the gulf between the lives of young white middle-class Georgians and their African American contemporaries. He learned more than he was able to articulate in *Negroes of Athens, Georgia,* and he was eager to do more for interracial cooperation, but he was completely unprepared for many of the sharper contrasts between black and white lives that he encountered in rural parts of the South as a Phelps-Stokes Fund investigator. His commitment to the idea of regional reform, his aptitude for research, and his appetite for hard, detailed work meant that he became a vital part of the enterprise that created *Negro Education,* a report that assumed immense significance in the growing tension between white liberals and radical black analysts of southern life.

The Phelps-Stokes Fund survey of southern black education was based on school visits and questionnaires, state surveys, and conferences, and loosely modeled on Abraham Flexner's critical 1910 report on American medical schools. Although

Thomas Jesse Jones concentrated on private schools offering elementary education to a total of 70,500 pupils, selective additional inspections were made of the private schools offering education at high school and college level (teaching 13,000 students), and the few public high schools and colleges (with another 13,000 students). This hardly represented a comprehensive survey of black education and youth in the South: the elementary pupils in private schools represented only 3.5 percent of the two million southern black children aged between six and fourteen years, and total black high school enrolment represented less than 2 percent of those between the ages of fifteen and nineteen. Nevertheless, as chief investigator, Jones believed some fundamental truths about southern life would emerge. The schools, he stated, would be judged against "the real educational needs of the people and the extent to which the school work has been adapted to these needs."[2] Jones insisted these "real educational needs" related to agriculture, industry, and domestic service. He favored a highly prescriptive elementary curriculum, with mathematics playing an important corrective part: "To emotional groups, prone to action without adequate thought, thorough practice in mathematical processes is essential." In secondary education, he prized the social sciences for developing citizenship, business skills, and aesthetic awareness, and wanted normal schools to train teachers capable of delivering the programs devised at Hampton and Tuskegee. Other tertiary education was for training wise leaders, doctors, and clergymen.[3] There was nothing new in this model—ten years earlier the southern Methodist Episcopal bishop in Mississippi, Charles Betts Galloway, demanded "the rudiments of an education for all, industrial training for the many, and a collegiate training for the few who are to be the teachers and leaders of their people."[4]

The novelty lay in Jones's determination to show what happened to the $3 million given each year by private individuals, charitable boards, and churches to black schools in the South. He noted, "Thoughtful people of the South and of the North, white and colored, have long been puzzled as to the merits and demerits of the many appeals for money and sympathy in behalf of all sorts and conditions of institutions for the improvement of Negroes." A lot of money was wasted, he argued—some very good schools had "achieved international fame for pioneer service in democratizing education," but there were others whose work was "of no value or whose so-called presidents or founders deliberately play upon philanthropy for their own personal gain." Ineptitude or fraud was compounded by a widespread reliance on a traditional curriculum, "with too exclusive emphasis upon bookish studies."[5] This was a complaint he made about southern education, as a whole, irrespective of race.

Jones urgently needed assistants. First, he hired Ocea Taylor, a thirty-two-year-old African American clerk in the Bureau of the Census, to maintain an office in Washington, D.C., and assist with field trips. Taylor had graduated from the State Agricultural and Mechanical College at Huntsville, Alabama, an institution devoted largely to training teachers, and afterward gained BA and LLB degrees at Howard University. He was making his way in the upper reaches of black Washington society and had been admitted to the bar in the District of Columbia. As a statistical clerk, Taylor liaised with the black press for the Census Bureau and dabbled in journalism, starting up a short-lived newspaper, the *Washington American*, in 1909, with another black government clerk, Oliver Randolph, a migrant from Mississippi. Taylor accompanied Jones to meetings of the Common Welfare Club and shared his interest in cleaning up Washington's notorious alley dwellings. Adding a black researcher to the *Negro Education* survey pleased the Phelps-Stokes trustees, who were "anxious that the point of view of the dominant race in the South should be adequately represented on its investigating staff, [and also] felt that the attitude and insight of the best type of educated colored man would be invaluable." By "best type," they meant someone who was unassuming, with some background in vocational schooling. Jones considered that Taylor's "training and disposition" would enable him to "discover many facts not available to a white man . . . [and] make it possible for the white investigator to avoid situations which might arouse the antagonisms of Southern whites." In material terms, it was a good move for Taylor, too; the Phelps-Stokes salary of $1,200 was $200 more than his government pay.[6]

Jones knew the junior levels of Washington bureaucracy were a racial minefield under the Taft and Wilson administrations and was "strongly inclined to the conclusion" that his office secretary should also be male. "My chief reason for this thought is that some of our extreme Southern friends might misunderstand if they found a white young woman and a colored man working in the same office." He was justifiably anxious: within a week of Taylor's recruitment, white clerks in the Bureau of Education began a protest about his presence. Jones asked Anson Phelps Stokes for a further $1,000 to rent a new office outside the Department of the Interior, "to avoid clashes with extreme Southern Whites and sensitive Blacks," but Stokes and education commissioner Philander Claxton deemed this an overreaction, so Jones told Taylor to work from Hampton Institute. By the summer of 1913, the fuss had died down, allowing Taylor to spend most of his time in Washington with Jones until the schools opened in September. Over the next three years, between periods of fieldwork, Taylor worked regularly in the Bureau of Education on the analysis of school financial accounts.[7]

Jones's second recruit was twenty-year-old Jack Woofter, setting the latter firmly on the path of race work and cementing his links with the Phelps-Stokes trustees, who knew his name through the fellowship at the University of Georgia. In the spring of 1913 he was still engaged in basic research on black life in Athens, but, from several points of view, he fitted the bill. Jones, Stokes, and Claxton agreed that their ideal office secretary should be a young southern white man "of the right attitude," whose race, gender, and origins would satisfy potential white critics of the project. The work of the University Commission on Southern Race Questions showed that men of this sort were to be had, since "the right attitude" seemed increasingly common among well-educated southerners. (The Methodist YMCA organizer Willis D. Weatherford, a tireless optimist and advocate of the Social Gospel regarding race relations, told the Y's general secretary in March 1913, "Quite a number of our choicest college men are volunteering to give their lives to this particular phase of work.") The Tennessean educator and health reformer Wickliffe Rose, who knew T. J. Woofter Sr. through the Southern Education Association and the Peabody Fund, was the first to recommend Jack Woofter to Jones and Stokes. Rose also addressed any concerns over Woofter's age: "I know him intimately and assure you that you need have no misgivings on this score. His maturity is far beyond his years. He is a young man of very unusual ability and character. He will be a credit to the work."[8]

After meeting Woofter for the first time in April 1913 at the second annual meeting of the Southern Sociological Congress in Atlanta, Jones told Stokes:

> The first impression [Woofter] gives is that of youthfulness. He is only twenty. President [Edmund T.] Ware [of Atlanta University] said that when he first saw Woofter a year ago, he was only a 'callow youth with sophomoric ideas on the race question.' When President Ware and others saw him last week, however, they were surprised at the development which had taken place. While he is young, he has a discerning mind and a good spirit. The quality which especially attracts me is the determination to study the situation first-hand and not to depend upon hearsay evidence.

Jones added that having an assistant with the same name as the dean of education at the University of Georgia "would be especially helpful in conferring with public officials of southern states."[9] In a further letter recommending the younger Woofter to Claxton, Jones noted, "The only question any one raises against him is his age. . . . As this is a condition out of which he will grow, I am not seriously impressed with it." Claxton, another old friend of T. J. Woofter Sr., suggested a salary of $1,000, "with the prospect of some increase in salary when he has demonstrated that he can do the work well." Jack accepted the job as a "special collaborator" in June 1913, but was allowed to spend the summer completing his Athens study and working as a sports editor on the *Atlanta Journal*.[10] Over the next four years, he discovered the rigors of fieldwork, the diversity of the South, the dynamics of different rural and urban communities, and the tangled interracial and intraracial conflicts that education, in particular, could provoke. Marching under the Hampton-Tuskegee banner and in the pay of northern philanthropy, Woofter acquired an identity that would benefit his career in the short term, but badly damage him in the eyes of black activists who saw Jones, in particular, as a baneful influence. For example, when Woofter published his memoirs in the mid-1950s, William M. Brewer, who succeeded Carter G. Woodson as editor of the

Journal of Negro History, wrote, "Unfortunately [Woofter] came under the indoctrination of Thomas Jesse Jones, Director of the Phelps-Stokes Fund and the most evil person that touched Negro life from 1902–1950!" From that moment, Brewer recalled, "Woofter, like his mentor and sponsor Jones, also became a white professional leader of colored people."[11] For his part, Woofter gladly acknowledged Jones's impact on his career and his skill as a social scientist, later recalling that it was from Jones that he gained a "respect for hard facts and impatience with pretense and false sentiment."[12]

Jones and his new assistants became nominal employees of the Bureau of Education, receiving annual payments of $1.00, while their actual salaries and expenses were provided by the Phelps-Stokes Fund. By the time Woofter arrived, Jones and Taylor had written a preliminary report on private black schools in Alabama, "to ascertain the value of our various lines of inquiry." From a base at Tuskegee Institute, they assessed each school against student achievement, the curriculum, management and finances, the buildings and equipment, and local esteem. Jones took an early decision that his final report, with little regard for the feelings of black educators, would depict a sector rich in unfulfilled possibilities. Like everyone involved in black education, he knew that public funding allocated by the states and divided by the counties was grossly inadequate. "The public school system is wretched," he wrote privately about Alabama, but he was surprised to find it was also corrupt: "While the number of southern [white] men interested in the education of the Negro is increasing, I am not only finding cases of neglect in these [public] schools, but also cases of actual fraud in the use of the small appropriations made." He knew private schools could "at best, only supplement the efforts of the state," but now he saw their potential social value, giving the black middle class an alternative and allowing northern philanthropists to insinuate their point of view and code of manners. (Indeed, as Adam Fairclough has noted, private schools heightened differences in class and speech between black southerners.) He was concerned, nevertheless, that badly managed schools would discredit the rest by wasting money and alienating white donors. He constantly looked for school principals who were lining their own pockets with charitable donations, but, in fact, he found very few. In Alabama, he was also shocked by the immorality and crime (including a murder) that accompanied summer closing exercises at several rural institutions. The numerous demands in *Negro Education* for strict military-style regulation of male dormitories stemmed from this experience.[13]

Jones preferred schools run by white people, especially white women of northern origin, such as the Calhoun Colored School in Lowndes County, Alabama, and the Penn Normal, Industrial, and Agricultural School on St. Helena Island, South Carolina, which were held up as paragons of useful learning in *Negro Education.* He regarded the Calhoun School's principal, Charlotte Thorn, and the

Penn School's Rossa B. Cooley as embodiments of the Christian spirit of Caroline Phelps Stokes and deeply regretted the replacement of northern white teachers by black teachers. It threatened to "complete the segregation of the Negro from the aid, influence, and standards of white people." White teachers, Jones asserted, showed "their colored pupils by precept and example that education is not only head knowledge but the formation of habits that guarantee such fundamental virtues as cleanliness, thoroughness, perseverance, honesty, and the essential elements of family life." He also liked the ethos of schools run by northern churches such as the United Presbyterian Church: "While they do not emphasize the industrial to the extent one desires, they are usually honest and clean and orderly. The importance of these qualities is being emphasized by their absence in so many of the schools." He lavished praise on particularly deserving schools, and was equally quick to tell the trustees about schools from which money should be withheld. For example, Miles Memorial College, run by the Colored Methodist Episcopal Church near Birmingham, was denounced for poor staff, dilapidated buildings, and a history of misusing General Education Board (GEB) funds. In the final report, after two more inspections and a change of management, the college was prescribed a radical financial overhaul and instructed to do more industrial work before it was fit to be supported.[14]

Woofter helped Jones and Taylor complete a further preparatory exercise in Georgia, giving special attention to Atlanta, with its five large private black schools and six smaller schools "of all sorts and conditions." They found a good deal of ignorance in the South about black schooling, and their attempts to clarify "the relation and attitude of the white people of Atlanta to these schools . . . brought out some peculiar misunderstandings on the part of the white people." Jones was nevertheless pleased with his new team: "Woofter and Taylor are both doing very good work. The three of us are working together in harmony and unity which has no regard for race, creed or color." Here was a small model of interracial cooperation, pursuing objectives that would benefit all. In the final weeks of 1913, the trio visited counties in other parts of Georgia and South Carolina. Jones inspected the larger schools and sent Woofter to survey southern Georgia and collect comparative data from white private schools, while Taylor audited school accounts. Claxton found their initial reports "astonishing" and predicted that the completed study would force the South into "a more just division of public school funds."[15]

In January 1914, Jones addressed the American Association for the Advancement of Science conference in Atlanta on black education and the southern economy, while Woofter and Taylor inspected small schools in Florida. From there, all three went to Mississippi, Alabama, Louisiana, Texas, and Arkansas, so that the Deep South surveys were largely completed by the end of the 1913–14 school year, with the summer set aside for analyzing their materials and methods. They planned to spend 1914–15 inspecting schools in Virginia, North Carolina, and the border states before revisiting selected schools and starting their final report. They invited opinions from other educationists and six "specialists" in "agriculture, manual training, household arts, school accounts, buildings, and grounds," who each visited up to fifty schools for verification.[16]

In June 1914, with Woofter proving an effective field investigator, Jones hired the University of Georgia's second Phelps-Stokes fellow, Walter B. Hill, for clerical work while the others were on the road. Jones told Anson Phelps Stokes, "Our feeling is that it would be better to have the office force entirely of men and of men who have a firsthand knowledge of the situation." Hill was the oldest son of UGA's late chancellor, Walter Barnard Hill, which delighted Jones: "I am very much impressed with the possibilities resulting from the employment of the son of Chancellor Hill in a work that has to do with the negro problems. His family connection, as in the case of Mr. Woofter, will always be a splendid introduction to the people whom he approaches. To give employment to such a young man in this work also helps to create the proper attitude towards this question."[17] Jack Woofter had known Walter Hill since the latter's father had brought T. J. Woofter Sr. to Athens in 1903. A year older than Woofter, and less precocious, Hill was from a family much like the Woofters—progressive-minded and Methodist, deeply rooted in slaveholding on one parent's side and with out-of-state liberal connections on the other. Hill's father was an outspoken advocate of black vocational education and his mother, Sallie Barker Hill, was the first president of the Georgia School Improvement Club (GSIC), established by the Georgia Federation of Women's Clubs (GFWC) to campaign for the physical renewal of schools and libraries. It set up seventy-six county committees and ninety-seven clubs between 1904 and 1906 and was a forerunner of the Commission on Interracial Cooperation. She visited and secretly funded black schools across Georgia on behalf of the GSIC and the GFWC and took up her late husband's campaign for local taxation for education. The younger Walter Hill completed a degree in electrical engineering in 1913 and became a schoolteacher until illness forced him to return home, where he accepted the Phelps-Stokes fellowship after the preferred candidate withdrew. Walter Hill's dissertation, surveying black landowning, tenancy, and schools in rural parts of Clarke County, was an extension of Jack Woofter's work on Athens. It was completed in 1915 at Anson Phelps Stokes's urging, with help from Jones and Woofter. Like Woofter, Hill's direction in life was fixed by his Phelps-Stokes fellowship and his work with Thomas Jesse Jones; he committed himself to a career in black vocational education, going on to work for the federal government, the Georgia Department of Education, and the GEB.[18]

In the spring of 1914, Taylor and Woofter worked in Arkansas, before joining Jones for work in the southwest. Jones had devised a relentless fieldwork program, sending his men into almost every southern county to visit substantial institutions with several hundred students one day and dilapidated little schools with a handful of pupils the next. After a year in the field, Woofter found rural visits hard going. In November 1914, he was too ill to join Jones, Taylor, and Hill on a trip to New York to meet the Phelps-Stokes Fund trustees for the first time. He recovered sufficiently to work through December in North Carolina, but revisiting Alabama with Taylor in January 1915 he was laid low in Montgomery by "the exposure of travelling." The first phase of state surveys was nearly over; after a further five weeks in Kentucky and Tennessee the investigators planned to complete their fieldwork in mid-March.[19]

Woofter was encouraged by Jones to be judgmental—writing to Stokes and his sister, Helen Stokes, from Fordyce, in Dallas County, Arkansas, he commended the public elementary school for black children—it had support from county officials, a Jeanes fund teacher, and local white people, and required no other assistance—but he dismissed the private Bradley District Academy, a Baptist school, as "deeply in debt, dirty, and small . . . [almost] too insignificant to report on." In the published report, Bradley was deemed "a low-grade elementary school," with a staff consisting of the principal and his wife, that "should be combined with one of the larger Baptist schools of the state." Other Arkansas Baptist schools were similarly criticized, and the Presbyterian schools fared even worse, with most condemned as "unnecessary."[20] Woofter also investigated tensions in North Carolina after a principal's home was dynamited. Parmele Industrial School was struggling before the attack, and Woofter was initially unimpressed by principal William C. Chance's "rather visionary ideas" for the cramped four-year-old school with a staffing budget well in excess of its income, despite a $2,000 donation by the Phelps-Stokes Fund. After Woofter's visits and discussions between Jones and state officials, Parmele gained new stability by merging with a black public school, so that by 1917 its sounder finances and larger catchment area drew only minor recommendations about agricultural teaching and industrial equipment in *Negro Education*. Parmele lost some autonomy through amalgamation with the public system, but continued to grow under Chance's pugnacious leadership until it was destroyed by fire in 1954.[21]

In Woofter's hometown of Athens, the newly founded J. Thomas Heard University, a two-story elementary school, where fifty pupils were taught by the principal's wife, had a more bruising encounter with Jones's survey. Two-thirds of its $300 annual income came from donations, as it competed with the public Athens Colored High School and a nearby private school. After two visits, the inspectors reported, "There seems to be no need for this school." Woofter had already implied something similar in his Phelps-Stokes fellowship report, but many years later he had more sympathy with what Heard, a black attorney, was trying to do: "At the time I could only see the ludicrous pretentiousness of calling it a university. It was not until later when the wife of the founder told me that it had been established with the hope that it would grow up to its name and become a force for the uplift of the race that I sensed that this was a groping for the stars by one who was too far down and whose arms were too short even to reach the treetops."[22]

Negro Education purported to be an objective, scientific, and comprehensive assessment of pedagogy and provision, but it was swayed by other research and the politics surrounding black education and philanthropy in the 1910s. In September 1913 the *Annals of the American Academy of Political and Social Science* special issue on "The Negro's Progress in Fifty Years" summarized Howard W. Odum's study of Philadelphia's elementary public schools. Odum, then a junior colleague of T. J. Woofter Sr. at UGA, attributed marked differences in academic achievement and attendance between black and white children after the age of eight to environmental variables such as health, housing, migration, and family influence. He concluded that since the environmental factors would not rapidly improve, and since the children could not quickly adapt to the existing curriculum, the curriculum must be changed to suit them. Although Jones worked in a different region, he arrived at a similar conclusion, so that Odum's work bolstered his arguments about special schooling for black children.[23] In 1914, Jones conferred frequently with Abraham Flexner of the GEB, and the following year he attended the organization's first interracial conference on black education. The GEB wanted more institutions in the Hampton-Tuskegee mold and more vocationally trained black teachers, and Jones's recommendations were clearly geared to providing large charities with opportunities to direct funds at such activities. This meant collaborating with the state supervisors of Negro schools. Funded by the GEB, white state supervisors were appointed in the departments of education of almost all the southern states, and some, such as Jackson Davis in Virginia, Nathan C. Newbold in North Carolina, and Louis Favrot in Arkansas and later Louisiana, looked set to become influential across the South. This strengthened the determination of Jones, who wanted to be seen as the key philanthropists' agent, to produce a report that would resonate throughout black education and the northern charities.[24]

An unexpected black challenge to Jones's preeminence appeared in the form of the Association of Negro Industrial and Secondary Schools (ANISS), a professional body for two dozen "industrial and agricultural schools for colored youth patterned after Tuskegee and Hampton." Ostensibly, ANISS grew out of a fear that the system of northern philanthropy for southern black schools was breaking down and a need to respond to the accreditation movement in American education that sought to define terms such as "high school" and "college." Booker T. Washington was invited to join ANISS in February 1913, but he was confident that Jones and his paymasters would deliver a Bureau of Education report to his liking and decided to squash ANISS before it became a distraction. His main objection to ANISS was that the NAACP supported it. The NAACP might be more vocal than the Tuskegee machine on lynching and segregation, but Washington was not going to let it wade into education. He told NAACP board member Oswald Garrison Villard that it had no business meddling with schools and that the association's unpopularity in the South could harm the social standing of white educationists and philanthropic agents. He told Robert Russa Moton, Hampton Institute's senior black figure, "These people are hiding the real purpose of their movement and everything else that they do from our [philanthropist] friends." He singled out W. E. B. Du Bois and told his secretary, Emmett Jay Scott, "my letter [to Villard] cuts all of the foundation out from under the thing. Their single object was to give the public to understand through [NAACP journal] the Crisis that they are taking charge of education and had drawn Dr. Frissell [of Hampton Institute] and myself into their movement."[25]

Villard blustered that education was part of the NAACP agenda: "We are, therefore, only steering our proper course in doing what should have been done by Tuskegee or Hampton years ago in getting the rural industrial schools together in a strong organization to standardize and systematize and weed out the unworthy. . . . I think your timidity is running away with you." Insults only deepened Washington's determination to stop ANISS. In 1914, he advised New York philanthropist and Tuskegee trustee William G. Willcox not to waste time and money on the ANISS, especially in view of Jones's survey. Villard again protested that he merely wanted "standards of instruction and model curricula and proper accounting. . . . I feel sure that if you could know about this work and understand its purpose . . . you would not be throwing cold water upon the enterprise," but Washington rebuffed him. Flexner assured Villard that the GEB regarded the Bureau of Education survey as sufficient, commenting, "Dr. Jones is a disinterested and competent outsider whose report will separate the wheat from the chaff. After its appearance the public will have a source of information the accuracy and impartiality of which cannot be discredited."[26]

When Washington discovered in the spring of 1915 that Villard was persisting with the ANISS scheme, he told Jones to publish a statement on what he and his staff were doing, because "a fake organization is at work and a good many people are likely to be led into it innocently because they do not know of any other organizations." Washington also suggested a bit of spying: "it might not be a bad plan to get [Ocea] Taylor to go into their meeting and get on the inside so as to know what is going on."[27] It was bad advice, born of Washington's inability to shrug off criticism, but Jones acted on it and produced a sweeping three-page statement claiming that American philanthropists had been misled into "much waste of money on unworthy schools" that that there was "a lamentable failure to give adequate support to worthy institutions." The statement was blocked by secretary of the interior Franklin K. Lane, who knew that white friends of southern schools thought Jones was too aggressive during his inspections. Lane feared Jones's outburst would "lead to an immense amount of disturbance, because it will throw all the negro schools under suspicion of being unworthy." The Bureau of Education, he said, should stick to publishing its report, "and great care should be taken that schools should not be condemned as fakes which have merit." It was a severe reprimand, but Jones pretended he was "rather pleased with Secretary Lane's attitude. . . . There is undoubtedly some danger of arousing the antagonism of some of the schools and their friends before we are ready to deal with their problems." It did not prevent Jones from being highly critical of named schools in *Negro Education*.[28]

The ANISS, meanwhile, succumbed to Washington's pummeling. Its executive secretary assured Anson Phelps Stokes that he was promoting collaboration between "the most progressive Negro schools," such as Fort Valley High and Industrial School in Georgia and Snow Hill in Alabama. He desired "no friction [and] no overlapping of functions," and looked forward to Jones's report.[29] The ANISS episode, one of Booker T. Washington's final skirmishes before his death in November 1915, revealed the gulf between, on the one hand, forward-thinking black educators in the South and the northern-based equal rights movement, and, on the other, the gradualist interracial cooperation movement, in which the Hampton-Tuskegee tradition was revered.

As the publication stage approached, Stokes decided Jones's work should continue and that Taylor and Woofter should be retained to conserve the data and revisit selected schools. Their salaries were to be raised by $200, to $1,800 and $1,400, respectively, but Woofter had other ideas. He wanted a PhD in sociology from Columbia University, like Jones's PhD, and needed higher-paid work to save for the fees. Jones was hurt by the suggestion that the Phelps-Stokes Fund was less than generous, especially since fieldwork payments relieved the staff of many normal living costs; he also thought Woofter failed to appreciate the practical training he had gained: "As a preparation for further study the experience which Mr. Woofter has had with us is far more valuable than he can possibly understand at present."[30]

The team's field trips in 1915 were designed for verification and included a few forays to outlying states, such as Indiana, where Taylor surveyed the segregated high schools and a correspondence school offering what *Negro Education* called "impossible courses," such as "PhD course" for $30 and "agriculture" for $20.[31] The last inspections in Texas were undertaken by Walter Hill, while Jones, Woofter, and Taylor worked on their conclusions. After attending the Phelps-Stokes Fund executive meeting in November 1915, Woofter agreed to continue on a monthly basis during the editorial stage, finally leaving the project in September 1916.[32]

The final report, with detailed entries on every state and the curriculum and finances of every school and county visited, took far longer than anticipated. The Phelps-Stokes trustees were assured in November 1916 that both volumes of *Negro Education* were at the printers, but two months later Hill apologized for further delays: "We have all worked long hours, nights, and holidays, but the work has really proved enormous and far beyond our expectation." Jones was desperate to publish before the end of the school year and asked New York banker George Foster Peabody to use his influence on Capitol Hill to push the U.S. Government Printing Office. In March 1917, Jones asked Claxton, Dillard, Frissell, and the new principal of Tuskegee, Robert Russa Moton, to check the final recommendations. Confident of the report's success, Stokes doubled the initial order of one thousand copies, paying Claxton $500 for advertizing and a launch, but delays in the final editing stages were nearly fatal. The Bureau of Education's editor, W. Carson Ryan, squeezed *Negro Education* out ahead of emergency war printing in the summer of 1917.[33] Otherwise, the report, so significant for southern education, African American politics, and the interracial cooperation movement as a whole, would have gathered dust.

In his preface, Stokes praised Woofter, Taylor, and Hill for displaying "complete harmony of spirit and purpose . . . , in spite of their differences of birth and education." Here was the essence of interracial cooperation, wherein "men of high character of purpose [,] trained to investigate facts [,] cooperate in removing the Negro problem from the realm of the emotions to that of dispassionate study."[34] This was the theme of the report's launch at the UCSRQ's eighth meeting in August 1917 in Washington, D.C., attended by Moton, Peabody, Julius Rosenwald, Morehouse College president John Hope, George E. Haynes of the Labor Department's Division of Negro Economics, and several young white southern scholars, including economists Tipton Ray Snavely and Francis D. Tyson. Snavely was the Phelps-Stokes fellow at the University of Virginia in 1915–16, and both he and Tyson worked with Jack Woofter on a separate black migration project in 1917.[35]

The Jones report had finally emerged from almost three years of field research and writing. The total of 790 inspected establishments were made up of 625 private schools, 28 state institutions, 67 public high schools, 27 county training schools, and 43 special institutions such as hospitals, orphanages, and reformatories. Of the private schools, only 266 (43%) were deemed to "form an important part of the educational system of their respective States." The other 359 schools were "comparatively unimportant," a crushing verdict on the efforts of thousands of teachers and tens of thousands of students. The two volumes ran to over 1,100 quarto pages, cataloging the consequences of the southern states' deliberate hindrance of black education at the turn of the century by diverting revenues toward white schooling. The Phelps-Stokes Fund and the U.S. Bureau of Education hoped to both pressure the South and persuade philanthropists to identify more rigorously those black private schools that deserved support. Jones's conclusions suited conservative blacks, northern philanthropists, and southern white professionals, but radical black observers were appalled and denounced the insistence on narrow industrial and agricultural education for African Americans as a formula for permanent serfdom.[36] According to historians Eric Anderson and Alfred A. Moss, *Negro Education* was "central to the transformation of northern philanthropy for black schools." It might be truer to say that it bolstered the suspicions and prejudices of many philanthropists and charities, and, while not deterring them from further donations, it made them feel justified in becoming more selective and prescriptive.[37]

The first volume offered an overview of the history, funding, and ownership of black schools, and summarized the physical plant and property of secondary, college, normal, industrial, and agricultural institutions. Here, the report showed how the inadequacy of public funding systems led to the growth of private and philanthropically aided schooling.[38] Jones made it clear that he saw white charity as a crucial driver of black progress: "No greater loss could befall the Negro schools than the elimination of northern philanthropy and northern teachers. It is the emphatic conclusion of this study of the actual conditions of schools for colored people that sound policy requires white management and white teachers to have some part in the education of the race." Jones displayed a zeal similar to that of American missionaries abroad, a spirit that he, himself, tried to impart during his later visits to colonial Africa.[39]

The second volume contained inspection reports, organized by state and giving income details for each private school with a commentary on its teaching, curriculum, record keeping, and buildings. These reports were offered in the context of existing state spending, so that comparisons could be made between the quality of private and public provision. U.S. Census Bureau population figures were combined with local data on black and white teachers' salaries to calculate state education spending per capita by race. The outlines provided in *Negro Education* on the black population in each state and in many individual counties represented one of the most informative assemblages of data on the distribution, schooling, occupations, and literacy rates of southern blacks before the New Deal. It remains a valuable report in many ways, but a tone of heavy condescension runs through it. The authors' stated aim—"the promotion of the cause of the best and most practical education of all colored people for better living, civic righteousness, and industrial and economic efficiency"—revealed a generalizing and utilitarian mentality that ruled out black ambition and agency.[40] Jones commended only secondary schools and colleges that emulated the Hampton-Tuskegee normal and industrial model. Of the several schools calling themselves universities, only Fisk University and Meharry Medical College in Nashville and Howard University in the District of Columbia were deemed worthy of the title, although several other colleges were found to be improving. Most colleges, it was stated, would be better off admitting they were secondary schools, while most private high schools taught only elementary grades. The investigators clubbed dozens of private schools with phrases such as "of little worth" and "no need for it," criticizing several school principals by name for academic mismanagement and financial irregularity. Liberal arts education for blacks was dismissed as largely unnecessary and potentially harmful—the line the GEB had been taking since 1913. Practical manual training, on the other hand, was said to be useful and logical, given "the Negro's highly emotional nature."[41]

Although the report objected to certain trends in black teaching and was generally skeptical about the capacity of black people to manage their own affairs, it was also an explicit censure of the states' unfair policies toward black schools between 1900 and 1912, when public education allocations in the South as a whole increased by 180 percent. (The gap between total northern and southern public expenditure on education remained huge; for example, Virginia spent less than one-third of what Massachusetts spent per head of its school-age population, and South Carolina less than one-fifth.) Public funds might be allocated to the county boards of education on the basis of population, ostensibly without regard to race, but, by examining sums spent on teachers' salaries per pupil, Jones was able to show the clear racial basis on which counties divided the money. Across the South, the average expenditure on teachers' salaries was $10.32 for each white child and $2.89 for each black child, and black teachers were often poorly trained or not trained at all. A key variable factor was the relative size of the black and white populations of each county. Three types of counties were identified—those with small black populations, those with more or less equal numbers of blacks and whites, and those with significant black majorities. A county with a very small black population might spend almost equal amounts per capita on black and white pupils, since white schools would not gain any great advantage from a reduction in the sum allocated to the few black schools for teachers' salaries. In contrast, counties with equal-sized black and white populations might spend up to three times more of their state allocation on each white pupil than on each black pupil, to allow white schools to hire more teachers for more months of the year and ensure that provision for white pupils matched that of counties with small black populations. Counties with big black majorities, often politically dominated by wealthy white planters, typically spent over ten times more per head on the schooling of whites than they did on the schooling of blacks, again to maintain the quality of provision in the white schools. For example, in counties with populations that were 75 percent black, the average expenditure was $22.22 for each white child and $1.78 for each black child. The widest gap discovered by Jones was in a Louisiana parish where annual expenditure amounted to $27.73 for each white child and 47 cents for each black child. Black children's work in the fourth or fifth elementary grades—the highest level offered by most counties—was even less advanced in reality, because blacks usually attended for fewer months each year than whites.

High school education from the public purse for blacks was so minimal that white high school students in the southern seaboard states outnumbered black students by twenty-nine to one.[42]

State education funds were raised from property taxes, largely paid by white citizens, and allocated on a per capita basis to county school boards and distributed locally according to school. In industrial cities, such as Birmingham, Alabama, where business interests supported the Progressive ideal of a well-trained workforce and blacks retained some voting power, public expenditure on black education did not fall drastically behind that of white education. Even so, it remained a source of tension. A Birmingham labor leader complained in 1917 that "The negro is a parasite[;] he pays no taxes, no school taxes," and another stated that educated blacks were "insolent, overbearing, contemptuous of white men, not amenable to discipline, and with a lurking disregard for law."[43] In rural counties across the South, white people overwhelmingly rejected calls for larger expenditure on black education, even though their allocations were boosted by the black population. Since the end of Reconstruction, white voters and politicians had argued that spending should reflect the relative contributions of white and black taxpayers and that school taxes, themselves, should be segregated. Only Kentucky enshrined this in law; in other states, such as Mississippi, Alabama, and North Carolina, legislators refused to back explicitly discriminatory tax laws, preferring local distribution of funds in the knowledge that black disfranchisement meant white children would be heavily favored. In Georgia, 40 percent of counties voted to establish local tax districts in response to the failure of the Redemption government to provide a proper revenue stream for rural schools, but the complex rules surrounding local levies meant that all primary education was underfunded— and inevitably, black schools received least, and the few rural public high schools were almost all white.[44]

Economist Kenneth Ng has argued that those who claimed blacks paid less toward their education than whites in the form of direct taxes were basically right— black southerners received $2 in education spending for every $1 they paid in property taxes—but, as George Washington Cable argued in 1892 and W. E. B. Du Bois demonstrated in *The Negro Common School* (1901) and *The Common School and the Negro American* (1911), when indirect taxes were included black communities often paid more into state coffers than the cost of black schools, with the widest disparity of all occurring in Georgia. And as James D. Anderson has noted, the direct donations in cash, labor, and land that black southerners often made to their local schools amounted to a "double taxation."[45] Plainly, the additional benefits enjoyed by white pupils were a glaring consequence of rural black disfranchisement and segregation, but if Jones made this connection it was not a point he chose to labor.

The inspection reports in *Negro Education* were not unremittingly negative. The most frequent criticism was that emphasis should be shifted away from liberal arts and toward agriculture and manual training, and better regulation of boys' dormitories was demanded everywhere. Harsh things were said about some teachers, but many were commended, and the recommendations for each school were largely constructive. The overall implication of the report, however, was that the chaff needed to be rigorously sifted. In South Carolina, for example, twenty-one schools were basically commended, with suggestions for improvement; six schools were sharply criticized, but deemed capable of improvement; twenty-two schools were advised to merge with others in their religious denomination or with local public schools; and twelve schools were condemned as unnecessary or unworthy of outside aid. The verdict on Harbison College at Irmo, with 89 students, was typical: "That the time spent on ancient languages be given to subjects properly belonging to a rural-life school." The main recommendation for Morris College at Sumter, with 160 students, read: "That emphasis on foreign languages be not allowed to interfere with provision for teacher training, gardening, and simple industrial training."[46]

Despite appearances, the report was far from comprehensive. Jones was conscious that it was the philanthropic boards and, to a lesser extent, the state governments, that would take most notice of his recommendations, so he omitted many schools maintained by churches, especially black denominations, the implication being that they could waste their own money if they wished. Only half of the ten Baptist schools and four of the seven Episcopalian schools in South Carolina were thought worthy of a visit, as were only eighteen of the forty-eight schools run by the Presbyterian Board of Missions for Freedmen, resulting in a general recommendation that these schools be merged for financial efficiency. In North Carolina, only fifteen of the twenty-five Baptist schools and fifteen of the thirty-one Presbyterian schools were visited, with the rest regarded as "in session irregularly," "little more than Sunday schools," or "transitory" and likely to move if the pastor took up a new ministry. Only one of North Carolina's nine Lutheran schools, the Immanuel Lutheran College at Greensboro, was visited (and heavily criticized). In Georgia, thirty-one of the forty-eight Baptist schools were deemed too frail to stand a visit. Everywhere, Catholic schools were virtually exempt—in South Carolina, three Catholic schools with combined rolls of 366 students were noted, but not visited, as were six Catholic schools in North Carolina with over 400 students. In Virginia, two wealthy Catholic boarding schools in Powhatan County were visited because little else existed there, but five other Catholic schools in the state with a combined student roll of nearly 600 were merely noted. In Mississippi, one German Catholic school was visited and commended, but another nine, with total student rolls of 535, were ignored. In Maryland, five substantial

Catholic schools in and around Baltimore, with nearly 900 students, were omitted, and in Louisiana, all of the twenty-four Catholic schools, ranging in size from 29 students to 350, and totaling more than 2,800 students, were similarly noted, but not inspected.[47]

The report was more than a purely racial or regional exercise: Jones's pleas for relevance, efficiency, and good management were consistent with national trends toward accreditation and consolidation, especially regarding rural schools. But, fundamentally, *Negro Education* amounted to the powerful instructing the powerless as to their needs and selecting schools for assistance on the basis of rigid criteria. During the fieldwork stage, W. E. B. Du Bois made it clear that he was hostile to Jones, warning in 1915 that the planners of the "new Negro curriculum" were "openly committed to any demand of the white South." He described the movement for industrial education as a "quiet insidious persistent attempt to keep the mass of the Negroes in America in just sufficient ignorance to render them incapable of realizing their power or resisting the position of inferiority into which the bulk of the nation is determined to thrust them."[48]

Du Bois found the final report to be exactly what he predicted—"a dangerous and in many respects unfortunate publication"—and masterfully tore it to shreds. Jones's triumphant obsession with vocational subjects and the "adaptation" of schooling to supposed community needs struck Du Bois as a "sinister" attempt to bar bright black children from a high-quality academic pathway and a recipe for permanent black rural dependency. He also objected to Jones's attribution of a single mindset to philanthropic and religious boards and his bias against independent-minded black teachers and principals. Du Bois thought the recommendation that many private schools be absorbed into the public system would be disastrous, if implemented. After all, the report showed clearly that the public system was rotten, despite Jones's silence on the most obvious cause, black disfranchisement. He remarked, "The white community, undoubtedly, wants to keep the Negro in the country as a peasant under working conditions least removed from slavery. The colored man wishes to escape from those conditions. Mr. Jones seeks to persuade him to stay there by asserting that the advance of the Negro in the rural South has been the greatest." If this was interracial cooperation, Du Bois wanted none of it: "Cooperation with the white South means in many cases the surrender of the very foundations of self-respect."[49]

Du Bois regarded Jones's silence on the effects of disfranchisement as a capitulation, but it was not realistic to have expected anything else. The northern philanthropists whom Jones represented were averse to controversy, and the Bureau of Education was subject to the whims of a southern-dominated administration and Congress. Overtly political statements would not have survived the editorial process, even if Jones, Taylor, Woofter, or Hill had tried to insert them. Du Bois's more telling charge was that black Americans were "practically unrepresented" in the creation of the report. He sympathized with Ocea Taylor, suspecting he was chosen for his youth and inexperience; he was "of excellent character but absolutely without weight or influence."[50] Du Bois mistook the process by which the report was written, but in essence he was right. Jones and Woofter, and to a lesser extent Hill, wrote the commentaries on each school's choice of subjects, teaching, and value to the community, while Taylor added to the final report as an auditing accountant and analyst of the informal records of income and expenditure kept by many school principals. He was given no role in judging the best curriculum for African Americans, or the pedagogical fitness of the inspected schools.

The African American historian Carter G. Woodson devoted a whole chapter of *The Negro in Our History* to Jones, under the heading, "The Tender Mercies of the Wicked." Woodson's resentment of Jones's eminence was deep-seated and long lasting; when Jones died in 1950, Woodson dubbed him "the most advanced agent of Negro control" and called his methods "narrow-minded, short-sighted, vindictive and undermining." (Woodson set up the Association for the Study of Negro Life and History [ASNLH] in 1915, and Jones had obliged him by serving on the editorial board, but they fell out and Jones was ejected. Thereafter, Woodson questioned the motives of "so-called friends of the Negro"—a brave stance, since he needed outside help to sustain the activities of the ASNLH and the *Journal of Negro History*.) Woodson conceded that *Negro Education* exposed some inadequate schools, but he accused Jones of prejudice against the idea of black people having control over their own education. He deplored the way in which Jones assumed the role of advisor to the rich and powerful on African American needs and extended this influence to cover missionary work in Africa. Woodson added, with some justification, that Jack Woofter and Jones's other assistants "had not been adequately trained in methods of scientific investigation."[51]

Not all blacks were critical, proof that the late Booker T. Washington's viewpoint lived on strongly. The *Fisk University News,* edited by Isaac Fisher, who would later work with Jack Woofter and the interracial cooperation movement in the 1920s, accepted that *Negro Education* would upset people, but predicted that "certain definite good will result to the whole country from the study." The *New York Age,* a Tuskegee mouthpiece, welcomed the report as evidence of the eagerness of black Americans for good education and the failure of the South to provide it.[52]

White readers were uniformly impressed by *Negro Education.* Abraham Flexner, on behalf of the GEB, called it "an epoch-making contribution to the subject of Negro education," congratulating Jones for displaying "infinite patience, skill, tact and devotion." The *Richmond Newsleader* declared that, unlike the usual advice on racial matters from "biased northern sources [which was] irritating in its cocksureness and narrow sectional viewpoint," the *Negro Education* report was "statesmanlike."[53] The white historian Broadus Mitchell, who grew up in Kentucky, Virginia, and South Carolina, saw significance in the type of person chosen to assist the investigation. Mitchell was the same age as Woofter and Hill and was a similarly college-bred liberal. He was completing his doctoral work on southern cotton mills at Johns Hopkins University when *Negro Education* appeared, and he appreciated the legwork involved, his own research having taken him around the Deep South at the same time as Jones's team were on the road. Congratulating Jones on his "broad statesmanship," Mitchell remarked that he "was fortunate and wise in gathering about him a group of young Southerners, in most instances graduates of state universities, who did much of the detailed field inspection, and who were able to bring to their task an intimate knowledge of the conditions and a keen sympathy with their problem. One of the most hopeful lessons from the work is that Southern men of training and responsibility and position were willing to enter heartily into such an undertaking."[54]

Negro Education remains an enigma. It was the product of months of grueling work by Jones and his men from 1913 to 1916, touring the remotest corners of the South, recording what they saw, and painstakingly compiling their results. As such, the report contains a wealth of factual information about the location, scope, management, and effectiveness of a liminal sector of American education in a pivotal period. It was also evidence of the massive task that northern philanthropists were determined to perform and their faith in Jones, personally. In 1920, on the eve of his three-month visit to Africa, Jones made overblown Wilsonian claims that *Negro Education* represented "an answer to the world challenge, 'How is American democracy to meet this test of its wisdom and idealism? Will the people of the United States work out an educational policy that will inspire the world to a more real sense of interresponsibility?'" He thought the war and the turmoil of 1919 had given the report "increased significance and value as a source book both of what to do and what to avoid in race relations and in the education of peoples handicapped by causes within or without the group." He considered *Negro Education* was a blueprint allowing "civilized governments of the world [to] establish common machinery for adjusting in some measure their educational systems [and] coordinating the effect of these systems upon more backward peoples."[55] In other words, it was the means by which the Hampton-Tuskegee model could be exported to meet the peculiar needs of native people and their colonial rulers.

The report was widely read and it undoubtedly influenced state, federal, and colonial government policies and the behavior of philanthropists; it also coerced black teachers and principals into an acceptance of certain narrow recommendations in order to secure funds. And therein lay its weakness. As Du Bois indicated, it was a manual written primarily by and for white people, about black people, many of whom were far from convinced that its findings were fair or that its recommendations were in their best interests. Critics claimed that the Phelps-Stokes Fund and the Bureau of Education misunderstood southern black aspirations and failed to anticipate future needs, but Jones maintained, "The real value of the report is in its statement of school conditions that have considerable permanency."[56] He was wrong; the war and consequent black migration and urbanization, and the continued rise of a black middle class, meant that *Negro Education* was outdated within a few years. African American publicists, preachers, teachers, students, and entrepreneurs shared in a changing consciousness after the war that made veneration of industrial education above all else increasingly untenable, even though the philanthropists and government educationists were determined that, as long as segregation reigned, schools would train black and white children differently. Young black people increasingly sought proper college education in the 1920s, and the kind of schools on which Jones reported fell out of favor with parents and students. Many closed or merged with the public system, so that in North Carolina, for example, out of the sixty institutions visited by Jones and his team, only five private secondary schools still existed in 1939. The two positive effects of the report were that it highlighted the physical decay of black schools and the weaknesses of black teacher education, both of which began to be addressed by the philanthropists and the states by the mid-1920s.[57]

*   *   *

Jack Woofter had slipped easily into the Phelps-Stokes fellowship and his job with the Bureau of Education through family and Methodist connections, without realizing that he was courting criticism by associating with Thomas Jesse Jones. He regarded the Welshman with admiration and gratitude, and Jones, in turn, was fond of the hardworking, open-minded young Georgian and took him under his wing, intervening on several later occasions in Woofter's career when professional hazards or unemployment loomed. It was partly Woofter's work on the *Negro Education* report and his recurring involvement with Jones in various projects in the 1920s and 1930s that caused Du Bois and other black intellectuals to distrust him. Certainly, they rarely gave Woofter the credit that he deserved for independent and thoughtful analyses of racial problems in subsequent work, and at times they singled him out for abuse.

Looking back on the *Negro Education* report in the 1950s, Woofter was unrepentant. The basic problem facing the South, he argued, was a chronically low tax base and a failure to accumulate capital, "since its economy was, in a way, a colonial appendage of the rest of the nation." He regarded the Jones report as a timely warning that, in a region handicapped by high interest rates, low crop prices, and poor transport, any underinvestment in black schooling would have a stagnating effect. He also maintained that the Jones formula—"agricultural and industrial training with emphasis on thoroughness and character building"—was right and pretended that Du Bois's criticism did not matter. However, it plainly still bothered him; compared to Booker T. Washington, he wrote, the *Crisis* editor was unrealistic and tactless.[58]

Thomas Jesse Jones's career was boosted in several ways by the *Negro Education* report. Its completion made the Phelps-Stokes Fund more determined to fulfill the overseas element of its founder's intentions and, as education director, Jones became the fund's main emissary to Africa. Practical education was an area in which American reformers felt they could advise European powers, and many colonial educationists looked across the Atlantic for guidance from experts on the supposedly analogous teaching of former slaves and their children. Du Bois had already noted this during the series of Pan-African Conferences after 1900 and, especially, the International Congress on the Negro hosted by Booker T. Washington at Tuskegee in 1912. When the American Baptist Foreign Missionary Society announced it was looking for an expert to undertake a survey of African education, the Phelps-Stokes Fund naturally volunteered Jones. He led two successive African Education Commissions and produced reports on vast regions of the continent that drove the education policies of the British Colonial Office after World War I. Without attempting to develop a detailed understanding of existing educational provision or local culture in East, West, and southern Africa, Jones promoted almost exclusively the value of Hampton and Tuskegee–style industrial and agricultural "uplift" for underdeveloped peoples.[59]

The months immediately following the publication of *Negro Education* were taken up with disseminating its findings and further inspections, but this all ceased when Jones and his remaining assistants were drawn into war service. Jones helped the War Department's Committee on Education and Special Training to identify schools and colleges able to deliver technical training to black military personnel. He also liaised with the special assistant to the secretary of war, Emmett Scott, on ways in which the Phelps-Stokes Fund could help with "maintaining good moral conditions among Negro soldiers." Jones became the resident white expert on all things African American in Washington, D.C., dealing with a stream of requests for his advice from various divisions of the War, Labor, and Agriculture Departments, including the Military Intelligence Branch of the General Staff. He commented confidentially on the loyalty of over one hundred black participants at a conference in the capital in June 1918, identifying twenty-five "Questionable" individuals. After the Armistice, he joined Tuskegee principal Robert Russa Moton on a tour of black army units in France, leading to accusations in the black press, especially by Du Bois, that Jones was there to keep an eye on Moton and report any subversive utterances.[60] In May 1919, the *Washington Bee* newspaper deployed one of Du Bois's descriptions of Jones as a headline, calling him "The Evil Genius of the Negro Race." The *Bee* recalled that Jones had "endeavored to use most arbitrary and unfair means to crush out those schools which did not bow to his sovereign will." The *Negro Education* report, it declared, was "manifestly so unfair and biased that its use even for waste paper could be seriously questioned." Jones and Walter Hill tried to laugh off the "evil genius" taunt and claimed to be more bothered by Du Bois's criticism of Moton. Hill told Jackson Davis of the GEB, "This is a joke as far as we are concerned, but the attack on Dr. Moton is no joke. DuBois is trying to shatter Dr. Moton's prestige, and also, it would seem, to poison the minds of the Negroes against their white friends. I am afraid he is succeeding only too well."[61]

Walter Hill was hired by education commissioner Claxton early in 1918 for a survey of public black elementary and high schools in Tennessee, before joining the Personnel Division of the War Department as an assistant to the Committee on Classification of Personnel in the Army. The committee included Beardsley Ruml, a psychologist, and Leonard Outhwaite, an anthropologist, who shaped American social science research after the war as director and administrator, respectively, of the $80 million Laura Spelman Rockefeller Memorial. The classification committee determined appropriate military roles for enlisted men and officers with experience in certain trades; Hill's task was to assess qualifications gained in black training schools. The Phelps-Stokes Fund continued to pay his salary on the understanding that he would resume educational inspections when schools ceased their army-training schemes. After the Armistice, Hill wrote another special report for the Bureau of Education on rural black schools in Alabama, which left him convinced that the underfunding of black education could not be defended. Increasingly unhappy about racial inequality, generally, he proposed further statistical work on the public school systems of the South, "to show the difference between the school facilities for white children and those for colored children." After five years with the Phelps-Stokes Fund, he resigned in the summer of 1919 when Claxton refused to make black school improvement part of the remit of the Bureau of Education. Hill returned to Georgia as a vocational adviser for Camp Gordon, at Chamblee, near Atlanta, helping disabled servicemen find work as they were discharged. He told Anson Phelps Stokes, "I am especially interested in the Negro soldiers, and I feel fairly competent to advise them as to what they should do. My work for the Fund qualified me for this." He managed the Federal Board for Vocational Education services for black people in Atlanta, before joining the Georgia Department of Education on January 1, 1920, as supervisor of Negro schools, on a salary provided by the GEB. Like Woofter, he had found the daily examination of black life in the South with Thomas Jesse Jones chastening. He continued to see things through the eyes of a gradualist charitable reformer; he had moved a long way from the heartless norms of white supremacy and was a committed lifelong supporter of interracial cooperation.[62]

Ocea Taylor's career was also furthered when the Phelps-Stokes Fund arranged eighteen months of accountancy training for him with a New York firm, so that he could "perfect himself as an expert accountant." He continued to provide specialist advice to southern schools, but, to Jones's dismay, he reentered permanent government service as an accountant in the Treasury Department. He was replaced as the Phelps-Stokes special accountant by Leo A. Roy, an experienced Hampton graduate, until he, too, joined the War Department as an inspector of student officer training, before rejoining Jones in January 1919 to continue the work of setting up new accounting systems for schools.[63] Taylor was arrested soon after the Washington, D.C., race riot of July 1919; defended by veteran black lawyer Joseph Stewart, his habeas corpus petition was dismissed by the District of Columbia superior court, but the outcome is unclear.[64] *Negro Education* undoubtedly changed Jack Woofter's life, and the three years he spent under Jones's wing opened his eyes to the responsibilities and power of the social scientist in an age of reform. Jones's example of doggedness and duty were lasting: when the Welshman completed twenty-five years of service with the Phelps-Stokes Fund, Woofter told him, "I count it one of the great privileges of my life to have been associated with you and to have felt the warmth of your interest in vital things and seen the vigor with which you shunt aside the irrelevant sentimentalities and the erroneous shibboleths." Jones, in turn, recalled Woofter as an "impartial, impersonal and fearless interpreter of social trends; . . . ever remembered for able services and staunch friendship."[65]

Jones trusted Woofter and made more use of him than the other assistants, and through Jones Woofter began to understand the social effects of the South's desperate education system and narrow-based economy. The complexity of life beyond Athens and the depth of the region's problems were now obvious—as Woofter recalled, "I was given the opportunity to move about the South in major cities and small towns, in plantation areas and areas of small farming. . . . It was readily apparent that the South was carrying a heavy load on a weak back."[66] He was struck by the lack of hard evidence available to state and federal government, charities, and universities about the extent and causes of economic backwardness, and he recognized that the South needed to change urgently, but concluded that change was impossible without interracial cooperation. He never subscribed fully to the dominant racist ideology in which white supremacy was a permanent necessity; as an agent of the Phelps-Stokes Fund, he distanced himself from it even further. Siding with the liberal minority of white southerners, Woofter accepted that the region's problems could be solved only with outside help, especially that offered by philanthropists in northern cities who devised and supported education programs that the states were politically and fiscally incapable of delivering. It was to be a decisive break. He would always identify personally with the South, but he deplored many of its practices and attitudes, and he was willing to endure the suspicion, at best, with which many southerners regarded white liberals. His readiness to commit himself to the postwar interracial cooperation movement showed in a review in September 1917, when he wrote that "the Negro must cultivate racial cohesion and co-operation, and must also increase his contact with the customs and institutions of the white man, so as to become articulated into the community."[67] "Articulated" here did not mean "integrated," but nor did it necessarily imply remaining subordinate.

Consciously or otherwise, in joining with the interracial cooperationists and accepting the terms and conditions of northern philanthropy, Woofter was setting out on a difficult path, both emotionally and in career terms. For the next twenty years, he was a prominent dissenter from the creed of total white supremacy and permanent black backwardness, and a fierce opponent of racial violence and injustice in the courts, but he failed to convince black social scientists and activists that he believed fully in black civil rights, and he endured repeated criticism of his writings on African American life. What he saw as his own realism concerning the pace of change in the South, others saw as a desire to rationalize the status quo. His talents as a social scientist and his contacts in education and the interracial cooperation movement sustained him professionally, but as a white Georgian man he was an enigma and not fully trusted by either his own people or African Americans.

3 Migration and War

Aꜰᴛᴇʀ ᴛʜʀᴇᴇ ʏᴇᴀʀs as a Phelps-Stokes researcher, Woofter applied for graduate study at Columbia University, where the sociologists and statisticians in the Department of Social Science rivaled those at the University of Chicago. He knew that Thomas Jesse Jones's career as a social scientist began with a PhD from Columbia, but his financial circumstances and the University of Georgia's lack of accreditation for admission to advanced work hampered him. Relying on personal connections and favors, he secured a one-year fellowship at the American University in Washington, D.C., with references supplied by Jones and U.S. commissioner of education Philander P. Claxton, who sat on the university's fellowships board. His $500 award for 1916–17 let him register for a probationary year in the graduate program at Columbia as a "Fellow of the American University," before enrolling properly as a PhD student with an intended dissertation on "Negro Farm Life in Georgia."[1]

Woofter's work at Columbia was supervised by the eminent sociologist Franklin H. Giddings, who, like his colleagues in psychology, anthropology, and economics, favored rigorous statistical analysis and use of the Burroughs adding and listing machine. Giddings believed social behavior and adaptation derived from the "evolution of a consciousness of kind" that individuals shared with members of their own group; he also held that most social conflicts and inequalities stemmed from innate differences between groups and that those tensions were logical expressions of collective identity and preference.[2] "Consciousness of kind," he contended, led people to "manifest a dominant antipathy" toward "variations" from their type: "Fundamental identities or similarities of nature and purpose, of instinct and habit, of mental and moral qualities, of capacities and abilities, are recognized as factors in the struggle for existence. To the extent that safety and prosperity depend upon group cohesion and cooperation, they are seen to depend upon such conformity to type as may suffice to ensure the cohesion and to fulfill the cooperation."[3] The rationale that the New England–born Giddings provided for degrees of segregation of American racial and ethnic groups struck Woofter as persuasive and reassuring. Woofter detached himself from many aspects of orthodox southern thought, including the ideal of total racial separation, but he remained wedded throughout his life to the conviction that the races should not mix at the most intimate levels and that harmony was best preserved by Americans spending their social lives in homogenous company. Giddings's elaboration of "consciousness of kind" appeared to rest on scientific investigation and reasoning, rather than the prejudice and bitterness that made Woofter uncomfortable in the South. As Giddings put it, "consciousness of kind" meant "that pleasurable state of mind which includes organic sympathy, the perception of resemblance, conscious or reflective sympathy, affection, and the desire for recognition." Woofter could see that both black and white Americans might derive satisfaction and comfort from a separateness maintained for positive reasons and not imposed out of antipathy and suspicion. According to historian George M. Fredrickson, Giddings and the "pioneers of the new discipline of sociology" were reacting against unmodified social Darwinist concepts of competition; instead, "the new sociologists posited a social order based on co-operation, compromise, and cohesion," while stressing basic differences between the cooperating groups.[4] The interracial cooperation movement drew heavily on this point of view.

Woofter knew that Giddings had supervised the doctoral work of both Thomas Jesse Jones and Howard W. Odum. Jones, in particular, regarded Giddings as his own great mentor and hailed Woofter fondly as another "disciple of Giddings."[5] In January 1917, Woofter told Claxton, "This year has been most profitable to me, and [I] am now practically assured that, with another year's work I can pass my Ph.D. examinations and receive the degree." He failed in his bid for another fellowship, but secured more money by reentering federal government service in June 1917 with a project that directly contributed to his doctoral dissertation and drew him even closer to the interracial cooperation movement. With the approval of the head of the Bureau of Immigration, Anthony Caminetti, and Assistant Secretary of Labor Louis F. Post, a spurious job title of "immigration inspector" allowed Woofter to be hired under the congressional appropriation for "Expenses of Regulating Immigration, 1917."[6] His actual task was to study black migration in Georgia from an office in Macon as part of a regional project led by James Hardy Dillard, entitled *Negro Migration in 1916–17.* Published after the war, this was the first significant U.S. government study of African American migration. In 1916, Secretary of Labor William B. Wilson had commissioned a short report by two black investigators, but the acceleration of migration after the United States declared war led the government to look again. In addition to Woofter, Dillard hired the Slater Fund's black field agent, W. T. B. Williams, who had degrees from Hampton and Harvard, R. H. Leavell, a white Mississippian who studied sociology at the University of Chicago, and economists Tipton R. Snavely and Francis D. Tyson from the University of Virginia and the University of Pittsburgh. The white investigators covered specific regions, while Williams provided general observations. (Williams, in the opinion of both Dillard and W. E. B. Du Bois, ought to have been hired for *Negro Education* report.) The Department of Labor wanted to know the extent and causes of the migration and its implications for the war effort, but Dillard went further and called for swift changes in the treatment of black people in the South, which he still regarded as "the best home for the masses of our Negro population."[7] (Despite the migration, it would continue to be the home of the great majority: in 1900, 90% of the U.S. black population was southern; by 1920, this had only fallen to 85%; and by 1930, the figure was 79%.[8])

James H. Dillard was the elder statesman of the Social Gospel as it applied to race relations. Born on his family's plantation in Virginia four years before the Civil War, he had a modest academic career as a classicist that took him in 1891 to Tulane University in New Orleans, where he took an interest in black education. He became president of the Jeanes Foundation in 1908 and the Slater Fund in 1910. When Edgar Gardner Murphy's health deteriorated in 1909, Dillard became the most eminent white activist in the interracial cooperation movement. A brilliant coordinator of philanthropic programs, he advanced a pragmatic southern version of Giddings's "consciousness of kind" that was echoed in Jack Woofter's later work on race. Dillard regarded strained race relations as a "natural" legacy of Reconstruction and spoke of "natural" segregation: "Negroes as naturally and inevitably flock together as do the whites." He believed firmly in "the universal fact of race" and considered that of all the racial differences in mankind, "the difference of the Negro and the white is most of all distinctly marked." Dillard saw this as no reason to spurn interracial cooperation as a medium for peaceful change, since blacks had "human rights" and southern white prosperity was dependent on black progress:

> Are we not, we whites of the South, also bound by peculiar claims of both nearness and necessity? The Negro served us as a slave; in the providence of God he is now by law among us as a man. For his good, for our own good, is it not well for us to be helping him on to useful manhood? Grant that in the mass he is low down, can any low class, black or white, lie in the ditch and all of us not suffer?[9]

White supporters of interracial cooperation repeated this creed during the interwar period, acknowledging that segregation and disfranchisement were painful for African Americans, but preferring to focus on other adjustments, such as law enforcement, schooling, and health care, in the belief that harmony was best preserved by preventing the escalation of incidental grievances—and because sudden regional change seemed impossible.

Woofter's chapter in the Bureau of Immigration report in the summer of 1917 reflected his changed outlook since graduating from UGA. In 1912, his decision to examine black life in Athens and the energy with which he approached his survey showed his humanity and eagerness to do good, but did not prevent him from arriving at jejune conclusions. After three years' fieldwork across the South and a further year's graduate study, Woofter was now a different man, trying to understand the thinking of both the black migrant worker and the white employer and willing to speak out against certain southern practices and beliefs. He grasped the interplay between race and economics in Georgia, and his observations on the damaging effects of racial oppression were radical for their time. He traveled to every corner of the state to accumulate material for a detailed analysis of rural and urban labor, interviewing more than two hundred planters and lumber bosses. He found the average workforce loss of 7 percent had prompted planters to use more child labor and switch from cotton to food crops, or hire migrants from Alabama. Overall, the movements of black Georgians caused critical shortages only in the supply of "day labor"—the lowest-paid seasonal workers—particularly in lumber and naval-stores businesses around Savannah, but the potential scale of the migration was significant. As the war went on, Georgian planters developed an exaggerated fear of wholesale loss of labor and demanded that drafted black men be furloughed so that they could return to agriculture, while the state (and many counties) introduced "work or fight" laws compelling black civilians to be "regularly engaged in some lawful, useful and recognized" work. Although mobility had been high among black Georgians since Reconstruction, and there were similarities between the causes of westward movement in 1866–68 and a rise in migration in the early 1910s, the new wave of 1916–17 suggested a different black consciousness at work. In many Black Belt counties, the boll weevil was a new push factor, but it was clear to Woofter that the migration also sprang from a deep sense of "social grievances . . . : Injustice in the courts, lynching, discrimination in public conveyances, and inequalities in educational advantages."[10] In this respect, he was admitting to something that few white southern commentators would concede, despite the clarity with which black Americans attributed the migration to historic oppression and new opportunity. Significantly, northern critics of Jim Crow, including staff of the National Association for the Advancement of Colored People, cited Woofter's contribution to the migration report with approval.[11]

His starting point was that migration was caused by better wages in the North, but he noticed that lynching counties showed some of the highest levels of black movement. He dismissed the idea that blacks were "moving to gain 'social equality[;]' it is fairly certain that they are merely seeking social advantages—advantages in safety, protection in the courts, and better housing and education." (He knew "social equality" would be understood to mean close association with white people, especially white women.) He suspected that migration was triggering broader changes in parts of the South, noting that African American leaders in Georgia were reporting better law enforcement and increased spending on black education. (Seventy-five years later, Stewart Tolnay and E. M. Beck, testing "a model of reciprocal causation between racial violence and black net out-migration," arrived at the same conclusions.) Woofter called for a government campaign to help planters adapt in the face of continual crop failures, so that they could offer peacetime levels of employment and tenancy that satisfied black labor.[12] His observations were objective and far-sighted: he acknowledged that several factors caused the migration, but he also saw it as a fundamental rejection of southern habits and attitudes. He implied as strongly as Dillard would allow that things needed to change and advocated many of the farm-demonstration approaches that would eventually be adopted by the Department of Agriculture during the interwar period. Thus, four key concerns that would drive Woofter later in his life came together clearly in the three months he spent working for the Department of Labor in 1917: opposition to lynching; the promotion of interracial understanding; the betterment of rural education and farm economics; and the acceleration of landlord-tenant reforms. Above all, he took away a new realization that when African Americans were given a fair chance and a sense of security they made swift progress. Any larger conclusions Woofter might have drawn were postponed by his participation in the war effort.

Military life provided him with further new skills and perspectives on the South. He spent two years as an army officer gaining an intensive training in statistical analysis and presentation, under constant pressure to provide information to senior American decision makers. On June 5, 1917, the day before his Bureau of Immigration job started, Woofter registered in Athens for the first wartime draft, claiming a class 5a deferral under the provisions of the Selective Service Act because of his impending federal government employment and expertise in "Negro Farm Labor." This delayed his induction until the black migration report was complete. In September 1917, on the advice of Robert E. Chaddock, the Columbia University professor who first taught him how to gather statistical data, Woofter resigned as an immigration inspector and joined the statistical division of the Council of National Defense (CND) in Washington, D.C. The following day, he was commissioned as an infantry officer and joined the staff of Colonel Leonard Porter Ayres, the chief statistician of the CND. Ayres's staff gathered data from the Adjutant General's Office (AGO) of the War Department to prepare weekly confidential reports for the Wilson administration on all aspects of American mobilization, including troop numbers, training throughput, procurements, and transportation. Ayres, who previously produced education studies for the Russell Sage Foundation, was unsurpassed in the succinct presentation of complex statistical data, a skill Woofter absorbed and used in later academic and government work.[13]

In December 1917, Woofter wrote Anson Phelps Stokes that his work in the new Statistical Division of the AGO required him "to put to use some of the training received from Phelps Stokes investigations." He expected a transfer to the aviation section of the U.S. Army Signal Corps to serve under the Andean explorer and future U.S. senator Hiram Bingham III, but General John J. Pershing demanded part of Ayres's Washington staff for data gathering and analysis with the American Expeditionary Force (AEF), and especially for transmission of accurate, timely information to and from the battlefield. In mid-February 1918, Woofter boarded a troop ship at Hoboken, New Jersey, en route to Pershing's headquarters in the vast barracks at Chaumont, 150 miles east of Paris. As part of the HQ battalion, Ayres's officers and clerks maintained station lists and processed strength returns of frontline and reserve units during the steady buildup of American combat regiments in the spring and summer of 1918. The paperwork was torrential, as new information poured in every hour concerning troop locations, movements, losses, and replacements. The AEF HQ Statistical Division monitored every change in the size and deployment of American forces, the "order of battle," railway movements, and communication codes. Woofter ran the division's Strength Returns Section and was responsible for organizing and consolidating data so that the adjutant general could give Pershing and the War Department daily and weekly statistical portraits of the American role in the fighting. In addition, the Statistical Division dealt with information concerning German and Allied prisoners, several categories of wounded men, the missing, nurses and other civilian personnel, supplies, the property of dead soldiers, war risk insurance matters, and press releases, and answered a stream of anguished inquiries from soldiers' relatives.[14]

Woofter's arrival at the AEF HQ contributed to a much more systematic approach to statistical analysis, especially regarding unit strength returns.[15] After complaining about the lack of clarity in graphs showing deaths, sickness, and arms supplies, he improved the general format and accessibility of AEF data. By May 1918, the Statistical Division was dealing efficiently with the most top-secret information in AEF circles, enabling the Americans to present reliable information at the Versailles meetings of the Allied Supreme War Council.[16]

In October 1918, when he was promoted to captain, Woofter commanded 160 men compiling different kinds of strength return. The cessation of hostilities a few weeks later meant the workload increased, since there was now a wider range of subjects on which figures were required. Data was more swiftly processed and better presented during the demobilization than it was during the war, so that in 1919 the Chaumont statisticians provided a complete picture of the ever-changing locations of American combatant and noncombatant units across Europe, and details concerning hospital admissions, new deaths, missing and repatriated men, replacement troops, pack animals, weaponry, and airplanes. The Statistical Division's final analysis for the official history recorded that in one week in April 1919 it handled 124,837 separate "papers."[17]

After the Armistice, like other American officers, Woofter studied briefly in Paris on the Cours de Civilisation Française de La Sorbonne and spent illicit nights in the city in February 1919 by exceeding the time permitted to transfer between railway stations. Typically, this involved an officer catching a train back to his unit twenty-four hours later than his orders dictated. If this was noticed, it resulted in a minor reprimand or, in Woofter's case, the denial of further leave. He left France in August as the last American division returned to the United States and was honorably discharged at Camp Gordon, where Walter B. Hill was working with demobilized men. Woofter had spent twenty-three months in uniform, far longer than most drafted men, and it built in him both personal discipline and the capacity to collate and interpret vast amounts of material, represent trends graphically, and describe clearly the relationships between different data sets to specialists and general readers alike.[18]

Woofter resumed work on his thesis at Columbia in the fall with a broader topic and a new title, "Rural Organization and Negro Migration," and gained the PhD in 1920 despite a heavy teaching load as an assistant.[19] The focus on black migration let him combine material from his Department of Labor fieldwork with extra research undertaken on his return from France. The final work, published as *Negro Migration: Changes in Rural Organization and Population of the Cotton Belt,* was one of four extended migration studies published soon after the war. Former assistant to the secretary of war Emmett Scott published migrants' letters and press reports; Henderson Donald developed a broad study from articles in the *Journal of Negro History;* and Hannibal Duncan wrote an anthropological PhD dissertation at the University of Pennsylvania with a northern focus on the 1919 riots. Woofter's book was identified by Howard Odum as one of the first demographic studies by an American sociologist. Using methods that were to characterize much of his later work, he tried to capture the nature, causes, and effects of black migration "in terms of current usage in social science." He preferred the statistical approach, "not only because it is the only satisfactory method from a scientific viewpoint, but also because of the growing belief that constructive work in race problems must, to a greater extent, be based on conclusions reasoned from verified facts, rather than upon those deduced from sentimental beliefs or traditional prejudices."[20]

Woofter believed the migration altered the whole of African American life. He attributed it primarily to southern patterns of land tenure and organization, devoting large parts of his study to this correlation, but he went much further, showing that prejudice and racial discrimination propelled many black families northward. This was a fuller, uninhibited articulation of ideas advanced in his contribution to *Negro Migration in 1916–17.* The confidence with which he wrote suggests that leaving Athens and seeing the rest of the South and northern cities, wartime suffering, and French society opened his eyes to the pettiness of Jim Crow and prompted a degree of empathy with African Americans. For example, the work of W. E. B. Du Bois now made sense to him. In his bibliography, he recommended *The Souls of Black Folk* (1903) and Du Bois's postwar deliberation, *Darkwater* (1920): "These give a side of race relations which should be known. They are remarkably written introspective accounts of the impressions of a colored man, but are extremely pessimistic." He also recommended work by Kelly Miller ("An illustration of the attitude of the cooperative group of colored thinkers."), Robert Russa Moton ("Full of the cooperative spirit of race relations. Well worth while."), and the late Booker T. Washington ("All of his works are of importance, especially *Up From Slavery*.").[21] He welcomed the southern initiative to foster local interracial committees that began while he was in France, and that was eventually given leadership by the Commission on Interracial Cooperation (CIC).

The first half of Woofter's book on migration analyzed southern land tenure and African American roles in agriculture since the Civil War; the second half concerned population movement. In an appendix, "General Statistical Method," his discussion of sociology as a discipline showed the influence of Giddings and Chaddock:

> The first objective of social science in accurately analyzing its problems is to state them in terms of definite forces which operate in well defined groups and are associated with resultants which can be measured and counted. The next is to group these elements logically and determine the real importance of each. When this is accomplished it can give descriptions of the elements of the problem which are as clear and significant as the diagram of a mechanical engineer.

Nodding in the direction of Émile Durkheim, Woofter declared, "the problem of scientific social research is to describe the true relationship between definite traits of group behavior and definite elements in the situations in which groups are found." Woofter's approach to the race question would involve gathering "social facts" and analyzing the "collective consciousness" of groups so as to pinpoint both sources of conflict and opportunities for cooperative interaction.[22]

The statistical content of *Negro Migration* was intense, but some of the methodology was facile. He argued that the previous and new circumstances of African Americans could be separately quantified and the relationship between them rendered numerically, removing "the necessity of discussing minutely each of the possible causes."[23] Black sociologists would later be irritated by Woofter's urge to verify facts. It told them little they did not know about black disadvantage and white prejudice; what they wanted were more critical conclusions and radical remedies that would arouse black readers, prick the consciences of white people, and resonate in policy-making circles. And yet, *Negro Migration* was not simply a dry socioeconomic analysis. Although Woofter relied heavily on U.S. census data (including Thomas Jesse Jones's summary of the 1910 census and a 1919 special report on changes in the black population from 1790 to 1915), he also discussed the morality of southern race relations and speculated as to the region's future. His interest in postwar change in American society ensured that his graduate work did not fall into the common trap, as Odum later put it, of treating race as an "elemental and relatively unchangeable heritage."[24]

Writing about black farmers, Woofter rejected Henry George's assertion that a rise in tenancy was evidence of downward social mobility. For all its problems, Woofter saw tenancy for a black farmer as a rung on the upward climb from laborer to landowner. The increases in black-tenanted and black-owned farms that accompanied the contraction of the average southern landholding were therefore to be welcomed. But, undoubtedly, racial discrimination made the lives of black farm families more complex than those of white tenants. Two streams—discrimination and opportunity—ran through any black farmer's life, wrote Woofter: "These two, flowing side by side, sometimes act on one another, and create queer cross currents and eddies of policy which are extremely difficult to understand."[25]

In his analysis of southern land use, mostly extrapolated from conditions he found in Georgia, Woofter showed that white and black farmers approached production in largely the same way, but the lack of secure tenancy meant blacks typically made fewer long-term plans. He also pointed to the impunity with which white landowners could exploit their black tenants, using contract laws to create "conditions on some plantations which amount to peonage or practical re-enslavement of share tenants." He advised planters hoping to retain farm labor to offer concessions to their waged employees and tenants—one effect of which was "to democratize the plantation." He pointed out that white and black migrants moved to new farms, or to cities, or to new regions mainly for common economic and social reasons. The significant variable was the prejudice and abuse encountered by blacks, which could be decisive when they weighed the difference between moving to a neighboring district and moving irrevocably to the North.[26]

Woofter showed that between 1900 and 1910 there was continuous movement within Georgia itself, to and from the counties of the Black Belt, Upper Piedmont, and wiregrass areas, and from Georgia into other southern states. This persisted after 1910 and was replicated across the South, as black families were pulled toward places giving them the best chances of becoming independent farmers. What was new, beginning in 1916–17, was the scale of additional movement to northern cities, as the boll weevil infestation spread and industrial opportunities grew. But this movement, Woofter suggested, was not just about economic advantage; it was specifically racial. It was pushed by "three of the worst lynchings ever seen in Georgia," as well as discontent over unsanitary housing, draconian courts, underfunded education, disfranchisement, and the squalor of Jim Crow cars. (He was referring to lynching outbreaks in December 1915 and January 1916 in Dodge, Early, and Lee counties in which a total of fourteen people had died.) He insisted that harsh treatment was operating "more and more as a cause for race movement as the Negro develops a fuller group consciousness" and predicted that, "unless effort is made to alleviate the social grievances of the Negro, no amount of effort to alleviate economic injustices is going to stop the movement."[27]

He stated that the social problems among African Americans that other observers attributed to innate racial difference (i.e., "abnormalities in sex distribution, fecundity, vitality, criminality, [and] insanity") were, in fact, caused by the high proportions of migrants present in all communities, North and South. In-fluenced by the Columbia University anthropologist Franz Boas, Woofter specifically warned against racial difference theories, pointing out that scientific investigation was still in its infancy and that "the same peculiarities also exist to some degree among other racial groups in the same circumstances." That did not stop him making some sweeping statements of his own, based on the slender evidence of his research in Athens and the U.S. census relating to the conjugal condition of black women in 1910. He claimed that, among African Americans, "low morality and looseness of family ties [were] due to the disturbance in the ratio of the two sexes through migration." He also predicted that migration would cut the birth rate and thereby "reduce the rate of increase in the Negro population tremendously," especially in northern cities, where numbers were sustained only by new arrivals from the South. He asserted that the typical black migrant was of "superior intelligence" to the mass of African Americans and pointed to the multiple layers of leadership to be found in urban churches, businesses, and newspapers. He also rejected the southern axiom that black criminality was innate or unusually frequent, arguing that environmental factors were crucial and that the crime rate among foreign-born migrants was twice that among native-born white citizens. Black criminality was higher in the North than the South, he argued, because of the "strain of urban life and migration," which also produced high rates of insanity and divorce.[28]

Like many whites in the interracial cooperation movement who were descended from slaveholders—Dillard, Odum, and Lily Hardy Hammond, for example—he could not rid himself of a deep-seated sense that white mastery was natural or a romantic view of blacks as both lovable and frightful. The romantic southerner emerged in Woofter's suggestion that migration relieved "the fear of Negro domination" where black majorities occurred and in his lament for "that personal relationship between families of ex-slave owners and ex-slaves which has been such a potent influence maintaining white sympathy for the Negro's problems and stimulating mutual aid."[29] Woofter always seemed to write primarily for a white audience, feeling it was his duty to reveal things that his readers normally failed to consider. He understood that his own views on race were diverging from the mainstream of anti-Negro thought in the South and had to be advanced carefully. He believed demands for immediate restoration of black civil rights would be counterproductive, but hoped that some facts from a southern writer like himself might persuade thoughtful whites that gradual change was necessary and just.

Early in 1920, Woofter interviewed northern industrial managers, most of whom welcomed black workers, even though they were hard to place in closed shops. He concluded that the readiness of migrants to work during strikes was not straightforward strikebreaking. When, on rare occasions, unions admitted members without regard to race, as had the longshoremen's union in New York, blacks would "play the game" and observe a strike, but most unions kept them out. "As a result, when white union men strike it means that by doing so they give the colored laborer the first opportunity which he has had to fill a job for which he is trained, but from which he has been previously barred by the very union which accuses him of being a scab." Woofter advised black workers to seek open shops, join company unions, and avoid federated unions, except in the building trades, or create their own organizations, such as the Dining Car Cooks and Waiters Association set up by employees of the Pennsylvania Railroad.[30]

The lingering influence of Thomas Jesse Jones and the Phelps-Stokes Fund was clear in Woofter's concluding section, "Constructive Measures," in which he called for changes in the way government at all levels treated black citizens. Noting that the race problem was now "national rather than sectional," he laid out a progressive, rational agenda that departed at almost every turn from politics in the southern states. He urged Congress to provide funds for permanent specialist work in the Bureau of Education, migration studies in the Division of Negro Economics (DNE) of the Department of Labor (created in response to the 1916–17 Negro Migration report), and new research and advisory work on black farming and cooperatives in the Department of Agriculture. He called on the states to improve African American health, housing, education, and legal representation, especially in juvenile delinquency cases. He condemned the white press for its trivialization and distortion of African American life, which had alienated "the larger and larger group of Negroes who read [and who] are almost entirely dependent upon more or less destructive [black] newspapers for news." He noted the condemnation of lynching by "the better classes" in the South, including "woman's clubs, the universities, Inter-racial Committees, governor's conventions and the press" and welcomed the enactment of state laws to "quell the outbreaks of the more unruly elements of the population," since a federal law would be unconstitutional. His final plea was for a "patient and sympathetic effort of the white and colored leaders in local communities." The South's task in the postwar era was to "create a saner community life . . . [in which] two races may live side by side without conflict—a task in which the democracy of the United States is being tested, while the civilized nations of the world who are 'bearing the white man's burden' in Africa look on, hoping to be aided by our experience."[31]

* * *

The African American scholar Kelly Miller, dean of arts at Howard University, sensed the emergence of a new southern scholarship in *Negro Migration,* in contrast to what had passed for academic rigor before World War I: "Mr. Woofter represents the best type of intelligence and character of the new generation of white college men of the South. His treatment is wholly without rancor and is free from the arrogant assumption which is so often met with in works by southern authors. There is a refreshing frankness and sincerity of purpose to promote the general betterment of both races."[32]

The leading white rural sociologist, Carl Kelsey of the University of Pennsylvania, called *Negro Migration* "one of the best studies of Negro life in the rural districts of the South that I have seen." Albert Jay Nock's short-lived magazine, the *Freeman,* carried a review by "H.J.S." (almost certainly Herbert J. Seligmann of the NAACP) thanking Woofter for showing the connection between economic injustice and migration, although he found parts of the book hard going: "Few laymen will be sufficiently addicted to the statistical method Mr. Woofter employs to want to read the volume; but it deserves cordial welcome for his evident desire to add a few hard facts to the current American fictions about the Negro." As an academic treatment from a press in New York City, the book was never going to attract many southern readers, but Sydney Dodd Frissell, the son of the late principal of Hampton Institute, Hollis Burke Frissell, gave it an enthusiastic welcome in the *Atlanta Constitution.* He credited Woofter with an "intimate knowledge of southern rural life, and the condition of the negro in the country and the city" and saw the book as evidence of the interracial cooperation movement's growing importance. He recommended it to any "southern planter and landlord whose cotton was unpicked and whose land was unworked during the great exodus of black folk to the north, in 1916–1917, or who still bemoans the instability of negro labor," and drew particular attention to Woofter's claim that "race feeling and grievances" were as important as wage levels in causing migration.[33]

Woofter briefly referred in *Negro Migration* to the issue of African American radicalism, having encountered it in the controversies surrounding the *Negro Education* report. He was in France during the war and the riot-torn summer of 1919, when black political consciousness and debate reached an unprecedented pitch, but he was intrigued by the factions emerging under the New Negro umbrella. It suited him to simplify the choices facing southern blacks into two conflicting ideologies—one "militant" and the other "cooperative." Paraphrasing Booker T. Washington, Woofter stated, "The school of militant protestors constantly holds before the public the sins committed against the Negro. They direct caustic criticism against lynching, injustice in the courts, the 'Jim Crow' car, . . . and their chief activity is litigation." The NAACP journal, the *Crisis,* was their primary organ. He contrasted that "militant" attitude with the demeanor of Robert Russa Moton at Tuskegee Institute and his efforts to promote "opportunity, training for citizenship, winning recognition through efficiency in agriculture and industry, and cooperation with the white race." Woofter's point was that, despite "the appearance of an inter-racial struggle," and notwithstanding "the gruesome facts as to lynching . . . there is a brighter side to the picture than that which appears in the public press,—the side in which constructive workers with Negro problems are primarily interested." Jack Woofter counted himself among the constructive workers, and during the remainder of the 1920s he aligned himself clearly with the "cooperative" tendency among "thinking Negroes and friends of the Negro."[34]

As "friends of the Negro," the Phelps-Stokes Fund remained firmly committed to its fellowships at the University of Georgia and the University of Virginia. Anson Phelps Stokes wanted the endowments to produce useful work by young southerners that spread enthusiasm for interracial cooperation. He was pleased with the output of the first three recipients at Athens—Woofter's thesis on black life in the city, Walter B. Hill's on local farmers, and Miley K. Johnson's study of Clarke County schools—but the next three UGA fellows were hampered by the war and produced no publishable work, despite Howard Odum's efforts as their adviser. The 1918–19 fellow, Frank Taylor Long, studied the war-related activities of blacks in Clarke County and his successor, Ruth Reed, the first woman to hold the award, wrote a survey of black women in Gainesville, Georgia, before proceeding to Columbia University and a PhD dissertation on black illegitimacy in New York City.[35] The completion rates of Phelps-Stokes fellows at UVA in the first decade were equally patchy (partly because the income was misused to fund a lecture program), but D. Hiden Ramsay studied blacks and crime, Samuel T. Bitting examined black landownership, Tipton R. Snavely produced original work on taxation, and Richard L. Morton completed a substantial thesis on the black vote after the Civil War.[36] In January 1920, as he neared the end of his doctoral work at Columbia, Woofter organized a conference of Phelps-Stokes fellows at Tuskegee Institute, chaired by Thomas Jesse Jones. The thirty people present included black and white students, teachers, philanthropic agents, state education officials, and members of the UCSRQ. It was a small gathering, but it was one of the building blocks of interracial cooperation in 1919 and 1920, cementing personal and institutional links and contributing to the formation of the CIC. Jones particularly welcomed the opportunity for "frank statements of the existing attitudes of white and colored people."[37]

As secretary of the Association of Phelps-Stokes Fellows, Woofter asked for a $55,000 grant from the GEB to extend the fellowships to other southern universities. He argued that several recipients, such as Walter Hill, were actively working for interracial cooperation in the South and that more research in every southern state would assist the new interracial committees now springing up. There was, he claimed, "no way in which the South can be more efficiently stimulated to take up these problems seriously than by providing a group of young southern men technically trained for the job." The fellowships were "a direct blow at ignorance and prejudice, and hence a very statesmanly move in bettering race relations." Anson Phelps Stokes (who sat on the GEB) added that eligibility ought to be widened to include southern women's colleges. Woofter began to receive enquiries from interested institutions, such as the University of North Carolina, where Odum, newly appointed as head of sociology, considered "the study of negro problems [was] most timely and urgent." However, GEB president Wallace Buttrick blocked the bid on the grounds that existing plans rendered Woofter's ideas not "practicable." What he meant was that the GEB was not interested in paying white students to gain second degrees. When the board announced its grants of over $2.5 million in March 1921, the allocation of $210,000 relating to African Americans in the South was solely for the salaries of county training school teachers, summer school teachers, and supervising teachers recruited by the Jeanes Foundation, all of whom were black.[38]

Having completed his PhD at Columbia, Woofter was reemployed as a field agent by the Phelps-Stokes Fund and, in effect, replaced Thomas Jesse Jones during the latter's first survey of African colonial education. Jones met with colonial and Red Cross officials in Europe in April and May 1920, before heading to West Africa for a tour that lasted until September 1921.[39] He entrusted Woofter with three broad tasks. First, Woofter was to examine the lives of black migrants in northern cities and the economic causes of racial friction following the riots of 1919. Although other investigations were under way, such as that of the Chicago Commission on Race Relations, Jones was eager to develop new philanthropic work in the North and promote urban interracial cooperation. Woofter understood that he would engage in northern city work, while Lewis B. Moore, the former dean of education at Howard University and now an agent of the American Missionary Association, would do six months' interracial work in southern cities, but Moore declined the job at the last minute. Secondly, Jones expected Woofter to revisit large southern schools and colleges to update the findings of the *Negro Education* report. The third task, and the most important in the long term, was that he should help with the organization of the CIC in Atlanta. This was an absurd set of instructions for one man, but Woofter mapped out a grueling program of travel and liaison in 1920. The results were uneven and he received little credit for his efforts, leaving him frustrated and homesick.

Woofter dutifully visited the northern cities with the eleven largest black populations and several smaller cities, trying to weld municipal, business, and welfare organizations into interracial networks that could identify and address racial problems. Only Chicago, Cleveland, and Cincinnati had recognizable structures already in place. He found it almost impossible to interest chambers of commerce in furthering interracial cooperation, but reported that the National Urban League (NUL), with well-established branches in many industrial cities, was already "growing into a clearing house for Negro work." Elsewhere, he found welfare agencies with black staff, such as the Children's Aid Society in Buffalo, providing links between white people of goodwill and the black community. His efforts proved worthwhile only in Ohio, where he worked with state officials to call an interracial conference at Columbus in January 1921, attended by welfare agencies from Akron, Toledo, Dayton, Cincinnati, Hamilton, Chillicothe, and Middletown. This led to the formation of the Ohio State Interracial Committee and the beginnings of black representation on statewide welfare bodies. The Ohio conference impressed on him the permanence of black migrants' decisions to move north and the sense of political liberation they experienced as a result, despite tension in northern industrial relations, ambiguous racial attitudes of the police, and the constant danger of unemployment. When the first National Interracial Conference was held in Cincinnati in March 1925, several local interracial committees and associated bodies were represented, showing that in Ohio, at least, Woofter's efforts had borne fruit.[40]

He wrote up his work in northern cities in the *Survey* magazine, edited and managed by Thomas Jesse Jones's friends Paul and Arthur Kellogg, and in the *Southern Workman* magazine, edited by W. T. B. Williams and published by Hampton Institute. He reported that only half the southern migrants who arrived in northern towns settled for any length of time; the other half moved on as soon as they heard about better opportunities, often drawn to factories where nonunion labor was welcome, such as the Pullman shops and yards in Chicago, employing fifteen thousand black people. He found twenty companies that had hired more than a thousand black workers and a further two hundred companies with workforces that included over two hundred blacks. The largest employers were in the iron, steel, automobile, meatpacking, and railroad industries, where skilled black workers could find work only in open shops. The American Rolling Mill Company, in Middletown, Ohio, exemplified the welfare capitalism through which some employers retained hundreds of migrant black workers. He saw the prospect of prewar levels of European immigration as the biggest threat to racial harmony; recalling the race riots in industrial towns in 1917, 1918, and 1919, he predicted recurrences unless black employment was maintained at a fair level. He hoped employers would show initiative and take decisive steps to promote "interracial peace," but feared it was too late; African American workers were already well aware of the hostility of white labor toward black apprenticeships and union membership. He noted, "These cases of discrimination have been widely discussed among the Negroes and have so galled them that they are very suspicious of the motives of unions." The black worker in the North had to help himself: "The question as to whether, in the face of increasing competition, he will hold his place in industry, will be largely answered according to the type of leadership which he is able to develop to aid him in opening up new opportunities, increasing his efficiency, and husbanding his earnings." Woofter welcomed the emergence of separate black railroad unions and the work of the NUL and the Young Men's Christian Association and called on the Department of Labor to use the DNE, led by black economist George E. Haynes, as a way of highlighting the special problem of industrial race relations.[41] Woofter's wartime experiences under Leonard Ayres had convinced him that the federal government needed clear, deep, statistical data on social and economic change, and he was outraged when "sheer political chicanery" and a budget-cutting Congress allowed the DNE to wither away.[42]

Woofter largely ignored Jones's instruction to follow up the findings of *Negro Education*. Jones hoped that regular inspections would allow each school's bid for charitable support to be assessed against its compliance with the report's recommendations, but a clear system never developed because of the war, the dispersal of the investigating team, the minimal staffing of the Phelps-Stokes Fund offices in New York and Washington, and Jones's growing interest in colonial Africa. Nevertheless, Woofter participated in one special visit that showed the inadequacy of the Flexner and Jones inspection model in which schools were forced to anticipate the preferences of remote charities. In January 1921, he was asked to represent the Phelps-Stokes Fund on a survey of academic standards and facilities at Southland College, in Phillips County, Arkansas, the scene of one of the worst outbreaks of racial violence in 1919, where dozens, possibly hundreds, of sharecroppers were hunted down by posses and soldiers near the town of Elaine, after a minor skirmish between sheriff's deputies and members of a sharecroppers' union. Since its creation in 1864 by the Union Army and Quaker missionaries from Indiana as a home for orphaned and abandoned black children, Southland College had been a significant provider of teacher training and industrial education. When Thomas Jesse Jones and Ocea Taylor visited in March 1913, they were impressed, and Southland, like many schools established by northerners, emerged well in the *Negro Education* report. By 1920, it was in a precarious position, despite the annual injection of Quaker funds and other donations and the tuition fees of the four hundred pupils. As a result, the Home Mission Board of the Five Years' Meeting of Friends announced a "careful and systematic study."[43]

The inspectors were led by Jackson Davis, whose methods as the Virginia state supervisor of rural Negro schools between 1910 and 1915 were followed by the GEB in its work with other state education departments. Davis took over as the general agent for the charity's black education division in 1917 and was one of the most energetic white advocates of the Hampton-Tuskegee brand of industrial and agricultural training. He was especially eager to raise the number of teachers produced by county training schools across the South.[44] His all-white team—Jack Woofter, Leo Favrot, the Louisiana state supervisor of Negro schools, his Arkansas counterpart, John A. Presson, and two Quaker representatives—concluded that Southland was "well managed [and that it] inculcated some of the white man's standards of work in the class room, and living conditions in the dormitories," but that "it was not quite up to modern school standards." It needed more staff, more upper-elementary and high school grade teaching, and an "increased emphasis upon industrial training, including farm mechanics and household handi-

Survey of Southland College, Phillips County, Ark., January 1921. Left to right: Jack Woofter (Phelps-Stokes Fund), John A. Presson (Arkansas supervisor of rural Negro schools), Jackson T. Davis (general field agent, General Education Board), Harlow Lindley (Society of Friends Board of Home Missions), Anna Wolford (Southland College), Ruthanna Simms (Board of Home Missions), Harry C. Wolford (Southland College), Leo M. Favrot (Louisiana supervisor of rural Negro schools). *Jackson Davis Collection of African American Photographs, Albert and Shirley Small Special Collections Library, University of Virginia.*

crafts [and] especial emphasis upon practical farming and principles of agriculture." In an obvious reference to Tuskegee, the inspectors wanted Southland to train more vocational teachers and "reach out into the community and develop as a center for the life of the Negroes . . . of Phillips County," despite the shattering effect of the 1919 riot. These recommendations led to the recruitment of new staff and a new director, but Southland's funding crises persisted, and in 1925, after it proved impossible to meet all Davis's demands, the Quaker Board of Missions closed the school permanently.[45]

The original aim of the Society of Friends when it created Southland College, according to Quaker social worker Ruthanna Simms, had been "to give invaluable help to the Negro race and also to the United States in its effort to adjust race relationships."[46] For the rest of the 1920s, the "adjustment" of race relations became Jack Woofter's calling, but with a clear regional slant. He was much more interested in the reasons why black people were leaving the South and how the lives of those who stayed behind might be improved than he was in the fate of those who went to the North. Thus, Jones's instruction to help the newly created CIC in Atlanta appealed to him strongly. It allowed him to return to Georgia, where he was more at ease than in northern cities. Moreover, Woofter's travels with Jones in the 1910s had given him a feel for the subregions of the South, whereas the North was foreign to him and he felt like an outsider with northern black and white people, alike. In the North, discussions of social problems were coded differently and his progressive paternalism sat badly with uninhibited black community leaders who were determined to effect change, with or without close white guidance. In the South, the nuances surrounding race, class, power, and religion were familiar to him, and he knew how to exploit them when dealing with competing interests. Working for the CIC under the leadership of Will Alexander allowed him finally to give free rein to his instincts and assert his identity as a scientific, forward-looking southern reformer.

4   Will Alexander and the Commission on Interracial Cooperation

Jack woofter joined the Commission on Interracial Cooperation (CIC) on a temporary basis, but his commitment to the work in Atlanta was so clear that Anson Phelps Stokes let him stay. During the early 1920s, as the interracial cooperation movement became more conspicuous, Woofter found his second great mentor in the CIC's Missouri-born cofounder and director, Will W. Alexander. A former Methodist minister, who worked in Tennessee before joining the YMCA's War Work Council in 1917, Alexander came to rely on Woofter's local knowledge and sangfroid, assigning him to special projects, involving him in key meetings, and entrusting him with increasingly important, and sometimes hazardous, missions.[1]

Woofter stayed for seven years with the organization that transformed the ambition and reach of white liberalism. He helped to change it from a religious initiative for lessening postwar local tensions into a regional campaign and education program against racial violence. He lobbied legislators; raised money; undertook research; published articles, handbooks, and a college textbook; liaised with the press and other campaigning bodies; assisted with the formation of the CIC's nine original state committees and its county committees; dealt with city and state governments; protected victimized black farmers; exposed and confronted the activities of the Ku Klux Klan; and led the CIC's successful fight against lynching, especially in Georgia.

In small, uneven, steps, the movement for interracial cooperation had grown since the 1890s, so that the CIC built on the groundwork laid by earlier regional groups, notably the Southern Sociological Congress (SSC) and the University Commission on Southern Racial Questions (UCSRQ), and several local associations, such as the Committee on Church Cooperation created in Atlanta after the 1906 riot. Although most of these organizations failed to expand beyond their initial memberships and faded away after 1920, a new momentum was already building for community-based and more truly *interracial* cooperation to reduce violence and foster black progress.

The CIC attempted to move southern race relations onto a new plane by giving interracial cooperation a practical and visible form, harnessing local energies and residual goodwill. Alarmed at recent changes in African American activism and expectation, and infused with the Social Gospel, the white founders of the CIC fostered a new mentality among many middle-class white southerners. For some white people, the spark was a desire to halt the migration of black labor by improving health care, personal security, and education.[2] Other whites were prompted by perceptible changes in the class structure of the black population and a greater sense of common interests. Every year, thousands of poorer families were abandoning tenancy or rural wage labor, so that one in four black Georgians now lived in a town or city. Since 1900, the number of black industrial workers in the state had risen from nearly 26,000 to over 68,000; those engaged in trade or transport rose from under 20,000 to over 43,000; and the number of black professionals had risen from under 5,000 to nearly 8,000. Almost as dramatic was the rate at which black families with accumulated savings were leaving tenancy or wage labor behind by becoming landowners, so that by 1920, fourteen thousand black Georgians owned nearly two million acres of farmland.[3] These trends complicated the master-servant social order, heightened the political awakening of the African American masses, and gave new resonance to the equal rights movement led by northern-based organizations such as the National Association for the Advancement of Colored People (NAACP) and the smaller National Equal Rights League. Opportunist white politicians, citing the growing radicalism of the black press, the rapid demobilization of black soldiers, continued migration, and the summer riots of 1919, called for the entrenchment of white supremacy. But the white response was far from monolithic; many southerners plainly hoped for a new postwar relationship between the races, and between the South and rest of the United States. In these circumstances, the loose association of individuals and groups that made up the interracial cooperation movement carved a role for itself in promoting peace, reconciliation, and modernization.

Without an organizational focal point, the movement had been forced to rely on education reform as a vehicle for improved race relations and black progress. For two decades, white northern philanthropists and their education agents had corresponded with southern black leaders, but arm's-length interactions created frustrations on both sides. The flow of charitable money from the North became vital to individual schools, but it provided no solution to the region's economic problems; nor did it affect the political status of black southerners or make white southerners generally more well disposed toward them. Will Alexander wanted meaningful face-to-face conversations between the races in the South. As he put it, "Goodwill is a by-product of contact and understanding."[4] Thus, the CIC set up state organizations and local networks of influential men and women who called openly for dialogue, respect, black economic progress, the rule of law, and local improvements. In doing so, the CIC created new networks of middle-class white southerners within communities and encouraged them to discover areas of common concern with their black counterparts. Many were looking for ways to lessen mob violence and were moved by the sense that interracial cooperation fulfilled a Christian duty.

John Hope, president of Atlanta's Morehouse College and a key black supporter of the CIC, applauded its white leadership for ceasing "the habit of even favourably disposed southern white people to think out what was best for Negroes and do that," without involving black people. He was more optimistic about white southern liberalism than his friend W. E. B. Du Bois, and believed the CIC's founders were determined to change the South and prevent the degradation of American civilization as a whole: "The little group of white men that met in Atlanta, Georgia, just after the World War faced the fact inexorably: A people cannot remain cruel and unjust and live."[5] Jack Woofter saw men like Hope as essential—and the CIC provided them with a new forum in which they could speak "freely and frankly" and initiate change through "conference and cooperation." Their involvement meant that "white people learned from the lips of Negro leaders themselves just how they felt about the racial situation, and Negro leaders learned of a sympathy and friendship which they had but dimly realized before."[6]

From the black perspective, the appeal of the CIC approach partly lay in the chance to have some say about local services, even on the most basic level, but many African Americans reacted skeptically to new white expressions of "goodwill." In March 1919, James E. McCall advised readers of the *Montgomery Emancipator*:

> We cannot drive out darkness, except by turning on light. Neither can we usher in interracial good will until the victory over injustice is gained. The time has come when the Negro masses are demanding their leaders to speak out frankly and fearlessly and ask for the fundamental things that the race is seeking here at home—the things for which Negro soldiers fought and died side by side with their white comrades on the bloody fields of France. Why ask for good will when what we really want is justice, democracy and a man's chance in life?[7]

Thus, the upheaval of World War I produced both the idea of the CIC and the circumstances in which it could grow. In 1918, over several months, white observers of the war effort in France and the United States, including officials and volunteers of the Young Men's Christian Association (YMCA), saw race relations deteriorating at the front and in the training camps. The student Christian movement, generally, was a longstanding proponent of the Social Gospel's relevance to the race question, and postwar interracial cooperation was central to its social justice agenda. Article 13 of the "Social Ideals of the Churches," adopted at the YMCA's first postwar convention, was a pledge to work for "justice, opportunity, and equal rights for all; mutual good will and co-operation among racial, economic, and religious groups." The YMCA's War Work Council supported the proposal of its official, Willis Duke Weatherford, for weeklong segregated "training schools" for young people on reducing racial strife in their communities. This was a reprise of the "Negro problem" meetings that Weatherford first organized on southern campuses in 1912 for 6,000 white students and the Negro Christian Student Conference in Atlanta in 1914, an international gathering attended by 600 black people and 70 white church delegates under the chairmanship of John R. Mott of the World Student Christian Federation. In the months after World War I, Weatherford accommodated 824 white men in eight separate schools at his Blue Ridge Assembly near Asheville, North Carolina, while Will Alexander led 509 black men in five schools at Gammon Theological College in Atlanta. Many of these men, half of whom were church ministers, became the first county-level organizers for the CIC, while more than half the founding chairmen of the state-level interracial committees in the South had YMCA connections.[8]

An important part of the CIC's strategy in the early 1920s was the practical demonstration of goodwill through selected legal cases. This work was coordinated by Jack Woofter and involved seeking redress for peonage, the defrauding of black farmers, and cases of racially motivated assault. Although the Ku Klux Klan began to attract adverse comment nationally by the end of 1921, after the investigative reporting of the *New York World* received wide exposure, the debate in Georgia on such matters was muted, with only one newspaper, the *Columbus Sun-Enquirer*, carrying the *World*'s revelations. The CIC, which had provided the *World* with much of its material, thus represented the loudest organized white opposition in the South to the Klan. Eventually, the editors of leading southern papers, such as the *Memphis Commercial Appeal* in 1923 and the *Montgomery Advertiser* in 1927, found the courage to denounce the Klan for corrupt election practices and rural brutality. As the commission challenged the general assumption that a white person could do anything to a black person, Woofter coordinated a handful of prosecutions that showed participants in racial violence that their identities might be revealed, in cases that did lasting damage to the reputation of the Invisible Empire.[9]

*   *   *

In December 1918, Thomas Jesse Jones of the Phelps-Stokes Fund and the principal of Tuskegee Institute, Robert Russa Moton, traveled to France at the U.S. government's request to test the mood of black regiments after military intelligence and other agencies reported unrest and conspiracies. Moton served on the Committee on the Welfare of Negro Troops of the Federal Council of Churches and was skeptical about such reports, but was anxious about the treatment black veterans would receive in the United States.[10]

One effect, ironically, of sending observers to visit the troops was to increase fears that racial unrest in the United States would inevitably follow the war, prompting concerned groups to prepare for a crisis. In January 1919, a group of liberal white ministers, industrialists, and educationists, calling themselves the "Committee on After-War Cooperation," invited Weatherford and Jones to attend their first meeting in Atlanta. The participants were connected by war work or other charitable activity and included Will Alexander, James Hardy Dillard of the Jeanes and Slater Funds, Wallace Buttrick of the Rockefeller-funded General Education Board (GEB), and senior YMCA official Richard Hayne King. They were joined by three Atlanta social gospelers: industrialist John J. Eagan, Baptist minister Meredith Ashby Jones, and Episcopalian minister Cary B. Wilmer. The most energetic of these was Eagan, who chaired both the War Camp Community Services and the Race Relations Commission of the Federal Council of Churches, and led the white half of the Committee on Church Cooperation in Atlanta, in which Wilmer was also involved. Dillard and Ashby Jones had served on the Committee on the Welfare of Negro Troops, along with Thomas Jesse Jones and the Georgia-born New York philanthropist George Foster Peabody.[11]

In February 1919, in New York, Thomas Jesse Jones hosted an interracial symposium between the Phelps-Stokes Fund, the YMCA, and the War-Time Committee of Churches regarding the "racial disturbances clearly pending." Soon afterward, Thomas Jesse Jones, Robert Moton, and U.S. secretary of labor William B. Wilson discussed the coordination of government and local voluntary efforts to head off trouble. When the Committee on After-War Cooperation reconvened in Atlanta in March, Thomas Jesse Jones and John Eagan predicted dire consequences of black wartime service, because white people expected trouble from black veterans, and black veterans would demand democracy. The meeting, attended by Jackson Davis of the GEB and Walter B. Hill, representing the U.S. Bureau of Education, showed the different directions in which the interracial cooperation movement was being pulled, as speakers proposed measures to either reassure whites or placate blacks. Thomas Jesse Jones stressed that the program—justice in the courts, an end to lynching, better travel accommodation, better schools, better housing, new parks and playgrounds, and fairer wages—required white people, not blacks, to change. To Ashby Jones, it was about giving the African American "his right to make his own place[;] we are not even thinking about social equality," while Will Alexander wanted to show black people they had white friends and that not all whites supported the "Ku Klux or night riders." Meeting again in April 1919, the committee began calling itself the "Interracial Commission," although its membership remained all white. (Weatherford referred to it as the "Inter-Racial Commission of the War Work Council of the YMCA," while Thomas Jesse Jones stressed its links to the Phelps-Stokes Fund.) An entirely voluntary body, it had no official status—several reforming organizations in Georgia called themselves "commissions," such as the Commission on Civics, created by the Christian Council of Atlanta.[12] Indeed, the CIC was part of a trend for southern reform bodies without the control of state agencies or politicians. In the 1940s,

UNC Woman's College sociologist Lyda Gordon Shivers listed twenty significant unofficial welfare organizations founded since 1900, including the CIC, the UC-SRQ, the SSC, the Conference for Education in the South, the Southern Woman's Educational Alliance, the Southern States Industrial Council, and the Southern Conference for Human Welfare. She noted, "A salient characteristic of the regional picture of social welfare in the South is the importance of the socially minded layman."[13]

The sense of doom in the Interracial Commission's meetings stemmed from the violent backdrop. Black veterans (dubbed "Frenchwomen-ruined niggers" by Senator James K. Vardaman of Mississippi) faced widespread hostility, and at least a dozen were lynched, while race riots occurred at Charleston, South Carolina, and Longview, Texas. Alexander, as executive director, and Eagan, as chairman, recruited additional sympathetic white men, so that by July 1919 the group had doubled in size to sixteen. As Atlantans, they knew the horrors of race rioting and saw the 1919 riots, the Red Scare, and the apparent assertiveness of African Americans as the start of a race war. After agonizing, they opened their meetings to mild-mannered black leaders such as John Hope and Robert Russa Moton. (Hope, too, worked in France during the war with the YMCA.) When the YMCA's National War Work Council gave Alexander $75,000 to form local interracial committees, he sent out teams of one black and one white agent to southern cities and towns to hold public meetings about race problems. They covered 452 counties, and by the end of the year 159 local committees had been created.[14] It was an encouraging start, but the next steps were unclear. As Ronald C. White noted, "A strength, and later a weakness, of the Commission on Interracial Cooperation, as it was now called, was that it had no ordered strategy. Blacks and whites did not have to say yes or no to a program. They were encouraged simply to talk together."[15]

Other, broadly comparable, organizations sprang up across the South at the end of World War I, but they lacked the altruism of the CIC and its connections in educational, religious, philanthropic, political, and commercial circles. The Tennessee Law and Order League, with branches in thirty counties, was formed in 1918 by white businessmen and college professors opposed to lynching. Its leaders included men committed to cooperation, such as Edwin Mims of Vanderbilt University, who joined the CIC, and less candid men, such as Memphis businessman and pamphleteer Bolton Smith, who fed lies about W. E. B. Du Bois to military intelligence during the war. Smith persisted in slighting Du Bois, telling the Tuskegeeite editor of the *New York Age*, "I confess to a difficulty in working for a cause when people keep saying all long that it is hopeless—as our friend of the Crisis too frequently intimates."[16] Smith's wife, Grace Carlile, also engaged in interracial cooperation work as president of the Bishop's Guild in Tennessee.[17] The Mississippi Welfare League (MWL) was formed in April 1919 under the leadership of planter and writer Alfred Holt Stone and the GEB-funded state supervisor of rural Negro schools, Bura Hilbun. According to Weatherford, the purpose of the MWL was to "keep down race troubles and lynchings; also to improve living conditions and encourage better rural school work, and for the general uplift of both races," but its main aim was to dissuade blacks from migrating northward and persuade those who had done so to return. (Hilbun was later jailed for embezzling Rosenwald Fund school-building money, but had genuine reforming instincts. He attempted to count all the blind black babies in Mississippi to assess their education and was surprised to find much smaller numbers of black babies than white babies blinded at, or soon after, birth by venereal and other infections.)[18] Other interracial cooperation groups operated on a local urban basis, such as the subcommittees of the Commercial Club in Nashville and the Chamber of Commerce in Memphis, the Colored Civic League in New Orleans and other Louisiana cities, and the City Relief Association in Fort Worth, Texas. The white businesses and charities that supported these efforts were concerned with managing the temper of African Americans after the war and minimizing "race friction." They showed little interest in pushing for fundamental reforms; in the case of Nashville, for example, the Commercial Club's interracial committee supported strict segregation on streetcars because of "the continuous danger involved in the mingling of the races."[19] Outside the South during the 1920s, in northern and western cities, such as Chicago, Philadelphia, and Los Angeles, students and youth workers set up several local interracial groups, but their focus differed from that of the CIC, with its regional scope.

As fears of a race war mounted in 1919, interracial cooperationists hoped desperately to discover the true feelings of black southerners. In April, two UCSRQ representatives were shaken by the militancy they encountered in black colleges. William Muse Hunley, a political science professor at Virginia Military Institute, and the GEB's James Dillard described a meeting at Fisk University in Nashville at which members of Du Bois's "Talented Tenth" condemned America for lynching, segregation, and other discrimination. The UCSRQ issued an open letter to white college students, entitled "A New Reconstruction," in which they declared that black wartime loyalty required whites to show "wise sympathy and generous cooperation" during demobilization. In particular, they asked young white southerners "for the control of careless habits of speech which give needless offense" and for a show of "cooperation between the best elements of both races, to emphasize the best rather than the worst features of interracial relations, to secure greater publicity for those whose views are based on reason rather than prejudice."[20]

The Phelps-Stokes Fund also appealed to white opinion through its Southern Publicity Committee (SPC), led by Clark Howell, the owner-editor of the *Atlanta Constitution*. The committee's main writer, Lily Hardy Hammond, who attended the March 1919 meeting of the Committee on After-War Cooperation, issued press releases covering interracial activities, war work by black people, education, and lynching to over a hundred newspapers and several hundred YMCA branches. When her husband's ill health obliged her to move to New York, the SPC hired Sydney D. Frissell to target the press.[21] The *New York Times* carried his account of the legacy of the Southern Education Board under Walter Hines Page, Charles W. Dabney, and George Foster Peabody, and the impact of the latest UCSRQ circular on the responsibilities of southern college men.[22]

The SSC, with a membership overlapping that of the CIC and the UCSRQ, also reacted to the sense of a looming crisis. In May 1919, at its annual gathering at Knoxville, Tennessee, the congress responded to the lynching of three black men and the burning of lodges and churches at Millen, in Jenkins County, Georgia, following the killing of two white lawmen during a dispute at a church picnic.[23] The SSC demanded "the immediate exercise of all possible state and federal power to put a swift end to these outrages throughout the country," but this call for federal action against lynching was highly unusual and was not repeated. Dillard opened the proceedings of the SSC's race relations section with a confident assertion that the war had increased "sensible cooperation and mutual good-will. . . . After such an exhibition of patriotism as this and such cooperation, it must follow that relations between the races are going to be further improved." John Louis Kesler, a North Carolinian Baptist who taught at the YMCA's Southern College in Nashville, was more pessimistic. The best he hoped for was better communication between rational well-to-do members of both races, because the lower end of the social scale was a racial powder keg. Kesler warned, "The greatest prejudice, with its incurable blindness, is found in the lowest types of both races. They occupy the danger zone, and they are in contact with each other. The finer types of both races are thinking in larger terms. . . . They are our hope, but they are not in contact with each other." He urged the South to strike a balance—he deplored disfranchisement and lynching (he was teaching at Baylor University in Texas when seventeen-year-old Jesse Washington was burned alive nearby at Waco in 1916), but he was all for "racial integrity and social separateness." The most important thing was to give black people hope:

> [that is,] an equal chance for personal and social development, equal protection and security under the law, equal opportunity—economic, industrial, educational; equal courtesies, equal conveniences and comfort in street cars, railway coaches. . . . It is a mistake to suppose that just anything will do for the Negro; that he does not understand, does not see. He does see and he does not forget[;] . . . he is to be an intelligent and efficient citizen or the nemesis of our neglect. We'll help him or he'll hurt us.[24]

This echoed Booker T. Washington's remark in 1896 that "The negro can better afford to be wronged in this country than the white man can afford to wrong him."[25]

Consciously or otherwise, Kesler also reprised the warning by the Atlanta newspaper editor and orator Henry W. Grady in 1887: "Let us give [the Negro] his uttermost rights, and measure out justice to him in that fullness the strong should always give to the weak. Let us educate him that he may be a better, a broader, and more enlightened man. . . . And let us remember this—that whatever wrong we put on him shall return to punish us. . . . But what we win from him in sympathy and affection, . . . out of it shall come healing and peace."[26]

The African American statistician and librarian Monroe N. Work of Tuskegee Institute, also addressed the SSC, warning that "the best element in the Negro race [was] more or less out of touch with the best element in the white race." He pointed to new opportunities for interracial cooperation afforded by education, agriculture, health care, and war veteran resettlement, adding, "It is very important in connection with the present efforts for interracial cooperation that the new South have a better understanding of the new Negro."[27]

Thus, the future of the South, itself, was a powerful theme in postwar interracial cooperationist rhetoric. When Will Alexander called for better treatment of African Americans, he was not motivated simply by humanitarian concern. He knew the war had been a transformative experience for many blacks and feared they would seek revenge for past and present wrongs. During the war, military intelligence officers and agents of the Justice Department repeatedly claimed that pro-German subversion was unsettling the black population; in 1919, the same agencies switched to stories about Bolshevik agitation, hoping to silence equal-rights activists by accusing them of disloyalty. Like many white liberals, Alexander accepted uncritically the government's propaganda. In July 1919, he warned an Interracial Commission meeting:

> There is a small group of radical Negroes who are trying to drive a wedge between Negroes and whites on the assumption that the white man is autocratic and that he means to dominate everything himself. They are trying to organize the Latin races and the Negro race against the white race. You see what you are up against if that idea is allowed to spread. The most important thing that can be done is the promotion of closer contacts between the right sort of Negroes in our communities and the right sort of white men. If we do not do this, this racial cleavage is going to broaden.[28]

Major outbreaks of race rioting in Washington, D.C., and Chicago during the following week seemed to add weight to Alexander's warning.

At the request of Woodrow Wilson, the riots were discussed at the annual meeting of the National Governors Association (NGA) at Salt Lake City in August 1919. The NGA invited the SSC to put forward its "Program for Improving Race Relations," a nakedly white supremacist document revealing the rootedness of the SSC in late-nineteenth-century liberalism. It was delivered by Episcopal bishop

T. D. Bratton of Mississippi, assisted by Dillard and SSC secretary J. E. McCulloch, but only two southern governors, from North and South Carolina, were in the audience. Bratton stated that "no enduring basis of good-will between the white and colored peoples in this country can be developed except on the fundamental principles of justice, cooperation and race integrity," but his idea of cooperation was hopelessly lopsided. It was the kind of thing that made W. E. B. Du Bois despair of the interracial cooperation movement. Although the presentation called for an end to lawlessness, Bratton attributed lynching to the rape of white women and suggested that the prime responsibility for reducing mob violence lay with black people. The first step, he said, would be "the enlistment of Negroes themselves in preventing crimes that provoke mob violence."

> [Black leaders have a] duty to trace out and run down the offender and hand him over to the proper authorities to see that justice is done. Then we as the governing race should be willing to see that this offender has a proper and a speedy trial, and that speedy execution shall follow the conviction of the offender. . . . We should impress upon the people that justice will be done in such cases . . . with the greatest possible speed, so that there will be no motive whatever for mob riots and acts of violence.

He called for "legislation that will make it unnecessary for a woman who has been assaulted to appear in open court to testify publicly . . . [and] legislation that will give the governor authority to dismiss a sheriff for failure to protect a prisoner." Bratton added that "the citizenship rights of the Negro should be safeguarded" in segregated trains, new schools, and new housing, but he made no mention of the vote or justice in the courts. Local interracial committees and the employment of black doctors, nurses, and policemen would create "closer cooperation between white and colored citizens . . . (without encouraging any violation of race integrity)." Governors were asked to promote "justice, good will and kindliness" through advisory committees on the causes of "race friction." He concluded, "Today there are a lot of things which we could do for the benefit of the 'Nigger' and which would tend to settle this race problem, if foolish people would not cause the negro to be inflamed from time to time. That has been our trouble right along." The audience responded by denouncing Bolshevik agitation. Only Governor Thomas W. Bickett of North Carolina spoke up for practical measures such as suppressing mobs by martial law and relocating trials of black people accused of assaulting whites.[29]

If interracial cooperation had been left to men like Bratton, nothing would have been achieved. The heart of the southern interracial cooperation movement in 1919 lay in the several hundred local meetings devoted to improving race relations. Most were attended only by white people, but over a hundred included black participants.[30] By the end of 1919, such activity regularly attracted national attention and began to look like a long-term strategy, rather than a response to a crisis. In a Sunday supplement article in the *New York Times,* Sydney Frissell described interracial meetings in southern cities and the new readiness of white southerners to condemn lynching, donate money for schools, and give black people a "square deal." He criticized the casual labeling of black radicals during the Red Scare. Too much attention had been paid to "certain negro leaders [who] heap abuse upon the South and stir race bitterness[, in contrast to] real negro leaders, like Robert Moton [of Tuskegee Institute], Isaac Fisher [of Fisk University] and John Gandy [of Virginia Normal School], specialists not in friction, but in co-operation, who preach good-will while they demand a square deal for their people."[31] Articles such as Frissell's were only glimmerings of goodwill and dialogue in a sea of gloom about race wars and radicalism, but they appear to have been influential: several southern governors spoke out against racial violence in 1920 and 1921, hosted their own interracial conferences, and formally sanctioned the state race relations committees of the CIC. Some white churches also endorsed the CIC in the spring of 1920: in quick succession, the Episcopal Church of South Carolina, the Southern Baptist Convention, and the General Assembly of the Southern Presbyterian Church encouraged their ministers and members to participate in interracial meetings.[32]

In March 1920, Thomas Jesse Jones told the CIC that Jack Woofter's "study of conditions in northern cities and his intimate knowledge of racial conditions in the South would probably be of value to you in your future plans." Jones made this offer for three reasons: to look after Woofter, to help the CIC, and to place his own man in the organization. Jones had attended only one CIC meeting since July 1919 and was about to depart to London for two months, before spending most of 1921 in Africa, but he was full of insistent advice and tried to shape the commission's central body. He wanted minimal African American influence and worried that new committee places for black members meant including Robert Elijah Jones, soon to be one the first African American bishops of the Methodist Episcopal Church. Thomas Jesse Jones told Richard King that he was "especially concerned with the election of Negro members to the Committee. There are great possibilities of good as well as great possibilities of misunderstanding in this step." Dillard, he said, had agreed "that the increase of that group on the Committee [should] be gradual." Thomas Jesse Jones had experience of the factions in African American politics and favored leaders from the Hampton-Tuskegee school of tact and compliance beloved by white philanthropists over activists who insisted on telling the truth. He feared that putting African Americans on the committee and letting them nominate new members risked "clique management" and would introduce "an element that represents a personal rather than a broad racial interest."[33] He partly got what he wanted: the three black men added to the central committee in June 1920 were not radicals—John Hope, John M. Gandy, and Isaac Fisher—

but Jones could not stop the CIC inviting more than twenty other black leaders as observers. In time, more blacks were co-opted onto the central committee, but they remained a minority; in 1924, there were sixty-five white members and only seventeen blacks, although the latter were generally more active.[34]

As one of eight original CIC state secretaries, Jack Woofter was given responsibility for interracial cooperation work in Georgia and Florida.[35] State secretaries' duties included helping the CIC meet its target of 759 local committees—one for each southern county in which African Americans exceeded 10 percent of the population. By June 1920, 562 local committees had been set up. Although fewer than half developed a lasting program of work, Woofter recalled them as having "accomplished something by just being in existence." Gradually, the CIC carved out a role as a regional advocate of community-based cooperation, so that interracial committees became a familiar feature of southern life, encouraging black citizens to speak out about local problems and inviting white people to offer solutions. The Wake Forest College historian C. Chilton Pearson spent the summer of 1920 organizing interracial committees in North Carolina towns, finding blacks and whites who wanted genuine dialogue, a reduction of friction, and improved services. There was no sense, however, that interracial cooperation entailed adjustments in the distribution of power or any guarantees concerning constitutional rights.[36]

In August 1920, the existence of the CIC was formally announced in *An Appeal to the Christian People of the South*, issued at the Blue Ridge Assembly. Members of eight religious denominations met with the YMCA, the YWCA, and the agents of several educational charities. Academe was represented by UNC sociologists Samuel H. Hobbs and Howard W. Odum. All of the seventy participants were white, and only three were women: Carrie Parks Johnson from Georgia, a member of the Methodist board of missions; Fannie Yarborough Bickett, of the YWCA, the wife of North Carolina's governor; and Susie Moore Brittain of Florida's Baptist board of missions. The signatories of the "Appeal" declared themselves "absolutely loyal to the best traditions and convictions of the South, and especially to the principle of racial integrity." They welcomed the formation of the CIC and its spreading network of local committees as a homegrown response to a southern problem, stating baldly, "It is a matter of common knowledge that grave injustices are often suffered by members of the Negro race in matters of legal procedure, traveling facilities, educational facilities, the public press, domestic service, child welfare and in other relations of life." They applauded the governors of states in which lynching had declined and called on the churches to "unhesitatingly and uncompromisingly condemn and oppose all mob violence." They also urged railroad companies, "under the laws of separation pertaining to public transportation, [to make] adequate and equitable arrangements for the safety and comfort of travelers of the Negro race," and especially for black women. They called for domestic servants to be offered "the maximum of moral as well as physical protection." They deplored "the unsanitary and bad housing conditions which prevailed in many sections of the South" and demanded renewed school buildings, "an equitable distribution of school funds," and better training for black teachers. The "Appeal" also publicly named the initial fifty-five members of the central committee of the CIC, drawn from thirteen states. Georgia, with ten members, provided the biggest delegation, including Will Alexander, Ashby Jones, John Eagan, Lily Hardy Hammond, John Hope, and Walter Hill. The next largest groups were from Virginia and Tennessee with seven and six members, respectively.[37]

By the mid-1920s, the CIC head office in Atlanta, the separate state committees across the South, and the local interracial committees at county level represented the most effective force for the reduction of lynching and other racial violence. Without the CIC, southern antilynching protests would have been sporadic and inaudible, for no other body offered regional leadership on this issue. In the heyday of Progressivism, southern universities had raised concerns about numerous social problems, but the UCSRQ and the SSC were now in decline. The YMCA gave seed money to the interracial cooperation movement, but would pursue a broader national reform agenda after the war. The NAACP campaigned vigorously against lynching from its base in New York and lobbied effectively in Washington, D.C., but was not up to the task of challenging racial oppression in the rural South. The CIC, on the other hand, through its contacts in churches, colleges, women's clubs, business groups, governors' mansions, and newspaper offices, was wired into the diverse reforming forums of the region, and in Will Alexander it had a director with a rare capacity to convince leading men and women of both races to put aside their reservations and work together.

At first, it even seemed possible the NAACP and the CIC would form a partnership. When the NAACP took the bold step of holding its annual convention in Atlanta in 1920, the two organizations made special efforts to acknowledge each other, but they differed fundamentally in philosophy and method. Ashby Jones, as chairman of the CIC's Georgia State Committee on Race Relations (GSCRR), addressed the NAACP convention on the need for "cooperation between the intelligent elements of both races," and Cary B. Wilmer, another white CIC founder, joined W. E. B. Du Bois on the platform to address the closing session on education and voting rights. But the leadership of the NAACP also met with other civic leaders to learn more about the Atlanta Plan of Inter-Racial Cooperation, which predated the CIC and held monthly joint meetings of the city's black and white church councils. The NAACP favored this approach over "the race committees that are growing throughout the South [because] the Negroes are chosen by their own people, not by the whites."[38]

The Atlanta city government was keen to attract the convention, as evidence of progress since the 1906 riot, but generally in the South the NAACP was regarded as an embodiment of outside interference and radicalism. It was so distrusted by most white people that it could never have attempted the work undertaken by the CIC. Alexander respected the NAACP and developed a good working relationship with its assistant secretary, Walter F. White, who was from Atlanta, but other CIC members had deep misgivings about the association's role in the South. Josiah Morse, a Jewish Virginia-born psychologist at the University of South Carolina, could not contain his resentment:

> I wish some one or some group could persuade the N.A.A.C.P. to go out of existence. Their activities hamper us greatly in our work. They have taken hold of the wrong end and gone at it in a wrong spirit. Their attitude gets our backs up. The South is not going to be coerced or directed by a hostile organization that confines its efforts almost exclusively to the Negro and puts notions in his head, which, if he had no better sense than to follow, would surely lead him to the shambles. The North can give moral and financial assistance, but the direct work must be done by ourselves. And we must be allowed to make haste slowly.[39]

Several new NAACP branches were created in Georgia during and after the war, giving the association a presence in sixteen cities and towns; in Atlanta the membership rose from seven hundred to three thousand, but this activity was not sustained. During the early 1920s, many branches folded in the face of white threats to the lives or businesses of their members. For example, the Thomasville branch, in Thomas County near the Florida border, boasted three hundred members at its peak, but disbanded in 1920 after its president was told he would be killed. Walter White, who liaised with Jack Woofter on cases concerning Klan violence and peonage, recommended a small NAACP donation to the CIC in 1923: "I think the money would be well spent for we could then refer to them more freely a great many cases which come to us and which they can handle much better than we, especially in view of the intimidation of our branches in southern states."[40] Eventually, according to historian Mary Rolinson, Marcus Garvey's Universal Negro Improvement Association (UNIA) outdid the NAACP in forming farmer-led chapters in a swathe of counties with bad lynching records in southern Georgia. The NAACP remained strong in certain cities and among black professionals, but its organizing attempts in many rural parts of the South faltered badly.[41]

By the summer of 1921, the CIC had instructed sixty-one white and twenty-six black organizers to identify receptive black and white community leaders, establish interracial committees, and survey local black needs. The ideal deployment was four workers for each state—a white man and woman and a black man and woman—but this mix was rarely achieved. In many places, CIC organizers were able to exploit grassroots disquiet about lawlessness after World War I, and a succession of communities declared themselves opposed to lynching and pledged to help law officers protect prisoners or arrest participants in mobs. In September 1920, after the killing of two black men taken from a jail in Alcorn County, Mississippi, a mass meeting of white citizens in a Baptist church issued a "stern condemnation" of the mob's "ruthless and inexcusable disregard of the courts."[42] In Kentucky, where interracial committees were formed in 60 out of the 120 counties, the CIC's black state secretary, James Bond, stated they had prevented at least five lynchings in the first half of the 1920s (when only one lynching actually occurred).[43]

* * *

The CIC's all-male founders initially excluded white women from their central meetings, claiming this would encourage both a white backlash and female fanaticism. Most of the first local interracial committees were also exclusively male, but the determination of southern women to become part of the CIC network led to the establishment of a central women's committee and several state women's committees.[44] This activism was born of twenty years of professional missionary work by southern women, particularly Methodists, who saw the necessity for interracial cooperation and found ways of approximating it before the CIC was formed. Lily Hardy Hammond, author of more than fifty articles and books between the 1890s and the 1920s, undertook publicity and research work for both the NAACP and the Phelps-Stokes Fund in 1917 and later worked on interracial cooperation materials for the YWCA and the CIC. The daughter of North Carolinian slaveholders, she was inspired by the Social Gospel and undeterred by the bile directed at other white liberals such as Andrew Sledd and Charles Lee Coon. She recognized that whites would be in control for the foreseeable future, but saw no justification for deliberate obstruction of black progress; she was especially clear on the need for white and black women to work together. In 1904, she challenged "unreasoning prejudice and unreasoning pride" and declared that the white race had forfeited any right to dictate the behavior of the former slave population:

> Outside of personal and often unreasoning kindness, where we are prone to take the attitude of feudal lords who give *largesse,* what is there in our treatment of the Negro to inspire him with respect for justice and the law? If we will lay aside our preconceived notions for a little, and go over all the complex web of racial relations in the South as they might appear to a gentleman from Mars, for instance, newly landed on the earth, what is there, outcome of the fifty years, commensurate with the obligation of a strong people to a weak one? What have we done to bind them to us? What to lift them up? What foundation have we as a people laid for dwelling with them in honour and mutual good will?[45]

By 1920, these questions were still unanswerable, but through the YWCA black women leaders seized opportunities to advance the case for better education, justice and safety in the workplace, reconciliation between the races, and equality and Christian sisterhood within the association itself.[46] It was an important step in the postwar construction of the interracial cooperation movement.

The Woman's Missionary Council of the Methodist Episcopal Church, South, forced Will Alexander to accord women a future role in the CIC by pledging early in 1920 "to show the whole world the power of Christianity to settle racial differences and to meet inter-racial crises everywhere." A subgroup began studying "the whole question of race relationships, the needs of Negro women and children and the methods of cooperation by which better conditions might be brought about." They were invited by the Atlanta black women's leader and YWCA official Lugenia Burns Hope to attend the convention of the National Association of Colored Women (NACW) at Tuskegee Institute in July 1920, where they witnessed "the splendid executive ability of those educated Negro women [and] realized that in that body was massed a potential power of which they had little dreamed." This should not have come as a shock. The southern black women's networks had been growing for thirty years, protesting against lynching and underfunded education, running special schools for black girls, opening clubs, sustaining churches, attending educational congresses, and making their voices heard in interracial forums. As historian Glenda Gilmore has noted, after black men were excluded from the political process, "black women's task was to try to force those white women who plunged into welfare efforts to recognize class and gender similarities across racial lines." And yet, most white women failed to grasp the scale of the southern black women's networks, despite points of contact such as the Women's Christian Temperance Union and the YWCA. During the Tuskegee conference, a new awareness began with an interracial women's meeting in the home of NACW cofounder Margaret James Murray, the widow of Booker T. Washington. Afterward, the white delegates persuaded Will Alexander to sponsor a Woman's Missionary Convention on "Southern Women and Race Cooperation" at Memphis in October 1920. The NACW prepared a discussion paper on "some of the unhappy conditions of the day," and four black women were invited to speak on "What It Means to Be a Negro."[47]

The black speakers were Margaret James Murray; Jennie Dee Booth, a teacher and wife of Tuskegee principal Robert Moton; Elizabeth Ross, a sociologist and YWCA official married to Department of Labor economist George E. Haynes; and Charlotte Hawkins Brown, the principal of Palmer Memorial Institute at Sedalia, North Carolina. They represented a range of views: Haynes and Brown were regarded as more outspoken, while the Tuskegee connections of Murray and Booth worried radical black activists, who doubted their commitment to ensuring that the Nineteenth Amendment applied to black women. Lugenia Burns Hope regarded Jennie Booth Moton as far too conciliatory on the vote question and described her as "weak, very weak. . . . She is too compromising in her attitude on race relationship."[48]

In a cramped YMCA hall, Charlotte Hawkins Brown spoke with extraordinary directness to the audience of ninety educators, social workers, and churchwomen, revealing how "crushed and humiliated" she had felt when, on her way to Memphis, she and another woman were ejected from a Pullman car in Alabama by a dozen white men. It was no longer 1880, she reminded the audience, and yet in some respects little had changed. She remarked that black mothers did not teach their children to hate white people with horror stories about slavery; equally, white mothers should not incite their children with "those horrible things of reconstruction." She challenged her audience:

> We have begun to feel that you are not, after all, interested in us and I am going still further. The Negro woman of the South lays everything that happens to the members of her race at the door of the Southern white woman. Just why I don't know, but we all feel that you can control your men. We feel that so far as lynching is concerned that, if the white woman would take hold of the situation that lynching would be stopped, mob violence stamped out and yet the guilty [black man] would have justice meted out by due course of law and would be punished accordingly. We do not condone criminality. We do not want our men to do anything that would make you feel that they were trying to destroy the chastity of our white women [but], on the other hand, I want to say to you when you read in the paper where a colored man has insulted a white woman, just multiply that by one thousand and you have some idea of the number of colored women insulted by white men.

She remained "a little bit discouraged," but she told the white women, "Thank God you are waking up today."[49]

The stunned white delegates called for "the exercise of justice, consideration and sympathetic cooperation" toward black citizens in relation to domestic service, child welfare, sanitation, housing, education, travel, lynching, the courts, and the press. They endorsed segregation, but called for "adequate accommodations and courteous treatment." Their commitment to interracial work resulted in a department of Woman's Work within the CIC's Atlanta office, under the direction of Carrie Parks Johnson, and the gradual formation of women's sections in the CIC's state interracial committees.[50] In the following months, black clubwomen also responded to the Memphis conference. In June 1921, the Atlanta-based Southeastern Federation of Colored Women's Clubs (SFCWC), whose leaders included Mary McLeod Bethune, Charlotte Hawkins Brown, Margaret Murray Washington, and Lugenia Burns Hope, issued a precise statement on black welfare issues, in order to "enlist the sympathy and co-operation of Southern white women in the interest of better understandings and better conditions, as these affect the relations between white and colored people." They were pleased that more southern white women were "determined to face the truth" and understood "the part which colored women must play" in improving conditions. They wanted action on all the areas highlighted by the white women at Memphis, but added a call for "the peaceful, orderly exercise of the franchise by every qualified Negro citizen." Having stated "frankly and soberly what in our judgment, you as white women may do to correct the ills from which our race has long suffered," they concluded: "We deeply appreciate the difficulties that lie before you." Carrie Parks Johnson refused to comment on granting the vote to black women, but others were explicitly opposed. Prior to the 1920 election, Fannie Y. Bickett and fellow interracial cooperationist Delia Dixon-Carroll, a physician and sister of the racist novelist Thomas Dixon Jr., had toured North Carolina encouraging registration of white women of the "right type" to ensure that any black women who might register were outnumbered.[51]

In 1922, Johnson called a joint meeting between the Woman's General Committee on Interracial Cooperation (incorporating the CIC's Committee on Woman's Work and seven white representatives of major religious denominations, women's clubs, and the YWCA) and the Interracial Committee of the SFCWC in Atlanta, to form "a plan by which the two groups could work together in greater usefulness." The black women at the meeting nominated seven of their number to join the Woman's General Committee, "to cooperate in constructive work for peace and good will." Johnson set out "the task of arresting the attention of large numbers of women and winning them to the work," and urged the women present to "work slowly and constructively, always bearing in mind that it is *all* the women and *all* the homes of both races which must be reached." As secretary of the GSCRR, Jack Woofter spent an afternoon speaking to the delegates on "Practical Plans of Cooperation," and encouraging them to focus on child welfare, education, and lynching.[52]

Women thus formed a key element within the interracial cooperation movement from the early 1920s, with 11 CIC women's committees forming by 1924 and 606 women's Methodist auxiliary committees working with black women to improve health care and recreation by 1927. The effectiveness of this work varied from committee to committee, as did the interracial bonds formed, but in many cases genuine partnership flowed and reform agendas merged. When the National League of Women Voters created a Committee on Negro Problems in 1924, several of the southern representatives were members of their local interracial committees. In South Carolina, as historian Joan Marie Johnson has shown, gender and religion interacted powerfully to reinforce the work of the CIC and other reform movements. The white chairwoman of the state interracial committee, Clelia McGowan, and her black deputy, Marion Wilkinson, both members of the Episcopal Church, formed an especially close cooperative relationship. McGowan was the first woman elected to the Charleston city council, in 1923, and Wilkinson, who attended the NACW meeting with white women at Tuskegee in 1920, led the Charleston branch of the Women's Christian Temperance Union. Both were active in the YWCA. Although the South Carolina diocese objected to full black participation in the Episcopal Church, McGowan and Wilkinson organized inter-racial work by women on a range of education and health projects.[53]

Despite progress, those white women who publicly identified with the inter-racial cooperation movement remained a small minority. The Boston-based writer Edith Armstrong Talbot, daughter of Hampton Institute's founder, knew from ex-perience that women with liberal views on race took greater social risks than men with similar views. Writing in the *Christian Science Monitor* in 1922, she declared that "women who take this stand are pursuing the path of martyrdom, not per-haps at the stake, but what is perhaps almost as hard to bear, the constant criti-cism and disapproval of their friends and neighbors."[54]

* * *

As soon as he was seconded to the CIC, Jack Woofter's abilities were recog-nized, and Alexander came to depend on him for moral support, as well and facts and figures. In February 1921, Alexander turned to Woofter when Robert Russa Moton asked the CIC to assist him in a meeting with president-elect Warren G. Harding. Moton was hoping to maintain the regular White House consultations and correspondence he enjoyed with Woodrow Wilson. Harding had made en-couraging noises to black journalists and women's antilynching delegations dur-ing the election campaign, while adroitly avoiding any statement that could alarm white southerners. After the election, Florence Harding thanked the black press and the Negro Women's Republican League and promised, "Senator Harding will give to the colored citizens of our nation a square deal."[55] In the approach to the inauguration, the CIC delegation hoped for clear policy indications, and Alexan-der's expectations were high. He recalled, "I also took along a youngster I had on my staff in whose mind I had a good deal of confidence—Dr. T. J. Woofter, in order to have his reaction afterwards about what had happened." Their encounter with Harding, in the Ponce de Leon Hotel in St. Augustine, Florida, was embarrassing and pointless. Moton had provided advance notice of proposals for government policy on race problems, but Harding, preoccupied with making appointments, was not briefed and seemed barely aware of Tuskegee Institute. Woofter wrote in his memoirs that Harding mistook the CIC group for southern Republican job-seekers, treating them to an expletive-laden monologue about the "nigger having made more progress in the past fifty years than any other people in history . . . always under white leadership." Moton replied, "Yes but we don't like to be told that," before the group departed without any discussion of race relations or co-operation. Alexander recalled that, as they left the hotel, "Woofter, who had said nothing during the conversation, said, 'If you'd eliminate damn from that fellow's vocabulary he couldn't do anything but stutter.'"[56]

After meeting Harding, a shocked Woofter wrote Anson Phelps Stokes. His letter merits quotation, both as a statement of what the CIC hoped to achieve at the national level and as the testimony of an idealistic young man in an age when American political leaders normally seemed remote and grave:

My most depressing experience of recent years was an interview with Mr. Harding three days ago. Some of the Southern men prominent in the Inter-Racial movement went down to "uphold Major Moton's hands" in a conference. Our main object was to make him realize that there is a strong body of Southern public opinion behind Dr Moton's cooperative ideas[,] thereby assuring Dr Moton of an audience on future policies relating to race relations. This we accomplished freely, because "backing" is one word [Harding] respects and "cooperation" is to him an open sesame. Our secondary object was to commit him as far as possible to avoidance of the advice of colored politicians and visionaries and to the principle of [appointing] expert colored advisors to the heads of his administrative departments. The principle which, during the war[,] was exemplified by the work of George Haynes and Emmett Scott. I don't think he caught even a remote idea of the significance of this. His mind was too preoccupied with the policies of the old fashioned "pie counter" involving postmasterships and minor jobs in Washington.

Plagiarizing from a recent statement of Mr. Taft[,] he assured us with much unction that he would not irritate the Southern people by appointing negroes to office where Southerners would be forced to deal with them. He said that he did not mind appointing negroes to positions in Washington and added that "no d–n radical was going to slip anything over on him." (He swore several times, not artistically[,] but solely from the paucity of genuine words[,] several of which he succeeded in mis-pronouncing.) Imagine our chief executive speaking the language of a ward politician at a level which, in America, is our nearest approach to an audience at court. One of our number was a minister.

The truly depressing feature of the interview was, however, the harangue which he himself delivered mostly for the benefit of Mr. Moton. Its text was you negroes have progressed wonderfully but should always remember that this is a white man's civilization. He squeezed himself dry on this subject in a few sentences and we left feeling very much humiliated at the contrast between him and Dr Moton. I was forced to remark that if he represents a white man's civilization, I choose Dr. Moton's. Dr. Ashby Jones (the minister) said that in place of his campaign pleas for the old time religion, he should have substituted a plea for a return to "that d–n righteousness." Mr. Alexander said he believed that if Mr. Harding lived in Georgia he would head some local Clan [sic] of the Ku-Klux, while Dr Moton said[,] "We will have to try to reach his cabinet members when they are appointed."[57]

Alexander and Moton may have been surprised, therefore, when in April 1921, in his first message to Congress, Harding let it be known that the interracial cooperation movement had succeeded in getting through to him. He referred to the "difficulties incident [to] . . . a condition which cannot be removed"—the large black population in the United States. He said it had been suggested to him that some of its difficulties might be ameliorated by a humane and enlightened consideration of it, a study of its many aspects, and an effort to formulate, if not a policy at least a national attitude of mind calculated to bring about the most satisfactory possible adjustment of relations between the races and of each race to the national life.

One proposal is the creation of a commission, embracing representatives of both races, to study and report on the entire subject. The proposal has real merit. I am convinced that in mutual tolerance, understanding, charity, recognition of the interdependence of the races, and the maintenance of the rights of citizenship lies the road to righteous adjustment.

To the delight of Moton and other black lobbyists, such as James Weldon Johnson of the NAACP, who had spoken to Harding about lynching a week earlier, the president went on to ask Congress "to wipe the stain of barbaric lynching from the banners of a free and orderly representative democracy."[58] The idea of a national study on race had been mooted in a bill introduced in April 1920 by Senator Selden P. Spencer (R) of Missouri. It provided for a commission made up of three white men from the South, three white men from the North, and three black men, whose task would be to recommend legislation to "relieve the Negro of many of the embarrassing conditions under which he now lives."[59]

Once Harding was installed, the impact of the lobbyists was intermittent, at best. He never again commented explicitly on antilynching legislation, and the national commission did not materialize. The following October, he gave a carefully worded speech to a segregated audience during the semicentennial celebrations of Birmingham, Alabama, which accorded with the line of the interracial cooperation movement in phraseology and sentiment. He spoke about the advantage and basic justice of granting educational and economic equality to black people, who should be allowed to vote "when fit to vote." He added that both races should "uncompromisingly" oppose "social equality," insisting that "racial amalgamation cannot be" and that "natural segregations" were beneficial. The white press generally commended Harding, but the speech caused a brief fuss among southern politicians, taken aback by his audacity in raising the subject at all in the Deep South and the enthusiastic applause he received from black members of the audience. The black press was generally skeptical, although Marcus Garvey quickly congratulated Harding. W. E. B. Du Bois, reckoning "The Year 1921 in Account with the American Negro" in the February 1922 Crisis, placed "Harding in Birmingham" in the debit column along with Marcus Garvey, Thomas Jesse Jones, fifty-nine lynchings, the Tulsa riot, and the murder of peons in Georgia. The rather longer credit column contained, among other things, Georgia's anti-Klan governor, Hugh Manson Dorsey, the interracial committees of the CIC, the Dyer antilynching bill, and three black women who gained PhDs.[60]

Harding's message to Congress and his Birmingham speech did not represent a policy, as such, and had no bearing on the administration's response to the race problem. Harding drew praise from black leaders for constructing an African American veterans' hospital at Tuskegee in 1922–23 and staffing it, in the face of Klan protests, with black doctors and nurses, but his mild disapproval of the Klan and his refusal to reverse fully the civil service segregation that spread under Wilson were disappointing. Charges of a "lilywhite" policy in the South began to appear in the black press within a few months of Harding's inauguration, as he appointed fewer African Americans to federal posts than was expected of a Republican president and failed to preserve the Division of Negro Economics in the Department of Labor.[61] Jack Woofter told Anson Phelps Stokes, "President Harding agreed in substance to the principle of expert advice in the federal departments, but I am afraid that he did not understand at all thoroughly the principle to which he was agreeing." In small ways, then, the moral force and political logic of interracial cooperation impinged on the thinking of senior Republicans, but not for long. In the St. Augustine hotel meeting, Woofter witnessed at close quarters the basic lack of interest and casual presumption that ultimately cost the GOP most of its black vote.[62]

After establishing the Georgia State Committee on Race Relations, the CIC moved swiftly to set up equivalent committees in other states. Woofter frequently traveled around the South, spreading the antilynching message, advising on the formation of new state committees, and attempting to ensure that they included black members.[63] In March 1921, for example, he went to Raleigh to help set up the North Carolina state interracial committee with G. G. Huntington of the YMCA's interracial department and William L. Poteat, a Baptist member of the interracial committee of the Federal Council of Churches. Governor Cameron Morrison gave the state committee his official blessing and named Poteat chairman. Other white liberals co-opted included Howard Odum and farmers' advocate Clarence Poe, previously a supporter of segregated farmlands. In the long term, such contacts were useful to Woofter; eventually, he would work with CIC supporters in Odum's Institute for Research in Social Science at Chapel Hill. The North Carolina committee prioritized public welfare, health, rural home demonstration programs, and education reform, rather than lynching. It was good at convening annual meetings, setting up subcommittees, and enunciating principles, but according to Odum's colleague and fellow CIC member Guy B. Johnson, its day-to-day work and local groups soon became weak and ineffectual.[64] Poteat's penchant for controversy did not help. As a eugenicist biologist and president of Wake Forest College, he clashed with antievolutionists, including his fellow Baptists, and was an outspoken critic of the Klan, declaring, "The K.K.K. with its fe-fau-fum, mumbo jumbo, [and] thirteenth century mummery is an insult to the intelligence of the time, and an out-and-out slap at the existing apparatus of justice." He was typical of the CIC's progressive white leadership in his unwavering confidence that segregation was good: "Race mixing is detrimental to the races themselves," he claimed.[65]

Alexander and his assistants ran the CIC from its central office in the Palmer Building in downtown Atlanta, but the commission's most dynamic arm was the Georgia state committee under the successive leadership of Jack Woofter, Clark H. Foreman, and Arthur F. Raper.[66] The state committees in Kentucky, Tennessee, North Carolina, Virginia, Alabama, and Texas were also active, whereas the committees in Oklahoma, Arkansas, and Louisiana were dormant for most of the 1920s, particularly in the latter state, where the committee was dominated by strongly segregationist white members and little work was done outside New Orleans. The southern state with the weakest CIC presence was probably Mississippi, where the deployment of agents was limited by a shortage of funds.[67]

In the summer of 1921, Woofter coedited the CIC's handbook, *Cooperation in Southern Communities,* an essential catechism for local interracial committees written by three black and nine white experts. It was his first major project for the CIC, produced in collaboration with the black academic Isaac Fisher, a member of both the central CIC committee and the Tennessee state interracial committee. If the CIC had allowed Woofter to edit *Cooperation in Southern Communities* by himself, it might have been a how-to manual, but Fisher and the other black contributors injected a political edge. Fisher was born on a farm in Louisiana in 1877, the sixteenth child of former slaves, and raised in Mississippi. One of the ablest graduates of Tuskegee Institute and Booker T. Washington's most devoted disciples, he was the Wizard's New England agent for two years, organized farmers' conferences in the South, and studied northern and southern school systems, before running normal schools in Arkansas and Louisiana. He helped found the *Negro Farmer* journal and taught journalism at Fisk University from 1916. In the eyes of northern equal-rights activists, Fisher was a lackey of the Tuskegee machine, and he was given little credit for the clarity with which he stated the case for change in the South. W. E. B. Du Bois, in particular, despised him. Perhaps best described as an urgent realist, Fisher was a gifted essayist. He encouraged black southerners to demand an immediate start to civil rights reform, even though its completion would be slow.[68] As far as he was concerned, white liberalism was on trial. He warned James Dillard at Fisk in 1919, "The Negro feel[s] that he is permanently to be regarded as inferior, second-rate, endured for his service but not respected for his humanity. . . . The Negroes no longer trust the white people to give them a fair deal."[69] He also told a meeting of the CIC central committee frankly in March 1921 that a few interracial meetings did not change the landscape of Jim Crow:

> No, I do not believe that Southern white people are the best white people on earth. No, I do not like the mob, and I do not like segregation. I do not want to be shut out from the right to vote, and I do not like anything that prevents me from doing or having all the things that others do [and] have; and, although I mean no irreverence, if the Good Master ever asks me I will tell him before

His face that I do not like any phase of segregation, nor any phase of mob rule and that it will never happen that I will like them.[70]

A few months later, in a more optimistic mood, he told CIC chairman John J. Eagan: "In the history of the South, this was the first agency set up to give Negroes and whites a chance to see into each other's hearts, on a large scale; and discover that there was a South of Christianity as well as a South of lynch-law; and that there was a body of Negroes as proud of themselves and the integrity of their own race as any Caucasian could possibly be."[71] Fisher stayed on the CIC central committee and was a popular speaker at state interracial committee meetings during the 1920s. He also assisted Alexander's efforts to keep the CIC financially afloat after the decision to make the commission permanent at the end of 1920, joining him on fundraising visits to East Coast sympathizers.[72]

In *Cooperation in Southern Communities*, Woofter and Fisher distilled the CIC's mission and its mantra of localism. They argued that the racial crisis was rooted in the South's peculiar history and could be addressed only by black and white southerners, working together. The race problem was essentially local; it was "the sum total of numerous local situations, and . . . these can be satisfactorily adjusted only by conference and cooperation between the white and colored leaders within local communities." The book revealed the CIC's asymmetry by presenting the seniority of the white race as normal in its guidance on the conduct of meetings. In his introduction, Woofter advised local committees to navigate around racial sensibilities by having black members agree in advance, "for clearness and conciseness," which of them would speak, and on what topic. Then, "when the colored members have made their presentation, the motion for definite action would come with better grace from some white member of the committee."[73] Woofter wanted CIC supporters to define clear local objectives and interracial projects to foster a sense of common purpose and reduce friction. It was all about preventing strife, not reacting to it. He observed that since race cut across all phases of Southern life—"religion, labor, law and order, education, health, housing, recreation, and care of the poor and delinquent"—the work of interracial committees was for the uplift of entire communities, not just their black segments. He recommended the recruitment of people from local government, churches, charities, and the press, and giving black leaders a taste of the public service from which they were normally excluded.[74]

Fisher, in his introduction, addressed black readers much more directly, asserting that the CIC offered a rare opportunity to connect with powerful elements in society. He assured black skeptics that interracial cooperation was not an attempt, "by giving the impression that all is well between the two races, [to] halt the movement for the securing of certain specific rights for the colored people . . . and for the curing of evils against which they unanimously complain." He dismissed fears that cooperation was "likely to result in an obscuring of issues, and

Isaac Fisher of Fisk University, photographed as a young man. Born in northeastern Louisiana in 1877 and trained at Tuskegee Institute, Fisher became one of the most committed African American members of the Commission on Inter-racial Cooperation. He co-edited *Cooperation in Southern Communities* (1921) with Jack Woofter and was relied upon by CIC director Will Alexander for help with fund-raising. W. E. B. Du Bois called Fisher a "'white folks' nigger" who represented "nothing but his own blubbering self." *Tuskegee University Archives.*

the acceptance by the Negro and by the nation at large of remedies which are expedients only, not going to the heart of the matters at issue." He pointed out that many whites would be uneasy about cooperation, "fearing that it may result in concessions to the Negro," but insisted that blacks sought only the "fullest opportunity" to develop. He represented the CIC as an alliance between "the most Christian white people here . . . [and] a small group of colored people who are not too much embittered by the past to give white people this latest chance to prove that they *desire fair play for the Negro.*" Before it could work, the white man had to stop telling the black man what to think and start listening to "what he actually feels and resents." He listed black grievances:

> That no Negro's life is safe from the mob, . . . That frequently equal protection of the laws are denied to the Negro, particularly where he and white persons are in controversy with each other, . . . That frequently laws are made without due reference to the Negro's welfare, . . . That frequently laws are enforced without due reference to the Negro's welfare or his racial pride, . . . That the customs of the South relative to the Negro, including various forms of segregation, and the mode and spirit in which the laws are enforced and the customs upheld, are unnecessarily and needlessly humiliating to the colored people, . . . That, and this is fundamental, generally deprived of the ballot, colored people are absolutely helpless to protect themselves, . . . That the most discouraging phase of race relations in the South is that on all matters mentioned here and others, the Negro has had no redress, [there being] no white people who seemed to understand the feelings of the colored people, or who were willing even to hear him state his case.[75]

Isaac Fisher realized that interracial cooperation would not eliminate the defects of southern democracy, and that progress would vary from state to state, but local committees were a chance for blacks to speak out and test white people. The impunity with which blacks were ill-treated and the apparent refusal of whites to see them as Americans with constitutional rights was crushing, but when the CIC talked with black leaders, called for judicial reform, and tried to prevent violence, the South seemed less monolithic to Fisher: "It has not revolutionized racial conditions here, but it has established the basis of race adjustment by providing for the co-operation and goodwill which spring out of perfect understanding." When he mentioned the ballot and southern customs, he was not predicting imminent mass voter registration or desegregation, but nor was he discounting them as eventual outcomes of interracial cooperation.[76]

The difference in tone between Woofter's tiptoeing optimism and Fisher's combination of anger and hope indicated the moods with which each race approached the whole issue of cooperation. Woofter and Fisher were writing in terms they imagined were acceptable to their own sides, and in that sense they achieved a skilful balance. White defenders of southern traditions would have been intrigued, but probably not alarmed, by Woofter's thoughts on the merits of interracial co-operation, whereas Fisher's vision was intended to engage his black readers with the prospect of steady change. The risks lay in what members of the opposite race would make of their respective words. Black readers of Woofter's introduction may well have concluded that white liberalism offered sympathy, but no real prospect of reform, and the hackles of all but the most liberal white readers probably rose as they read Fisher's complaints about the status quo. The minefields that Woofter and Fisher crossed to reach their readers typified the efforts of the inter-racial cooperation movement as a whole, and the CIC in particular, to ingratiate itself with both the black and white middle classes in the interwar period.

Each section of the *Cooperation* handbook was written by a southern special-ist. The three African American contributors were Methodist bishop Robert Elijah Jones, Robert Russa Moton, and Burwell T. Harvey Jr., a young Morehouse Col-lege science professor and athletic director. The African Americans' analyses and recommendations were unsentimental and pointed, whereas some of the white-authored essays were ornate and general. Jones gave advice on interracial church cooperation, citing the regular meetings of black and white preachers at Chatta-nooga, Tennessee. He wanted more white clergymen to visit black churches, but only if they could preach "a pure gospel without seeking to give the Negroes pa-tronizing advice. Nothing is more objectionable to Negroes than to have some white preacher fill a pulpit and build his entire sermon on the 'black mammy' ro-mance. However sympathetic this may be it always puts the Negro audience in a bad humor." He acknowledged that, "for the present, this pulpit exchange will be one-sided" and that white congregations would rarely accept spiritual guidance from a black preacher, but they could be won over by "folklore songs . . . sung with the beauty and pathos characteristic of Negro choirs and quartettes."[77] Moton, in the book's most significant chapter, argued that economic justice was the key to black self-help and changing white perceptions. Racial prejudice would persist, but it would be easier to bear if hard work was fairly rewarded. He argued that lo-cal committees should push for more black farm and home demonstration agents in counties with big black populations, instead of the current provision of, at best, one black agent for every 2,500 black farmers in Alabama, and, at worst, one agent for 16,000 farmers in South Carolina. Committees should persuade landlords to provide better homes and gardens and abandon "lax methods of accounting and irregular terms of settlement" if they wanted a stable tenant population. He noted that many blacks wanted to buy land; if this was financially easier and socially more acceptable, a forward-thinking community could be built. He supported calls for protection of the health and morals of domestic servants and attacked the notion that blacks expected low living standards and could be paid accord-ingly. Moreover, "Negroes are often required to provide for themselves those fa-cilities for recreation, for education and for public welfare that other members of the community receive from the public treasury, to which both black and white contribute as taxpayers."[78] Burwell T. Harvey Jr. discussed the hazards of urban life for young black people and urged interracial committees to improve recreation facilities, "as an antidote for degrading motion pictures, vulgar vaudeville, questionable dance halls, dives, bootblack stands, camouflaged soft drink stands and the ambition-deadening influences of the public pool room." Most cases of syphilis and other contagious diseases were caught and spread by "misguided and unintelligent recreation," whereas sports, "singing, debating, drilling, domestic science contests," and outdoor activities such as campfires and scouting would preserve the virtue of the young.[79]

Wooter roped in David C. Barrow, chancellor of the University of Georgia, to comment on white ignorance about African Americans. If Woofter was a Progressive Era southern liberal, Barrow was a liberal representative of white middle-class men who reached adulthood at the end of Reconstruction. He believed southern black people had made great progress since emancipation by disguising their actual ambitions, so that "the Negro [was] undergoing a change of which his white neighbors were not aware. He, on the contrary[,] had the white man as an open book." It was time for "those who come in contact with the Negro . . . to deal with [him] on a basis of individual merit rather than racial characteristics. . . . It would seem to be the plain duty of the more advanced race to inform itself and lend a hand."[80] James Banks Nevin, editor of the Hearst-owned afternoon daily the *Atlanta Georgian,* provided a practical chapter on the power of the press. A member of the Georgia state interracial committee, he stressed the importance of local newspaper reports on interracial activity and getting journalists to "work for the principle of cooperation through their editorial columns." Newspapers should be persuaded to avoid sensation: "It is certain that if the news concerning Negro crime is constantly paraded before the public and emphasized by flaring headlines containing the word 'Negro' a very unhealthy state of mind is brought about." He cited yellow journalism's role in the riots at East St. Louis in 1917 and Omaha in 1919. Black interracial committee members should approach black newspapers; there was no need "to muzzle their press, or persuade colored editors to take stands in which they do not thoroughly believe, . . . [but] many of the newspapers are in the hands of a non-cooperative group of men, . . . [given to] constant controversy and unbridled vituperation [who could] . . . show more wisdom as to when and where to take these stands and more accuracy and temperance in their method of expressing themselves."[81] In 1922, Nevin's advice was heeded in particular by the Virginia state interracial committee, which claimed to have persuaded newspaper editors that "the press could help . . . in this dawning era of good feeling by making an effort to secure and publish more negro news of a character which would be stimulative and helpful to him and less chronicling of the crimes of negroes."[82]

James Dillard contributed a chapter on the improvement of rural schools since the publication of the *Negro Education* report—the school year was now generally longer, black teachers were paid more, and the accommodation and supervision of schools was better. The philanthropic funds were still shelling out vast sums, but the contributions of the states were also increasing. Continued improvements in schooling were plainly in the South's interests, and Dillard encouraged local committees to monitor school boards and state officials.[83] Ludwig T. Larsen, a Norwegian-born missionary-educator and secretary of the Mississippi state interracial committee, submitted suggestions for "wholesome" rural recreation, noting that new schools for white people were community centers, often with "an auditorium with opera chairs, a stage, and sometimes a steropticon or a moving picture machine, or both. Some schools have shower baths, and even swimming pools." These things should be sought for black people, incorporating playgrounds, libraries, and meeting rooms for demonstrations. Burr Blackburn, secretary of the Georgia Department of Public Welfare, advised local committees to demand that states gave blacks the same poor relief and care for children and the disabled as whites received. He also wanted more black social workers. G. Croft Williams, secretary of the South Carolina Department of Public Welfare, wrote about the historic environmental causes of African American delinquency, attributing crime to poor housing, urban temptation, and the lingering effects of "the Negro's traditional background," which had filled black people with "emotions fitted to their tribal life." Impressions of black criminality were made worse, he wrote, by "unsympathetic and unscrupulous arresting officers [who] too often arrest for petty offenses and exploit the Negro for fees which they receive on the basis of arrests and fines." Interracial committees were advised to inspect jails and penitentiaries, raise funds for black reform schools, encourage the creation of prison farms, and oppose the convict-lease system. To prevent crime, committees should demand improved social work among black families and the appointment of black probation officers.[84]

Edwin Mims, the CIC's first director of education, advised interracial committees to help deter and dissuade lynch mobs by raising the awareness of mayors and sheriffs, creating special police reserves, and equipping jails with hoses and machine guns. If a lynch mob formed, men of goodwill could avert a tragedy by addressing the crowd, encouraging law officers, and contacting the state authorities. If such efforts failed, they could demand the prosecution of participants in lynchings and foster antilynching and anti-Klan sentiments in their community. The idea was to turn "thoughtless and indifferent citizens into men with a determined purpose to oppose any outbreak of lawless passion."[85] Twenty years earlier, Mims's exhortations would have seemed fanciful, even foolhardy, but in 1921 such resolve in confronting the mob was beginning to be shown by middle-class whites across the South. Over the next few years, many local committees stepped up to deflect lynch mobs, embolden sheriffs, and testify.[86] For all its practical advice, however, *Cooperation in Southern Communities* dodged the main causes of black vulnerability—enforced separateness and disfranchisement. The emphasis was on "the principle of leaving [it] to the home folks."

* * *

In announcing the publication of *Cooperation in Southern Communities,* the CIC exaggerated the number of county committees, claiming that 800 existed by November 1921, involving upward of seven thousand people, whereas this was the target; the actual number of committees was 676, and large parts of the South were untouched.[87] In his memoir, Woofter maintained that the spread of local interracial committees represented a great achievement in the forbiddingly racist atmosphere of the early 1920s. Of the men and women of both races who joined committees, he wrote:

> Their outstanding characteristic was courage. We must keep in mind that this venture was made in the heyday of the Ku Klux when it was impossible in many communities to be elected or appointed to even a minor office without the endorsement of the Klan. The white leaders, therefore, had to be secure enough in their position or serene enough in their belief to ignore the scurrilous attacks based on the appeal to prejudice. Negro leaders had to be courageous for another reason. They had to step cautiously to avoid offending the white people on the one hand or losing their own following through overcaution on the other.[88]

Clearly, the interracial committees were something new, and their steady spread across the South in the early 1920s reflected grassroots desires and the energy of individuals such as Alexander, Woofter, and Fisher. In the committee meetings, forward-looking white people often encountered black professionals for the first time. As Woofter recalled, "Often in the early days of the movement you could hear the expression, 'I did not know that such people existed.' . . . The white leaders were not only surprised to discover such intelligent Negro neighbors but some were surprised to discover likeminded men of their own race." This was truer of the county committees than the state committees, since "men of statewide prominence knew a little about one another. Strangely enough it was in the smaller places where everybody is supposed to know everybody else that contacts between the leaders of the races had been least." When isolated white liberals, who normally bit their tongues on the subject of race, were brought together, "an esprit de corps arose. They gained courage from each other." Out of such meetings, respect could develop along with "a realization of mutual interests arrived at through the realization of mutual dependence."[89]

In 1928, Alexander could claim plausibly, "Today, through the Interracial Movement, intelligent white and colored men know more about each other than at any time since the Civil War."[90] Although whites still expected to be deferred to by blacks in discussions and unequal forms of address were never relaxed, the interracial committees educated their white participants. As Woofter put it, "The members learned that Negro leaders, in their role, were as efficient in leading their own people as the white leaders, that the skilled labor, the art and the music of the Negro were making real contributions to southern communities."[91] Black observers largely agreed; senior YMCA official Jesse E. Moorland argued that interracial committees "actually changed the [white] attitude from one of hostility to respectful consideration in more than one place."[92] Local committees also stopped rumors, according to Woofter. "During the exciting times attending the re-patriation of white and Negro soldiers from the World War there were many disturbing rumors as to what the returning soldiers might do," he wrote, but a decade later one of the CIC's most important contributions to the reduction of violence was "the prompt and energetic application of the true facts where they are needed most."[93]

The matters on which blacks and whites actually sought cooperation were often minor, such as repairing a road from Main Street to a cemetery, or a street cleaning drive, but Woofter believed that "a few successes instilled in the committees a real pride in working together."

> I know that these were not earth-shaking accomplishments. Many of them fell into the category of removing the gravel from the shoe of the Negro who wished to progress. On the other hand, the lesson of cooperation was learned and the improvement of the racial climate was real.
> The Interracial Commission did not conceive its mission to be solving the race problem by grandiose and sensational moves but believed that the so-called race problem was the accumulation of a large number of problems growing out of day-to-day relationships which, if not handled with sympathy and understanding, mounted up to an accumulation of misunderstanding, irritation, and even bitterness.[94]

Thus, local committees delivered practical improvements and reduced the isolation of white dissenters, but did not transform race relations. White men—typically, they were social workers, ministers, and college presidents—chaired all the state interracial committees and most county or town committees, where local needs were ultimately determined by the white membership. Committees collaborated with existing agencies, chambers of commerce, community chests, parks commissions, farm bureaus, and education departments to provide new roads, street lighting, schools, and sanitation, and they persuaded newspapers to avoid sensational reports, but none of this was a substitute for the right to vote. The effects of reforms were often temporary, and the committee attrition rate was high—perhaps only half did anything tangible, and many folded as quickly as they formed. The white Kentuckian writer George Madden Martin, a founder member of the CIC, wrote frankly in *McClure's Magazine* in 1922 that of the eight hundred committees the CIC claimed to have set up, only "forty per cent are functioning with fair efficacy." By 1927, when the District of Columbia's interracial committee was set up, the CIC claimed to have more than a thousand local committees in the southern and border states, but the spark had already gone out of the local cooperation program, and there were more inactive than active committees.[95]

Initially, local committees had multiplied so fast that some state committees knew little about work done at community level and the central CIC office in Atlanta knew even less. In 1923, the Virginia and Carolinas state secretary, R. W. Miles, tried to collate information from four states, where there were two hundred members on state committees and up to five hundred county committee chairmen. He appealed repeatedly for news about interracial contacts, no matter how trivial, "even if no meetings have been held," or for reports about "the little friendly acts of helpful cooperation between the leaders of the races in local communities that make up the real program and work of the Inter-Racial Commission." CIC educational director Robert Burns Eleazer emphasized the importance of small gestures in a pamphlet entitled "An Adventure in Good Will." He insisted the CIC, itself, had "no program of race relations"; true interracial cooperation meant that "in every community where race relations are an issue the best people should take the matter seriously in hand, with the determined purpose to seek a Christian solution of every problem as it arises, and to substitute good will and justice for the spirit of distrust and suspicion that is fraught with so great danger to both races."[96]

Although local committees set up between 1920 and 1922 often failed to sustain programs of work for more than a few months, Alexander refused to be downhearted. He argued that any well-intentioned interactions between black and white members of a community created new empathy and spread the idea that racially exclusive progress was impossible. He wrote in Howard Odum's new journal, *Social Forces,* "Negro welfare is fundamental to all community welfare in the South. There is no better training in social-mindedness for the average southern white person than to be led to work out some of the social problems that affects [sic] Negroes. There is, therefore, a double significance in thus using these committees."[97]

The first years of the CIC were characterized by intense, often disorganized, local activity and sincere efforts to improve race relations. As a field agent, researcher, and publicist, Jack Woofter played a key role in promoting the local cooperation principle. The resulting dialogue challenged entrenched attitudes in some rural communities and churches, sections of the press, certain court circuits, and state capitals, but basic racial inequality remained a destabilizing factor in southern life. A sympathetic northern reviewer of the CIC's work between 1920 and 1930 recalled that in the wake of the war and the race riots that followed it, the commission attempted to "tide over the immediate emergency . . . and remove as much as possible the fundamental causes of friction between the races. It was recognized that the race problem was perhaps insoluble and certainly would not be solved in this generation, but it was believed that definite steps could be taken to make it less dangerous."[98] For Alexander and Woofter, this meant confronting racial violence in the South and entering a national debate over lynching in order to regain the initiative. They took a controversial stand against federal legislation that was crucial to the CIC's success in gaining support in the upper reaches of southern political and judicial systems, but it also raised serious doubts in the minds of African Americans about the sincerity and value of white liberalism.

5   Dorsey, Dyer, and Lynching

Physically slight and carefully spoken, Jack Woofter was an unlikely adversary, and yet as secretary of the Georgia State Committee on Race Relations (GSCRR) he showed courage and determination. An acquaintance recalled him as "very quiet, rather blond, of medium height. His face was sensitive, the features delicate yet masculine. When the commission had board meetings, at Blue Ridge or elsewhere, he usually sat at the back of the room, slightly slouched down on his spine, with a perfect poker face. He was a southern gentleman who knew his way around in both the rural and urban South."[1] In 1922 and 1923, Woofter's character was tested in a public disagreement with the National Association for the Advancement of Colored People (NAACP) over federal antilynching legislation and in the CIC's attempts to defend black farmers in Georgia by prosecuting members of the Ku Klux Klan for night-riding.

In the fall of 1923, Woofter claimed the southern campaign against lynching was "a citizen's fight" requiring no outside help, since only the states and their white electorates could solve the lynching problem and the disorder that it represented.[2] He exchanged correspondence with the NAACP about the CIC's work, but the positions of the two organizations on the prevention of lynching were irreconcilable. NAACP assistant secretary Walter White was convinced that the inability of most southern states to suppress mob violence required federal antilynching legislation, for which public opinion in northern and western states had to be mobilized. The CIC's response was that a federal law would be unenforceable, unconstitutional, and counterproductive. Some black Americans concluded that this stance demonstrated the ineffectiveness of southern liberalism and that Woofter, personally, was an apologist for glacial change. The two politicians who most clearly represented the respective positions of Woofter and White were Hugh Manson Dorsey, a progressive Democrat who denounced racial violence during his second term as governor of Georgia, but opposed federal intervention, and Leonidas C. Dyer, a Republican congressman from St. Louis, Missouri, who repeatedly sponsored a federal antilynching bill in the first half of the 1920s.

During Woofter's youth, mobs killed African Americans at a rate of about one a month in Georgia, including some of the worst atrocities committed anywhere in the South. No lynchings had occurred in Clarke County, however, and Woofter regarded the city of Athens as "an island of peaceful race relations even though there were rough places nearby."[3] When he entered high school, he began to hear stories about killings in other counties, and he was intrigued by the embarrassment that asking about such events could produce in adult company. Shortly after his twelfth birthday, the horror of lynching was vividly impressed upon him when he found himself standing on the spot where a mass killing had just occurred. He was left shaken by his proximity to the incident and the realization that most white Georgian men regarded black people with varying degrees of malice, fear, and cruelty—feelings he never shared. In the summer of 1905, he was part of a group of boys from Athens traveling by horse and wagon to a YMCA summer camp. When they stopped to rest in a small town, a white resident proudly showed them a row of wooden posts:

> "There boys," he said, "is where we lynched seven niggers last week. There was one in that there jail accused of rape and when the crowd went in it was dark and they warn't shore which one he was so they cleaned out the jail and took all seven that was in there and tied each one to a fence post here and shot the whole passel. That's the way we teach niggers to behave here."
>
> I have a vivid imagination but I did not need half of it with that row of fence posts in front of me—some bullet scarred—to see the mob moving inexorably by lantern light, to hear the frantic protests followed by hopeless cries when the victims began to realize the brutality of their captors, and finally the agonized screams as the burst of gunfire cut them down. Only a small boy's dread of showing weakness enabled me to control a wave of nausea.

When he got home, he found the slaughter was common knowledge in Athens and generally disapproved of—"but there did not seem to be the slightest idea that anything should be done to invoke a penalty on the mob-crazed men who had set themselves above the law by willful murder, or that anything could be done to keep the State clear of such disgraces in the future." His attempts to tell people outside his family what he had seen were met with "a kind of shocked silence which soon taught me that it was not fashionable to discuss such subjects publicly." He recalled no ministers or newspapers speaking out against the murders: "A veil of reticence enveloped the people who might have molded public opinion. They did not stand up to be counted."[4]

The town where the killings occurred was Watkinsville, about fifteen miles south of Athens. They were carried out in the early hours of June 29, 1905, by a mob of between forty and a hundred masked men. In all, eight men were killed—seven black men and a white man implicated in a double murder as an accomplice of three of the black men. A ninth black prisoner was wounded, but survived. (The only other southern lynchings with as many victims occurred in Barnwell County, South Carolina, in 1889, where eight men died, and Sabine County, Texas, in 1908, where nine died.) Although Woofter correctly recalled that no action was taken against the Watkinsville mob, he was wrong in thinking that no white people cared. The killings were reported nationally and condemned by unanimous resolution in the Georgia House of Representatives. The state offered rewards of $500 for evidence leading to the ringleaders' conviction and $200 for the names of other mob members; a grand jury investigation was also held, but there were no arrests. It was this massacre that provoked the Reverend Henry Stiles Bradley to attack white supremacy from his pulpit in Atlanta.[5] The murders also contributed to Oconee being among the ten Georgia counties that lost the highest proportion of their black residents through migration between 1900 and 1910.[6]

The Watkinsville atrocity, the state's failure to deal with it, and his fellow Athenians' apparent refusal to talk about the South's most glaring flaw made a deep impression on the young Jack Woofter and shaped his responses to injustice and prejudice as an adult. Ronald C. White has drawn attention to the almost invariable impact on those who subscribed to the Social Gospel of some "personal encounter with human misery that, upon reflection, is seen not to be an individual problem but one of society," and perhaps this sudden brush with the lynching problem helped to determine Woofter's outlook.[7] The white reaction in Athens also sharpened his sense of being out of tune with most of his peers. In 1920, he would be one of the few white men in Georgia prepared to stand up openly against the lynching mentality and call for perpetrators of racial violence to be identified and prosecuted. Within a few years, many more white Georgians took a similar stand, and by 1930 the state's lynching problem had declined sharply, partly due to Woofter's efforts.

White-on-black violence was part of the racial fabric of the South, from day-to-day cuffs and kicks meted out to servants, tenants, and strangers, to maiming assaults and murders carried out by angry individuals and mobs. Lily Hardy Hammond, one of the few whites to imagine aloud what this meant for black people, commented in 1914, "The possibility of illegal violence, the fear if it, is an ever-present thing in their lives. It hangs, a thick fog of distrust, between our race and theirs."[8] Such reflections were rare, despite lynching claiming the lives of some three thousand black people between 1890 and 1930, mostly in the old Confederacy. Mob murder was condemned periodically by state governors, judges, and reform groups, such as the Southern Sociological Congress, as a sorry reflection on society, but it was frequently treated in the white press and by many politicians as the forgivable expression of communal outrage over an unpardonable transgression.

The standard justification for lynch law—that it defended white womanhood and southern honor against the depredations of black rapists—was weakened when white women themselves began to reject it. Hammond recorded her own pleasure at hearing the 1913 annual meeting of the Woman's Missionary Council of the Methodist Episcopal Church, South, declare that "as women engaged in Christian social service for the full redemption of our social order, we do protest, in the name of outraged justice, against the savagery of lynching." The delegates called on legislators and law officers to "recognize their duty [and] . . . arouse public opinion against mob violence, and to enforce the law against those who defy it."[9] When Willis D. Weatherford organized a law-and-order conference at Blue Ridge in North Carolina in August 1917, Kate Herndon Trawick, the white general secretary of the YWCA in Nashville, derided suggestions that lynching could be chivalrous and noted that it was often a consequence of unrest following attacks by white men on black women.[10] In the same year, the convention of the Georgia Federation of Women's Clubs supported state legislation against lynching, calling on "enlightened women of the state to create a public sentiment in favor of law and against the continued blight of mob violence," and issued an "unqualified condemnation of lynching as a means of punishment for crime of any character."[11] At the conference called in Memphis on "Southern Women and Race Cooperation" in 1920, the delegates called on law enforcement officers and the courts "to prevent lynchings at any cost," insisting that "proper determination on the part of the constituted officials, upheld by public sentiment, would result in the detection and prosecution of those guilty of this crime."[12]

As the interracial cooperation movement grew, more well-connected white women, deeply affected by meetings with black women, hammered away at the standard exculpation of the lynch mob—that it acted in defense of white womanhood. With clarity, they restated their abhorrence at the idea that lynch mobs offered them comfort and protection. Thus, denunciation of lynching in these terms by white southern women did not begin with CIC, although it became louder and more consistent under the commission's leadership during the 1920s. In September 1921, the women's section of the GSCRR condemned mob violence and the cant surrounding it in language that set the tone for women's sections in other states. They rejected any chivalrous connotations of lynching and stressed the especially vulnerable position of black women, rather than white women. The Georgia women's section was led initially by Ella Beckwith Lawton; other members included the highly effective chair of the Race Relationships Commission of the Southern Methodist Church, Carrie Parks Johnson, and Jack Woofter's mother, Callie Gerdine Woofter. In a swipe at the new Ku Klux Klan, they called on Georgians to "speedily banish self constituted groups and agencies which presume to usurp authority." Lynching, they declared,

> undermines constituted authority, breaks all laws and restraints of civilization, substitutes mob violence and masked irresponsibility for established justice and deprives society of a sense of protection against barbarism.
>
> Therefore, we believe that no falser appeal can be made to Southern manhood than that mob violence is necessary for the protection of womanhood, or that the brutal practice of lynching and burning of human beings is an ex-

pression of chivalry. We believe that these methods are no protection to anything or anybody, but that they jeopardize every right and every security that we possess.

The double standard of morals which society passively permits is rapidly producing results that imperil the future integrity of our national life and we are persuaded that this problem can never be solved as long as there is a double standard for men and women of any race. We appeal for the creation of a public sentiment which will no longer submit to this condition, and declare ourselves for the protection of womanhood of whatever race.

We are convinced that if there is ever to be a solution of the race problem there must be an intensive and sustained campaign to instruct whites and negroes to respect both moral and civil law.[13]

Women on other state committees echoed these ideas. In February 1922, at a conference in Nashville called by Johnson on behalf of the CIC and attended by Jennie Booth Moton, Will Alexander, and W. D. Weatherford, the women's section of the Tennessee state interracial committee declared, "We appreciate the chivalry of white men, but deplore the fact that a colored man must suffer violence in seeking the protection of the women of his race. Justice can never be realized until there is a single standard of morals for all, and a sentiment for the equal protection of all women."[14] The North Carolina women's section declared, "We resent the assertion that criminality can be controlled by lawless outbreaks, and woman's honor protected by savage acts of revenge," and the Texas women's section, led by Jessie Daniel Ames, stated, "We condemn every violation of law in the taking of life, no matter what the crime."[15] When the Dyer antilynching bill was defeated in Congress, the CIC's central women's section renewed its commitment to a southern solution, deploring, "with a deep sense of humiliation[,] that this hideous crime is heralded abroad as the only means available to men for the protection of womanhood." The women of the Southern Methodist Episcopal church, meeting in Atlanta, agreed that the U.S. Senate had "thrown the responsibility back upon each state for removing this hideous crime."[16] These ringing denunciations of mob violence by women across the South gave the interracial cooperation movement added legitimacy and challenged myths surrounding lynching before Ames formed the Association of Southern Women for the Prevention of Lynching in 1930. In a doctoral dissertation at the University of North Carolina in 1928, John Roy Steelman noted the importance of women's interventions: "Some have claimed this to be the last 'tack in the coffin' of lynching—southern women in large groups have repudiated the idea that men are lynched for their protection."[17]

Until the CIC gave such calls wider currency, the preference of many southern political leaders, courts, and newspapers had been to look away when gross acts were committed, as if denouncing lynching invited other unwelcome questions about the social system, so riddled was it with violence. In 1916, William Pickens, dean of Baltimore's Morgan College and later NAACP field secretary, noted that wealthy, well-educated white southerners sat untroubled atop an inherently vicious racial hierarchy, believing that their own hands were clean:

> It is hard really even for the best white people to tell just exactly what position they do want the Negro to occupy. But this seems true: that the majority want him down and under, but do not wish to brutally mistreat him in any other way,—they would not hang and burn him without law. They fail to see, however, that brutality and murder are the necessary sequel to their own finer forms of repression: if the better whites keep the Negro down, the inferior whites will take care of the hanging and burning.[18]

The Reverend M. Ashby Jones, a CIC founder and chairman of the GSCRR, echoed Pickens's views in 1922, when he commented on the attitude of former slave-owning families: "To my mind it is this dehumanizing of the Negro in the thought of the better class which is responsible for the dehumanizing of the Negro in the thought of the lower class, which in turn is responsible for the unspeakable record of barbarities committed against this weaker race."[19] The challenge facing the CIC was how to make the southern elite take responsibility for leading the campaign against lynching. Mounting calls for political action from employers of black labor, churches, and related groups such as the YMCA, generated a debate over new powers and whether they should be wielded by state officials and courts, or by agents of the federal government. In Atlanta and Washington, D.C., Hugh Dorsey and Leonidas Dyer offered very different and equally controversial answers.

Most southern governors endorsed the broad aims of the CIC, but none so spectacularly as Dorsey, whose intervention in April 1921 transformed the commission's regional profile. Dorsey's opposition to mob violence stemmed partly from his legal career and a case in which the state of Georgia notoriously failed to protect a citizen. In 1913, he led the successful (and almost certainly mistaken) prosecution of Leo Frank, the Jewish manager of an Atlanta pencil factory, on a charge of murdering one of his own employees, thirteen-year-old Mary Phagan. As the Fulton County superior court's solicitor general, Dorsey let local anti-Semitism influence Frank's trial and subsequent appeals, insisting on the correctness of the verdict and the death sentence. The trial judge afterward admitted to doubts about the prosecution's evidence, prompting the outgoing governor, John M. Slaton, to amend Frank's sentence to life imprisonment. In August 1915, a gang of masked men, incited by former Populist presidential candidate Thomas E. Watson, took Frank from a prison hospital in Milledgeville and hanged him in Phagan's hometown of Marietta. The lynching provided impetus for the rebirth of the Knights of the Ku Klux Klan, which received an official charter from the state of Georgia in 1916. Dorsey denounced the lynching, but the trial plainly assisted his political career.[20] Running on a law enforcement platform with the support of Tom Watson, he was elected governor in 1916 and pursued a reform program that included an illiteracy commission and the addition of 25,000 children to the school rolls through Georgia's first comprehensive attendance law.

In May 1918, Dorsey was appalled by a five-day lynching mania in Brooks and Lowndes Counties, near the southern border with Florida, where violent disputes over working conditions saw at least eleven, and possibly eighteen, blacks killed, including a heavily pregnant woman, Mary Turner, who was hung upside down, burned, and butchered. Dorsey declared martial law in the area, but resisted calls to take more lasting measures against lynching. Instead, he accused African American leaders of failing to condemn crimes committed by black people, and specifically rape, "this supreme outrage upon law and civilization, which too often provokes communities to substitute summary vengeance for the form of organized justice recognized by law."[21] Such facile comments were intended to deflect criticism by potential white rivals, but after his unopposed election to a second term in November 1918 antilynching campaigners pushed him into a direct attack on brutality and exploitation suffered by black Georgians. In May 1919, he proposed special grand and petit juries for the prosecution of lynching cases, declaring, "I have long recognized that the matter of lynching is a crime against the sovereignty of the state, and as such, the state should have the first jurisdiction over the criminals—that it should not be left to the hands of the particular community, where the crime occurred." He asked the legislature for the power to remove sheriffs who failed to protect prisoners, an idea supported by some lawyers and judges. Dorsey was not unique; other southern governors took stands against lynching, including Thomas W. Bickett of North Carolina and Edwin P. Morrow of Kentucky. In April 1919, former governor Emmett O'Neal of Alabama, in a Founder's Day address at Tuskegee, uttered what Principal Robert Russa Moton considered "very brave words." O'Neal declared, "The South should set its face like flint against all forms of mob violence and lynch law. . . . The act is none the less murder, however flagrant or odious may be the crime which has been committed." O'Neal later admitted that the states would never deal with the problem alone and that an amendment was required to the U.S. Constitution empowering the federal government to act. As he saw it: "Lynching has grown until it has become a national evil, a blow upon our national life and a shameful reproach to our civilization. It is a horrible and inexcusable wrong for which the whole country must bear its just share of responsibility."[22]

Dorsey never proposed moving jurisdiction outside the state, but he went further than other southern governors in the vividness of his denunciation of racial persecution, becoming astonishingly outspoken in his final months in office. He had been embarrassed in October 1920 when Governor Albert E. Sleeper of Michigan refused to allow the extradition of Thomas Ray, a black man accused of murdering a white man in Wilkinson County, because of fears that he would be lynched. The NAACP, which fought Ray's case in Detroit, stated that the Georgian authorities had been "forced to realize that a long period of mob rule and disregard of law has created the impression, and a correct one, that a colored man in a southern state accused of any offense against a white man has little or no chance of securing a fair trial."[23]

Having been defeated by Tom Watson in his attempt to win a seat in the U.S. Senate in 1920, Dorsey chose to act decisively on the race question in the early months of 1921. In January, he sent the adjutant general of the National Guard and a special deputy to Hall County, in northeastern Georgia, to investigate reports of organized efforts by the Ku Klux Klan to drive black families out of the area north of the Chattahoochee River. Houses, churches, and lodges were shot up and burned, and agricultural and industrial employers of black labor threatened. Letters signed "K.K.K." were sent to white people, asking whose side they were on, and to black people with the warning "Get out you damned nigger. We give you ten days to get south of the Chattahoochee or have your house blown up." Imperial Wizard W. J. Simmons admitted that the Klan sent such letters "when it is impossible for our representatives to see a man personally." These threats destroyed black wealth and added to that of whites, since many African Americans who left Hall County were taxpaying landowners who simply abandoned their land or sold it cheaply to whites. One of the two white men arrested in connection with the letters was indicted, but acquitted by a superior court jury. Driving out black farmers was not the preserve of the resurgent Klan—during the previous ten years, whites had expelled almost all the blacks from several counties in Georgia, but the latest wave of disturbances was repeated in six counties, in all, suggesting a new pattern. That was how it appeared to U.S. district attorney Hooper Alexander, who was equally concerned about the rising number of peonage cases. One day, as he dictated a letter to the U.S. attorney general about peonage in Georgia, six black people entered his office to complain about being driven from their homes by hooded men in Gwinnett County.[24]

In February 1921, a gruesome lynching of a prisoner seized from law officers attracted national attention. John Lee Eberhart, a twenty-three-year-old African American laborer, was held in Clarke County jail in Athens on suspicion of having murdered his employer's wife in neighboring Oconee County. White men smashed their way into the supposedly mob-proof building, took Eberhart back to the woman's farm (where her body was displayed on a bier), and slowly burned him to death before hundreds of onlookers. The commissioners of Clarke County offered a $1,500 reward for the identity of the ringleaders, but no action was taken.[25]

Even more shocking were the horrors uncovered in Jasper County in March 1921, when federal agents began investigating allegations of peonage. During the war, landowner John S. Williams and his sons dealt with the labor shortage by acquiring field hands from jails in Atlanta, Macon, and elsewhere. The abuse-ridden system of leasing convicts to private companies in Georgia had been abolished in 1908, but Williams simply paid the convicts' fines in return for their promised labor. The planter and his black overseers forced the men to continue working long after they had paid their debts, housing them in stockades and hunting them with dogs if they ran away. In November 1920, an escapee sparked an investigation by the U.S. Justice Department's Bureau of Investigation (BI), which had already received a complaint from a black farmer that his house had been shot up by Williams and a gang of white men. The BI investigation led Williams and his black enforcer, Clyde Manning, to dispose of the remaining peons, killing at least eleven men over several weeks and hiding their remains in ponds, creeks, and fields. When three bodies were recovered from the Yellow River on the Newton County side of a bridge, Governor Dorsey persuaded the local judge and prosecutor to hold a grand jury investigation, allowing the state to take over the case and leading to the indictment of Williams and Manning and the discovery of more bodies. Although the unsupported testimony of black witnesses was normally insufficient to convict a white man in Georgia, Williams was sentenced to life imprisonment on April 9, 1921. Manning received the same sentence after two trials in which the CIC paid for lawyers to both prosecute and defend him.[26] The Williams case made nationwide front-page headlines and was a rare prosecution success. It sparked similar action in other states, including the arrest of four white men for holding seventy-five laborers at a highway construction camp in Tennessee. Most other attempts in the 1920s by state or federal authorities to pursue landowners for buying and holding indebted workers failed due to reluctant witnesses, lack of judicial zeal, or the refusal of white juries to convict.[27]

On April 22, near the end of his governorship, Dorsey called a conference of thirty-nine white Georgian CIC supporters at Atlanta's Piedmont Hotel, where he issued a statement "as to the Negro in Georgia," which he had been considering for several weeks. Using four headings—lynching, peonage, the driving-out of black people by "organized lawlessness," and "individual acts of cruelty"—he listed "135 examples of the alleged mistreatment of negroes in Georgia in the last two years." He accused law officers of permitting anarchy and white citizens of condoning inhumanity. According to Dorsey, "If the conditions indicated by these charges should continue, both God and man would justly condemn Georgia more severely than man and God have condemned Belgium and [King] Leopold for the Congo atrocities. But worse than that condemnation would be the destruction of our civilization by the continued toleration of such cruelties in Georgia." He provided a chilling list of mob murders, beatings, threats, terrorism, and bondage, and minimal intervention by the authorities. These were the cases that Dorsey had been told about; he suspected that many acts of viciousness went unreported and was sure "the better element" in each locality wanted such behavior prevented. He did not name the places concerned, but he made clear references to the Eberhart lynching and the Williams trial. The measures he called for echoed steps taken or proposed by other southern governors—better education to improve race relations, new laws governing labor contracts, and extra powers for governors and judges to prevent lynchings, prosecute participants, and punish derelict officialdom. He was determined that any "investigation and suggestion of a remedy should come from Georgians, and not from outsiders." To that end, he invited his audience to create a state committee on race relations, which, as he knew, they had already done. His speech and a pamphlet detailing his charges produced national headlines.[28]

Given Georgia's easily ignited racial politics, the tone and scope of Dorsey's denunciation of the behavior of thousands of white people was surprising. Historian John Dittmer has called it "probably the most candid and courageous attack on racial injustice issued by an American governor."[29] The black press and some white papers, including the *Atlanta Constitution*, applauded Dorsey, but he was condemned for shaming his own people by governor-elect Thomas W. Hardwick and reactionary members of the judiciary. In the coming weeks, the Klan and elements of the press whipped up a grass-roots vilification campaign, accusing Dorsey of gross exaggeration. A Macon group calling itself the "Guardians of Liberty" wanted Dorsey impeached because "Georgia—our mother—is being defiled before the world," and a Klan front organization, the Dixie Defense Committee, attacked his failure to mention "the white women ravished and butchered by black brutes of uncontrollable passion." Even Dorsey's friends, such as the *Macon Telegraph*, wished he had worked quietly with the federal district attorney to investigate peonage. Opinion elsewhere in the South was more balanced; the *Birmingham News* commented, "Better to let the light of publicity play over these cases than to damn Dorsey out of hand."[30]

Dorsey defended himself vigorously, pointing to new evidence of night-riding in Taliaferro County (where a black population of 6,450 in 1910—nearly three times the white population—declined through migration to 4,222 by 1930). In the eyes of many, the outgoing governor had opened a can of worms. He had few defenders, and those who supported him, such as the NAACP and District Attorney Alexander, were no help politically. Black Georgians, such as Fort Valley High principal H. A. Hunt, privately hoped the "gnashing of teeth in Georgia" would yield results, but maintained a diplomatic silence. Meanwhile, rumors of another "murder farm" in the southern part of the state, the indictment of a Pike County farmer on peonage charges, and news that the Justice Department was about to send fifty agents from Washington to probe the peonage problem dismayed many white Georgians.[31]

The chairman of the CIC's Georgia committee, Ashby Jones, let the governor soak up punishment for a month, before giving an opaque account of how the speech and pamphlet had come about. He ridiculed those who demanded the suppression of Dorsey's allegations, especially Sam L. Olive, the state senate president, who openly defended lynching as a response to black violence and denied the existence of peonage. Jones claimed civilized nations were watching: "And we must come to see that it is the Georgia mob, and not Georgia's governor, which is ruinously advertising us around the world as a lawless people." A few days later, fifty-two members of the CIC's Georgia committee came out in support of Dorsey, admitting that they prepared his statement and had it printed, "and that they are taking the entire responsibility for the act."[32] This came too late to help Dorsey, who left office amid intense recrimination. The episode showed CIC director Will Alexander the internecine nature of state politics and the danger in inviting the rest of America to comment on southern racial problems. This was why Jack Woofter later made it clear in his dealings with Walter White that the CIC and its friends were vulnerable and that any information supplied to the NAACP or the American Civil Liberties Union should be used discreetly.

The validity of Dorsey's charges was shown when a mob in southern Georgia deliberately taunted him for his outspokenness. On June 18, after being found guilty by a jury of the murder of a twelve-year-old white girl at Autreyville, John Henry Williams was seized from the Colquitt County sheriff and deputies on the steps of the courthouse. White and black newspapers gave differing accounts of what followed. The *Atlanta Constitution* described Williams's immolation as an orderly affair: "Williams calmly smoked a cigarette as the match was applied to the fuel around him. . . . Not a shot was fired by the tremendous mob, all standing about quietly, watching the negro burn. . . . The mob quietly dispersed after the lynching." Black newspapers told another story: the *Baltimore Afro-American* reported that Williams was tortured for an hour, and the *Washington Eagle* carried an eyewitness account of black residents being terrorized and their churches burned, after a carnival-like lynching that began with Williams being castrated and made to eat part of his own genitals. "Another portion was sent by parcel post to Governor Dorsey, whom the people of this section hate bitterly."[33] This was not unprecedented; Georgia's antilynching governor in the early 1890s, William J. Northen, was sent parts of victims' bodies, and in 1899, after the notorious lynching of Sam Hose in Coweta County, a member of the mob handed Governor Allen D. Candler a slice of his heart.[34]

Dorsey left office a week after Williams was burned, repeating his horror at Georgia's record and listing the fifty-eight mob murders during his governorship. He called for a state constabulary, nonresident juries, movable court hearings, and stronger executive powers. The cases to which he referred plainly answered those who condoned lynching on the grounds that it protected white women; the record showed clearly that lynching persisted because of racial hatred and oppression. Fourteen cases involved allegations of rape or other offenses relating to white women; three lynchings were said to have followed incendiary statements by a black person, but by far the largest category, thirty-seven lynchings, were caused by disputes between a black man and a white man, including employers and law officers. (The causes of four lynchings were unknown.) Dorsey's parting shots drew a withering response from Governor Hardwick at his inauguration. He insisted that race relations in Georgia were "harmonious. . . . There is no State or country in the world where a good, law-abiding, peaceable negro can live with more security to his life, his property or his rights than the State of Georgia." He acknowledged some unrest during the war, but said Dorsey's "indictment of the whole State and all of its people for mistreating the black race [was] an unspeakable slander." Hardwick especially objected to allegations concerning peonage. The white Georgian farmer, he said, despite the boll weevil and low prices, had "taken care of the negro, fed him, clothed him, sheltered him, doctored him, and now, in a year like this, when he has made every imaginable sacrifice to help the negro, to be charged on high authority with holding the negro in peonage is almost more than he can bear."[35]

Hardwick's denials were pure politicking. Even the most antiblack governors, such as Hoke Smith, had admitted lynching was a problem and called for the law to be upheld, and in time Hardwick would be forced to concede that Dorsey was right. Although he praised the Ku Klux Klan in August 1921, Hardwick was so shocked by the organization's growing lawlessness and arrogance that he was its leading critic by the end of his term as governor. Bidding for reelection in 1922, he was heavily defeated by a known Klansman and failed to gain a seat in the U.S. Senate in 1924 partly due to Klan opposition.[36]

*   *   *

In calling for a "remedy . . . from Georgians, and not from outsiders," Dorsey was commenting on attempts in Washington to make lynching a felony punishable by federal law. The Dyer bill, which was introduced on several occasions, would have allowed United States courts to punish mob members and any culpable local officials and to impose forfeits on the counties concerned, payable to the victims' families. It closely resembled a bill drafted by former Massachusetts attorney general Albert E. Pillsbury and sponsored by Senator George F. Hoar (R-Mass.) in 1901. The Hoar bill, which historian Adam Burns has called "the most significant anti-lynching bill ever drawn up in the United States," foundered on the issue of state jurisdiction, but it widened debate about the federal government's power and duty to defend citizens' constitutional rights.[37] In January 1922, after intense lobbying led by the NAACP's James Weldon Johnson, the Dyer bill was passed by the House of Representatives (230 votes to 119, with 78 members not voting). The chamber divided along party lines, only eight Democrats voting in favor and only eighteen Republicans against, following debates in which southern congressmen described lynching as an inevitable consequence of rape and the bill as an unwarranted interference in states' affairs. Representative Hatton Summers (D-Tex.) called its supporters "hired Negro agitators and white negroettes."

Faced with predictions that such attacks would see the bill succumb in the Senate, the NAACP prepared for a massive increase in lobbying.[38]

Since no southern state wanted Washington's jurisdiction enlarged in an area of criminal law, most governors took their own steps to reduce lynching when momentum built for federal legislation. The southern press and church opinion also called increasingly for law officers and courts get a grip on the lynching problem. In that sense, the Dyer bill clearly had an impact on the problem, even though it was never enacted. In Georgia, the *Atlanta Constitution* took a significant step in January 1919, after the burning of a condemned man, Bragg Williams, in Hill County, Texas. Two decades earlier, the *Constitution* had joined in the ritual denunciation of the Hoar bill as unconstitutional and unnecessary, but now it doubted the capacity of the southern states to solve the problem:

> It is such barbarity as this that is cursing this section, and if public sentiment does not put a stop to it the federal government will inevitably assume control of the punishment of such offenses.
>
> The national escutcheon is blackened by such acts of outlawry and the civilized world holds the whole American people—not an isolated community—accountable for such doings.
>
> And if the day ever comes when the federal government does step in the sleeping public sentiment that now tolerates such outrages will have none else to blame than itself.[39]

When a grand jury failed to indict anyone for killing Williams, the *Houston Post* expressed almost identical views, adding, "Federal action would be less hampered in dealing with the peculiar difficulties surrounding mob violence than State processes have been." The *New York Times* cited the *Post*'s "remarkable editorial [as evidence] that the wish and purpose to put an end to lynching are a force to reckoned with."[40] Following the lynching of black prisoners on consecutive days in May 1919 at Vicksburg, Mississippi, and Johnson County, Georgia, the *Constitution* became even more direct: "Brutal business; barbaric business; dangerous business; intolerable business! And it is a type of business which must be stopped by the States which now permit its practice if they expect Uncle Sam—the American people as a whole—to keep hands off and continue to respect their sovereignty."[41] In Savannah, Roman Catholic bishop Benjamin J. Keiley took a similar line. Keiley was a Civil War veteran who sneered at Theodore Roosevelt in 1902 for choosing to "sit cheek by jowl with an Alabama negro," but he warned white Georgians in November 1919 that the violence had to stop: "If appeals to right, to justice, to Christian morality, do not avail to put a stop to this injustice to the Negro, and protect him against the murderous lynchers, then Georgia will see Federal bayonets giving him protection."[42]

The *Atlanta Constitution* returned to this theme after the Dyer bill passed the House. In an editorial, it congratulated an Oklahoma judge for sentencing members of a mob to life imprisonment: "A general administration of that sort of justice throughout the country would have killed the Dyer bill before it was even thought of."[43] The prominence given by *Constitution* to the lynching problem reflected an acknowledgement by its publishers, the Howell family, that the press could positively influence racial attitudes, having failed in this regard before both the 1906 Atlanta riot and the murder of Leo Frank. Will Alexander had befriended Clark Howell Jr. in 1917 at Fort McPherson near Atlanta, where the former managed the YMCA facilities and the latter underwent officer training. In 1920, Howell, who was in the Chi Phi fraternity with Jack Woofter at the University of Georgia, became business manager of the *Constitution,* which gave full coverage to the CIC's meetings and public statements.[44]

The growing sense that the surest way to defeat the Dyer bill was for the states to take action—an argument that Jack Woofter and the CIC put forward strongly—partly explains the increasing frequency of prosecutions (if not actual convictions) in state courts across the South and the introduction of new legal devices. This approach showed in the chorus of middle-class disapproval that met each new lynching. Thus, although mob violence was not quickly eradicated and some of the killings in the 1920s and 1930s were among the most fiendish in post-Reconstruction history, the looming possibility of federal legislation was a powerful spur to southern action to confront lynching as both a judicial and a moral problem. The prospect of federal legislation also led to criticism of the Ku Klux Klan for encouraging outrages with which most southerners no longer wished to be associated.

An important new factor was middle-class southerners' increasing sensitivity after World War I to international opinion concerning lynching. Foreign comment had begun long before the war, with Ida B. Wells's visits to Britain in the 1890s leading to sensational news coverage and the formation of two organizations, the Society for the Recognition of the Brotherhood of Man and the London Anti-Lynching Committee.[45] The International Socialist Bureau in Brussels condemned lynching in 1903, and the European press frequently asked why the United States took no action to protect its international reputation.[46] The London *Spectator,* hailing Woodrow Wilson's inauguration in 1913, offered a gentle warning:

> A man of high political courage in the Chief Magistracy should stop lynching if America is to retain its title of a civilized country; and passionately do we who love her desire that she should retain it. She must put down lynching. We do not say to marry them (the negroes) or to ask them to dinner, or even to sit in the same cars with them. What we do say is, stop burning them alive.[47]

After the Armistice, Americans understood that the United States, through the War for Democracy and the Versailles settlement, had exposed its own social and political practices to closer foreign scrutiny. The recognition that barbaric features of life in the former Confederacy were shaping European perceptions injected a new urgency into efforts to eliminate them. In 1919, the popular British travel writer Stephen Graham toured the South before writing *Children of the Slaves* (published in America as *The Soul of John Brown*), which was serialized in *Harper's Magazine*. He had witnessed the persecution of minorities all over the world, especially in Russia, but he was so astounded by the viciousness of lynching that it became the book's dominant theme. The few hopeful things he noted concerning black-white relations in the South included the interracial committees of the CIC in Alabama.[48]

Woodrow Wilson's embarrassment at Versailles was the main point of an address given by Edwin Mims of Vanderbilt University to the May 1919 meeting of the Southern Sociological Congress at Knoxville: "Do we ever think how this great man must feel at the Peace Conference [when he] refers to the atrocious crimes of the people of other countries, when he has the consciousness that back here in his own country just as great lawlessness is going on and members of our own [American] race are committing such great injustices against each other[?] Europeans cannot understand this thing."[49]

The eradication of lynching was the CIC's constant priority during Jack Woofter's years in Atlanta, but it never supported the Dyer federal antilynching bill. Many opponents of the bill, including northerners such as Senator William Borah of Idaho, declared it to be unconstitutional, but the CIC's stance was based on practical objections. Mindful of the Dorsey furor, Will Alexander and Jack Woofter were convinced that a federal law would be impossible to enforce and might weaken the states' own efforts, and even incite mobs to murderous acts of defiance. No subject, including segregation, caused a deeper rift between the black and white supporters of the interracial cooperation movement, despite the lengths to which southern white liberals went to explain their position.

Ashby Jones tried to reconcile his definite wish to see lynching cease with his opposition to a federal law in a series of Sunday sermons in the *Atlanta Constitution* in 1922. The son of Robert E. Lee's chaplain, Jones had a long record of opposing lynching and the extension of segregation during his previous ministries in Virginia. He was as proud of his southern heritage as he was appalled by the behavior of many of his countrymen, and he was certain that the federal government had the right to take action against lynching if it chose to: "For a mob in Georgia to kill a man without a legal trial is unquestionably to rob him of his right as a citizen of the United States, and thus to commit an offense against the government of the United States." In 1876, in *United States v. Cruikshank*, the Supreme Court had upheld the states' rights after the federal government protected freedmen against white terrorism under the Fifth, Sixth, Seventh, and Eighth Amendments. However, Jones pointed to the Fourteenth Amendment, requiring each state to guarantee "to any person within its jurisdiction the equal protection of the laws." If a state failed, Jones argued, "the federal government has the right to assume jurisdiction by special statute over the offense of the mob murder whenever it shall so decide." Far better, then, for the states to police themselves than to allow the enactment of the Dyer bill—"It will not help, it will only hurt." The South was at a crossroads, and the states could take responsibility for curbing lynching, or they could do nothing and invite imposition of a constitutional, but damaging, law.[50]

Jones's stance no doubt impressed many white readers as resolute and forward-looking, but it frustrated leading black southerners such as Robert Russa Moton, who insisted that lynching was the most crushing feature of white supremacy and that federal intervention should not be delayed while the South stirred itself into action. He reminded James H. Dillard, another liberal white opponent of the Dyer bill, that each lynching was a hammer blow to the confidence and security of every black person, including well-connected people like himself. "I, or any one of us, may be taken from a train or elsewhere and lynched without Judge or jury, should we come near the description as given of a Negro charged with a crime in that locality. . . . Our most intelligent and upright Negroes are ever conscious of the fact that at any hour they may be hurled into eternity."[51] The lynching of 240 black people and 27 whites between the Armistice and the end of 1922, many for trivial alleged transgressions, proved his point. Although Moton never gave up on the CIC and credited it with "a radical change [that] has taken place throughout the south in public opinion [on lynching]," other black activists saw no sense in associating with white liberals who would not support federal action on lynching and who refused to challenge segregation. As W. E. B. Du Bois commented, the real test of the interracial cooperation movement's value was its readiness to "face the fundamental problems: the Vote, the 'Jim Crow' car, Peonage and Mob-Law."[52]

In the summer of 1922, amid uncertainty over the Senate vote on the Dyer bill, Ashby Jones saw a "supreme opportunity for Georgia to enact its own anti-lynching legislation, and back it up with the full force of a justice-loving people." A fifteen-year-old murder suspect, Charlie Atkins, had just been slowly burned to death in Washington County, watched by a crowd of two thousand people. (In 1926, Charlie's parents, now in New Jersey, sought help from the NAACP in seeking damages for his death and their own imprisonment; Walter White referred the case to the CIC, but without success.) How Georgia responded to such an outrage, wrote Jones, was a test of "the Anglo-Saxon civilization of the South."

> We have in our midst and absolutely under our power, an infant race, without history, traditions, or material wealth. This race is at the mercy of the Anglo-Saxon race. By all the traditions of our past, the very genius of our race demands, if we hope to maintain our supremacy, that we grant to this weaker race, the protection of our magna charta, and gladly grant to them those "inalienable rights of life, liberty, and the pursuit of happiness."[53]

Robert Russa Moton, principal of Tuskegee Institute, Alabama, from 1915 to 1935. Born in Virginia in 1867, he spent twenty-four years as an instructor and administrator at Hampton Institute before succeeding Booker T. Washington at Tuskegee. In 1918, he visited black troops in France with Thomas Jesse Jones at the request of the Wilson administration. He was one of the first African American leaders to collaborate with the Commission on Interracial Cooperation and remained a prominent member throughout the interwar period. *Tuskegee University Archives.*

The Dyer bill foundered in November 1922, after Republican leaders yielded to a threat by southern senators to choke all congressional business with a filibuster. Jones saw this as the culmination of a "legislative farce":

It is another expression of a type of political hypocrisy which trifles with serious social problems, and plays its petty partisanship with tragic situations.

> The republicans proposed the bill in order to win the negro votes in the north-
> ern and western states, and the democrats heroically and violently opposed the
> bill in order to win white votes in the southern states. But in the meantime ne-
> groes are put to death without any legal trial, and in many instances with in-
> describable brutality.

He was glad that the "lynching bill was lynched," but not for the partisan, legal,
or racist reasons put forward by its opponents. It was a matter of honor: "I should
be horribly humiliated to see my beloved south forced by federal authority to do
that which we know to be right. It would rob us of our democracy, and steal from
us the precious privilege of voluntarily rendering justice to the weak." He called
on the state assembly to end "the anarchy of lynching [through] some adequate
police legislation" of its own.[54]

The *Atlanta Constitution* congratulated itself on the failure of the Dyer bill, but
warned against complacency, since the bill was merely dormant and plainly constitutional. Meanwhile, Georgia's lynching record and its contribution to black
migration were deeply troubling: "[I]f the state cannot cope with the mob situation, and bring to justice terrorists who take innocent lives at will, and who drive
peace-loving residents from their homes, then we may expect the federal government to step in in the interest of protecting the lives and property of American
citizens, as guaranteed under the federal constitution."[55] The CIC sent a release
headed "It's Up to Us," containing similar editorials from eight leading newspapers, to six hundred daily and weekly publications in the South. A piece from
the *Charleston Post* was typical:

> The Dyer Bill is a symptom of which the States would do well to take serious
> account. The crime of lynching is a disgrace and a danger to the whole Nation,
> and the States must find a way to put an end to it. If they do not show their ca-
> pacity to deal with this evil, ultimately some measure of the general character
> of the Dyer Bill will be enacted by a stretching of the Constitution.[56]

Thus, the debates surrounding the Dyer bill in 1921 and 1922 convinced a wide
range of white southern sentiment that state action was imperative. For African
Americans, the campaign for federal legislation was generally unifying and represented common ground for normally divergent camps, such as supporters of
the NAACP and the adherents of Tuskegee. However, few pinned all their hopes
on the Dyer bill, and some openly expressed doubts. In December 1922, the leaders of the Colored Methodist Episcopal (CME) Church, meeting in Atlanta, indicated they would settle for state laws, since "lynching and mob violence is of
deeper concern to us than the method of eradication [and] more grave than dis-
puted rights as to national and state authorities."[57] The CME Church was financially dependent on the Methodist Episcopal Church, South, which sanctioned
its organization in 1870, and was generally more conservative than the African

Methodist Episcopal Church, which had northern affiliations. Other black skeptics included the Republican vote-catcher, Perry Howard, who disapproved of the NAACP threatening GOP congressmen with the defection of voters unless the Dyer bill was passed.[58] The bill's most vocal black critic was the New York-based nationalist Marcus Garvey, who saw it as an improbable and unworkable vehicle for NAACP publicity.[59] In the South, explicit criticism of the Dyer bill came from the Reverend P. Colfax Rameau, an African Methodist Episcopal Zion Church minister in Athens, Georgia, and president of the Alabama-based Southern Afro-American Sociological Congress. Condemning criminal acts by both races, he argued that legislation "would simply intensify the prejudice which results in lynching." Education, commerce, and segregation were the ingredients of good race relations, according to Rameau.[60]

An antilynching bill was introduced in the Georgia General Assembly in 1922 by Senator Alexander R. Lawton of Savannah, who was influenced by his wife, Ella Beckwith Lawton, an active supporter of the CIC. Alexander Lawton, a railroad owner, president of the Georgia Bar Association, and son of a Confederate general, saw the eradication of lynching as the duty of a superior race: "We know that we are in the ascendancy and that the negro's fate is largely in our hands." The legislature had passed a law "to Prevent Mob Violence" in 1893, requiring law officers to protect prisoners from mobs by force or face prosecution, but it was disused. Lawton's bill went further, requiring Georgia to remove or suspend negligent sheriffs, and won the approval of the judiciary committee, but it was never voted on. If Thomas W. Hardwick been reelected in 1922, he would have supported a new state law, but under the regime of his openly racist successor, Clifford Walker, it was doomed. Jack Woofter led a vigorous campaign in support of the Georgia bill in 1922 and helped to develop new versions of it in 1923, 1924, and 1925, all of which made early progress but failed to pass, despite support from a broad coalition of activists, politicians, and newspapers. The 1925 bill, on which Woofter testified before the lower house's judiciary committee, allowed sheriffs to be sued and removed and provided for a special state commission to investigate lynching.[61]

*   *   *

Antilynching bills sponsored by the CIC's state committees also failed in Texas and Mississippi, but elsewhere state legislatures and public officials showed that an effort to combat lynching could be effective. New measures were adopted in Tennessee, for example, including the formation of a state constabulary in 1926, while a law enacted in Kentucky in 1920 provided the death sentence or life imprisonment for lynching and jail terms of between two and twenty-one years for attempted lynching. A further Kentucky law required the removal of law officers who surrendered prisoners, and during the next five years, the state witnessed only one further lynching. In South Carolina, where an existing law allowed the family of anyone murdered by a mob to sue county officials, a low rate of lynching was achieved in the 1920s, with a dozen mob murders, and in Virginia, the persistence of lynching after World War I resulted in a state law in 1928. In North Carolina, the readiness of Governor Thomas W. Bickett and several sheriffs to use force against mobs led to the effective suppression of lynching between 1921 and 1930.[62]

During 1922 and 1923, NAACP assistant secretary Walter White expressed "warm personal regards" to Woofter in correspondence about the CIC's efforts on behalf of black Georgians. By the end of 1923, however, Woofter's open opposition to federal antilynching legislation and his insistence on state-based solutions had strained that relationship.[63] Woofter said the Dyer bill was unenforceable, smacked of Yankee meddling and Republican scheming, and might provoke more violence, but his main objection was that lynching was already declining. In October 1923, in the reform-oriented pages of the *Survey*, he discussed at length the drawbacks of a federal law and merits of the local approach. He welcomed a national discussion, because it "contributed to the growth of the feeling that state and local officials are placed under a moral obligation to stamp out the evil," but he was convinced that the Dyer bill would be counterproductive. He wrote that Republicans and Democrats had been "playing politics with the measure," and while there were "honest doubts on both sides as to whether or not it is constitutional," the wrangling on this issue obscured a crucial point—that "the federal courts would, in all probability, be less effective than state courts." Woofter noted that prosecutions under the Dyer bill would still depend on local investigators, and most Bureau of Investigation agents in the South were themselves southern and often former county law officers. Even if a lynching case reached a federal court, the jurors who weighed the evidence would usually identify with the defendants. Woofter concluded that a federal law would be a setback, since it would "lessen the very essential sense of responsibility now developing among state and county officials." He drew on several CIC statements and publications in constructing his article, congratulating the southern states on their efforts to tackle lynching and predicting success through a mixture of voluntarism and proportionate state legislation. Essentially, his argument was that the Dyer bill was punitive and external, whereas the CIC's approach was preventative and communal.[64]

Having asserted that lynching was starting to decline across the South, Woofter offered Georgia, one of the worst offenders historically, as a positive example, crediting Governor Hugh M. Dorsey with changing the attitudes of the courts, the press, and the churches, all of which, in turn, were persuading ordinary white citizens to change their behavior. The CIC's establishment of county interracial committees and its support of state law-enforcement leagues, as in Tennessee, had also created a new local determination to oppose mob violence. He pointed out that other southern states with falling lynching rates, such as South Carolina, Alabama, Kentucky, Florida, and West Virginia, had already empowered their governors to remove negligent sheriffs, a trend that made the Dyer bill's provisions superfluous. Woofter's CIC experiences with state superior courts had also convinced him that engaging with "prominent local leaders . . . [would] help create such a sentiment against lynching that grand juries will indict and petit juries will convict mob members." He ended his *Survey* article with uncharacteristic tub-thumping:

> Another ten years of vigorous propaganda and prosecution will see the mob spirit thoroughly controlled in the United States. This much to be desired goal cannot be reached, however, without the expenditure of a great deal of effort and energy by the average citizen in the communities where the evil is now localized. It will require daring and skill, and there is enough adventure in matching wits with a mob or facing it boldly to appeal to the American spirit. It is a citizen's fight: the need of waging war against this enemy which attacks our civilization from within is as great as was that for curbing the raids of the red savage against the early pioneer settlements, for mob violence flouts the law and, if unchecked, it weakens all laws. If the fight is not won there can be no safety under legal institutions and democracy itself is in danger.[65]

Instead of the strenuous, but misdirected, legislative efforts of the NAACP, he invited *Survey* readers to support the approach of southern interracial cooperation. He failed to mention the difficulty that the CIC was having in getting a state antilynching law adopted in Georgia or the fact that black supporters of the CIC strongly disagreed with the commission's stand on federal legislation.

Woofter's article apparently impacted journalistic perceptions. Early in 1924, the *Survey* drew optimistic conclusions from a report by Tuskegee Institute that lynching had fallen to a new low of twenty-eight deaths in 1922 and that on forty-six occasions the removal of a prisoner had been prevented:

> Perhaps the lynching fever has passed its crisis. . . . Only succeeding years can show whether this reduction is mere chance, a temporary reform in the face of threatened legislation, or a new grip on that foundation of all government, law and order. While the killing of 28 persons by mob force is still an anomaly among the civilized nations of the world, the record gives a basis for hope, which is strengthened further by the very real and earnest work toward a better racial readjustment which has been apparent in the South.[66]

Walter White and his associates were stung by Woofter's criticism, having once regarded the CIC as a potential ally in the South. The NAACP's director of publicity, Herbert J. Seligmann, sent the *Survey* a petty reproach. Two years earlier, in his trenchant study of racial discrimination, *The Negro Faces America*, Seligmann had been impressed by Woofter's willingness as a southerner to attribute migration to discrimination and lynching. Now, Seligmann carped at Woofter's reference to lynching as "murder"—it was worse, according to Seligmann; it was "anarchic dethronement of government," hence the need for federal intervention. He complained that constitutionality was a matter for the Supreme Court, not southern critics, and that Woofter had wrongly played down the change-of-venue provision in the Dyer bill. Seligmann's more salient points were that "the local anti-lynching campaigns in the South, of which Mr. Woofter writes so informingly, have been immensely stimulated by the congressional campaign" and that the congressional debates had dispelled many myths, making it impossible to condone lynching on traditional grounds, such as the defense of womanhood. All Seligmann's points were valid, but they did not address Woofter's argument that the states were making better progress than could be expected of the federal government.[67]

Woofter disliked being lectured by northerners who lived without the day-to-day challenges involved in promoting interracial cooperation in the South. He was also irked by the failure of NAACP publicists to give credit to others for creating antilynching sentiment. Thus, Woofter had men like Seligmann in mind, and perhaps James Weldon Johnson, when he complained in 1925 about "obdurate individuals, with more zeal than wisdom, who think that they alone could direct this great task of racial adjustment. In the North, this phenomenon occurs in the man who can see nothing good in the South's dealings with the Negro, and who accepts any unverified rumor of the wholesale slaughter of Negroes as typical of the attitude of all Southerners."[68] For Woofter to accuse NAACP officials of failing to appreciate the realities of southern life was deeply unfair. It was true that Seligmann was a northern white liberal who relied on secondhand information about the South, but other leading figures in the NAACP knew the South well: Johnson grew up in Jacksonville, Florida, taught in rural Georgia schools, and attended Atlanta University; Walter White was from Atlanta, where he helped organize one of the association's most active southern branches, and had been thrust into the investigation of southern lynchings almost as soon as he joined the national office in 1918; and W. E. B. Du Bois taught in a rural school in Tennessee when he was a student at Fisk University and lived in Atlanta for twelve years.[69] Such men needed no lessons from a white professor's son about the realities of working for better race relations in the South.

The first interwar campaign for a federal antilynching law effectively expired at the end of the 67th Congress in March 1923. Although Leonidas Dyer and the NAACP continued to fight for the underlying principle and new versions of the bill were introduced, the surrender of the Republican leadership in the Senate to the southern minority was complete. After Harding's death in August 1923, the Coolidge administration paid lip service to the idea of action against lynching, but avoided opportunities to endorse Dyer's bills in 1924, 1926, and 1927. In his first message to Congress, Coolidge referred to racial tension as "local problems which must be worked out by the mutual forbearance and human kindness of each community," adding, "Such a method gives much more promise of a real remedy than outside interference." (When the lynching issue resurfaced with the Costigan-Wagner bill during the New Deal, the political infighting was more complicated, but the results were similar.) Southern antilynching campaigners, meanwhile, focused on state courts, and there was talk of a southern law-and-order commission through which state governors could develop a workable model that could be presented to the separate legislatures.[70]

There were several other areas in which the CIC and the NAACP could have collaborated, despite their differences over the pace of change in southern life, but the dispute over the prevention of lynching drove the two organizations apart. From the northern "equal rights" point of view, the distinctions between interracial cooperation in the South and reactionary racism became blurred, with the CIC's refusal to give primacy to the Dyer bill looking like collusion with white supremacy. From the southern interracial cooperationist point of view, northern black radicals and their white sympathizers seemed unable to appreciate either the caution with which the racial status quo had to be questioned or the provocative nature of federal legislation. The irritation felt by CIC supporters when northern equal-rights activists belittled their efforts found expression in 1925 in a letter to W. E. B. Du Bois from James Bond, the African American director of the Kentucky interracial committee. Bond considered that Du Bois's remark that the CIC's work was mostly "advertising" showed a "narrow, biased attitude." Bond would have welcomed passage of the Dyer bill, but only after local interracial committees had prepared the ground by changing opinion on lynching: "It must be clear to you that these thousand Inter-racial Committees throughout the south[,] enlisting the active and out-spoken support of the local press, the local churches and over a million white women throughout the south and thereby tremendously affecting public sentiment[,] cannot but be exerting far-reaching influence in the matter of prevention of lynchings." He felt "certain that the Inter-racial Commission and the Inter-racial Committees throughout the south are doing a work which the N.A.A.C.P. has never done and can never hope to do."[71] In the mid-1920s, at least, the efforts of CIC activists such as Bond had some impact on Du Bois, whose tone concerning the southern interracial cooperation movement noticeably softened; later, he would later resume his skeptical stance.

* * *

The causes and meaning of lynching intrigued Jack Woofter all his life. As the civil rights movement gained momentum after World War II, he looked back on his years with the CIC in an attempt to analyze the functions of mob violence. He knew that the lynching habit had taken root at the end of the nineteenth century because it was effectively sanctioned by leading elements of white society, and he understood that lynching was not simply a mentality to which some rural communities were prone; rather, it was a logical consequence of the system of discrimination and repression erected after the Civil War. He rejected the cliché that race relations in the South were normally placid, and rather than seeing lynching as an aberration, he saw it as the tip of an iceberg. Writing in 1956, Woofter recalled, "For every lynching there were dozens of unreported non-fatal insults, damage to property, or beatings."[72]

In 1922 and 1923, Woofter worked directly with victims of night-riding and observed their persecutors at close quarters. His experiences in troubled districts of Georgia convinced him that lynching persisted for three main reasons. The first was psychological: "These mobs were symptoms of a lurking fear of the Negro, and . . . lynchings were not so much for the punishment of an individual as for a show of force to keep an abused people under control, a reaction to a deep subconscious fear of reprisal for abuses and indignities heaped on him before." The second reason was political: "The law officers were put there by the electors who were voters in the white Democratic primary. Without the protection afforded by the power to vote and serve on juries, the Negro was helpless." And the third reason was essentially economic and reflected the poverty of the Deep South: "Interracial violence flourished most in backward rural communities—small, isolated counties where the law enforcement machinery was weak."[73] In 1922 and 1923, Woofter experienced all this firsthand, when working to combat stifling injustice in places where the law often provided little assistance. The CIC's efforts would have been short-lived without the growing resolve of black southerners to improve their own circumstances. Their participation in local committees and their courtroom testimony in lynching and peonage cases made widespread interracial cooperation a reality, whereas before World War I it was only an ideal. Moreover, Woofter and other CIC officials would not have found the moral and physical courage to oppose the Klan by word and deed without witnessing the fortitude of black farmers and their families who faced their fears day and night.

In time, Will Alexander, Robert Eleazer, and Jack Woofter won over sections of the white press and news agencies, providing information by telephone and trying to deal only in facts. They persuaded the editors of leading papers such as the *Atlanta Constitution* and the *Chattanooga News* to support interracial cooperation, denounce lynching, and present positive images of African American life. When an editor responded that, although he could not always carry the stories supplied by the CIC, his views were affected by them, Alexander was satisfied: "So, although we do not get it in the columns all the time, we are talking to the editors and little by little there is a change in the attitude of the newspapers, making it better."[74]

At the end of 1922, Woofter produced a hard-hitting report for the CIC in an attempt to revive the anti-Klan mood created by Governor Dorsey. He reported a fall in the annual number of lynchings and the fact that for the first time courts across Georgia were actively pursuing mob members. He knew of only one indictment for lynching in Georgia between 1885 and 1921, and yet half of the eight lynchings in 1922 were followed by charges involving of a total of twenty-two men, four of whom served sentences in a state penitentiary, while another fifteen men awaited trial. In two cases, black people who survived attempts to lynch them brought suits for damages against mob members, resulting in further charges against eight men.[75]

Such cases strengthened Woofter's belief that federal antilynching legislation was a red herring and that Georgia would pass a new law of its own.[76] It never did, but Woofter's optimism that his home state could sharply reduce mob violence was justified, and it seems clear that the publicity generated by the work of the CIC, especially during 1922, was a decisive factor. Between 1920 and 1922, there were forty lynchings in Georgia (an average of more than thirteen a year), whereas between 1923 and 1926 only ten occurred (equivalent to two or three a year). In 1926, only one black man and two white men were lynched in Georgia, and in 1927 the state had its first lynching-free year since 1882, a record it maintained until 1930.[77]

Lynching also declined across the rest of the South after 1922, although the pattern was uneven—North Carolina witnessed none between 1922 and 1929; nine occurred in Florida in 1926 and none in 1927. Although there would be a temporary resurgence with the onset of the Great Depression, the number of black people killed by southern mobs in any calendar year fell permanently below thirty from 1922 (including just seven in 1929 and six in 1932), whereas the first two decades of the century saw an annual average of more than sixty black victims.[78] The fall in the number of lynchings broadly corresponded to a steady rise in the number of mob members being indicted in state courts. Historian W. Fitzhugh Brundage has shown that several legal milestones were reached in Georgia in the 1920s, including injunctions, indictments, and a handful of convictions of white mob members for assault, attempted murder, and murder itself. The sentences handed down by state courts ranged from a few months behind bars for attacking a jail to several years for assault. It was true that prosecutions following lynchings usually collapsed, as in the cases of seventeen defendants acquitted in Florida in May 1926 after witnesses refused to testify, but the number and nature of the indictments were unprecedented, and court appearances for mob-murder were widely publicized. Anonymity and immunity, important parts of the appeal of joining in a lynch mob, were no longer assured.[79] Two men were sentenced to life imprisonment for murder in 1926 when the victim and killers were white. W. E. B. Du Bois insisted that it was "not a real case in point, because the man lynched was white. If he had been a Negro these lynchers in all probability would have gone scot-free."[80]

The slowly changing attitudes of Georgian politicians, journalists, judges, and grand juries toward the lynching problem represented a response to three things: black migration and labor shortages; the threat of federal action; and the spirit of interracial dialogue fostered by the CIC. Most lynchings went unpunished, as Du Bois stated, but a powerful consensus now formed that mindless hatred and contempt for the law could never be excused and that lynching was a damaging symbol of southern backwardness and immaturity. There had been earlier attempts to build an antilynching movement, such as the law-and-order committee set up in 1911 by the Georgia Chamber of Commerce following the murder of two black prisoners in Walton County. The antilynching campaign after 1919 was different in its grassroots and interracial qualities. It was also assisted by the removal from the political scene of racists such as the Georgians Hoke Smith, defeated in the U.S. Senate election of 1920, and Tom Watson, who died in September 1922, and the Mississippian, James K. Vardaman, who failed in his bid for reelection to the U.S. Senate two months later. The "Negro subversion" hysteria that caused an increase in racial violence during the German and Bolshevik spy scares subsided quickly after 1920. In the face of facts provided by campaigners, whites found it harder to rationalize lynchings as understandable lapses born of communal outrage or deflect the blame for mob violence onto black people. More sheriffs went to unusual lengths to protect black prisoners; more southern judges began to give grand juries explicit instructions to indict those who usurped the law.[81] A new mentality had thus emerged since 1904, when *Atlanta News* editor John Temple Graves could advise readers of the *New York Times* that there was no "remedial agent as effective as the mob for the intimidation of the criminal classes and for the protection of Southern women."[82]

Commenting in the 1950s on the CIC's campaign "to discredit violence as a method of settling racial differences," Woofter was careful not to overstate its significance, preferring to focus on other aspects of interracial cooperation:

> [Antilynching work] was the most spectacular part of [the CIC's] program, [but one] that was negative and defensive. [The CIC's] more basic objectives were to spread the philosophy of cooperation between the leaders of the races on the basis of frankness, man to man; to secure the participation of Negroes as full participants in constructive programs; and to create a climate of public opinion favorable to the operation of other organizations concerned with progress in the South.[83]

He was trying to suggest continuities between, first, the CIC's efforts to widen the debate on race and region after World War I; second, the New Deal's social reform agenda; and third, the South's gradual acceptance after World War II that African Americans could no longer be treated as second-class citizens. In terms of approximating specific constitutional rights, this was stretching a point, but he was also excessively modest about the way in which the CIC's efforts to reduce racial violence helped the later civil rights movement to grow. The critical achievement of the interracial cooperation movement was not simply that of making race work respectable; its undermining of the lynching mentality was essential to all other progress.[84]

Jack Woofter was also being modest about his own role as a quick-witted investigator and strategist. Until the mid-1920s, thousands of white men in Georgia were prepared to participate in lynchings in the certain knowledge that no action would be taken against them. They were also persuaded that Klan membership and night-riding were honorable pursuits and that, in certain circumstances, murder served a useful function. In his efforts to create local interracial committees, expose the truth, support black victims, cajole prosecutors, and place white defendants before courts, Woofter played a major part in challenging not only white supremacist behavior, but also the beliefs that underlay it. This work came together in his attempt to help black farmers stand up to the Klan in Barrow and Oconee Counties in 1922.

After the lynching of three black men in Oconee County in December 1921, Sheriff Clarence T. Maxey and the western circuit judge, Blanton Fortson, attempted to have four white men prosecuted for murder. They were acquitted after a victim's widow failed to identify the first defendant, but the trial indicated the judiciary's willingness to act in cases of lynching.[85] In the following months, as racial tension grew in neighboring Barrow County, a series of "whipping parties" descended on a black preacher and several black farmers, mostly at night, near the town of Winder. Jack Woofter was sent to investigate these events, and specifically the cases of Asbury McClusky in Barrow County and Willie and Odessa Peters in Oconee County, who were driven off their farms after exchanging shots with the same gang of hooded men in May 1922. Woofter arranged for McClusky and Willie Peters to be kept safe in Atlanta and discovered evidence to corroborate their versions of events, before persuading Fortson and an ex-Klansman who served as grand jury foreman to initiate the prosecution of eight white men. McClusky also began a private suit for damages. Woofter was entrusted with protecting the black witnesses, driving them to the courthouse in Winder each day from Atlanta. Not unexpectedly, the prosecutions and damages suit failed and both black families had to move to other counties, but the cases made national headlines and damaged the reputations of the defendants, making it clear that the anonymity of mobs could no longer be assumed. Woofter also investigated the lynching of two men in Liberty County, following their conviction for rape in Wayne County in July 1922. He established that they were almost certainly innocent and that the Wayne County sheriff and deputies conspired to have them murdered. Again, white men accused of involvement in the lynchings were tried and acquitted. These events played a major part in convincing Governor Hardwick to condemn the Klan and demand that it reveal its membership and cease the wearing of hoods in public. Woofter told both the American Civil Liberties Union and the NAACP about the progress of these cases, but asked them to treat the information confidentially.[86]

On August 11, 1922, after the CIC's summer retreat at W. D. Weatherford's Blue Ridge Assembly in North Carolina, Woofter gave Will Alexander a summary of his efforts to help black victims of injustice in Georgia, including the Barrow and Oconee County cases. He took on an excessive workload in his eagerness to maintain momentum for the changes in judicial circles he believed were under way. He placed a greater emphasis than other people in the CIC on an energetic program of litigation and prosecution, believing that if he could publish the facts, involve the right lawyers, embolden the plaintiffs, and engage local interracial committees, a dramatic breakthrough would occur. The Williams peonage "murder farm" trials in 1921 gave him hope, and the integrity of judges and grand juries in Oconee and Barrow Counties (and also Schley and Colquitt Counties) in the first half of 1922 indicated a new determination to confront the Klan. The cases Woofter worked on showed what could be done in the face of immense opposition, but only if they were followed up. As he told Alexander, "These cases hold out encouragement, but indicate the crying need for more vigorous action. The Williams case was only the opening gun in a long fight." He was certain of two things: "That no force for justice is so powerful as an aroused local sentiment" and that, ultimately, "justice is a luxury to be secured only by the man who can afford a good lawyer." The problem was not simply prejudice in the courts against black plaintiffs; it was the "inability of the party imposed upon to get the true facts before the [court] officers because of the handicap of poverty and ignorance."[87]

His investigations bore out these conclusions and showed that local interracial committees could sometimes intervene effectively. The first concerned a black farmer who agreed to buy land from a white man in installments totaling $4,500, but failed to make the first payment after a poor yield in 1921. The farmer offered to return the land with $320 interest, but the vendor ordered the farmer to raise a mortgage on his wife's farm to complete the payments. According to Woofter, the white man, who stood to gain $4,500 and foreclosure rights on two farms, "visited their house at night, threatening dynamite, Ku Klux, and other vague horrors." When the purchaser sought help from the CIC in Atlanta, the local interracial committee persuaded the white man to accept the original offer and cease the harassment. "They also expressed hearty disapproval of his methods." In the second case, Woofter paid a lawyer $35 to help a black woman recover her late mother's twelve-acre farm from a white man who seized it as payment for a mule.

The third case followed a complaint by a white woman that a white farmer had enslaved a black boy to settle a family debt, and was beating him. The U.S. district attorney failed to help, so Woofter collected affidavits and began habeas corpus proceedings. He visited the farmer to explain the law on peonage and secured the boy's removal to an orphanage in Atlanta, where the National Urban League found him a job and a place at night school. The fourth case proved hopeless: some white men had been able to trick a black man out of his small farm because the deed he was given when buying the land twelve years earlier from a black man had been fraudulent. The fifth case was already two years old, and concerned a "feebleminded Negro girl [who] was arrested on complaint of the white woman for whom she worked, on the charge that she had stolen a ring. She was given the third degree and very badly beaten. The ring was found. It had been misplaced by the owner." Released from jail, the girl was beaten again by a mob and was now disabled. Woofter abandoned the case; it was too late to sue for damages and, above all, "the Ku Klux is very strong in this county and our committee is weak. There is not enough local sentiment to lend any hope of convicting the officers of negligence."[88]

The Barrow County indictments produced an upbeat mood at the meeting of the GSCRR in the YMCA headquarters in Atlanta in October 1922. Jack Woofter's report to the meeting, released in advance to the press, indicated real progress in areas such as lynching, legal aid, health, and education. He contrasted the hostility toward Governor Hugh Dorsey's statement about injustice in Georgia in April 1921 with the frequent acknowledgement by politicians eighteen months later that conditions were indeed dire in parts of the state. Woofter thought that for many white Georgians, the governor's home truths "came as a clap of thunder from a clear sky. The [white] people were not prepared for such startling disclosures." He also detected a changing attitude in news stories and editorial comment in the white press, often generated by his own work. "In spite of politics and organization which capitalize [on] prejudice there seems to be less violence and more of a tendency to punish violence." At a local and state level, the CIC's commitment "to create an atmosphere of cooperation and a spirit of mutual helpfulness in solving community problems" was making a difference, and, whereas few of the incidents listed by Dorsey were investigated, Woofter identified many examples of tangible progress in similar cases in 1922.[89]

The state committee thanked Woofter "for his tireless and successful efforts" and his account of interracial work, especially the twenty-two indictments relating to lynching, and commended local committees for their support during investigations. Expressing "great surprise and gratification," GSCRR member Rabbi David Marx of Atlanta's Reform Temple commented, "As a southern man, I think the south can make no greater contribution to civilization than by working out amicably its inter-racial problems, and I am [now] sure that the goal is much nearer than most of us suppose." Black members of the GSCRR, led by the CME Church's Bishop R. S. Williams of Augusta and Principal Henry A. Hunt of Fort Valley High and Industrial School, "pledged the negro leadership of Georgia to hearty co-operation in the effort to uphold the law and improve conditions." The anti-lynching bill introduced in the Georgia assembly in the summer of 1922 was out of time, so the GSCRR drafted a new version, adding the power to impose penalties on counties, an idea lifted from the Dyer bill and the existing law in South Carolina.[90]

Assaults of the sort that rocked Barrow and Oconee Counties in 1922 and the harassment of black farmers by Klansmen were repeated across Georgia in the early 1920s, but Woofter's work encouraged more county law officers to see it as their duty to investigate and deter such behavior. Although vivid memories of mob violence and night-riding would fortify white supremacy and Jim Crow for another twenty years or more, the lynching epidemic in the South entered its final phase in the mid-1920s. The tipping point was reached in Georgia because white middle-class sentiment and black economic progress persuaded local and state-wide commercial and political elites, the churches, the press, and the judiciary that mob rule, particularly in terms of what Grace Elizabeth Hale has called "spectacle lynching," had to be broken.[91]

6 The Limits of Interracial Cooperation

In February 1926, W. E. B. Du Bois told readers of the *Crisis* that the Commission on Interracial Cooperation (CIC) represented "the definite breaking up of the effort of the South to present morally and socially a solid front to the world."[1] He arrived at this judgment gradually, knowing that many equal-rights activists would disagree, and despite mixed signals regarding the interracial cooperation movement's stand on segregation, black welfare, education, the vote, and lynching. Du Bois felt certain, at least, that the movement was more than a postwar reaction to migration, riots, and radicalism, and that it sincerely opposed the Klan and enjoyed the support of many southern black leaders; less clear were the movement's democratic aims, its economic outlook, its ultimate social objectives, and its views on race itself. At the close of the decade, Du Bois would conclude with disappointment that, in fact, white southern liberals such as Jack Woofter were dishonest and incapable of leading real and lasting change.

By the beginning of 1923, the CIC had established itself as a significant presence in southern life, and it continued to grow across fifteen states, with a core membership of fifty-nine white and black leaders. The previous summer, at one of its regular gatherings at the Blue Ridge Assembly, the commission decided that more public information should be generated through an improved news service, directed by the Methodist evangelist Robert B. Eleazer.[2] A circulation list of eleven hundred southern dailies and four hundred national and regional publications widened the CIC's reach and promoted liberalism among young white journalists on a range of issues.

The cost of maintaining a regional profile was enormous, and Alexander knew he could not rely indefinitely on the resources of the YMCA, which gave the CIC over $500,000 between 1919 and 1921. He secured new backing from churches and the Phelps-Stokes Fund and later from the Laura Spelman Rockefeller Memorial (LSRM), the General Education Board, the Carnegie Corporation, and the Rosenwald Fund. The LSRM, for example, gave $210,000 to the CIC during the 1920s, because Leonard Outhwaite, the charity's race programs administrator, was impressed by Alexander's ability to get moderate blacks and whites working together. He noted Isaac Fisher's comment, "Through the agency of the Interracial Commission, the saner members [of each race] are being brought into contact with each other and are encouraged to find that there are so many of their kind." Jack Woofter later remarked that heavy reliance on northern philanthropy excused the CIC from having to try harder in the South, whereas in the long-term a "greater effort to build indigenous financing would have been more effective."[3] This was ironic, given that Woofter's recruitment by the CIC had increased its dependence on northern charities for staff salaries.

Alexander struggled constantly to meet the CIC's operating costs, totaling well over $1 million for the decade. In 1923, alone, the budget was $117,000: the central office in Atlanta cost $55,500, half going on the salaries of Alexander ($6,000), Eleazer ($4,800), the director of women's work, Carrie Parks Johnson ($3,600), and six office staff; the salaries of the eleven state secretaries cost $31,500 and their office and travel expenses a further $30,000. The six white secretaries were paid more than the five black secretaries, so that Woofter received $3,000 annually for running the Georgia State Committee on Race Relations (GSCRR), while Kentucky state secretary James Bond earned $2,200, and their respective office and travel expenses were similarly graded.[4]

After three years as secretary of the GSCRR, Woofter sought a new role within the CIC. He had struggled with the traveling involved in the position of state secretary and in January 1923 asked the CIC to hire a black assistant secretary, "as he could not get around to the different local committees." The necessary funds were not forthcoming, so he devised a membership scheme for the GSCRR to generate income. In 1924, the Atlanta branch of the National Urban League agreed to release the Reverend J. W. Jackson to work full time "in cooperation with Dr. Woofter on this gigantic task of blending the races into a solid Americanism." A year later, Woofter described Jackson's appointment as an experiment and claimed there was insufficient work to justify it, revealing that some of the local interracial committees were flagging. Woofter was also clearly disheartened about the value of the investigative fieldwork he had undertaken in 1922. He still believed in "giving legal aid in cases found to be worthy" and collaborating with the NAACP where possible, but he thought the legal efforts had fallen short: "The first case we took was probably the hardest case we could have taken—the Barrow County night-riders, and if we had gone into it wholeheartedly instead of experimentally we could have done as much about it as the people at Mer Rouge [Louisiana] are doing. This would have meant much to the law and order of the State."[5]

Certainly, Woofter rarely engaged in work of the Barrow and Oconee County kind after the acquittal of the Klansmen involved. The work of the Georgia state committee shifted toward welfare, church, education, and health issues, as the CIC lowered its expectations regarding interventions for individual plaintiffs. Although Woofter agreed to go to southern Georgia in November 1923, to advise a black taxi operator who was being harassed by white bus drivers, Alexander warned NAACP secretary James Weldon Johnson not to expect much action: "It is possible that pressure can be brought upon them by letting the matter be known around the town and if not, that the courts can be appealed to to protect him. [However, d]ue to the migrations it is a poor chance now of getting a case like this handled by local sentiment and authorities as in the past."[6] Another example of a more laissez-faire tendency on the part of the CIC, at least in the opinion of John Hope, was its failure to arouse the business community of Atlanta to rescue the black-owned Standard Life Insurance Company when it began to collapse in 1924.[7]

Woofter's routine work for the GSCRR had included fundraising from individuals, serving on the board of the community chest in Atlanta, and liaising with community chests in other cities, such as Savannah. He also produced guides for local interracial committees and campaigning pamphlets, attended conferences, lobbied the state assembly, organized a student interracial forum, spoke on the *Atlanta Journal*'s WSB radio station, and arranged public appearances for black speakers such as Robert Moton.[8] Woofter represented the CIC in May 1923 at the fiftieth National Conference of Social Work in Washington, D.C., speaking on "Organization of Rural Negroes for Health Work." He also secured more government spending on black citizens by collaborating through the Georgia Council of Social Agencies with the state's departments of education, health, and public welfare, delivering improved schooling for delinquent black girls and new measures to tackle tuberculosis, venereal disease, and infant deaths. He worked particularly closely with Rhoda Kaufman of the Public Welfare Department, herself an active member of the GSCRR, and helped her to secure northern funding for the salary of a designated black children's welfare worker in Atlanta. The CIC also worked with the Georgia Federation of Women's Clubs on health and education, finding that even small changes could have large effects. For example, the GSCRR helped Methodist missionary women raise funds for the employment of a black public health nurse, who visited 785 homes in a single year and addressed over three thousand people in eighty-two meetings. Her instructions to midwives in ten-lesson courses significantly cut infant mortality rates.[9]

Woofter also engaged in wider debates about good government and the regional economy. As a self-styled "progressive citizen" more familiar than most with the inadequacy of the state's roads, hospitals, asylums, schools, and college buildings, he called on the assembly to raise a thirty-year $40 million bond to supplement existing revenues, auto tag sales, the gasoline tax, and federal appropriations: "It is necessary to borrow to build. . . . The farmer wants to ride comfortably, wants advantages for his children and care for the unfortunates in the community. He wants to be reasonably proud of his home state."[10] He devised rural initiatives, including a foray into cooperative farming when he persuaded an interracial cooperation conference in Atlanta to back his plan to give each locality a "community cotton patch making possible intensive cultivation, the revenue from which would [go] toward any worthy effort in the community—the building of better schools, employing of teachers, etc."[11]

As the CIC's influence spread, tension with the Ku Klux Klan deepened, especially in Georgia. The Klan attempted to entrap Alexander in hotel rooms, and later threats were made to his family by the Black Shirts, a fascist organization, forcing him to hire Pinkerton agents to guard his home in the Druid Hills neighborhood of Atlanta. Ashby Jones was also denounced by the Klan for calling a black man "Mister" in front of a "body of fair womanhood of Atlanta" and threatened when he responded. His wife was insulted by the Klan, and Jones later confessed to the CIC annual conference that he felt intimidated: "I never know when the white caps will come to my door."[12]

A common form of attack was the accusation that liberals were naïve, irresponsible, or disloyal. Historian J. Douglas Smith notes that definitions of racial liberalism in the south "evolved in the 1920s and 1930s, but in 1921 a liberal might have been anyone who advocated interracial dialogue and emphasized the need for harmony and understanding."[13] Conservative critics complained that liberal attempts to promote understanding between the races encouraged middle-class blacks to insinuate themselves in places where they were unwelcome. Activists like Alexander and Woofter were also warned that the formation of local committees and youth groups would lead to physical proximity and familiarity. White liberals were sensitive to such charges, aware that the entire interracial cooperation program could collapse if it were characterized as a campaign for "social equality." W. E. B. Du Bois knew what white liberals were fearful of provoking: "All subconsciously, sex hovers about race in Georgia. Every Negro question at times becomes a matter of sex. Voting? They want social equality. Schools? They are after our daughters. Land? They'll rape our wives. Continually the secrecy, the veiled suggestion, the open warning pivot on sex; gossip rages and horrible stories are spread."[14]

"Social equality" was such a potent, if ill-defined, phrase that many liberal whites, who genuinely sought better race relations through cooperation between the races, insisted that preserving racial "integrity" or "purity" was essential and that aspects of segregation had to be firmly retained. Thus, it was a long-standing rhetorical device for white supporters of interracial cooperation to preface remarks celebrating black progress with the assertion that "social equality" must be opposed and that segregation benefited both races. For example, Joseph H. Choate, the former U.S. ambassador to Great Britain and Ireland, told a glittering Carnegie Hall fundraiser for Tuskegee Institute in 1906, "The maintenance of the integrity of the races, which, with the approval of both races, has formed the basis of Southern civilization, has given opportunity to negro lawyers, negro doctors, and ministers in every profession and industry, and the negroes are making the most of it." Choate's defensiveness stemmed from the knowledge that racist demagogues would use the cry of "social equality" to discredit interracial cooperation. And sure enough, as the *New York Times* reported, when Booker T. Washington entered Carnegie Hall that evening a messenger handed him a note from the author of *The Clansman,* Thomas Dixon Jr., "in which the writer said he would contribute $10,000 to Tuskegee if Mr. Washington would state at the meeting that he did not desire social equality for the negro, and that Tuskegee was opposed to the amalgamation of the races. When asked what he had to say on the subject Mr. Washington said: 'I will make no answer whatever. I have nothing to say.'"[15]

The following Sunday, Dixon caused a disturbance at a symposium entitled "What Shall We Do with the Negro?" in a Baptist church in New York. Black and white participants were angered by his call for "peaceful colonization" in Africa: "We must remove the negro or we will have to fight him. He will not submit long to the injustices with which we treat him both in the North and in the South. And this thing, half devil and half child, is supposed to be your equal, and actually claims that equality. He does not get it now, but fifty years from now 60,000,000 negroes will claim those equal rights, and will take them if they are refused."[16]

Despite the best efforts of black and white reformers, the "social equality" trip-wire was almost impossible to avoid. In the 1890s, the phrase reflected a south-ern obsession with the status and class of white citizens, but it acquired purely racial connotations during the next two decades and became the rallying cry of Jim Crow. It permitted race-baiters to make wild allegations, forcing white lib-erals into mealy-mouthed connivance and barring black leaders from express-ing themselves honestly. The African American academic and journalist Kelly Miller called it a "savage warwhoop . . . the shibboleth which divides the races asunder." It was not only crude scaremongering, he stated, but also "the crux of the race problem. . . . The charge that the educated Negro is in quest of social af-filiation with the whites is absurdly untrue. His sense of self-respect effectively forbids forcing himself upon any unwelcome association." Moreover, to prevent "social equality," Miller protested, the South "would rob [black people] of politi-cal and civil rights, as well as of educational and industrial opportunity."[17]

Inevitably, the CIC's unwillingness to question segregation as the basic ar-rangement of southern life, partly because of anxieties about a "social equality" backlash, raised doubts in the minds of African Americans about the commis-sion's sincerity and commitment to black progress. Former associates of Booker T. Washington, such as Isaac Fisher and Monroe N. Work, took a charitable and op-timistic view. Work saw the CIC's approach as a step forward "in a general way to secure social justice, a square deal for the negro and to bring about the coopera-tion of whites with negroes for the best interest of the south and of the nation."[18] He also understood the predicament of the black middle class, who depended on local white goodwill for their survival—men, for example, such as Linton Stephens Ingraham, who founded Sparta Agricultural and Industrial Institute in Hancock County, Georgia, in 1910 and struggled to keep it going. Ingraham, cruelly lam-pooned by Jean Toomer in *Cane,* enthusiastically embraced interracial coopera-tion as the key to "peaceable relations between the two races." In a coauthored let-ter to his local newspaper, he reacted to the Williams "death farm" peonage case not by denouncing racial oppression, but by declaring, "We fully realize that no county can prosper where it's [*sic*] citizens do not, as a whole, cooperate. As citizens we wish to assure the law-abiding white citizens that we stand for law and order and our every interest is for the uplift of our county."[19]

Northern radicals such as W. E. B. Du Bois were intolerant toward such appeasements, but across the South black community leaders who might privately agree with the NAACP about integration and equal facilities knew that anyone demanding them in the heartland of Jim Crow would face a furious reaction. President John Hope of Morehouse College defended Alexander and the CIC in those terms to friends like Du Bois and in the black press.[20] Another observer was Benjamin E. Mays, who served Morehouse for thirty years, becoming its president and inspiring Martin Luther King Jr. Mays began teaching in Atlanta in 1921, at the start of the tension between the CIC and the Klan. Looking back during the 1980s, he understood why some people criticized the CIC for being too conservative and wedded to segregation. He had once asked the CIC to help him seek redress for discrimination by the Pullman Company, but he was rebuffed: "I was aware of the 'ideal' aims of the Commission and so I was deeply hurt and disillusioned when Dr. Alexander advised me to drop the case." Later, he came to appreciate Alexander's position: "The Commission never sought to abolish segregation; it worked to improve conditions between the races *within the segregated system.*" Mays conceded that since many whites regarded the CIC as dangerous and radical, its approach was necessarily discreet: "If Alexander had set out in 1920 to abolish segregation, the Commission would never have been allowed to function; and Will Alexander would have been considered insane if he had insisted on it. If he had tried to abolish segregation, the Ku Klux Klan would have had the support of most white Southerners who would have abolished the Commission."[21]

Thus, black people who supported the CIC generally avoided critical remarks on segregation, conscious that an explicit challenge could harm themselves, their institutions, and interracial cooperation as an ideal. None of the black officers and assistants of the CIC's state committees in North and South Carolina, Tennessee, Louisiana, Oklahoma, and Kentucky forced the issue on segregation. James Bond, a Congregationalist minister who served full time as Kentucky state secretary from 1920 to his death in 1929, wrote a weekly column in three leading white newspapers in which he promoted goodwill and cooperation, but rarely mentioned the effects of segregation. He campaigned against lynching, and struck a political deal to fund black high schools in Louisville, but when controversy arose over access to public parks, he supported the creation of new spaces for black citizens, rather than free admission to all the city's parks and playgrounds. The CIC's black adherents in Kentucky were several decades older than more militant supporters of the NAACP and Marcus Garvey, and this was part of a growing generational division across the southern states.[22]

The CIC approach to issues of segregation was shown in December 1925, when Woofter helped to organize a performance by the black tenor Roland Hayes at Atlanta's five thousand–seat City Auditorium. The son of former slaves, Hayes was born in northern Georgia in 1887, grew up in Tennessee, and studied at Fisk University. The Georgia state committee hosted the fundraising concert to show "the white people the possibilities of the colored man and serve for the colored people as an example of what a member of their race can do." Hayes sang to a packed black and white audience, with seating "divided strictly in half [i.e., down the middle], giving to each race exactly the same opportunities of hearing him." This satisfied both the CIC's idea of progress and Hayes's determination not to sing in venues that excluded blacks from the best seats.[23]

The best-known black leader associated with the CIC, Robert Russa Moton, hated segregation, but waited until the late 1920s before he would criticize it openly. When he did so in *What the Negro Thinks*, his complaint was unequivocal and heartfelt. He found the shabbiness of segregated facilities tiresome, but what tormented him was the thought that Jim Crow, merely by existing, invited white southerners to think that black people had accepted their inferiority and the offensiveness of their presence. This was what made segregation "the most humiliating form of racial discrimination, with the least substantial excuse or justification."[24] W. E. B. Du Bois was surprised by Moton's bluntness, remarking, "This is a book that would have been unthinkable ten years ago and would have caused something like a riot twenty years ago.... It is extraordinary that a book like this can come out of Tuskegee, Alabama, even in 1929."[25]

Will Alexander understood the humiliation caused by segregation, and his statements of the CIC's cautious position did not fully reflect his personal preference. He allowed the student dining hall to be integrated at one of the CIC's interracial conferences in Missouri in 1922, but he kept the matter secret afterward.[26] Just once, in answer to a question following an address to the Interdenominational Young People's Conference in Birmingham, Alabama, in 1926, did he feel bold enough to speak out, saying, "I believe in the repeal of any unjust law, and [segregation] is unjust." The conference rounded on him, and the next day the white Methodist ministers of Birmingham declared Alexander "unsuited to take the lead in the discussion and direction of race relations." It almost caused him to be removed from the CIC, and it was the last time he said such a thing openly.[27] One of the CIC's most prominent Georgian supporters, Marion Jackson, resigned over Alexander's speech and the "disastrous course" it seemed to indicate. Other prominent white CIC members either explicitly endorsed segregation, or avoided the subject. In 1925, CIC chairman M. Ashby Jones was quick to distance the commission from interracial meetings of young people of both sexes under the auspices of the YMCA and the YWCA in southern cities. When the CIC annual conference applauded the desire of young white southerners for better race relations, Jones forced through a resolution declaring that mixing young men and women of both races was dangerous on several levels. It stated that "too great haste in this direction might result in misunderstanding and friction that would jeopardize all the good will generated by the commission in six years of patient effort." As Jones put it himself, "There is still too much suspicion and there are too many immature minds in both races to permit our assuming a position whereby we might be held responsible for any trouble that might arise out of badly handled meetings of this character."[28]

By the end of the 1920s, Jones willingly endorsed calls for fuller rights of citizenship for blacks, including the vote, but he never abandoned his belief in the wisdom of segregation.[29] His fear of a racist reaction if the CIC relaxed its position too soon was borne out in March 1930, when the *Southern Methodist* accused his successor, Robert B. Eleazer, of having "Socialistic leanings" and charged that the CIC was out to destroy segregation. In reply, he left room for debate on the subject, saying, "The Commission is definitely on record as being opposed to the further extension of the principle of segregation and to the stiffening of the segregation laws now prevailing. On the other hand, it has not deemed it wise or desirable to seek the abrogation of these laws at present."[30] Thus, the white leadership of the CIC declined opportunities for radical pronouncements, but clearly did not see segregation as a permanent fixture of southern life. It is evident from the language Alexander used in his controversial Birmingham remark, from the statement by Jones that there was "still too much suspicion and . . . too many immature minds," and from Eleazer's advice against "the abrogation of these laws at present," that all three men expected the South to make fundamental adjustments over time, but they were hesitant about taking the first step. As late as 1945, in debates in the Southern Regional Council, which replaced the CIC, Will Alexander was reluctant to take a public stand against segregation, although he chaired the Federal Council of Churches race relations board in 1946 when it called for "a desegregated church in a desegregated society."[31]

In their refusal to challenge segregation, the CIC's leadership clearly helped to perpetuate what Patricia Sullivan has called the "white racial dreamworld in which the status of blacks was forever separate and inferior." However, for some white liberals this was not an automatic reflex, especially among those whose approach to interracial cooperation was basically religious.[32] The veteran Methodist social gospeler Arcadius McSwain Trawick, of Wofford College at Spartanburg, South Carolina, agonized for years over how God, on the one hand, and the South, on the other, wanted black people to be treated. He was from Tennessee, where his brother, Arch Trawick, his former brother-in-law, W. D. Weatherford, and his sister-in-law, Kate Trawick, were all active members of the CIC. Arcadius Trawick had previously served as a national officer of the YMCA and organized the important Negro Student Christian Conference in Atlanta in 1914. He was a member of the War Work Council, and his wife, Maude Wilder Trawick, was an outspoken president of the YWCA, which, as an organization, took an earlier lead on interracial cooperation than the YMCA. The YWCA actively encouraged black representation and interracial student meetings, and the interracial education department of the National Student Council's Southern Division allowed black and white student secretaries to work and travel together across the South.[33] Arcadius Trawick gradually shifted from a belief in "superior and inferior races" to the view that any "attempt to classify races as superior and inferior is both unscientific and unchristian." He decided that respectable and accomplished black people deserved to be treated the same as their white counterparts. In 1925, he wrote in the *Methodist Quarterly Review*, "A man of conscience faces no more serious ethical problem than that which is raised by the presence of another race. Which master shall he serve, God or Race? . . . Will he love kindness only so long as he looks into the face of men of his own color? Will he walk humbly with God until a man of another race calls up his love of vanity and superior privilege?" Trawick concluded that although race prejudice seemed natural and could even be "a safeguard to morality and race integrity," its main effects were hatred and cruelty. His quandary was how to square his respect for certain black acquaintances with his sense that "Negroes are, so far as the bulk of the population is concerned, a backward, superstitious, improvident, and irresponsible people." He blamed white people for causing these deficiencies by enslaving Africans in the first place and then denying them the "right to be conscious of [their] Americanism." It was time for the white South to acknowledge the "honest, hardworking, unheralded numbers [of blacks] who are achieving success in the pursuit of things worthwhile."

> Most of us sympathize with the one negro in the Jim Crow car, but because of the race we keep him there. . . . On the one hand is the law of love and a high regard for human worth; on the other the stone wall of race discrimination, where love and courtesy and mutual tolerance come to an abrupt end. . . . Spiritually, the color line is nothing; mentally it is a barbed-wire entanglement.[34]

As a Baptist minister and chairman of the GSCRR, and later chairman of the CIC itself, Ashby Jones also wrestled with "the Christ test." To Jones's mind, the flaw in southern race relations was the conviction of "the average man in the South . . . that the Negro was something less than human . . . a slave kind of man. This kind of man is only fitted to fulfill a social function of service within a limited sphere. To allow him to step outside of that sphere would be to render him inefficient and hurtful to society in general." Jones wanted whites to accept fully the humanity of black people: "This can only come from a Christian consciousness. If the Negro is human then he is God's child and he is my brother." As such, he could not be denied "some 'inalienable rights' . . . [even though] the races should be separated by such social barriers as are necessary to preserve the purity of the blood of the two peoples."[35] This was the recurrent style of white religious interracial cooperationists—anguishing over the merciless penalty of white supremacy and seeking solace in the biological soundness of segregation. Thus, Episcopal bishop Kirkman G. Finlay of South Carolina, a CIC supporter, abhorred the subjugation of black people through "injustice in courts, unfavorable living conditions and surroundings, lack of educational opportunities, and the white man's tendency toward mob violence," but still insisted that "parallel development of the negro and white races was . . . the only practicable solution of the race problem," even though Jesus, himself, "accepted no barriers of race or color."[36] The small minority of white male theologians and ministers who meditated on the race problem found the humanitarian imperative impossible to reconcile with their profound sense that race meant hierarchy. Under such leadership, even the most liberal white churches remained evasive on civil rights. White women Methodists and Baptists, however, found it easier to form alliances with their black counterparts and translate ideals into action.[37]

Speaking in the 1970s, southern historian Broadus Mitchell recalled both the CIC, which his father, Samuel Chiles Mitchell, supported, and the Southern Regional Council, which his younger brother, George, directed. He regarded the interracial cooperation movement as principled (but mistaken) in its belief in the power of goodwill, and he understood its reluctance to start doomed legal battles against white supremacy over constitutional matters,

> because they felt that it would take a long time and many adjustments and that it was important to keep peace and to avoid doing damage which it might be hard to repair. They were patient. . . . It was a kindly attitude . . . not one of justice but of duty. You see? It was your responsibility to be friendly and to entertain hopes of [black] progress. But you weren't going to see it tomorrow, and anything like a lawsuit would be unfortunate. You didn't appeal to ultimate things.[38]

Thus, the CIC's public position was that a degree of segregation was necessary, but that is not to say that it had no impact on Jim Crow. Merely by allowing the subject to be aired from time to time, the interracial cooperation movement made a number of young white southerners think about whether it was just or necessary. As Grace Elizabeth Hale has observed:

> Despite the mild and moderate nature of its protest . . . the CIC opened up a space for the beginning of white questioning of the culture of segregation. While [the] CIC drew most of its white leaders from the generation that pre-

ceded Lillian Smith's and Margaret Mitchell's contemporaries, young white southerners sometimes cited their participation as college students in YWCA and YMCA CIC-related activities as the beginning of their racial conversion.[39]

Seen from the perspective of progressive northern integrationism, or that of later generations of civil rights activists, the CIC seems overly cautious, but for their time Will Alexander and his associates represented the most radical end of the white southern liberal spectrum.

The CIC embodied the Social Gospel, but it was a creed that also attracted those who had essentially conservative purposes and who believed in profound black backwardness. In 1925, for example, the joint endowment fund of Hampton Institute and Tuskegee Institute put together a southern committee to promote "constructive industrial Negro education." Hampton's appeal was issued by its white principal, James E. Gregg, and former U.S. president William Howard Taft, while the Tuskegee appeal was led by Robert R. Moton and the New York philanthropist William Jay Schieffelin. It was the kind of exercise that weighed on Moton's conscience. The African American population was portrayed to potential donors explicitly as the region's main problem: "This work is in behalf of better citizenship; that which helps to make the Negro a better citizen helps the community in which he lives, reducing crime and elevating the general standard of citizenship."[40] The president of the University of Virginia, Edwin A. Alderman, joined in, applauding philanthropists who supported industrial education as "high-minded men who see in the presence of ignorant masses of African people a menace to our national life, and who are seeking not only to minimize that menace, but to contribute affirmatively to the good energies of the nation." He cautioned African Americans who believed they were entitled to the full rights of citizenship: "The hardest experiences of the negroes are yet to be, for the world will demand of them that they develop not only manual and industrial power, but those moral qualities necessary to win freedom through competition and self-effort."[41]

In contrast, Will Alexander was less concerned about shaping black behavior than changing white attitudes, especially among the college-educated, but he lacked suitable material. Most post-Reconstruction literature on the American Negro with academic pretensions was venomous, and the sympathetic studies for students in the early 1920s often lacked rigor or relevance, having been written before the boll weevil's spread, the war, migration, and consequent shifts in black political outlook. After 1924, Alexander tried to encourage fundamental research by social scientists and a new engagement with race as a subject in southern universities. He needed a research director who could articulate the commission's objectives, not only at the state and local levels, but also from a regional perspective. He could have selected one of several rising black social scientists for this work, but if such a thing even occurred to him, he would not have entertained the idea for long—he was uncomfortable with people who wanted to move at a faster pace than he thought wise, and he flinched at generalized attacks on the morality and attitudes of southern white people. The CIC preferred to issue appeals couched in Christian missionary language to potential converts to interracial cooperation (which blacks were assumed to favor) from a target audience of white academics, clergymen, bureaucrats, businessmen, and clubwomen. In Jack Woofter, the CIC had a dogged investigator with a PhD, a Methodist upbringing, and a commitment to interracial cooperation.

In 1924, following the death of CIC chairman and guiding spirit John J. Eagan, the commission was restructured; the Reverend M. Ashby Jones assumed the chair, and Woofter was promoted to research director, working closely with Alexander. Woofter was already engaged in gathering data on black schools for an analysis of the underfunding of public education in Georgia, which he compared unfavorably to spending in nine other southern states.[42] He was familiar with the funding problem from the *Negro Education* project and his studies with Robert Preston Brooks on the disinclination of white taxpayers to give black education a subsidy. The issue on which he focused was the disparity between the taxes that black southerners actually paid and the sums the states budgeted for the education of black children, and this became a recurrent theme in his work. Although funding in some states had risen since 1917, Woofter found a minimalist approach persisted everywhere regarding African American normal schools, teachers' salaries, and school buildings. He protested that black people in Georgia paid 9 percent of the city taxes that supported schools, but saw only 4 percent of the state's education expenditure. He never called for identical levels of per capita state provision, but, as he had stated in his annual GSCRR report for 1922, the current arrangement "means that Negroes are taxed to build white school buildings, which is unfair and undemocratic."[43]

The CIC continued to lobby for increased education spending in the South, with some success, notably in Tennessee, Texas, and Kentucky, where additional funding was secured after 1925 for black colleges and normal schools. Compared to the situation in 1913, the year Jack Woofter joined the Phelps-Stokes Fund, southern black education had improved by the late 1920s. Charities still made major essential donations, especially the Rosenwald Fund, but in ways that encouraged the states to increase their own spending. In 1921, Alabama had 234 Rosenwald schools (to which the contribution from public funds was $108,201), Louisiana had 135 ($161,812), Mississippi had 141 ($265,141), North Carolina had 175 ($260,342), Tennessee had 112 ($245,929), and Virginia had 105 ($163,163). Georgia's contribution to its 53 Rosenwald schools was just $31,465. States with a similar number of Rosenwald schools, such as Arkansas, with 54 schools, and Kentucky, with 52 schools, contributed $119,036 and $175,841 respectively from public funds.[44] Within a few years, thousands of new buildings were erected and equipped; the number of black high schools more than doubled; enrollments and attendance were up; illiteracy and class sizes were down; the number of black teachers rose from under twenty thousand to over thirty thousand, and their salaries, training, and annual periods of employment improved. And yet, across the South, comparative underfunding and segregation still excluded black children from common systems of state education and accreditation. Per capita spending on black children was under 30 percent of spending on white children in Alabama, Florida, Georgia, Mississippi, Louisiana, and South Carolina. In the latter state, blacks received a smaller share of education funds in the late 1920s than in 1911. In 1934, 2,568 of Georgia's 3,434 black schools still had only one teacher; another 566 had two teachers, and fewer than half the black teachers in the state held teaching certificates. Despite gross inequalities and limited progress in the 1920s, the professionalism of black teachers increased and the expectations of parents rose, adding to pressure for fundamental change in the Jim Crow system.[45]

It was the problem of southern education that initially drew Jack Woofter into the interracial cooperation movement in 1913, and both the fieldwork experiences he shared with Walter B. Hill and Ocea Taylor under Thomas Jesse Jones and his training in statistics and sociology helped him as research director for the CIC. As Will Alexander's biographers wrote of Woofter's work: "No dull, dusty research this, but firsthand exploration in a field charged with passion, crying out for serious documentation and understanding. . . . Alexander considered himself fortunate to find a man who could collect facts and at the same time sense the atmosphere surrounding a situation." Woofter, in return, appreciated Alexander's "thorough practicality in the mechanics of social change."[46] The research directorship became another turning point for Woofter, bringing him to the attention of southern policy makers and universities and setting him on a path of public service in education and government. He was to remain with the CIC until beginning of 1927, when he joined the University of North Carolina.

A lasting element of Woofter's work for the CIC was his success in persuading southern universities to confront racial issues in their teaching. In conjunction with Robert B. Eleazer, he arranged for colleges to be sent current information and literature and began a lecture series in which African American academics such as George Washington Carver and Isaac Fisher spoke on all-white campuses, a completely new and sometimes controversial experience for students and faculty alike. Eleazer said of the effect on white students, "The transformation in the viewpoint has been remarkable in many cases. They have been introduced to an entirely new type of colored people, who give them a new conception of the capabilities of colored people." Interracial student groups also began to hold more frequent discussions.[47]

Alexander's eagerness to generate new research through Woofter reflected his fear that most young middle-class white people were as ill-informed as their parents. In a survey of white southern colleges, Woofter found a high level of student interest in race, but hardly any meaningful teaching outside general sociology courses. There was a shortage of materials, the only widely available texts being three quaint contributions by W. D. Weatherford. Woofter commented that Weatherford's first two books on race, *Negro Life in the South* (1910) and *Present Forces in the Uplift of the Negro* (1913), were "excellent reading for beginners," but they were outdated and inaccurate. Weatherford wrote them after meeting black and white educators, Methodist missionaries, and YMCA officials at a conference in Atlanta in 1908 that helped cement the interracial cooperation movement. His books were transitional; they condemned lynching, criticized explicitly antiblack propaganda, looked for the best in "the Negro character," and embraced cooperation; but they were also riddled with spurious science about the value of "pure blood," the alleged "lack of self-control" among blacks, and the problem of "social impurity." Weatherford was very clear on one thing: "There must not be any mingling of the races."[48]

In his most recent book, *The Negro from Africa to America* (1924), Weatherford responded to a rash of popular racist texts promoting Nordic virtues over those of all other groups, including Madison Grant's *The Passing of the Great Race* (1916), Lothrop Stoddard's *The Rising Tide of Color against White World-Supremacy* (1920) and *The Revolt against Civilization: The Menace of the Under Man* (1922), Clinton Stoddard Burr's *America's Race Heritage* (1922), and Charles Conant Josey's *Race and National Solidarity* (1923). These books, and to some extent Weatherford's, fed what Matthew Pratt Guterl has called a "deepening national popular fascination with whiteness and blackness." *The Negro from Africa to America* was well received by white reviewers—Guy B. Johnson of the University of North Carolina called it "a triumph of the scientific attitude over prejudice"—but black critics were not grateful for Weatherford's attempt to defend the race. E. Franklin Frazier called it a "scrap-book," full of southern white "resistances." W. E. B. Du Bois, who preferred to debate race issues directly with writers like Stoddard, reckoned that *The Negro from Africa to America* was "the best thing the white South has produced," but that Weatherford was too smitten with "the smoother phrases" of Washington and Moton: "The net impression of Mr. Weatherford's scheme of treatment is that of a well-meaning man who in spite of himself is oleaginous and patronizing." Carter G. Woodson thought Weatherford had tried to cover too much black history that he did not understand; he was equally disdainful of Lily Hardy Hammond's gallery of black leaders, *In the Vanguard of a Race* (1922), but he appreciated her attempt to inform white readers about African American achievement.[49]

According to Woofter, by the mid-1920s, "College faculties and students were increasingly open-minded on race questions but had little ammunition in the way of systematically compiled facts."[50] Alexander therefore set him the task of writing a new textbook on race, *The Basis of Racial Adjustment*, published in 1925 by Boston textbook specialists Ginn and Company and eventually adopted by sixty colleges.[51] "Racial adjustment" had meant various things since Reconstruction, including the advancement of the freedmen through industrial education, and Woofter would certainly have encountered the phrase as a student. In American debates on race relations in the 1910s and 1920s, the terms "race adjustment," "racial adjustment," and "adjustment of race relations" were used frequently to indicate progressive reform in the South. The word "adjustment" itself enabled change to be discussed without the suggestion of anything drastic, and it allowed writers to avoid loaded words such as "rights," "social," "political," or "equality." For example, in 1917 Lily Hardy Hammond published *Southern Women and Racial Adjustment*, a pamphlet urging white women to do more to train and assist black women. She offered an anecdotal critique of the evils of prejudice and discrimination that was brave and outspoken for its time, while also advocating "racial integrity" and "racial separateness." One chapter was entitled "The Basis of Adjustment." Some black writers also used the language of "adjustment." For example, in 1908, Kelly Miller published *Race Adjustment: Essays on the Negro in America* (which Woofter praised in the published version of his PhD dissertation), and in 1925, in a special Harlem issue of the *Survey Graphic*, Miller referred again to the possibility of "race adjustment" resulting from greater self-sufficiency in northern ghettoes.[52] Woofter's use of the term "adjustment" was closest to its use by Monroe Work of Tuskegee Institute in his report on the interracial cooperation movement in *Social Forces* in 1924, in which he highlighted the molding of southern opinion, the reduction of friction, and an increase in face-to-face discussion between blacks and whites.[53]

In *The Basis of Racial Adjustment*, Woofter questioned white supremacy and segregation as much as the racial climate and his own sensibilities would allow. Will Alexander's subsequent assessment of the book was that it "had some value. It gave them something to use in the colleges. It was the beginning of an effort to create a working literature on this subject." He added, "Dr. Woofter tried to get underneath to see really what was making the trouble. It was an effort to do that sort of thing. It was not too successful, but it was fairly successful. But it seemed to me fundamental [to do research and publish]."[54] Alexander's comments seem harsh, given the scope of Woofter's efforts and the fact that so few other books in print at the time dealt competently and rationally with race. In 1925, *The Basis of Racial Adjustment* was rare and almost prescient, and it cemented Woofter into a new generation of white writers. The fact that Woofter was working outside a university department and seeing daily the impact of racism on black lives in the South, a region he had crisscrossed as a researcher since 1913, meant that he arrived at his critique of white supremacy sooner and by a more immediate set of observations than most white social scientists. Although he was deeply influenced by

his own family background and education, and the narrow mentality of the philanthropic funds regarding the capabilities of African Americans, he had become
much more open-minded and inquisitive than most white southern men. For example, when he declared at the CIC's annual conference in 1925, "Southern [white]
students should know as much about the poems of Paul Laurence Dunbar as they
do about those of Henry Wadsworth Longfellow," very few white people in the audience would have agreed with him.[55] It showed the ways in which his experiences
as a Phelps-Stokes field agent, government researcher, army officer, graduate student in the North, and CIC activist in the South had sensitized him to things far
beyond the experiences of most white men of his age and background. As Morton
Sosna observed, "An important influence upon Southern liberals was their experiences outside the South. Even when they returned home, they found that residence elsewhere had added new dimensions to their views about the South's racial situation."[56] This was certainly true of Woofter.

   The Basis of Racial Adjustment was a step in Woofter's reemergence as a social
scientist in the late 1920s. Race was an important strand of work in the major university departments of sociology, where it tended to be dominated by an attitude
of scientific racism in which explanations were sought for the "backwardness" of
African Americans. For example, Frank A. Ross, who completed his PhD at Columbia University alongside Woofter and continued to teach there, wrote in 1925:

> Out of the vague and ill-defined field of the social science of former days there
> are emerging specific problems which collectively are coming to be generally
> accepted as sociology. One of these is the subject of race relations. While an-
> thropologists and ethnologists have taken unto themselves the investigations
> of elemental peoples under primitive surroundings, sociologists have been pur-
> suing studies of backward peoples in civilized settings. Research bodies have
> been studying the Oriental in American populations and the negro as a factor
> in American political and social life.[57]

   That approach was evident in a wave of academic publications on race by soci-
ologists and other social scientists that followed *The Basis of Racial Adjustment*.
Woofter later confessed that his book suffered from an "immaturity and lack
of systematically developed facts," but he noted that it preceded many studies:
"It was not until the late 1920s that extensive, systematic, factual books became
common." Subsequent contributions by white anthropologists such as Melville J.
Herskovits (of Northwestern University) and white sociologists such as Ross,
Edward B. Reuter (of Tulane University, and then the University of Iowa), Jerome
Dowd (University of Oklahoma), and Frank H. Hankins (Clark University, and
then Smith College), were conscious attempts at objective, largely egalitarian,
and rigorous work, although they dwelled on sexual promiscuity and physical
form. All of the white liberal writers on race in the 1920s, including Woofter, and

some black scholars such as Frazier and Charles S. Johnson, were later taken to task by Melville Herskovits for playing down the significance of African culture in American life—"the perpetuation of the legend concerning the quality and lack of tenaciousness of Negro aboriginal endowment."[58] Although postwar literature on race expanded less markedly than the 1930s "race relations bulge" that David Levering Lewis has described, Coolidge-era scholars exhibited a new tendency to question longstanding assumptions about race and society, and *The Basis of Racial Adjustment* shows Woofter moving more swiftly than the established white social-scientific community in rejecting ideas of a biological hierarchy and racial difference in intelligence. Black disadvantage in America, he argued, was attributable not to inferiority, but to a combination of a cultural lag caused by slavery, discrimination in the workplace and education, and a legal system riddled with prejudice. Such statements did not strike sociologists like Frazier or Johnson, or black economist Abram Harris Jr. as novel or perceptive, but Woofter's book was a moment of relative clarity from the pen of a white commentator, and it contributed to a changing mood in white higher education. By 1930, thirty-nine southern white colleges were offering specific courses on "The Negro," and interracial collegiate forums continued to spread.[59]

The Basis of Racial Adjustment condensed various arguments for the fairer treatment of blacks in the southern states and the wider recognition of their rights as citizens. In several respects, Woofter's analysis of the economic, legal, political, and social circumstances of black Americans broke with the orthodox southern mentality, and his prescriptions for progress were, for their time, radical and constructive. In some of his other work on race and rural conditions, he offered factual information in a detached and politically neutral fashion, but on this occasion he picked apart the fabric of white supremacy, rejecting some of its core beliefs and attacking widespread injustice.

Although *The Basis of Racial Adjustment* was laid out as a textbook, with end-of-chapter further reading and questions, it was not a neutral survey of race relations. Woofter offered a qualified argument for racial liberalism, couched in terms intended to persuade white readers of the need for change. Here and there, he noted that race was a national issue and that the federal government's interest had grown because of migration, war, farming subsidies, education and health programs, and labor issues, but his focus was firmly on the South. The underlying theme was the value of patience and reconciliation, but in Woofter's vision the pace of change would be determined by white people. For example, when he discussed democracy, white precedence was implicit:

> The evolution of the Negro's place in government must be by the processes of growth rather than by any sudden universal enfranchisement, especially in those communities where the most ignorant and the most backward colored

people are massed and constitute a majority. Any agitation on the part of Negro leaders for sudden enfranchisement of the masses only tends to cement the determination of these communities to go to any lengths rather than permit it. On the other hand, the more rigid the regulation against Negroes voting the more they want to vote and the more they magnify the demand for the ballot out of all proportion to its real significance as a means to progress.[60]

Although Woofter did not mention the Klan, he frequently reminded readers that excessive haste regarding the adjustment of black participation in politics could reignite Lost Cause passions and caricatures.

Woofter was plainly influenced by the work of biologists and anthropologists, including Franz Boas. Rigid classification of individuals into races on the basis of appearance, Woofter argued, was a falsehood; cultural differences were more important than any superficial physical variations. He stated that scientific evidence did not "warrant the assumption of an inborn, ineradicable superiority of one race over all others" and for all whites to assume they were superior to all blacks was "a blind error." He argued that the African American population had to be patient and wrote unequivocally about "backwardness" and the need for a "dynamic viewpoint" that embraced changes taking place among black people as a race. Both races would have to rise above old fears, and white Americans, especially, had to overcome "the feeling that what is the Negro's gain must of necessity be the white man's loss."[61] Woofter saw sharp differences between the cooperative school of black leadership—mainly teachers and preachers "advocating hard work and gradual advance"—and the radical school—including northern editors and politicians—that was "insistent in its demands for equality, and constantly agitating and litigating for the immediate realization of its desires." The radical type was rarely encountered in person in the South, whereas moderate leaders such as Moton had earned wide recognition and respect. Without naming Marcus Garvey, Woofter especially denounced selfish leaders "for whom the weakness and gullibility of the great mass of colored people is too great a temptation." He believed the work of the CIC had proved that it was always local leaders who were "the primary factors in racial adjustment."[62]

Like almost all white American social scientists, including adherents of the Social Gospel, Woofter accepted that human races were at different points in the process of civilization and that some innate difference must therefore exist. Nevertheless, he envisaged a partnership—interracial cooperation, no less—for the purpose of "developing the Negro in harmony with American life and traditions. . . . The white man's tasks are those of self-control in difficult situations and of adjusting American institutions so as to give the maximum service in aiding the belated race; the Negro's tasks are those of self-development, of cultivating family life, industry, thrift, and moral stamina."[63] Those paternalistic sentiments revealed that the racist core of the CIC's key concepts of cooperation and goodwill. Woofter's writing echoed that of earlier liberal writers, such as the late-nineteenth-century critic of social Darwinism, Lester F. Ward, who attempted to prove that society was made up of groups, rather than competing individuals, and that cooperation between groups benefited both them and society. Woofter's use of phrases such as "aiding the belated race" smacked of Thomas Jesse Jones, but he could have pointed to black scholars who sometimes used such terms. For example, Kelly Miller, in 1913, declared, "The highest call of the civilization of the world to-day is to the educated young men of the belated races."[64]

The fact that 1924, the year in which Woofter researched and wrote most of his book, was the pinnacle of Ku Klux Klan influence in the United States, must have affected his judgment about the capacity of the South to allow reform and black progress. Nevertheless, he subtly questioned assumptions upon which white supremacy rested, while recalling and predicting changes in the racial landscape. In successive chapters, he outlined the rate of growth of the black population, the causes of migration (i.e., landlord exploitation, the boll weevil, lynching, the Klan, and the lure of the city), the multiple causes of ill health (i.e., poverty, rotten housing, lack of specialist care, and poorly equipped hospitals), the problems of "ignorant, improvident, and constantly shifting" farm labor, the role of black workers in industry and domestic service, the challenges facing black businesses in seeking white custom and attracting investment, issues relating to law enforcement and the courts, the questions that race posed about American democracy, the duties of the southern states regarding education, the value of black self-help organizations, the shortcomings of black churches, and the questionable validity of certain kinds of segregation. Many of the reforms Woofter called for grew directly from his experiences in the field with the CIC, particularly concerning economic conditions and justice in the courts. Wherever possible, he stressed environmental factors, rather than racial characteristics. In his chapter on health, he cited Frederick L. Hoffman's *Race Traits and Tendencies of the American Negro*— an actuarial study based on the 1890 census, which asserted that black ill health was so chronic that the group was uninsurable—in order to refute such claims with more recent census and insurance data showing that "the Negro is dying principally of diseases which arise from filth, poor living conditions, and exposure. In other words, the Negro race is not greatly inferior to the white physically, but it lives under very inferior health conditions."[65]

With regard to farming, Woofter called for new tenancy laws requiring written contracts and proper accounts, the reimbursement of tenants for soil improvements, the replacement of the crop-loan nexus with a proper rural credit system, larger investment in black farm demonstration agents, and more urgent action by the Department of Justice to eradicate peonage. Regarding the urban economy, he regretted the need for black women to work long hours in industry and domestic service, instead of devoting themselves "to rearing moral, intelligent, and thrifty families." He divided unskilled urban male labor into "the worst type of shiftless day laborer," on whom common stereotypes were based, and the more representative "ambitious man who moves in from the country without a trade." In the wake of immigration restriction, he pointed to black industrial labor as an untapped resource and attacked the restrictions on black skilled workers seeking work, equal pay, or union membership.[66]

Woofter declared that white supremacy's biggest failure was the South's unfair legal system. (Twenty years later, the Swedish sociologist Gunnar Myrdal was struck by the continuing relevance of Woofter's assertion that without the right to an impartial jury trial, "democracy itself rests on quicksand." Myrdal, who headed the Carnegie-funded project that produced *An American Dilemma* in 1944, held that "Woofter eloquently expresses the view of Southern liberalism today.")[67] Woofter tried to address persistent myths regarding crime, again stressing environmental factors. He accepted that many blacks were "as yet poorly adapted to the codes and institutions of the white civilization in which they live," but regarded inveterate black criminality as a white invention that gave free rein to prejudice in the courts: "The arrest and conviction of innocent Negroes, therefore, swells the commitment rate beyond the actual volume of crime." High rates of conviction and long sentences reflected harsh attitudes toward black defendants, especially the "feeble-minded," while prison tended to "debase, brutalize, and increase criminal tendencies." He attributed the behavior of southern courts partly to the unreliability of "ignorant and excitable" black witnesses who lacked the necessary "training and self-control [to give] statements . . . under emotional stress," but he maintained that black criminality was "not excessive . . . [and] not attributable to racial tendencies." He devoted special attention to mob violence and argued that the CIC's local approach had been the key to its reduction. He was still certain that federal legislation would never work, but acknowledged that the Dyer bill had "stimulated discussion and wide publicity" and called on all states to pass laws "strengthening the hands of the sheriff and providing penalties for his negligence."[68]

In discussing the qualities of African Americans, Woofter paid eloquent tribute to their record in uniform, especially in the trenches and behind the lines during the world war. He recalled wartime doubts about black loyalty and the "fear frankly expressed . . . that if the Negroes should be called upon to fight for the country they might demand as recompense more privileges than the country was willing to grant." In fact, black soldiers had never shirked, despite being "denied the fullest participation in the privileges and liberties of America." He never forgot the attempts to discredit black soldiers in 1919, which, as an officer in the AEF headquarters, he knew to be "gossip based on sheer fancy." He noted the immense charitable work of black churches and fraternal organizations, aided by the community-chest movement, although he wished such institutions would "place greater emphasis on the social importance and sanctity of normal family life." He also threw in the kind of gratuitous remark that angered black readers: "Neither African tribal customs nor the customs of slavery tended to inculcate into the Negro the highest ideals of family life" and made other references to the supposed polygamous traditions of black men.[69]

Woofter trod a fine line on the vote. He attempted to explain disfranchisement in terms of the different attributes of the southern and northern black populations. Echoing his college professor Robert Preston Brooks, he described the relative "intelligence" of separate black groups:

> In the very areas where the Negro is in the majority, his group is less intelligent, less familiar with American institutions, farther down the economic scale, and most likely to constitute the corrupt mass-voting element. In the areas where the Negro is distinctly in the minority, he is more intelligent, has had more chance to observe the workings of the white man's institutions, is higher in the economic scale, and more fitted in every way to perform the duties of citizenship.[70]

While not denying that blacks should vote, he argued that America should let the South "work out this extremely important and extremely delicate question in the way in which they have begun." He advised black people to be patient and have "faith . . . that participation in the government will be extended as rapidly as it can be done without the precipitation of reactions which would be harmful to the community as a whole and to the Negroes themselves." He warned the white South that "the bugaboo of Negro domination" did not justify keeping what Edgar Gardner Murphy had called "a serf class, a fixed non-voting population" by means of literacy tests, poll taxes, and white primaries. Woofter wanted the South to commit itself to eventual "fairness, a determination to enforce suffrage tests equitably on white and black alike, and a resolve to break away from the one-party system."[71]

He argued that since blacks contributed to the finances of southern states through their own property taxes and rent paid on other taxpayers' property, they were being shortchanged: "Justice and honesty should demand that the Negro get from the government services at least in proportion to the amount of tax which he pays directly and indirectly." This was especially true in education: if black taxpayers supported white schools, then "common justice demands the more liberal support of colored institutions." He argued that blacks were entitled to proportional state expenditure on separate high schools, normal schools, and colleges, since "sentiment will not permit them to attend the same institutions as white people," although he did not share that sentiment. Regarding the education process itself, Woofter maintained there were "differences in the native mental ability or intelligence of the two races, but just what these differences are, in quantity or in quality, is not known." Certainly, the wartime intelligence tests conducted by Robert M. Yerkes and others had not substantiated "the previous popular assumption of the essential inferiority of the Negro mind" and did not themselves justify different kinds of education for whites and blacks. The South's urgent need of well-trained people meant that white anxiety about an overeducated black population was illogical, especially in view of the southern states' average per capita expenditure in 1922 of only $7.12 on the education of each black child aged between six and fourteen years, compared to $29.72 on each white child. Although this represented a two-and-a-half-times increase in black education spending in the region since 1916, the trebling of spending on white schools meant the gap had widened. The southern black illiteracy rate of 22.9 percent was "a menace," he wrote, and it was absurd that the smallest per capita expenditure on black schools occurred in the states and counties with the largest black populations. He called for a curriculum that emphasized "history, civics, economics, and the natural sciences, so that everyday life will be more intelligently appreciated." Black children should study black writers and "the accomplishments of colored men of mark" and know more of their own history, for the "stimulation of race pride." Better vocational training was still needed, of course, and in this regard he cited the ten-year-old *Negro Education* report. He applauded the work of state supervisors, such as his friend Walter Hill in Georgia, and surveyed the assistance provided by the Jeanes Foundation, the Slater Fund, the Rosenwald school building program, the General Education Board, the Phelps-Stokes Fund, and the northern missions that established institutions such as Fisk University. None of these good works relieved the South of its own responsibilities, however; the states had to choose "between providing a separate system of higher education for Negroes and shirking the moral responsibility for developing a Negro leadership."[72]

Woofter's one major concession to his white southern readership was his attempt to present social segregation in a positive light. He was not defending Jim Crow in all its forms, but he was definite about the desirability of some separation for "race purity." In a concluding chapter entitled "Race Contacts," he stated his personal opinion: "There are forms of segregation which are cruel and others which are useless. Too often the separation of the Negro simply affords an opportunity to give him inadequate accommodations for the same pay, and does not help in preserving race purity." Questioning aspects of Jim Crow in this way was a bold departure from the southern white consensus in favor of complete segregation, which was, in some respects, becoming stronger. (When *The Basis of Racial Adjustment* was published in 1925, Georgia was in the process of enacting several new statutes and penal code adjustments to tighten rules on segregation in commerce and education; Virginia had just passed its Racial Integrity Act and was about to enact the extremist Public Assemblages Act.) It was pointless, Woofter argued, to segregate the races in education, health care, the workplace, religious observance, charitable organization, and local government. Such separation prevented better race relations, for "it is impossible to work consistently with a man and hate him." However, the one point on which he was unmovable was "the preservation of racial integrity." This was paramount. He said that white aversion to "social intermingling" was not prejudice; rather, it was a function of "the fundamental sociological principle of consciousness of kind, of pleasurable association with similars. The 'we-group' always sets up protective taboos and restrictions against intermarriage and to some extent against intermingling with the 'other-than-we-group,' especially if there is a wide ethnic difference between the two." The establishment of separate Christian denominations, he asserted, was an expression of "we-group" preference by blacks.[73]

The "consciousness of kind" idea was taken from the work of Franklin H. Giddings, under whom Woofter had worked at Columbia University. Woofter was also echoing Robert Ezra Park's argument that acceptable levels of intimacy between groups varied and that a preference for "social distance" should not be confused with prejudice. Woofter wrote:

> The solution of this situation would seem to rest in the imposition of only such forms of segregation as aid in the preservation of racial integrity, and in the administration of the system with absolute justice. If, in the long run, the wisdom and justice of such a system is not recognized by the Negro himself, there will either be constant discontent and friction or amalgamation. There is no alternative to these two, except the systematic minimization of social contacts.[74]

By "social contacts," he meant circumstances that might lead to sexual intercourse. Woofter wanted orderly change in the South, and he saw no point in encouraging notions that the majority of white people were not going to suffer. It is possible to attribute Woofter's rationale for social separation of the races to his peculiarly southern progressivism and his sociological training at Columbia University, but a close reading of *The Basis of Racial Adjustment* indicates his deeply felt unease at the idea of interracial sexual relations. On an intellectual level, he drew his arguments from Giddings, but his feelings on the matter were also visceral. He could discuss miscegenation in an academic manner (e.g., "anthropologists have been unable to agree on the physical results of race mixture, but the sociologists agree that the social cost of the mixture of heterogeneous types is prohibitive"), but interracial sex also provoked a degree of fascination and revulsion in Woofter that was typical of white southern men of his background and generation. As a child, he heard "big boys talk of what the young white men and colored girls did at night and often wondered what their mode of address was or how they felt

if they happened to meet on the street next day." He insisted that he never engaged in "youthful misconduct," himself. In 1956, when presenting an overview
of Jim Crow in his lifetime, he was still convinced that "wide differences between
the average individuals of the two races in health, morals, manners and education [meant that] . . . the white man will put as much social distance as possible
between his family and the family of the Negro."[75]

One of Woofter's concerns as CIC director of research was the weakness of
sociology in the South. He compiled a report for the conference of southern social science teachers in which he drew a straight connection between "the South's
backwardness in social thinking [and] the barrenness of social science teaching in Southern colleges." Of the sixty college-grade institutions in the South,
only twenty-two offered sociology. Woofter visited them all and found that of the
18,000 students at these institutions only 1,400 (7.5%) studied sociology in a basic
class, and only half of that number took it to a more advanced level. Only a handful of departments engaged solely in sociology, and the subject consisted mainly
of empirical studies of American society or the examination of key concepts and
a few specific groups. Woofter found that in more advanced courses, "the family,
immigration, races and labor problems seem to be the most popular," with social
work classes offered here and there. He called for three things: proper integration of sociology into the curriculum, so that all southern colleges could offer social science majors; the popularization of sociology so that resources flowed to it;
and the gearing of programs specifically to the needs and interests of the southern people. Consciously or otherwise, with a widely adopted textbook on race and
a cogent analysis of the discipline, he was making himself into a candidate for an
associate professorship somewhere in the South.[76]

This was confirmed by the enthusiasm of white reviewers of *The Basis of Racial
Adjustment*. The *American Economic Review* commented on its refreshing lack
of sensationalism and dogma, calling it "far and away the best balanced and san-
est survey we have seen of the American race (negro) problem. As a text book it
is all that could be asked. It covers the ground accurately, without prejudice, and
with a thoughtful sympathy for both whites and blacks." To the *American Political Science Review*, it was "informed and temperate," while the *Catholic World*
called it a "very readable and fair-minded attempt to throw light on existing conditions among the Negroes, with some excellent suggestions regarding the solution of problems confronting both their race and ours." Frank Ross, in the *Political Science Quarterly*, considered Woofter's southern birth and northern training
especially equipped him "to present a comprehensive discussion of the adjustment
of the races, black and white, to one another." Ross was pleased to find echoes of
their old mentor, Giddings, adding, "Segregation is a well recognized sociological
principle. Like invariably tends to associate with like." The *American Journal of
Sociology*, in a review that may have been by Edwin B. Reuter, was more doubt-

ful than Woofter that it was "possible for black and white people to live together in peace, without either amalgamation or extermination of the black racial minority."[77] In Woofter's home state, Clark Foreman, as secretary of the GSCRR, gave the book an enthusiastic puff in the *Atlanta Constitution,* which his grandfather founded and his uncle, Clark Howell, owned and edited. Calling Woofter "one of the best posted students of the race problem in the country," Foreman said the book was more than a textbook and that reading it would be "necessary for anyone making a study of the American negro." He compared it to Edgar Gardner Murphy's *The Basis of Ascendancy* (1909), a book that Woofter admired and that certainly influenced him as a young man.[78] In contrast, James Hardy Dillard was disappointed. Writing in 1927, after Woofter's book had been followed by several others on "problems of race, or of racial adjustments," Dillard expressed the kind of longing that drove New York's philanthropic coterie ten years later to hire Gunnar Myrdal: "These books all have their value in one or another direction, but in spite of their excellence a place yet remains for a still more comprehensive work. It will be written by one man—where shall he be found?—a man capable and available, a man of fairness and vision, and with power of style and exposition, who can perhaps command the co-operation of the scientific ability of men in colleges of both races."[79]

The *Survey,* which had a largely white northern readership, was equivocal. The reviewer, "B. L.," (probably former associate editor Bruno Lasker) considered that the factual central chapters of Woofter's book placed it immediately in "the front rank among textbooks available for study and discussion of this subject." He was congratulated on "a fair and—considering the present state of public opinion—on the whole courageous survey of the situation and . . . many wise suggestions for improvement," but the reviewer considered northern universities and churches were so "far in advance" of Woofter that his endorsement of segregation meant this could only be a book for southern classrooms. Textbooks tended to respect regional cultural differences, the reviewer acknowledged, and "a loud protest is the only possible answer to any attempt to impose southern view-points on the rest of the country."[80] Mary White Ovington, a co-founder of the NAACP who chaired its board of directors, penned a lukewarm review in the *Baltimore Afro-American.* She welcomed Woofter's finding that black migration was driven by more than economic considerations and his elaboration of the underfunding of black education, but concluded, "While the book is an admirable compendium of facts, it is nevertheless disappointing. What one wants to know is the way out of these conditions, and Mr. Woofter offers, as his title suggests, interracial cooperation. But he tells us very little about it."[81]

The most enthusiastic African American reviewer was W. E. B. Du Bois, who discussed *The Basis of Racial Adjustment* in the *Crisis* magazine. He had digested scores of disquisitions on race since the 1880s and expected to be unimpressed this time, especially in view of Woofter's origins, but he was agreeably shaken. He judged that it was

> far and away the best thing on the relations of the races in the South, that has come from a Southern white writer in our day. It is singularly fair and thoughtful; so eminently fair indeed, that after glancing at the first pages and noting the catholicity of treatment I was compelled to go through the rest of the book with a fine-tooth comb to find the lurking surrender to Southern race hate. I did not find it. . . . I know of no book by a Southern white man with which I so thoroughly and heartily agree.[82]

He reproduced approvingly several of Woofter's remarks on taxation, racial difference, and the vote. Either Du Bois had not read the book as carefully as he claimed, or he was holding out an olive branch to the interracial cooperation movement—and certainly Will Alexander was grateful for the positive comments in the *Crisis*.[83] Normally, Du Bois would have scoffed at Woofter's veneration of "cooperative" black leaders such as Moton and his demonization of "the agitating type of leader." He would also have been repelled by the positive slant Woofter gave to segregation, but what appealed to him was the sight of a young white southerner attacking the denial to African Americans of constitutional rights, proper health care, equal education, and economic opportunity, and Woofter's loud condemnation of mob violence. Having advised others strongly against interracial marriage himself (although agreeing that people had a right to do it), perhaps Du Bois overlooked Woofter's aversion to it.[84]

Du Bois had become increasingly interested in the interracial cooperation movement since the formation of the CIC, remarking in April 1921 that the interracial committees in Louisiana, Tennessee, and Kentucky were "the most forward and promising steps which the South has yet taken." The following month, he claimed the CIC was a response to the black radicalism generated by the NAACP: "The Inter-racial movement sprang from the fight we have made." He also had some barbed advice for "our Inter-racial friends—do not fill your committees with 'pussy footers' like Robert Moton or 'white-folks' niggers' like Isaac Fisher. Get more real black men who dare to look you in the eye and speak the truth and who refuse to fawn and lie. . . . Do something. Do not dodge and duck." He seemed to be hinting at the promise of the CIC later that year, when discussing desegregated schooling: "In some parts of the land . . . racial feeling is so strong that it would be impossible to carry on schools of this sort. But the community suffers from this and must, if it will keep down riot and race hatred, substitute other bonds of social sympathy to take the place of public school common training." He welcomed other expressions of southern white liberalism, such as Robert T. Kerlin's appearance at the 12th Annual Conference of the NAACP in Detroit, in June 1921. Kerlin, a Missouri-born professor of English, who published a compilation of assertive black writings in 1920 entitled *The Voice of the Negro*, was under threat of dismissal from Virginia Military Institute at Lexington for protesting to the governor of Arkansas about death sentences passed on black sharecroppers after the riot at Elaine in 1919. In a speech that Du Bois described as "in many respects, epoch-making," Kerlin warned that his fellow white Americans were "a dangerously uninformed and misinformed people on the Negro." Two months later, he was sacked.[85]

Du Bois was thus intrigued by southern white liberals and the risks they took, but he reserved judgment in the first half of the 1920s because he doubted their efficacy and sincerity. As he wrote in *Nation* in January 1925, he knew that the "determined group called 'inter-racial'" faced a conservative "politico-economic alliance . . . like a rock wall in the path of real reform," but he wondered how much white liberals really wanted the South to change.

> Most of them would mean by this the stopping of lynching and mobbing, decent wages, abolition of personal insult based on color. Most of them would not think of demanding the ballot for blacks or the abolition of Jim Crow cars or civil rights in parks, libraries, and theaters or the right of a man to invite his black friend to dinner. Some there are who in their souls would dare all this, but they may not whisper it aloud—it would spoil everything; it would end their crusade. Few of these reformers yet fully envisage the economic nexus, the real enemy encased in enormous profit. They think reform will come by right thinking, by religion, by higher culture, and do not realize that none of these will work its end effectively as long as it pays to exalt and maintain race prejudice.[86]

This kind of skepticism had drawn a rebuke from one of the CIC's leading black activists, James Bond, in February 1925. Now, just a few months later, *The Basis of Racial Adjustment* seemed to have changed Du Bois's opinion. He was so impressed that in October 1925 he invited Woofter to write a short piece for the *Crisis* "on the attitude of the younger generation of educated Southerners toward the younger generation of educated Negroes." He went on: "I would leave the phrasing of the subject and the treatment of it entirely to you but I have watched with interest evidences[,] culminating in your new book, of a change in the traditional attitude of the white South toward Negroes of education and ambition and would be glad to have a white Southerner indicate this change, in the pages of this magazine." He enclosed the issue of the *Crisis* containing his review and sent the letter to Ginn and Company in New York, although the NAACP had Woofter's office address in Atlanta.[87] Woofter may not have received the letter; at any rate, he did not reply, even though it was the sort of invitation he would normally have accepted. If he did receive it, he may have felt resentment toward Du Bois for his pitying portrayal of white Georgian liberals in the *Nation,* or he may have feared that penning an article for the *Crisis* would pose too great a risk to the reputation of the CIC in the South. This was one of the rare occasions in this period when Du Bois went out of his way to engage with white southern liberalism, and the ensuing silence may have irked him and help explain why Du Bois soon displayed a very different attitude toward Woofter, the CIC, and its Tuskegee-leaning black support.

Other African American reviewers of the *The Basis of Racial Adjustment* were more measured than Du Bois, and perhaps more percipient. Carter G. Woodson, in the *Journal of Negro History*, was disappointed by Woofter's failure to challenge segregation and by what this said about the CIC. He thought Woofter's book had "the merit of bringing together interesting information in handy form [but it was] worked out on the basis of opinion rather than of science."[88] In *Opportunity*, the monthly magazine of the National Urban League (NUL), Eugene Kinckle Jones called *The Basis of Racial Adjustment* "one of the most liberal books by a Southern white man. . . . But residing in Georgia, and in a professional way meeting almost daily the problems which he describes, one would naturally expect him to fail in his effort to treat the *whole* subject objectively." He found Woofter weak on black health and the work of organizations like the NAACP and the NUL, and regretted Woofter's strictures against excessive social contact.[89]

These differences of opinion about *The Basis of Racial Adjustment*, in which reviewers divided largely on racial lines, partly reflected the fact that where Woofter and other white sociologists failed most obviously was in their interactions with black academics and activists. Outside of the University of Chicago, where Charles S. Johnson developed his career, collaborations between black and white sociologists were virtually nonexistent, and this showed in the unthinking way in which white writers pitched their ideas to white-only readerships. The increasing numbers of white specialists on "the Negro problem" in the late 1920s were employed by exclusively white institutions, or occupied influential positions in white-dominated philanthropic bodies. White and black writers occasionally engaged in discussion in forums led by the CIC, or the Federal Council of Churches, or at the annual social science conference at Dartmouth College, but few lasting attempts were made to narrow the racial divide in academic endeavor. Thus, an all-white team of knowledgeable specialists in racial matters could coalesce under Howard Odum at the University of North Carolina, while African American scholars such as E. Franklin Frazier and Gordon B. Hancock were confined to colleges with all-black student bodies, such as Morehouse, Fisk, and Virginia Union. The rigid norms of segregation prevented black scholars from teaching white students, especially female students, or instructing white secretarial staff, so their chances of an appointment to a wealthy southern school were nil.[90]

The distance maintained by white social scientists from their black counterparts is exemplified by Frank H. Hankins, the book review editor of *Social Forces*, asking Howard Odum, "Would it be O.K. to have Frazier—Director Atlanta School of Social Work—review Woofter's Basis of Racial Adjustment? Have you any objection to reviews by negroes? There have been several times this question has come to mind but I have always found some one else." (Hankins supervised Frazier's dissertation at Clark University.) Odum replied that he would "be very glad indeed" to print a black scholar's review, and the result drove a permanent wedge between Woofter and black academe.[91]

If Odum expected Frazier to give Woofter's book an easy ride, he was wrong. Frazier had been appointed acting director of the small Atlanta School of Social Work in 1922 and worked hard to increase its income and bring much-needed professionalism to social-work training among African Americans. He secured a substantial Rockefeller grant in 1924 and worked with a new board of trustees, including Jack Woofter and Will Alexander, to give the school a new stability. One of Frazier's white colleagues, Helen Pendleton, was the school's supervisor of fieldwork and one of its trustees—thus, both subordinate to Frazier and one of his employers; she also was a member of the CIC's Georgia state committee. A series of disputes between Frazier and Pendleton over his powers as director and treasurer meant that her request that he write a "favorable review" of *The Basis of Racial Adjustment* irritated him, but he found the book disagreeable in any case.[92]

In a covering letter with this review, Frazier remarked to Hankins, "We know that race problems are not caused by ignorance, poverty, and lack of ability on the part of the repressed group." This simple statement summed up one of Frazier's fundamental objectives—wresting an acceptance from white Americans as to their responsibility for the nation's racial history and an acknowledgment that it was *their* attitudes and failings, not those of black people, that were the causes of strife.[93] Published in the December 1925 issue of *Social Forces,* Frazier's review of *The Basis of Racial Adjustment* was a devastating lament on the inability of even the most sympathetic white southerners to go the full distance in embracing the idea of African American citizenship. It also said much about Frazier's relationship with the South, his childhood in segregated Baltimore, his work as a teacher in Alabama, Virginia, and Georgia, and his graduate study in Massachusetts, New York, and Denmark. He was pleased that the southern interracial cooperation movement had spoken through Woofter's book, "as it will indicate the position of these men and women who have never formulated a creed." He appreciated that Woofter had worked hard and shown "the coolness of scientific investigation," in a way that was "strikingly free from the usual hysteria that characterizes southern writers on the race problem." This made the book a marked improvement on W. D. Weatherford's efforts, but Frazier was depressed by Woofter's tendency to dwell on "the lower cultural level of the Negro" and his fixation with "the Negro's finding a niche in American civilization. Beneath this we see the ever present attitude of assigning a place to the Negro, instead of leaving his social function to be determined as other citizens." Frazier was effectively repeating his assertion a year earlier in the *Crisis* that "the greatest crime of the age [was] the denial of personality to the Negro." He absolved Woofter of open bias, but charged him with "too much of an attempt at rationalization of the southern position." Southern liberals seemed to expect credit for saying that discrimination was wrong, but they were willfully blind to its origins in "the refusal to recognize [the African American's] rights as a citizen." Frazier complained that liberals imagined blacks objecting to segregation because it provided poor facilities, whereas, "Most Negroes whom I know object because it stigmatizes them as unfit for human association." Frazier thought the pleasure that conservative black leaders in the South would take in *The Basis of Racial Adjustment* only proved his point:

> This book may offer consolation to a group willing to remain serfs because there are [white] men who will protect them from the grosser forms of injustice and violence, but it offers no hope to that growing number of self-respecting and intelligent Negroes who want to be treated as other people. The intelligent Negro will not accept the present arrangement as due to some "fundamental sociological principle." I do not know one intelligent young Negro who intends to stay in the South longer than to accumulate and get a start in life. . . . The ambitious Negro must go elsewhere.[94]

Frazier's review of *The Basis of Racial Adjustment* did not endear him to the interracial cooperationist nucleus in Atlanta, which had already experienced his blunt speaking style in board meetings of the School of Social Work and at a CIC Georgia state committee meeting, when he lambasted police brutality in the city. (The CIC did not closely monitor assaults on blacks by the all-white police force until the 1930s.) By the end of 1926, the trustees of the School of Social Work were after his resignation, and he began looking elsewhere, eventually securing a Rockefeller-funded scholarship at the University of Chicago, despite reservations expressed by Will Alexander and John Hope about his ability to get along with others.[95] He would probably have had to leave Atlanta, anyway, after the furor caused by an article he published in the *Forum* in 1927, entitled "The Pathology of Race Prejudice," in which he likened race prejudice to madness and suggested that white Americans were in the grip of a "Negro-complex," the most volatile element of which was sexual desire. The white newspaper editors who turned on Frazier ignored the fact that controversial passages in his article were mostly quotations from others, such as Walter Hines Page's remark that "The Negro-in-America . . . is a form of insanity that overtakes white men," and Friedrich Nietzsche's dictum that "insanity in individuals is something rare—but in groups, parties, nations, and epochs it is the rule."[96]

Frazier's review was Jack Woofter's first experience of being dismantled by a black critic, and he must have wondered whether there was an ad hominem aspect to it. He would have been wrong; Frazier disliked Woofter as a type, not an individual. The two men knew each other and worked with each other's organizations; they attended the same conferences; and, although Frazier may have resented the connections and easy life that Woofter enjoyed because of his race, church, family, and the CIC, there was no animosity in the review. Frazier already knew the shortcomings of white interracial cooperationists, and Woofter's book merely confirmed his opinion. In reviews of Woofter's other work in the late 1920s, Frazier was, if anything, even more damning of what he saw as the tendency of white liberals to report "facts" and their failure to analyze situations rigorously, but even then he did not attack Woofter personally.

The first sign that W. E. B. Du Bois's brief ardor toward interracial cooperation had cooled was a peculiar letter to CIC educational director Robert Eleazer in March 1926. Eleazer had written in the following conciliatory terms: "If it is unfortunate for white people to be cynical and pessimistic about Negroes, it seems to me unfortunate, also, for Negroes to be wholly pessimistic and cynical about white people. . . . Bad as conditions are, we feel that colored people are entitled to know that justice is not wholly dead, nor bitterness and hate wholly regnant in the hearts of white people." In reply, Du Bois avoided direct criticism of white southern liberals, but he tore into their black supporters, instead:

> Of course you will realize that our greatest objection to the Interracial Commission is the kind of Negro that you pick to go on it. Isaac Fisher represents nothing but his own blubbering self. Major Moton is a fine fellow, but weak in the presence of White folks. John Hope is an excellent representative, but he stands almost alone. Mrs. Charlotte Hawkins-Brown represents the White South and so on.
>
> Of course it is not be expected that you can have radicals and extremists upon the Commission: That in the very nature of the case stands for compromise, but you have favored too much the sort of Colored men that we call "WHITE FOLKS' NIGGERS[.]" I think[,] however, undoubtedly that we are all moving nearer understanding.[97]

Ten years later, when Du Bois invited Frazier to cooperate on an "Encyclopedia of the Negro," Frazier declined, partly because he saw black scholars being sidelined by "interracial 'politicians' or 'statesmen,' white or black. It is no task for so-called 'big Negroes' or whites because of their good-will."[98] Du Bois understood this; by the mid-1930s, he fully shared Frazier's view of the intellectual and moral limitations of interracial cooperationism, but he admitted he could see no other source of funding than the charitable boards. Woofter, however, by now an established scholar on the brink of a new career as a government social scientist, was moving on, seemingly untroubled by criticism from African Americans.

7   Northern Money and Race Studies

In march 1925, at the first National Interracial Conference in Cincinnati, Jack Woofter and Will Alexander discovered how ambivalently African Americans regarded the interracial cooperation movement. The conference was held under the auspices of the Commission on Interracial Cooperation (CIC) and the Federal Council of Churches (FCC) and organized by black economist and social gospeler George E. Haynes, who ran the FCC's Department of Race Relations. His co-chairmen were George C. Clement, an African Methodist Episcopal Zion Church bishop who led the FCC's Commission on the Church and Race Relations (CCRR), and two white clergymen, CIC chairman M. Ashby Jones and the English-born president and cofounder of the FCC, S. Parkes Cadman. Other organizations represented at Cincinnati included the YMCA and the YWCA, along with sundry churches, public health associations, fraternal organizations, and student bodies. The Russell Sage Foundation also sent several delegates, including Mary van Kleeck, the New York social reformer who directed the foundation's Department of Industrial Studies.[1]

Many of the 216 participants (114 blacks and 102 whites) at the Cincinnati conference knew each other through war work, religious committees, or social work networks. Woofter, Alexander, and Ashby Jones were accompanied by the CIC's director of publicity, Robert B. Eleazer, and David D. Jones, a young black administrator recently appointed to be CIC general field secretary. Several CIC state interracial committees were represented, as were unconnected interracial groups outside the South. No one attended from the leadership of the National Association for the Advancement of Colored People (NAACP) or the National Urban League (NUL), but the latter's southern field secretary, Jesse O. Thomas, from Atlanta, and its Philadelphia secretary, Forrester B. Washington, participated throughout the conference. The small number of academic participants included E. Franklin Frazier and John Hope from Morehouse College and the white Chicago-trained sociologist Earle E. Eubank of the University of Cincinnati. Apart from Haynes, the best-known black leader present was the Reverend W. H. Jernagin of the National Race Congress, a second-division organization based in the District of Columbia and dominated by church ministers. The black press was represented by Nettie George Speedy of the *Chicago Defender*, Chandler Owen of the socialist *Messenger* magazine, and Nahum Brascher of the Associated Negro Press.[2]

Haynes opened proceedings with a gibe at new theorists of race in the social sciences, such as Franz Boas and Melville J. Herskovits, and organizations like the NAACP (and, implicitly, the Socialist Party and the Universal Negro Improvement Association). His point was that a national profile did not bestow local relevance: "The danger now arises that communities, organizations and individuals may lose sight of the fact that the problems consist of concrete relations of the two races in industry, in education, in church, in state, in neighborhoods and in other relations of life. The danger is that such a movement may become more or less theoretical and generalized rather than practical and localized."[3]

This attitude marked one of the differences between the 1925 National Interracial Conference and the better-known 1928 National Interracial Conference held in Washington, D.C. The latter was well funded, scientific, and more representative of the different groups studying and debating racial issues across the United States, whereas the significance of the Cincinnati conference lay partly in showing that an interracial cooperation movement existed and that it went beyond southern initiatives. The Cincinnati proceedings were captured in verbatim records of each session, in which personal testimony was as prevalent as research data. Religion and the "Golden Rule" were much in evidence during sessions on constitutional rights, integration, and equality. The conference showed how interracial leadership varied according to region, with whites to the fore in southern delegations and blacks speaking for northern groups. When northerners issued blanket denunciations of all racial differentiation in hospitals and YMCA facilities, southern black delegates responded that since separate services were all they could get in the South the key was not to decry them, but to make them as good as possible. Lynching was hardly mentioned, perhaps because any discussion would have opened up splits between different camps on the still-raw subject of federal legislation.

The critical division at the conference arose between those who prioritized improving the physical conditions in which black people lived and those who saw the primary challenge as removing race prejudice. The first group argued that slums and slum lifestyles caused prejudice and that urban reform could solve many problems at once; the second group, led by Frazier, saw all the material problems originating from the entrenched attitudes of white people, which, if left unchanged, would undo any other progress. The conference's overall conclusion, written up by Eubank, favored the former approach. He wrote that "racial antagonism arises fundamentally from social conditions, and that as such it is remediable through changes in those conditions, which will lead to revised social attitudes." This was not a consensus view, although most of the speakers at the conference adopted this missionary, Social Gospel mode, asserting that manifestations of inequality such as poor housing and unemployment were the most urgent problems, and that their improvement would bring concord. Frazier plainly found this aspect of the Cincinnati conference frustrating, telling the delegates that little would change until white prejudice was confronted in thought and deed. (To illustrate this, he said he was almost thrown out of a Pullman car coming from Atlanta to Cincinnati and anticipated further problems on the return.) Frazier's outlook was supported, after a fashion, by the white sociologist Herbert A. Miller of Ohio State University, who put his faith in a combination of "scientific facts" and "religious motive." He stated, "The race problem is the product of attitudes.... Modern science is now able to take away all the basis for prejudice, and sooner or later when its data have seeped into the popular mind practically all the attitudes which now prevail in race prejudices will be so contrary to common knowledge that one will have to advertise himself as a fool if he holds them."[4] The subsequent discussion revolved around tackling racism head-on through education, an idea that featured in the final resolutions of the conference.

Delegates cheered progress regarding medical care in the North, but Frazier, always quick to puncture misplaced optimism, tilted the session toward the inadequacy of segregated medicine in the South, especially in Georgia. He demanded that speakers confront segregation, until other young black participants began to support him. Forrester B. Washington agreed segregation was the fundamental problem and that it produced "a vicious circle" of bad housing, low pay, and separate care facilities: "Personally, I would be willing to put up with a little ill health for a while if it meant stamping out the symbols of segregation which over the long period are the cause of the special difficulties of the Negro." David D. Jones of the CIC, recalling his experiences in St. Louis and Atlanta, stated that black patients preferred the way black doctors and nurses behaved toward them—"They get better service; they are treated as human beings; they are not made to feel that they are the scum of the earth"—but he warned against the assumption that this meant they liked segregation itself. Dr Charles V. Roman of Meharry Medical College in Nashville, the leading center for the training of black physicians, gently reminded delegates that white people in the North were not necessarily nicer: "What [whites] do in Nashville by direct force, they do in Boston by innuendo." High black mortality rates were blamed on ignorance, migration, racism, insufficient cooperation, and insufficient "Negro aggressiveness in demanding their share of attention." The latter point was included at Frazier's insistence, although he knew it would annoy interracial cooperationists. As the historian John T. Kneebone has remarked, "Southern liberals had no place for black pressure groups or protest."[5]

The housing discussion showed the value of black loan associations and the shortage of properly maintained accommodation at fair rents in northern cities. Frazier pointed to the problem of opportunist landlords, intent on cramming in masses of poor black tenants. Jewish slum landlords were specifically criticized and equally vigorously defended. When a white speaker wondered why blacks wanted to move out of their areas and associate with white people, she was told firmly that the urge was for better housing, not better neighbors: "That is Americanism, and the Negro is seeking and looking for it." With regard to the South, A.M.E.Z. Church bishop William J. Walls of Charlotte, North Carolina, observed three kinds of segregation: "involuntary segregation," like the laws trapping blacks in Charlotte in a ghetto; "accepted segregation," as in Winston-Salem, where the courts allowed blacks to move, but "a system of great cooperation" meant they avoided certain areas; and "voluntary segregation," as in historically black districts of Durham, where extensive housing improvements by bodies such as the North Carolina Mutual Life Insurance Company meant that blacks had no wish to live outside their areas.[6]

Jack Woofter ran the session on welfare agencies and race with Mary van Kleeck. He gave a woolly introduction about social work having relevance to the whole community, not just the "race problem," before Frazier pulled the discussion into focus. This was his specialism, and he drove home the need for more black social workers in the South, chosen by black people. If whites appointed them, he argued, they would just pick the sort of black people they knew, citing a judge who made his chauffeur a probation officer. He described his own institution, the Atlanta School of Social Work, as "an achievement on the part of colored and white people in the schools and social agencies and the interracial commission." He commented that the CIC's local committees would benefit from "the technical knowledge which is given in schools of social work" and chivvied Woofter's subcommittee into calling for equal pay for qualified black and white social workers and black representation on the boards of welfare agencies.[7]

In the session on churches, George E. Haynes tried to present race and religion as inseparable, "because we need the dynamic which Christianity gives [us] to deal with such problems." The discussion turned, however, on world affairs. Delegates fresh from the Foreign Missions Convention in Washington, D.C., were convinced that race was "the great battle point of the Christian forces throughout the world," while others were captivated by Mohandas K. Gandhi's "interpretation of life [which was] so interesting, so complete, so unusual."[8]

The longest debate centered on industry, and particularly the nexus between skilled labor, unions, and black migrant workers. Questions of equal pay, women wage-earners, the effects of war, displacement of immigrant labor, and education for black workers related almost exclusively to northern industry and conflict resolution. The only southern operation discussed was the cast-iron plant at Birmingham, Alabama, bequeathed by the CIC's late chairman, John J. Eagan, to its mixed-race workforce, who labored on an integrated factory floor.[9] The session was chaired by the veteran Bishop C. H. Phillips of the Colored Methodist Episcopal Church in Cleveland. Born a slave in Jasper County, Georgia, he held three degrees, including one in medicine. He had worked all over the United States and abroad and was attempting to unite the black Methodist denominations. He was encouraged by equal rights activism, but he warned those present, including many students, that progress would be slow.

> It is going to take years, many years, to solve the problems which we are now studying. They will not be solved in my day, and, may I further add, they will not be solved in your day. You will never live to see the Negro given all the rights and privileges of this country which a white man enjoys. Personally, I never wished that I was a white man . . . [and think] we ought to have a movement of larger sympathy for the white man. I sympathize with him. I am sorry for him. I was once a slave. It is mighty hard for him to look upon me as his equal. . . . Race prejudice is one of the worst perils we have to contend with, and . . . there can be no peace for this country until prejudice is abolished.[10]

On law enforcement and the courts, there was agreement that when a white person's interests or testimony conflicted with those of a black person justice was nigh impossible. Frazier said bluntly that if he were arrested in the South he would have no qualms about putting up bond money and absconding, "and that would not be a racial characteristic but the easiest way out of the situation." Other delegates insisted the behavior of southern courts was a consequence of black disfranchisement, noting that treatment in Chicago's courts began to improve with the appointment of black officials, itself a product of the right to vote. The CIC was asked to make special efforts "to create a public sentiment in favor of giving the Negro his constitutional right [to vote] wherever it is denied him"—an idea that the commission failed to follow up, although individually its leaders agreed with it.[11]

In the education debate, John Hope pinned his hopes on the future behavior of young black and white people, now that the interracial cooperation movement made it possible for them to meet: "I say we do now have an interracial relationship that has not before come to pass in this country." What was needed was "downright honesty in thinking." The conference agreed that increasing "interracial contact and first-hand knowledge of each other" through schools was essential. Will Alexander also alluded to this, celebrating the "growing number of courageous [southern] people who are determined that . . . justice shall be done to all citizens, regardless of race or color [and who were] . . . trying to experiment in changing the racial attitudes of individuals, organizations, and communities." He cited Woofter's findings on the lack of social science teaching in southern colleges and widespread ignorance about the origins of racial injustice: "It is very easy to say that prejudice and meanness are responsible for it, and yet, we need to get closer to the economic, political, and social facts." Alexander was an optimist, but he was still baffled by the problem of converting goodwill and empathy into action: "The majority of Americans are capable of tolerance and can be made to believe and support justice. What we need is a method by which this can be done, and there is very much more value in experimenting for the discovery of such methods than in denouncing racial intolerance and injustice." As usual, Alexander's points were made without rancor, but he was laying a clear dividing line between his approach and that of black radicals. He rejected Frazier's approach of direct criticism, insisting that "patient study" held out more promise than "moral heroics"—precisely the kind of southern liberal comment that exasperated black scholars and activists and would eventually lead them to turn on researchers such as Woofter. So far as Frazier was concerned, "denouncing racial intolerance and injustice" was an essential starting point.[12]

At key points in the conference, the differences between the worlds inhabited by the black and the white participants and the ways in which they addressed key problems were brought into sharp relief. While Woofter, Alexander, van Kleeck, and Eubank talked about the need for more research, Frazier, Hope, Washington, and Jones described events they had experienced or knew about. The effect was surreal—one group at the conference, enjoying huge economic advantage and political privilege, behaved as if it possessed a heightened awareness and expertise concerning the other group's plight; the second group, with daily experience of the actuality, was forced to interject to demonstrate the underlying problem. The white participants presumed to stand up and tell black participants to wait until a way could be found to make society nicer; it was a frustrating encounter that revealed the nature of interracial cooperation in 1925.

The National Interracial Conference finally resolved that in all walks of life opportunities for interracial contacts should be maximized, that black people should be positively presented in the curriculum and in the press, and that all Americans, everywhere, should enjoy justice in the courts and the right to vote. Under the heading "Local Communities," the conference demanded that "compulsory segregation of Negroes be abolished."[13] Woofter, Alexander, Eleazer, and the other white supporters of the CIC were comfortable with all of these conclusions, except the last. From E. Franklin Frazier's point of view, the conference was a small victory, in which the foot-dragging tendency of the CIC was exposed and certain basic democratic principles were embraced.

* * *

Jack Woofter gained a new research assignment from the interracial conference that owed much to the CIC's close associations with Methodism and the YMCA. Alexander announced at Cincinnati that the CIC would assist a nationwide "dispassionate and scientific" study of housing and segregation—a task "for high social engineers, as well as moral crusaders." This developed into a major project under Woofter's direction, entitled "Studies of Negro Contacts in Cities," paid for by the New York–based Institute of Social and Religious Research (ISRR), an organization personally supported by John D. Rockefeller Jr. and led by the Methodist missionary and YMCA administrator John R. Mott. During World War I,

Mott recruited Alexander to run YMCA facilities in southern training camps, and later he authorized the first of a series of large-scale donations to the CIC. Between 1921 and 1934, the ISRR commissioned forty-eight research projects, resulting in seventy-eight books, including Robert and Helen Lynd's "small city study" of Muncie, Indiana (although the ISRR disliked the detached style of the completed work, *Middletown*). Woofter's new project produced another widely cited book, *Negro Problems in Cities*, in 1928, after he had left the CIC.[14]

Will Alexander promised that the research for *Negro Problems in Cities* would be "exhaustive and trustworthy" and that the final study would "probably prove to be the most important study of Negro conditions that has yet been made."[15] From September 1925 to June 1926, Woofter was scarcely in Atlanta as he moved from one city-center hotel to another, doing fieldwork, followed by months of writing and editing in New York. For the whole of Woofter's working life up to this time, except for his eighteen months in uniform, he was supported by philanthropic funding, but this was the first time he benefited directly from the Rockefeller millions. Between the early 1920s and the early 1930s, the administrators of several Rockefeller funds and associated agencies, including George E. Vincent, Edwin R. Embree, and Beardsley Ruml, injected huge sums into the social and biological sciences across the United States and abroad, in the hope that scientific examination of lingering problems would test hypotheses and effect change.[16] This funding produced few immediate revisions of government policy, but the preference for quantitative studies radically influenced social science research methods and led numerous economists and rural sociologists to seek further training in statistical analysis. There was a decisive move away from the older style of social surveys, such as Woofter's graduate work in Athens as a Phelps-Stokes Fund fellow. The sociologist Stephen P. Turner, calling this an "ideological struggle for quantification," notes the emergence of a new academic elite favored by the Rockefeller-funded Social Science Research Council (SSRC), set up in 1923, and typified by the work of the Columbia-trained sociologist William F. Ogburn at the University of Chicago.[17] In putting together *Negro Problems in Cities*, Jack Woofter demonstrated his academic promise to this select group, although the structure of the final work made it an uneven hybrid between a reforming social survey and an objective sociological study.

Woofter's replacement as CIC research director, Clark Foreman, had previously succeeded him as secretary of the Georgia State Committee on Race Relations. A well-connected young white Atlantan, whose views on race were rocked by watching the lynching of John Lee Eberhart near Athens in 1921, Foreman was a great networker and motivator, but he was restless and disliked living in Georgia.[18] As Alexander put it, "He turned out to be essentially a man of action. He wouldn't do the kind of research I wanted." In 1927, after three years with the CIC, Foreman left to work with Thomas Jesse Jones at the Phelps-Stokes Fund in Washington and New York, while studying part time at Columbia University. He later moved to the Rosenwald Fund, where Edwin Rogers Embree gave him paid leave to become Harold Ickes's special adviser on race in the Department of the Interior. To replace Foreman at the CIC, Alexander hired one of Howard W. Odum's brightest students at Chapel Hill, the rural sociologist Arthur F. Raper, initially as Georgia secretary and then as director of research.[19] These changes of personnel perpetuated the lily-white nature of the CIC central office. A few of the state secretaries were black, but following the departure in 1926 of the commission's field secretary, David Jones, to take up a college principalship, all the central staff members were white. Black activists, including NUL executive secretary Eugene Kinckle Jones, thought an avowedly interracial organization with an all-white staff was absurd, and Alexander was sensitive to the mounting criticism. He repeatedly claimed to be "seeking a colored man" to work with, but by 1930 he had still not appointed one.[20]

Jack Woofter was beginning to be perceived as a researcher on national race relations problems, rather than a southern interracial cooperation movement activist. In 1925, when the Social Science Research Council's Committee on Problems and Policy appointed an advisory committee on "Problems Relating to the Negro" (later amended to "Inter-Racial Relations"), Woofter was invited to be one of its all-white membership under the chairmanship of Columbia University's Frank Ross. Unlike Woofter, the others present at the first meeting in May 1926 all held academic jobs: Clark Wissler (at Yale), Robert Ezra Park (Chicago), Melville Herskovits (Columbia), and Sterling Spero (New School for Social Research). When Will Alexander became chairman of the advisory committee, he retained Woofter and, at Howard Odum's suggestion, added three black members: Charles S. Johnson, Carter G. Woodson, and Monroe N. Work.[21] As if to emphasize his readiness to move on from the CIC, when Woofter joined the American Statistical Association early in 1927 he described himself as "Research Secretary, Institute of Social and Religious Research, 370 Seventh Avenue, New York, N.Y." He was soon negotiating a move to a university department.[22]

Negro Problems in Cities was based on investigations in sixteen cities—seven in the North and nine in the South—and data provided on a further six cities by other agencies, including the NUL. By choosing big, fluid communities in the North and established communities in the South, Woofter engineered a theme of northern turmoil and southern stability. He wrote the first one hundred pages on "Neighborhoods," while his collaborators covered "Housing," "Schools," and "Recreation." Madge Headley, the white author who wrote the housing chapters, had worked on other northern urban studies, including *The Negro in Chicago* for the Chicago Commission on Race Relations. (She and Woofter cowrote a short preparatory study concerning Philadelphia, on which *Negro Problems in Cities* was modeled.)[23] The education section was undertaken by William Andrew

Daniel, a black sociologist from Atlanta, whose doctoral dissertation at the University of Chicago was published by the ISRR as *The Education of Negro Ministers* (1925) and in 1926 won one of the first Harmon Prizes for distinguished achievement by an African American. The final part of *Negro Problems in Cities,* on recreation, was entrusted to another black scholar, Henry Jared McGuinn, the holder of a PhD from Columbia University who taught social science at Virginia Union University for over fifty years.

African American migration, during and after World War I, was one of the most remarkable voluntary movements in the industrial era, and yet its effects had not been well studied by the mid-1920s. Apart from a handful of immediate postwar studies, including the Chicago Commission report and Woofter's own PhD dissertation, the *Negro Problems in Cities* study was the first extended examination of the rise in the black urban population from 750,000 in 1870 to 4 million by 1925. The migration was discussed in polemical works on racial tension, such as Herbert Seligmann's *The Negro Faces America* (1920), and its local effects were considered in the work of Abraham Epstein on Pittsburgh (1917) and George E. Haynes on Detroit (1918), while social scientists had begun to ask in short discussions what the migration might mean nationally, but there was no attempt before Woofter's to analyze large accumulations of multiregional data. Edward B. Reuter's study of black life in America in 1927 relied on material collected by others and devoted little space to migration and the city. In the same year, Charles H. Wesley published *Negro Labor in the United States,* but it was largely concerned with industrial problems and the labor movement. Alma Herbst's study of black women workers in Chicago was under way, but would not appear until 1932, amid a wave of new studies from several disciplines in the early years of the Great Depression. Thus, *Negro Problems in Cities* stood out, both as a source of information and as a summary of municipal responsibilities; hence the heavy reliance on it by commentators in the late 1920s and the 1930s and by post–World War II scholars, despite the book's uneven quality.

The chief weakness in *Negro Problems in Cities* was Woofter's selection of sixteen cities. He attempted too much in the time available and provided insufficient depth on any one problem or place. His own "Neighborhoods" section contained two maps for each of the sixteen cities, giving the location and size of the black districts before and after 1920, highlighting the concentration of northern black communities in tightly defined areas (with the exception of Philadelphia), while blacks in southern cities lived in scattered pockets (with the exception of Winston-Salem). According to Woofter, African Americans after 1910 and Mexicans in the late 1920s were repeating the urban experience of European immigrants: "Since the Negro city population is relatively new, it is now possible to see this process of migration, segregation, concentration, neglect, self-improvement, and amelioration at work." Woofter expected the movement of two million rural folk into cities to produce "profound cultural change and . . . multiple readjustments," but the actual outcome would depend on connections that emerged between different groups "when the newcomers settle into more or less solid racial colonies."[24] He was offering a starting point—"a summation of some of the most obvious interactions between the city and the incoming colored citizens"—and asking whether city governments were meeting the migrants' needs. He focused on housing, education, and recreation, but was aware that other areas needed detailed examination.[25]

Woofter dealt succinctly with the scale, distribution, and rate of black movement, noting instances of tension, but gave little attention to the motives of the migrants or the prejudices that constrained their residential distribution. Urban historian Stephen Grant Meyer charges Woofter with using the "rhetoric of invasion" to describe the movement of black residents into new areas. Woofter wrote, "The advance is somewhat like that of an army. A small outpost is thrown out ahead, and, if the terrain is favorable for occupancy by larger numbers, the mass advances." However, this was a brief, unrepresentative comment on the process by which black families spread into formerly Jewish and Italian districts.[26] His treatment of rioting was perfunctory: "Each city has one attack and afterwards seems to be immune[;] . . . the [Chicago] riot seemed to clear the atmosphere and bring about the realization that the rapid expansion of Negro population makes the expansion of residence areas inevitable." He showed that urban segregation ordinances could effectively persist, despite a 1917 federal court judgment against them, and that aggressive white residents' associations were multiplying, although they usually failed to prevent black settlement in new districts. A bigger problem was the failure of cities to maintain the infrastructure of streets newly occupied by black families. In this regard, Woofter noted with apparent approval that in Dallas and Winston-Salem, where black residents agreed to remain in certain areas, the cities undertook improvements.[27] The chief problem he associated with segregated city life was overcrowding and exploitative rents, especially in the larger cities, and the consequent increases in tuberculosis and pneumonia. Woofter wrote, "This fondness of the Babbitts for speculative profits in land has created cesspools in the midst of American cities." The problems of overcrowding were intensified by the taking in of lodgers, which Woofter saw as a cause of high levels of illegitimate births.[28]

He found migrants' expectations in northern cities differed from those who left rural life for southern cities; the latter just wanted more money, whereas the typical migrant to a northern city was more adventurous and sought a better quality of life that lay in "wider experiences, and in the opportunities that lessen hardship. Migration to the North has been impelled in part by the desire for these contacts, experiences and opportunities, especially for the children of the family." He drew sharp contrasts between the worst slums, where shiftless blacks endured foul housing and vice, and the better districts, to which "good" or "ambitious" families moved, especially if they could afford to buy a house. This contrast was found in both the North and the South: he found the "bungaloos" of Gary, Indiana, and the hovels of "Wild Cat Chute" in Indianapolis as unpleasant as the alley houses of Louisville, Kentucky, where "satisfied or ignorant families live in houses not fit for work animals [and] children are familiar with vice before they start to school. . . . No child who lives in such an environment has any decent chance, and the adults are beyond redemption." He urged municipal action on tenancy laws, schools, paving, sewerage, and lighting to eliminate slums and to prevent "these civic ulcers from poisoning the whole city." His understated point was that racial tension in cities derived from the restlessness of black residents who were "determined to progress" and their search for better housing. Woofter argued, essentially, that cities could reduce racial conflict and stabilize existing black districts by improving them enough to make black migrants stay in one place. He plainly regarded the existence of more or less exclusively black districts within cities as normal and to be expected, just as residential integration did not occur to him as viable or desirable.[29]

In her chapters on housing, Madge Headley summarized the information on separate survey cards for twelve thousand homes, showing that migrants' dwellings were often defective, small, and ill-equipped, especially when rented. Local groups, such as the YMCA and state interracial committees, assisted her by canvassing black districts. She found the shortage of accommodation made renting expensive relative to average earnings and that obtaining a mortgage was difficult. She doubted whether many migrants understood the implications of buying a home, but real estate dealers reported that they were no more likely to default than any other group.[30] Local charitable organizations, black community associations, and model homes projects provided practical advice, repairs, and health care, but such assistance could not match the growth in population. The basic problem was lax application of zoning ordinances, sanitation standards, and building codes, which she attributed to the "racial prejudices and slave-holding psychology . . . inherent in the treatment accorded to an emergent race."[31]

The most effective section of *Negro Problems in Cities,* in terms of addressing problems, was W. A. Daniel's education study. He observed northern school systems under sudden pressure, less from the actual number of migrant children than from the indifferent education they had received in the South. School principals looked for opportunities to suspend migrant children for minor infringements and move them on elsewhere, because their attendance was erratic due to a lack of suitable clothing, poor communication between families and schools, frequent changes of address, and the long hours parents worked to afford high rents. Daniel revealed a process of deliberate educational segregation in the North, springing from schools' policies and white parents' negative reactions to the influx of black children. Several cities, including Philadelphia, Gary, Indianapolis, and Dayton, made separate provision for black pupils (in the case of Dayton, through segregated classes for supposedly "retarded pupils"). In Indianapolis, the separateness policy led to construction of a large black high school in 1927, and Gary followed suit after a white students' strike at Emerson High School.[32] Criticizing "the main fallacy of separating races on the basis of [individual intelligence] tests," Daniel pointed to improving test scores by migrant children in the North. He found that a minority of black parents favored segregated schools, even in the North, believing that their children would be more motivated and that black teachers would have better opportunities, but most parents objected strongly to separation. Their views, as summarized by Daniel, read like a catechism of the future civil rights movement:

> 1. "Separate but equal accommodations" is a fiction. Nowhere has segregation inspired the Negro with the hope of a square deal.
> 2. Segregation is, and is intended to be, symbolic of the Negro's unfitness to associate with white people on the assumption that he belongs to a lower order of beings.
> 3. One form of segregation hastens the adoption of other forms.
> 4. If Negroes and whites are to live together satisfactorily in America, the public schools should not neglect this phase of their avowed purpose to train children for future citizenship.
> 5. Segregation increases the distances children have to travel to school, in some cases making it necessary for them to pay carfare, and in some cases subjecting them to dangers and delays in crossing streets with heavy traffic.[33]

In southern cities, schooling for black children was improving, but, Daniel noted, "Negro schools are a secondary consideration" and the racial divide persisted in funding, although the gap was narrower than in rural counties. Several cities, such as Atlanta, Richmond, Lexington, and Lynchburg, had provided modern black high schools in the 1920s, although they were all too small. Across the South, black urban schools made do with temporary structures and annexes, poor sanitation, and inferior equipment, while the cities enforced few standards for buildings, room sizes, record keeping, or teachers' pay and qualifications. Daniel also found that, given a choice, newly urban black parents and youngsters rejected industrial education. He drew this conclusion, paradoxically, from Indianapolis, "where [segregated] conditions more nearly approach those of a southern city than do the conditions of any other northern city included in this study." Black high school pupils in Indianapolis could choose their own curriculum and showed "a noticeable avoidance of the industrial subjects." The most popular subjects were English, mathematics, history, Latin, modern languages, science, and music; the least popular were domestic science, mechanical drawing, auto repair, and "general shop."[34]

In some respects, W. A. Daniel's voice in *Negro Problems in Cities* revealed the divergent discourse of interracial cooperation in the 1920s, in which black contributors tried to promote a meaningful reform agenda alongside more conservative white collaborators, such as Woofter and Headley. Just as Isaac Fisher, in *Cooperation in Southern Communities* in 1921, had dissented from Woofter's mild tone, the logic of Daniel's findings and the way he expressed them pointed in a different direction from that preferred by Woofter, whose approach to education and segregation still bore the hallmarks of the racist social science of Thomas Jesse Jones and Franklin H. Giddings.

Negro Problems in Cities concluded with Henry J. McGuinn's prudish examination of urban recreation. The inclusion of a section on recreation played well with Rockefeller fund administrators, who strongly supported the playground movement, and especially the Playground and Recreation Association of America. Tension arising from a lack of recreation facilities in northern cities was seen as a major problem in race relations following mass migration. However, Woofter should have taken a much firmer editorial approach with this section. McGuinn presented several nuggets of valuable information, but his anecdotal approach and dependence on the views of white social workers and court officials contrasted sharply with the methods of the other authors. Causes he advanced for "the excessive delinquency among Negro children," included broken homes, low incomes, "western pictures and crude vaudeville," and a lack of familiarity with "the traditions of Puritan morality which we have known for three hundred years." Despite such meanderings, McGuinn presented a picture of an urbanizing nation that excluded African Americans from opportunities for relaxation and personal growth that other groups took for granted. Separate, substandard, and poorly policed city parks for blacks were found throughout the South, but some northern cities were just as discriminatory. City beaches in Buffalo, Chicago, and Gary were segregated, while in Dayton blacks were limited to certain days for use of tennis courts and dance pavilions. Four large cities—Indianapolis, Louisville, New Orleans, and Atlanta—built separate swimming pools for blacks, while in Gary separate access was provided on two evenings per week. Access to children's playgrounds was restricted in many cities, and play leaders were in short supply. In the South, public library facilities were either separate or, more commonly, nonexistent for African Americans. The YMCA and YWCA attempted to meet the needs of young black city-dwellers, but almost all branches suffered from a lack of space, equipment, and funds. Small numbers of northern black boys joined the Boy Scouts, but scoutmasters blocked the raising of black scout troops in the South, and the only comparable work was sporadic provision of boys' clubs by charities and recreation programs run by churches.[35]

Segregation discouraged black adults from attending theaters, even in the North, and McGuinn described the mixture of blatant and subtle devices by which managers separated audiences. He regarded all-black theaters as inept and vulgar, and denounced dance halls and poolrooms in wide-eyed detail as scenes of drinking, fighting, and lewdness. He knew an "investigation of white dives would probably reveal conditions as shocking," but at least whites had a choice, whereas the restricted entertainment open to law-abiding blacks often forced them to frequent "dens of vice and crime."[36]

The reviews of *Negro Problems in Cities* split along racial lines; white readers generally applauded it and blacks condemned it. The white theologian Samuel C. Kincheloe called the book "one of the most significant books on Negro problems since the publication of *The Negro in Chicago* in 1922."[37] In the *Journal of Educational Sociology*, the anthropologist E. E. Muntz, who studied damaging effects of European contacts on "inferior cultures," welcomed the book as an antidote to the Carl Van Vechten school of Negroana. Muntz wrote: "At a time when it seems to be the fashion to depict Negro life in a halo of idealization and mysticism it is especially refreshing to chance upon such a straightforward and accurate description of the Negro's actual life conditions."[38] Another anthropologist, Melville Herskovits of Northwestern University, welcomed the book as "of great value to students of the Negro problem"—it was "a kind of continuation" of the work that W. E. B. Du Bois had done twenty years earlier in his Atlanta University studies of African American life, with "much of the detachment, careful collection of data, and sound appraisal of results which characterized that excellent series."[39] High praise indeed, but it contrasted sharply with the verdict of Herskovits's black friend and erstwhile colleague, E. Franklin Frazier, in the *American Journal of Sociology*: "Here and there we catch a sparkle of human life; but it is immediately smothered by an avalanche of for the most part meaningless statistics." Frazier saw "no excuse for a book as dull" and accused Woofter of a "monotony of vague generalities." By this time, Frazier had completed most of the research for his dissertation on the black family in Chicago and begun to publish some of his findings. He conceded that a general reader might find *Negro Problems in Cities* was "a ready reference" on the distribution of black urban populations, but it was deficient as an investigation of urban problems. Frazier was right in some respects; the book offered a selective snapshot of black urban life in the mid-1920s, rather than a close analysis of the causes of slum conditions, but Frazier ignored Woofter's admission that it was only a starting point for such work.[40] Carter G. Woodson published a terse review in the *Journal of Negro History*, stating that *Negro Problems in Cities* was "not scientific. . . . [depending on] too much hearsay and opinion" and that Woofter "undertook too much and, therefore, did not do it all well." Sociologist Ira De A. Reid in *Opportunity* agreed regarding the "limitation of breadth and possible haste that mark the entire book," but conceded that was "the only work of its sort hitherto undertaken, and should serve as an index to the potent possibilities for exacting research in the field of Negro urban neighborhoods." NAACP director of branches Robert W. Bagnall, writing in the *Nation*, found "surprisingly few inaccuracies," but considered that Woofter should have said more about industrial problems.[41]

Despite its shortcomings, *Negro Problems in Cities* remained a standard reference work for scholars for decades. It had less impact on urban studies, generally, than another book published in 1928—Louis Wirth's *The Ghetto*—but it was regularly raided for statistical information, including Woofter's fifty tables showing black urban population changes and density, mortality, tenancy, ownership, education enrolment and expenditure, mothers' occupations, and delinquency. As such, it clearly influenced academic work, charities, and, ultimately, government bodies. For example, when Charles S. Johnson prepared the report of the Committee on Negro Housing for President Herbert Hoover's conference on American housing in 1932, he relied heavily on Woofter's data and classifications.[42] In the mid-1960s, Karl and Alma Taeuber, in their study of segregation in 207 cities, acknowledged Woofter's book as "[t]he first important comparative study of residential segregation," although they thought it lacked "supporting analysis" and questioned the usefulness of Woofter's maps, compared to their own more sophisticated diagrams.[43]

Woofter was still committed to the investigation of southern problems. As he embarked on the cities project, he also tried to initiate a study of welfare work in deprived rural counties. He wanted answers to some basic questions: "What contribution to social progress is made by the agencies working for a higher standard of life among Negroes in rural districts? What results are obtained from the rural schools, farm and home demonstration agents, [and] the health agencies?" In December 1924, he gathered representatives of the agencies working among black people in a typical southern county to an interracial conference at the CIC offices in Atlanta. It was attended by Leo Favrot and Jackson Davis of the General Education Board (GEB), the Georgia Negro schools supervisor, Walter B. Hill, and the Rosenwald Fund general field agent, S. L. Smith, as well as representatives from the Georgia council of social agencies and members of the state board of health. Three black officials joined them from Tuskegee: Monroe N. Work, the institute's head of research, Thomas Monroe Campbell of the Colored Farm Demonstration Service, and G. Lake Imes of the Bible Training School. The key white participant was P. F. "Pete" Williams, the energetic county supervisor of Coahoma County, Mississippi, who was attempting to transform black lives through a building program in collaboration with S. L. Smith. Using a countywide tax especially for black education, Williams had created a new rural high school and fourteen junior high schools and replaced half of Coahoma County's seventy elementary schools with Rosenwald schools. Williams had become nationally known, and Coahoma County attracted administrators from across the South looking for ideas.[44]

Woofter's group proposed quinquennial surveys in which trained investigators would ask detailed questions about schools, health, farms, churches, and crime to track the impact of state agencies, charities, and interracial cooperation programs. They would start these dynamic county studies in Coahoma County, where the 8,000 black farmers greatly outnumbered the 800 white farmers. Local white control of the county was already changing, with ten thousand acres in the ownership of a northern syndicate headed by Stuyvesant Fish, president of the Illinois Central Railroad Company. The study would determine whether, and how quickly, Williams's new county school system improved social and economic conditions over successive years, and indicate the value of such surveys in other counties. The idea received strong support at a further conference in Memphis attended by education, health, farm demonstration, and welfare officials from Tennessee, Virginia, North Carolina, Arkansas, Mississippi, and Alabama. A three-man committee of Woofter, Leo Favrot, and C. H. Lane, chief of the Agricultural Education Service of the Federal Board for Vocational Education, petitioned the Laura Spelman Rockefeller Memorial (LSRM) and the GEB for $7,000 for the Coahoma County survey and sought a provisional commitment of $42,000 for surveys in another five counties. The LSRM was skeptical; by the mid-1920s, argues historian Alfred Perkins, the Rockefeller trustees were wary of "scatteration" of funds into unrelated projects. Although Woofter, Favrot, and local officials in Coahoma County kept pressing for support, delays in communication with the LSRM and long gaps between its board meetings prolonged the process for a year. The fund paid the expenses of the participants in the planning stages, but refused to make a greater commitment without more detail and a sense of who would manage the project, now that Woofter was heavily involved in the survey of black life in cities.[45]

Woofter hoped that Frank Ross would assume directorship of the county surveys, but his contract with Columbia University barred outside work. Ross considered doing the surveys without fully informing Columbia, but according to Woofter "his New England conscience has been having the bellyache since he received the impression that he might have to waive his university salary." In the end, the scheme was undone by Pete Williams's retirement and his successor's ambivalence, but the county surveys idea indicated Woofter's continuing determination to find out what was needed (other than the vote) to improve the quality of life for African American families in the rural South and stem migration from the land.[46]

If the proposed 1925 county surveys had gone ahead, with follow-up studies in 1930 and 1935, the rates of progress they revealed across a wide range of social indicators would have been invaluable to academics, welfare agencies, and political activists. They might have shown changes in the racial attitudes of whites and blacks between World War I and the Great Depression and shed light on the causes and effects of educational underfunding and racial violence. For example, the Coahoma County report could have analyzed local reaction to the lynching in Clarksdale in 1925 of Lindley Coleman, after a jury acquitted him on a charge of killing a plantation store manager. As a result of demands for action against the mob by leading white citizens, including an ex-governor's wife, a grand jury indicted the county sheriff, a planter, and two other white men. At their trial, the jury took twenty-seven hours, instead of the customary ten minutes, to return its first not-guilty verdict.[47] Pete Williams's work and the attempt to prosecute Coleman's killers appeared to show that monolithic white supremacy could be challenged by interracial cooperation and that the CIC's message was getting through in unlikely parts of the South. Although juries consistently acquitted white men accused of lynching, the act of getting defendants into court and reporting their names sent a clear message that they could no longer be confident of remaining "parties unknown."

In drawing up the Coahoma scheme, Woofter drew on his survey experience with Thomas Jesse Jones on the *Negro Education* report in 1913–16, his migration work for the Bureau of Labor in 1917, and the creation of the CIC's local interracial committees in 1921–24. The county survey scheme, in turn, helped to shape approaches he would apply in the 1930s in local surveys for the Tennessee Valley Authority and the assistance he gave colleagues at Chapel Hill in their surveys for the North Carolina Emergency Relief Administration.[48] The latter studies would lead to Woofter's recruitment by the Federal Emergency Relief Administration and his permanent employment with the federal government.

One of Woofter's final assignments for the CIC was an essay on the background and scope of interracial cooperation in the United States, to be presented by Will Alexander and John Hope at the International Missionary Council's Easter meeting in Jerusalem in 1928. Alexander and Hope traveled at the invitation of John R. Mott with W. B. Beauchamp, resident bishop of the North Georgia Methodist Conference, who sat on the CIC's executive committee. Alexander and Hope shared a cabin on the SS *Adriatic,* but Beauchamp avoided any contact with nonwhite people throughout the trip.[49] Woofter's task was to capture the American experience for a largely European and colonial audience and his essay was published in the International Missionary Council's report, *The Christian Mission in the Light of Race Conflict.*[50] Comparing "the situation of the Negroes in the United States and the situations of other belated peoples who are in contact with western civilization," he fell back on the old saw that "contacts" between individuals of both races were the critical variable. Using guesswork as much as anything, he argued that in India or Africa "the representatives of western culture are relatively few in number and . . . direct contact with the masses is very limited [whereas] the population ratio [in America] is almost perfectly adapted for the maximum number of contacts."[51] This vague ecologism aside, Woofter's views had clearly progressed since he wrote *The Basis of Racial Adjustment,* suggesting that he was affected by the reservations expressed by black critics such as Frazier and Eugene Kinckle Jones. His Jerusalem paper was scrutinized by a committee of Hope, Robert Russa Moton, and Thomas Jesse Jones. Having tried to reconcile their perspectives, Woofter concluded that white southerners ruled over a fundamentally unfair system. He described segregation in transport, schools, and public places such as hotels, restaurants, and theaters as illogical, unreasonable, and insulting, showing he had finally grasped that it was not the *quality* of segregated facilities that hurt.

His views on the Jim Crow system had shifted steadily since he left the University of Georgia in 1913, but he had no easy remedy for race prejudice. Middle-class white liberals such as Woofter and Alexander embarked on a moral journey to the point where they could look at segregation and discrimination and know that those things were wrong, and say why, but they were still afraid of conflict and unable to contemplate anything other than slow, peaceful change. They could look beyond Jim Crow and lynching to a time when white people were ready to grant racial equality and black people were ready to assume new roles and responsibilities; then, the South would be freed from the grip of history. But in the 1920s the idea that this might be accelerated by disobedience from below and the South forced to change by internal strife and outside pressure filled them with dread.

Woofter presented the Jerusalem conference with two views of segregation as honestly as he could and then chose to sit squarely on the fence:

> To the mind of the white man favouring segregation, separation is a symbol of the resolution to maintain racial integrity and a means of reducing racial friction. To the mind of the intelligent Negro, separation is an unnecessary degradation, a badge of inferiority. He feels that any lessening of contacts robs him of the chance to assimilate culture. On the other hand, Negroes realize that separation in schools and in churches creates opportunities for Negro preachers and teachers which otherwise would not be possible, and it enables them to gain experience in administering their own institutions which otherwise would be difficult to secure. There is little doubt that segregation, no matter how carefully worked out, usually results in discrimination against the segregated group. All in all, the problem of segregation has many angles and will probably be solved by time alone. In the last analysis it would seem that friction and dissatisfaction will arise from any form of contact or of enforced separation of the races which is not mutually agreeable to both.[52]

Woofter attributed lynching primarily to "economic jealousy" and said it was declining because of the "cultivation of a law-abiding public sentiment, and of courage and determination among law enforcement officers." He devoted special attention to interracial cooperation in religious organizations like the YMCA, but admitted that they had "not revolutionized race relations, nor have they always lived up to the hopes of their most advanced members."[53] He also detailed the aims and expenditures of the various philanthropic bodies for black education and described recent changes in black health care, farming, industrial employment, and property ownership. Referring to the unanimous Supreme Court decision in *Buchanan v. Warley* (1917), he claimed that residential segregation had been done away with, except where it was "based on social pressure and upon the cohesion of the Negroes themselves" (a more sanguine assessment than he had offered in *Negro Problems in Cities* and one that ignored practices such as the municipal zoning plan permitted in Atlanta by a 1928 amendment to the Georgia constitution).[54] He praised the NUL for its professionalism and the National Federation of Colored Women's Clubs for its "spirit of cooperation," and expressed respect for the NAACP. The latter had

> probably . . . done most towards arousing the race consciousness of the American Negro. . . . On account of its policies of agitation and protest it has naturally not made so many white friends as other more co-operative organizations and has gained the reputation of being a radical group. Though it has alienated people by these methods, it has been successful in focusing attention on conditions which need to be corrected.[55]

Attracting attention by "agitation" was one thing; getting things done was another, and here Woofter gave pride of place to the CIC. Its practical, local approach, he declared, was based on "conference and cooperation, rather than on agitation and conflict"; thus, the state committees ensured that state education, penal, and health agencies recognized black citizens' needs and white newspapers reported their achievements. Woofter was clear: "The Inter-racial Commission never loses sight of the fact that it is primarily an opinion-making body [for developing] a goodwill which is powerful in changing the racial attitudes in the mass."[56]

In the mid-1950s, as the civil rights movement increased its pace, Woofter looked back on the CIC with pride. He knew that both he and the organization had made many mistakes and that "with considerable justification" the CIC could be accused of being "not bold enough, that it was prone to implant the philosophy of cooperation without pushing for more spectacular action." However, as he recalled it, "the conscientious conviction of the members was that its modest gains would have been endangered by trying to push ahead too rapidly in the atmosphere of hostility which was encountered from formidable powers."[57] He thought universal lessons could be learned from the 1920s about the power of people of goodwill to effect change by sticking to certain beliefs. When he looked at the pressures on the southern civil rights movement of the 1950s, he was strongly reminded of the problems the CIC faced in defending its peculiar interracial principles against attacks by radical and conservative critics of both races:

> In truth nothing but altruism could then, or now, induce comfortable Southern people of either race to advocate moderation. [Reformers] cannot expect to be popular or gain any personal advantage. The rabid race haters castigate them for going too far, and from their pleasant ivory towers in the North, the starry-eyed professional sympathizers sneer at them for not going far enough. I am convinced, however, that it was a social miracle that, in the vexed crisis of the 1920's, anything at all was accomplished.[58]

By the late 1920s, state interracial committees still functioned in Kentucky, Tennessee, North Carolina, Virginia, Georgia, Alabama, and Texas, and a new one was finally founded in Florida, but the state committees had folded in Louisiana, Arkansas, Mississippi, and South Carolina. The attrition rate of the county-level interracial committees was even higher; by this time, the CIC was in direct contact with only twenty-three active committees, although Will Alexander insisted that many carried on their work without any contact with either their state committee or the Atlanta office—thus, he claimed, interracial cooperation was "becoming in many communities indigenous and spontaneous." That was wishful thinking, at best. Essentially, the fieldwork approach of the CIC had run its course, and Alexander's emphasis had shifted toward liaison with schools, colleges, and state conferences of social work. He was heartened by the response to the CIC's essay competition for high school students—269 entries on the subject of race relations were submitted by 139 white schools—but he was dismayed by the failure of the white churches to provide better leadership:

> The indifference, timidity, and lack of clear thinking on the part of the church is a discouraging feature of this work. The majority of ministers in the South exercise no influence whatever on the race situation either directly or indirectly, nor do they seem conscious that this is any part of their task. The effectiveness of certain outstanding ministers and the women's organizations of the church is an illustration of how far-reaching could be the influence of ministers, particularly in backward sections if their cooperation and interest could be secured.[59]

The white community leaders who seemed to have changed their attitudes most markedly were county sheriffs. According to Alexander, more sheriffs appreciated the importance of protecting prisoners as a result of the CIC's efforts, and they now knew they would receive public support. Between 1926 and 1928, the CIC awarded medals to more than twenty sheriffs for standing up to mobs. In Arkansas and Mississippi, the frequency of lynching appeared undiminished, but several states witnessed no lynchings in 1927. Alexander attributed this in part to the CIC's work with governors. Fewer lynchings were being attempted, more were being prevented, and when they did occur they were widely condemned; what was still needed was some successful prosecutions. In 1931, state field workers of the CIC were laid off, after a review concluded that working with churches, schools, state agencies, and the press would be more effective and cheaper than trying to organize or sustain local committees. Publicity, rather than organization, became the preferred approach.[60]

This change in direction signaled the end of a bold, passionate phase of the interracial cooperation movement. Jack Woofter had been at the forefront of the CIC's work in the rural South, entreating whites and blacks to establish interracial dialogue at a local level in the face of widespread intimidation and scorn. He had also helped to confront and expose the Klan, but in the second half of the 1920s, as the CIC concentrated on education and research, he looked for opportunities to build his own career, and that meant leaving Atlanta for good.

8 Howard Odum and the Institute for Research in Social Science

In 1913, JACK Woofter's father, T. J. Woofter Sr., gave the sociologist Howard W. Odum a much-needed job in the school of education at the University of Georgia, where he stayed until 1918, gaining a reputation as an energetic scholar and administrator. After a brief tenure at his alma mater, Emory University, Odum moved to the University of North Carolina, where he repaid the favor by hiring Jack Woofter to work in the expanding Institute for Research in Social Science (IRSS) in 1927.

Odum and the younger Woofter both believed in the social scientist's duty to secure definite facts about the "Negro problem" and accelerate the pace of change in the South, but Odum's zeal resulted from a more profound conversion than any experienced by Woofter. They were both Methodists and the grandsons of slaveholders, but came from different generations and different Georgian settings. Odum was ten years older than Woofter and was brought up about fifteen miles from Athens, in a district with strained race relations, until his father acquired a new dairy farm thirty miles to the south, near Covington, in Newton County.[1] After moving to Chapel Hill in 1920, Odum developed his vision of southern studies, but university administration initially occupied him as much as scholarship. He founded the Department of Sociology and the School of Public Welfare, began the liberal journal *Social Forces,* and fostered a collaborative research ethos. By 1927, he had edited a collection of biographical essays and coauthored three books about Negro songs and public welfare and was about to publish *Man's Quest for Social Guidance.*[2] Over the next decade, he would play a leading part in cementing sociology as an academic discipline in the South and mount a challenge to the subject's domination by the University of Chicago and Columbia University.[3]

Faced with a shortfall of state funds during the 1920s, UNC was reluctant to make a long-term commitment to regional social studies, forcing Odum to compete for donations by wealthy individuals or philanthropic bodies. He proved adept at raising money, although he found the process nerve-wracking. In 1924, the Laura Spelman Rockefeller Memorial (LSRM), an immensely rich New York charity founded in 1918 by John D. Rockefeller to commemorate his wife, gave Odum a three-year grant totaling $97,500 to create the IRSS, and a further $15,000 in 1925 specifically for research on race relations. The LSRM had noted in its social science policy in 1922, "All those who work toward the general end of social welfare are embarrassed by the lack of that knowledge which the social sciences must provide." In 1925, LSRM director Beardsley Ruml, who set up the Social Science Research Council (SSRC) in 1923 and enjoyed great discretion in the allocation of funds, indicated that race was now a priority and invited proposals by social scientists on "the problem that arises in connection with the tendency of human beings to associate (or dissociate)."[4]

Odum took heart from his first LSRM grant, but feared for the institute's long-term future. Seeking larger grants required burdensome correspondence and meetings with Ruml and other officials to satisfy them that he could deliver. They, in turn, knew that he was "apprehensive that the Memorial was going to fail the Institute" and that he worried that UNC social scientists were perceived as "too provincial; . . . [and] that their energies were too scattered and at other times that they attempted to produce too much." He had hired a number of young southern researchers, but he was short of experienced, qualified staff and was struggling to convince senior colleagues at Chapel Hill that investment in the social sciences would enhance the university's reputation for excellence in teaching and research.[5] In the spring and summer of 1927, he was under huge pressure—trying to run the IRSS, publish his work, edit that of others, and launch several new projects to justify the LSRM's donations. According to John H. Stanfield, "Odum's eagerness to please his benefactors at the memorial bordered on obsequiousness," but it was more a case of anxiety. He was engaged in ongoing battles against reactionary religious and political groups in North Carolina who were outraged by deliberately provocative articles in *Social Forces* on race, religion, and the origins of man. In addition, his wife was hospitalized for several months, leaving him with three young children to care for, and he suffered a further blow when his closest colleague, Jesse F. Steiner, was lured away to New Orleans to head the sociology department at Tulane University. To cap it all, Odum learned of rumors in other universities that he was having a breakdown. Throughout this, he reassured Ruml, "We are not downhearted. We have just begun. In spite of a series of difficulties you can count on us."[6]

For a mixture of professional and personal reasons, Odum made Jack Woofter's recruitment as a research associate the keystone of his IRSS development plan. On a professional level, the case for Woofter was threefold: his research on racial matters, his expertise in statistical analysis, and the fact that Odum needed relief from his teaching on black America.[7] His younger colleagues, including Guy Benton Johnson, a Texan research assistant, and Arthur F. Raper, a graduate student from Nashville, Tennessee, were keen, but inexperienced, so Odum persuaded the LSRM that the IRSS needed mature staff to undertake detailed work on the economics of African American life and especially the effects of migration.[8] Woofter's PhD from Columbia, his Phelps-Stokes connections, his practical experience with the CIC, and his role as director of the *Negro Problems in Cities* project for the Institute of Social and Religious Research made him the ideal candidate.

On the personal level, Odum was doing more than just a favor to Woofter's father; he was also helping his friend, Will Alexander, who needed to reduce CIC spending amid growing uncertainty over the intentions of the large philanthropic funds. In 1926, the Phelps-Stokes Fund supplemented its annual $2,000 donation to the CIC with an extra $1,500, effectively covering Woofter's whole salary, but for one year only. Alexander complained to Thomas Jesse Jones, "I cannot continue from year to year the personal responsibility of finding the money out of thin air for a staff of workers." He faced a "constant nightmare of possible loss of support at the end of each twelve months." In his 1927 letter seeking donations from CIC members, he warned, "This was never more necessary than for the present year, both because of the increasing opportunity and because of the financial depression throughout the country." For the first half of 1927, Woofter's salary came from his secondment to the International Missionary Council, but his future employment was uncertain. Alexander was fond of Woofter and admired his work, but replacing the thirty-three-year-old research director with a younger man made sense. At the end of 1926, Alexander told Odum that Woofter wanted a university job and would be available once the cities project was completed. They agreed that if he moved to UNC he could perform an advisory role for the CIC and that it would help the commission to develop strong links with Chapel Hill.[9]

For some time, Alexander had wanted to increase the number of experts on racial matters in southern universities and felt that efforts to address the South's problems would be harmed if people with Woofter's experience and contacts were lost to northern universities or government agencies. As Alexander recalled in the 1950s, "It seemed to me very fundamental to get more trained social scientists at work on this thing." Woofter primarily wanted a settled position, instead of the uncertainty surrounding the CIC and his itinerant work on *Negro Problems in Cities*. He declined an approach by the University of Denver in 1926, but when he expressed an interest in UNC or the University of Florida Odum and Alexander swiftly secured LSRM program administrator Leonard Outhwaite's agreement that it "would be very important to keep Woofter in the South." Outhwaite was an anthropologist from California, whose wartime work with Ruml for the Committee on Classification of Personnel in the United States Army brought him into contact with the interracial cooperation movement in the form of Thomas Jesse Jones and Walter B. Hill. Outhwaite met Woofter during a southern tour in 1923 and was familiar with the proposed Coahoma County study; according to Alexander, he had formed "a very high estimate of Woofter's ability."[10]

Odum met with Woofter and Ernest R. Groves of Boston University and offered them jobs immediately, before consulting the IRSS board. He pleaded with the LSRM for the additional salaries, telling Ruml, "With these men we shall have a rare opportunity; without them we shall be very much crippled" and warned Ruml's colleague Sydnor Walker, the most prominent woman in the field of philanthropic support for the social sciences, that the IRSS faced "what might be called a crisis in the need of men like Groves, Woofter, and others to help us distribute the load."[11]

The LSRM obliged with an additional grant of $240,000 over five years, taking its total donation to UNC for the years 1925 to 1932 to $353,000 and transforming the prospects of the IRSS. Set against sums that the LSRM gave for social sciences at other elite white institutions, UNC's grant was not extraordinary—the University of Chicago received $2,564,000; the SSRC, $2,554,000; the London School of Economics, $1,450,000; Vanderbilt University, $775,000; the Brookings Institute, $490,000; Harvard University, $340,000; Columbia University, $319,000; and the University of Virginia, $137,000; and various visiting professors shared $920,000. Black institutions fared less well: Fisk University got $184,500; Tuskegee Institute got $12,000; and the Association for the Study of Negro Life and History got a total of $62,800 in the years 1922 and 1926–29. All told, the LSRM gave the social sciences $12,778,000 and business subjects $2,285,000 before the fund was wound down in 1929.[12]

To Odum, this was manna from heaven and a huge boost to his confidence. As well as developing numerous potential projects, he could now afford Woofter, Groves, and several assistants who were to have distinguished careers at Chapel Hill, including Guy Johnson and his wife, Guion Griffis Johnson, Rupert B. Vance, and Fletcher M. Green. Further donations from the New York banker George Foster Peabody allowed Odum to hire Woofter's friend and former Phelps-Stokes Fund publicist, Sydney D. Frissell, to study farm cooperatives. Relieved, Odum told his New York publisher, Henry Holt and Company, that with his new staff, "next to Chicago, we shall be able to put into the field perhaps the most comprehensive functional program of sociological study and social work." Woofter, in particular, was "in the creative mood" and would give the institute new strength in statistics.[13] In announcing Woofter's appointment, Odum made much of his time as a "former statistician of General Pershing."[14]

Woofter's eagerness for a higher-paid academic post with more security and structure than the CIC research directorship was partly due to his marriage. In June 1924, at the age of thirty, he wed Ethel Ophelia Mays, a successful businesswoman five years older than him. A trained schoolteacher who left the classroom after ten years to enter Atlanta's burgeoning insurance industry in 1921, Ethel Mays was one of the New York Mutual Life Insurance Company's best agents, selling over $300,000 worth of life insurance annually. Three months after she married Jack Woofter, she was put in charge of the company's Atlanta office and the territory's agents. The *Atlanta Constitution* business pages hailed her success as evidence of "Woman's advance in the business world, her new-born tendency to step into places formerly consigned to men by popular and insistent consent. . . . Mrs. Woofter's rise in the business world has something of the Horatio Alger tang to it—so meteoric has it been."[15] The hints of Algerism in Ethel's life were stronger than the journalist probably knew. She had struggled upward from difficult beginnings, effectively reinventing herself, and her marriage to Jack Woofter further elevated her social standing. She was born in Opelika, a notoriously lawless town in eastern Alabama, where her father was a tenant farmer, and was the oldest girl among her mother's twelve children. When she was about twenty years old, the family gave up farming and moved to the crowded Ensley township, situated on a major coal seam just west of Birmingham, where in 1907 the U.S. Steel Corporation took over a rival plant and built new mills and hundreds of small workers' cottages. By 1910, Ethel's father was working in the pattern shop of a steel mill and Ethel and one of her sisters, having taken classes at the University of Alabama normal school without graduating, were teaching in the public school system of Jefferson County. For three years, Ethel attended University of Chicago summer schools, taking classes in composition, literature, and history.[16] Her move to the booming city of Atlanta in 1920 may have been prompted by three months spent working at the YWCA mountain summer camp run by Lillian Smith's father at Clayton, with girls and staff drawn largely from Fulton County. She secured a teaching post at the elite Washington Seminary for girls in Atlanta and continued to assist with music classes at the YWCA, before becoming an insurance agent. She was an active member of the Atlanta Woman's Club and played a leading role in the new Atlanta Club of Business and Professional Women, attending the state convention of businesswomen in 1922. She may have met Jack Woofter through one of these organizations or the functions of the State Federation of Women's Clubs, which he attended for the Georgia State Committee on Race Relations.[17] Jack and Ethel were married in her Atlanta apartment in a ceremony conducted by the CIC chairman and cofounder, the Reverend M. Ashby Jones, in the presence of their immediate families.[18] When Jack's post in the IRSS was formally confirmed at an annual salary of $4,000, they began construction of a substantial new home on the outskirts of Chapel Hill. They had no children, but for a time one of Ethel's nieces lived with them.[19]

When Woofter left the CIC offices in Atlanta for the last time, "with a lot of books under his arm and a somewhat dejected air," Alexander told Odum, "I can assure you that his final going left me feeling very much like I did when my father sold the family horse. My personal affection for Woofter has grown over the years and I have always felt better when he was around. He is a great fellow and the eagerness with which he enters into his work at North Carolina promises great things, I am sure."[20] Woofter looked set for a stellar future at UNC, with a publication record, friends in important charities and the interracial cooperation movement, and now his status as a protégé of Howard Odum. He was a key player in an enterprise of regional, and potentially national, importance. On Wednesday, June 15, 1927, Odum thanked Alexander for giving him Woofter—"He is going to be a great utility man for us as well as a specialist, because he can help us out in planning methods for all our research."[21]

Later that day, disaster struck, and Woofter's academic career was nearly extinguished before it had begun. In his study of black migration in 1920, he had called for southern judicial reform and especially the "abolition of the system of payment of fees to local officials on the basis of the number of arrests they make and the consequent cooling of their ardor for filling the local jails."[22] He now found himself at the mercy of just such an official in Virginia, in shameful circumstances. He had driven from Odum's house at Chapel Hill to meet a northbound train at Danville, en route to an International Missionary Council meeting in New York. At 10:30 p.m., Danville police officers, investigating reports that "a car crazily driven had been seen wig-wagging on the Yanceyville road," found Woofter's Pontiac dangling over a thirty-foot embankment. The *Danville Register* reported the next morning that Woofter was found "very deeply into his 'cups' [and] blissfully unconscious from too much research into the chemistry of North Carolina 'corn' or at least that is the charge against him." The police claimed they saved his life—"that car was just hanging over the embankment by a hair, and the professor was snoozing away inside," said one. Woofter reportedly maintained he had swerved to avoid an oncoming vehicle. He was arrested and appeared briefly in the local justice court the same night, giving his occupation as "research work for the Rockefeller Foundation" at UNC. The *Danville Register*'s account was ominously jocular:

> Whether the man arrested is really on the faculty of the University of North Carolina or not, is not known. When he arrived at the police station his tongue was very thick, and he was put to bed in the jail after a brief interview—but not without spirited remonstrance! "You can take my car, but don't put me in jail," Mr. Woolford [sic] said, with something like a pathos in his voice. "Don't put me in jail, because I am on my way to New York to attend some important business for the Rockefeller Foundation."
>
> But the professor was a little muddled on a point of law. There was no whiskey in the Pontiac car in which he was suspended over the bank, and he can have that back after his hearing—even if he cannot recover his professional dignity.
>
> The man had $60 in his pocket but told police he had $80. The police believe that his heavily inebriated condition accounted for the slip in his calculations. He will be given a hearing this morning.
>
> The Pontiac had a Georgia license, but Woolford said that could be explained at Chapel Hill.[23]

In court the following morning, Woofter stated that he was from Atlanta and was going to New York to work for the Rockefeller Foundation, thereby linking himself with an organization that epitomized Yankee meddling and two cities with negative connotations in southern Virginia. He pleaded guilty to a charge of "being drunk and driving an automobile within one mile of the city" and was sentenced by the police magistrate to thirty days in jail and fined $100. He asked for the sentence to be suspended, but the magistrate refused, claiming that Woofter's was one of ten such cases that month. The following day, Friday, June 17, damning accounts of his arrest and conviction, giving his correct name, were carried in the southern press, including the *Atlanta Constitution* and the *Washington Post*. His friend and housemate, IRSS researcher Sydney Frissell, rescued him, prompted by either an appeal from Woofter or the report in the *Raleigh News and Observer*, Chapel Hill's nearest daily newspaper. Frissell, who had a law degree, paid the fine and persuaded the magistrate and the assistant commonwealth attorney to suspend the jail sentence and instead ban Woofter from driving in Virginia for a year. Woofter traveled on immediately to New York by train, wiring his father mid-journey in Washington that he was "wrongly accused, [and] that the newspapers grossly exaggerated[,] giving him a horrible experience, but that it is all straight now." T. J. Woofter Sr. persuaded their hometown evening paper, the *Athens Banner-Herald,* to report that Jack's arrest and sentence had been only for speeding. Ethel Woofter, visiting family in Birmingham, Alabama, was wrongly informed by friends in Atlanta, who contacted the sheriff in Danville, that her husband was still in jail. When Thomas Jesse Jones met Woofter's train in New York, the latter explained that he had been delayed by an accident and briefly detained for an infringement of traffic laws. On Saturday, June 18, he wrote Odum a routine letter about getting funding from the Institute of Social and Religious Research to support Frissell, as if nothing untoward had occurred, but Odum already knew the situation and discovered that Woofter's plight was being discussed in philanthropic circles in New York. Odum attempted to limit the damage to himself and the IRSS by telling the press that Woofter—"one of the most capable research men in the South today"—was "engaged in religious and social research work for the Southern Inter-Racial Commission of Atlanta [sic]." He blurred Woofter's connections with UNC, claiming he had "not been engaged in research work at the University of North Carolina, but was to have come to that institution in the fall for a short period of work." It was true that Woofter's UNC contract did not officially begin for another two months, but it was not true that the appointment was to be short-term or that Woofter still worked for the CIC. His UNC contract was for five years, and he had left the CIC to complete various bits of writing and make an early start at Chapel Hill, but Odum's dissembling seems to have worked; in its report on Woofter's release from jail, the *Raleigh News and*

Observer made no mention of UNC and described him only as a "research worker for the Rockefeller Foundation."[24]

Odum's initial assumption was that the Danville affair had killed Woofter's appointment, for the stigma attached to a drunken driving conviction during national prohibition would be too great for him to be entrusted with the teaching of undergraduates. Acquiring a criminal record was bad enough, but flouting the temperance code that bound all shades of southern evangelical opinion made Woofter appear reckless and immoral. The leadership of UNC had already spent too much time in the 1920s fending off negative stories about the university's staff and their modern ideas and developing an understanding with the press in North Carolina. Woofter's troubles were therefore most unwelcome, and his position seemed hopeless.[25] Almost despairing, Odum wrote Jesse Steiner, who knew the small-town mentality of Chapel Hill in the 1920s:

> On the same day that we lost you we lost Woofter. While he received a very severe deal at the hand of the Danville police and judge, the publicity has been very bad, and he could not live down the atmosphere here now. If he were a member of the Chapel Hill community already, they would stand by him, but as an outsider, a new comer, and especially a Georgian, his task would be too hard for him, and I am sure he will not want to try it.[26]

On the Monday after his arrest, while still in New York, Woofter received a newspaper clipping about his case, probably from his father. He confessed to Thomas Jesse Jones, who sprang into action, ordering Odum and Alexander to meet him the following day in Greensboro, North Carolina. They agreed that things looked bleak for Woofter and the IRSS, but hoped that if the story were handled carefully it might eventually fade away. They decided that Woofter had no future at UNC, but Odum insisted that he should remain in Chapel Hill and live in Odum's home until a solution emerged. Once Ethel Woofter and their domestic staff had arrived, a house would be made available where "his father and mother will visit him here. During the summer here he will carry out the plans already worked out. In the fall plans will be worked out for an adjustment elsewhere." Odum wanted nothing done that could provoke the Danville judge into applying the original sentence, "and we must not injure Jack by giving publicity that would have them start out on his trail again." His main concern, however, was that more bad publicity would harm the IRSS.[27]

Despite the mess, Odum did not lose faith in Woofter. When he sent newspaper clippings about the case to the LSRM's Beardsley Ruml, he insisted that "the story is exaggerated, and Jack got an undeserved severity for what was really a minor accident. I am hoping you will be sympathetic. . . . Our plans are going ahead." But when he wrote again to Ruml a few days later about the IRSS and its staff members' forthcoming work, Woofter's name was conspicuously absent.[28] He told Woofter to collect his car from Danville and move in with the Odum family so that they could assess the situation together and to discuss other career options with Thomas Jesse Jones: "While it will not be wise to continue our plans here at the University as originally worked out, there are other very important tasks elsewhere that must be done, and which will need your skill and technique."[29]

The turning point was the arrival of T. J. Woofter Sr., who told Jack's old history professor, Robert Preston Brooks, "Odum has not [the] courage to handle a situation calling for much assertion." He traveled up from Athens to challenge the defeatist mood, and a burst of networking ensued, so that the same connections that secured the UNC post for Jack Woofter now rallied to save his career. As letters shuttled between Odum, Thomas Jesse Jones, and Will Alexander, a convenient proposal arrived from the white president of Fisk University, Thomas Elsa Jones (no relation). Odum reported to the others, "He asked us to release Jack for a while. I think this will make a sort of combination southern effort that we all have been wanting and that we had hoped would come to pass."[30] Helped by the fact that Thomas Jesse Jones was a trustee of Fisk and a member of its executive committee, a deal had been done. The plan was that Woofter would lie low in Nashville and not teach students during the coming academic session. Odum could reasonably claim that shifting Woofter to Nashville supported the overall objectives of Outhwaite and Ruml, since the LSRM had just awarded Fisk University money for the development of a social science program over a five-year period.[31]

For future reference, Thomas Jesse Jones produced a summary of the events surrounding Woofter's arrest, stating that the latter was obviously innocent because he had gone directly from Odum's home to Danville on June 15th. According to Jones, "these facts prove conclusively that Dr. Woofter could not have been under the influence of liquor."

> In view of the above facts and of our knowledge of Dr. Woofter's sterling character and splendid personality, it is our conviction that we should give every possible support and encouragement to Dr. Woofter so that he may be able to continue his remarkable services for interracial peace and for sound knowledge of human society. We emphatically agreed that to permit this unfortunate incident to limit Dr. Woofter's usefulness would be not only an injustice to him personally but a most serious loss to social science in relation to both white and Colored people in the United States.[32]

Will Alexander was relieved to receive Jones's assessment that the affair was "the work of a sensational newspaperman and a hard-boiled traffic officer," but even he must have recognized that Woofter's innocence had not been conclusively demonstrated.[33]

The neat solution offered by Thomas Elsa Jones offered an insight into how the southern professional classes looked after their own, but in the end it was not pursued, apparently because Jack Woofter rejected it. Three weeks later, an alternative plan was agreed, entailing his absence from Chapel Hill on fieldwork in South Carolina. The South Carolina project has since been construed as a quick fix, devised to sweep the Danville conviction under the carpet, but in fact it was something Woofter had been working on for several months. Even people close to Odum and Woofter seem to have formed the wrong impression about this. In their history of the IRSS, former staff members Guy and Guion Johnson stated that Odum, Alexander, and Thomas Jesse Jones were "determined to search for a project that would take [Woofter] from Chapel Hill for a year or so" and that, at Jones's probable instigation, they suddenly dreamed up and secured funding for a major interdisciplinary, multi-institutional study of the black community of St. Helena Island, one of the old plantation sea islands. It was to be directed on-site by Woofter and would involve a half-dozen other researchers, including the Johnsons.[34]

Historian Daniel Singal and folklorist Lynn Moss Sanders are among those who have repeated this erroneous version of events.[35] It was compounded by the testimony given by Guion Johnson to the Southern Oral History Program during a series of four interviews in 1974, two years after Woofter's death. Johnson clearly resented what she saw as Woofter's special treatment and the inconvenience of having to relocate herself to St. Helena while pregnant. Understandably, Johnson misremembered some details about what had occurred in 1927, but the amusement with which she recalled exaggerated accounts of the Danville affair and its aftermath suggests that Woofter was much gossiped-about at UNC and that he was never entirely rid of the matter. She told her first interviewer:

> Well, this is the story about how the project was started, and it was extremely interesting. And it [the project] was simply to whitewash the man who was the director who had got in trouble. He was being brought here to the University and there was a big banner headline, all the way across the newspapers, about how this man who was coming to the University had got into trouble. And well, there was a movement to see that he didn't come to the University. . . . And Dr. Odum very quickly began scurrying around getting research funds. He had always been interested in having something done about the St. Helena Island area, and he got the money. He was very clever at getting funds, got the money, and then just bundled us all up and sent us to St. Helena Island to begin on the project. We had to complete it in a hurry so that this man's good name would be brought back and he would be accepted into the University.[36]

Asked for details in a subsequent interview, Johnson gave unflattering elaborations:

I don't really want to do that because it was most unfortunate and a pathetic aspect of a very fine mind. Well, the basis of the whole difficulty was that he was an alcoholic. . . . Simply . . . well, since I have gone this far and said that he was an alcoholic, I will have to tell you that the incident was that he was leaving Atlanta—they had not moved to Chapel Hill—he was leaving Atlanta for a conference at Dartmouth College. He was driving, and on the way he was arrested in Danville, Va., because he was found drunk, asleep in his car on the city dump with the front wheels of his car extending over the abyss. So he was clapped in jail and the headlines were all over the papers of the South.

[INTERVIEWER]: Oh, and this was right before he was to come to UNC.

. . . Yes. So Dr. Odum scurried around and obtained a grant to study St. Helena Island. [Odum] had always wanted to explore the situation.[37]

This was hearsay. None of those trying to help Woofter retrieve his reputation in the summer of 1927 hinted that he was an alcoholic, although Odum did not try to discount all the allegations made by the police at Danville. The only other person who worked with Woofter at this time who recalled that he drank to excess was a UNC graduate student, Clyde V. Kiser, who used the St. Helena project to initiate a PhD dissertation on sea island migration at Columbia University under the supervision of Woofter's friend Frank Ross. In an interview in 1973 for an oral history project on the Population Association of America (PAA), Kiser praised Woofter as "a very astute man" who gave him good advice, before adding, "Unfortunately, Woofter was addicted a little too much to the bottle; you've probably heard of some of the things he got into." However, Kiser was ill-informed on other matters concerning Woofter—in a further interview in 1976 he wrongly thought Woofter had come to Chapel Hill to teach sociology and cultural anthropology and that Frank Ross had "hatched up the idea of studying Negro culture in St. Helena Island" with Woofter. No doubt, Kiser read the press reports about the Danville affair or heard whispers at Chapel Hill about origins of the St. Helena project, but after he moved permanently to New York in 1928 he had little contact with Woofter other than correspondence about the island study, and it is plain from the PAA interviews that they were not especially well acquainted.[38]

None of Woofter's more senior colleagues appears to have thought his work was impaired. Long-serving IRSS staff member Harriet L. Herring, a research associate and later sociology professor, knew Woofter well (better than Guion Johnson, for example) and continued to work with him after he moved to Washington in the 1930s. Interviewed in 1976, she recalled him warmly and did not suggest any problems:

I had known him ever since he came to Chapel Hill, and then his wife both;
knew him socially, and we had offices right next to each other and everything.
[laughter] This sounds ungracious: I was very fond of him, but if he wanted to
talk about something he'd come in no matter what you were doing. If you had
a fire on he would have to talk about what he wanted, what he was interested
in. Then he'd stroll out. If you wanted to see him about something you couldn't
corner him to save your life. He wouldn't pay you any attention, or he'd have
to go somewhere, you know. He had a good sense of humor and I liked him;
he was a very able man. . . . Well, he was a very quiet sort of person, except, as
I say, when he had something on his mind he could stand and talk to you 'till
your biscuits burned! [laughter][39]

The St. Helena Island project was not simply Howard Odum's quick solution
to an embarrassing situation. His correspondence indicates that he and Thomas
Jesse Jones preferred the Fisk isolation plan and that it was Woofter who was unhappy about it and wanted to discuss it with others.[40] The St. Helena alternative
also appears to have come from Woofter—unsurprisingly, since he had been developing a research proposal concerning the island for almost three months from
the time his appointment to UNC was agreed and had been keeping Odum fully
informed. Thus, the project was much more slowly developed than either the
Johnsons or Kiser apparently realized or cared to recall.

Woofter had been aware of St. Helena Island for ten years, in all, beginning
with his work on Thomas Jesse Jones's *Negro Education* report, in which the island's Penn School was held up as a paragon of community-based education.[41]
With beginnings not unlike the Port Royal experiment, the former slave community on the sixty-four-square mile island had survived numerous hardships since
Reconstruction, remaining largely free of white landlordism and domination. The
Penn School was founded by Quaker missionaries at the end of the Civil War and
provided the independent black farmers and their families with advice on cultivation, health care, and housing improvements. The five thousand islanders included a few dozen people of mixed race and around twenty whites, making St.
Helena Island and the adjoining Lady's Island places of fascination for a stream
of folklorists, musicologists, missionaries, and foreign colonial officials wanting
to observe the interplay between a largely autonomous native black population
and a small white guiding presence. Woofter was convinced that a detailed social
and economic study was needed because the imminent construction of a bridge
to the mainland threatened the culture of the islanders.[42]

In April 1927, Woofter took Leonard Outhwaite on a tour of Georgia, showing
him "a number of characteristic rural and small town situations which . . . present
both favorable and less fortunate examples of work in Negro education, social
work and general health and welfare." They made a special detour to St. Helena Island, where they visited the Penn School's long-serving director, Rossa B. Cooley,

and her assistant, Grace Bigelow House. Woofter told Cooley at this time, long before his conviction at Danville, that Howard Odum was intrigued by St. Helena and "the possibilities for a very valuable piece of research. From what he said it may be possible to work out some plan to make this study sooner than I had expected." Odum was interested in the challenge that modernization posed to black southerners, a theme he explored with Guy Johnson in *The Negro and His Songs* and *Negro Workaday Songs* and would revisit in his Black Ulysses trilogy of novels between 1928 and 1931. He told Woofter in May 1927 that St. Helena would be a good subject on which to deploy the Johnsons, now that new IRSS's funding had secured their positions. At first, Woofter envisaged a year-long folklore study by Guy Johnson, but he soon mapped out a larger "unified presentation of social and economic life on the Island, including linguistics, folk lore, significant social customs and institutions, as well as progress made in the assimilation of American culture through improved farm life and home and health conditions."[43] He was the latest in a succession of racial reformers to be seduced by the possibility that an idyllic balance had been struck on St. Helena Island between black autonomy, cultural purity, and white guardianship. Woofter cleverly summarized his intention as that of "demonstrating the improvability of a group of people whose opportunities have been limited in a very peculiar way . . . [and] who are, up to date, backward in assimilating American culture." This purpose struck a chord with the Penn School board of governors, including its treasurer, George Foster Peabody, a friend of the Woofter family. The board consented, so long as the researchers did not disrupt the work of the school.[44]

In August 1927, in an ostentatious show of support following Woofter's arrest, Odum took him to the annual two-week social science conference at Dartmouth College, in New Hampshire, where they discussed the St. Helena project with the race committees of the SSRC and the science-oriented National Research Council (NRC). Both groups, Woofter reported to Cooley, "enthusiastically endorsed the proposed study." Several scholars offered to help, convincing Woofter that a multi-disciplinary project was feasible. Thus, the St. Helena Island study was not cobbled together so that Woofter could be quickly packed off to some remote corner, as has been suggested by participants and subsequent students. Although the IRSS board considered the matter sooner than was originally planned, and its submission to the SSRC was brought forward, the project had been under consideration for three months before Woofter's mishap at Danville. It was not until the end of August that Odum knew for certain that funding had been secured, and Woofter did not depart for the island until November 1927, a further three months after his conviction. In the meantime, he did not hide himself away, and murmurings of disapproval at Chapel Hill subsided faster than Odum expected, hastened, no doubt, by the way in which IRSS colleagues rallied round and involved Woofter in their research during the remainder of the summer.[45] By October, Woofter's participation in IRSS seminars led Odum to call him "one of my most brilliant men." He invited Woofter to read drafts of his novel, *Rainbow Round My Shoulder: The Blue Trail of Black Ulysses,* and told Sydnor Walker about the new man's abilities as a statistician: "I knew he was good, but he is even better than I thought."[46]

All the same, it was fortunate for both Odum and Woofter that the president of UNC, Harry Woodburn Chase, was in London at the time of the Danville affair. Chase, an old friend of Odum from their graduate student days at Clark University, defended his staff whenever an article in *Social Forces* outraged fundamentalists, but academic freedom and personal morality were different. Had he been present, Chase might have concurred with Odum's initial reaction to Woofter's conviction.[47] Odum knew that impropriety could cost people their jobs in universities, as in the case of sociologist William Isaac Thomas, fired by the University of Chicago in 1918. (Thomas was not convicted, but allegations of disorderly conduct, violation of the Mann Act, and false registration at a hotel resulted in his dismissal.)[48] A month after Woofter's arrest, Odum sent Chase an account designed to close the matter. Making no reference to a crashed automobile, Odum gave the impression that Woofter was largely to blame, but everything had been sorted out:

> A few weeks ago Dr. T. J. Woofter, Jr., was arrested in Danville while under the influence of liquor. There is no doubt that he was unfairly treated, that part of it was a frame-up of a plain-clothes officer and a fee judge, and that it was an incident which would not happen once in a thousand years. There has been no publicity about it to hurt the University, but it was very clear that we could not proceed with his work this fall as usual, and so we have gotten him on to some research work for the Social Science Research Council. We have had him personally come back down to our house and stay with us and have stood by him. So far as I know, there has come no injury to the university at large. I think [UNC executive secretary Robert] House agrees with me in this conclusion, and we have worked the thing out together quietly.[49]

For all Odum's protectiveness, Woofter must have found the Danville experience harrowing and shaming, and the chance to spend time away from Chapel Hill on the St. Helena project was probably a relief. Shortly before setting off for South Carolina, he visited Will Alexander, who told Odum, "I was glad to see Jack today. He is looking better and gave good reports of his work." As the director of the St. Helena study, Woofter spent the final two months of 1927 alone on the island in accommodation provided by the Penn School, undertaking preparatory research and occasionally journeying by rail to Durham to confer with Odum and the research team. His wife and the other investigators joined him in January 1928. The seven-month gap between his conviction and the convening of the research team contradicts Guion Johnson's recollection that Odum "just bundled us all up and sent us to St. Helena Island to begin on the project. We had to complete it in a hurry so that [Woofter's] good name would be brought back and he would be accepted into the University."[50] Woofter was arrested in June 1927, Guion Johnson's appointment as an IRSS research associate did not start until September, and it was further four months before she and her husband arrived on St. Helena. Odum certainly allowed others to believe that he had devised the sea island project, but there was no unseemly haste about it.

For the best part of six months on St. Helena, Woofter coordinated the work of specialists in history, psychology, anthropology, farm economics, crime, and taxation, using a team of local enumerators to gather microscopic details about community life. The St. Helena freedmen and their descendants were described in the original bid to the SSRC as "one of the most primitive and isolated groups of Negroes in the United States." The project would capture their "unique culture pattern . . . [and] the organization of a truly homogenous community rather than a bi-racial community or an owner-tenant community," and examine the effects of the Penn School and migration. The Union Army had given land titles to the islanders, who engaged in yeoman farming for three generations, and now their families were spread across forty-four former plantations, each with an average occupancy of a hundred people. Between 1900 and 1920, the population fell from around 9,000 to 5,157, and it continued to fall after the infestation of sea-island cotton by the boll weevil in 1918.[51]

The sixteen-page preliminary report provided by Woofter to the Penn School trustees in 1928 made depressing reading. It showed St. Helena's residents facing the same problems as African Americans elsewhere in the South and deriving no special benefits from their peculiar history and location, in terms of education, family life, or economic prospects. The Penn School provided an acceptable education to those it reached, but the nine other public schools scattered across the island opened for only five months of the year, and all but two were "dilapidated one-room shacks" holding up to seventy-five children each. Beaufort County extracted much more in taxation from St. Helena Island than it put back in the form of teaching and roads, and the bridge to the mainland was not requested by the islanders, but was built to allow speculative development of shorefront lots. One-third of the island's families were headed by widows, living in dire poverty with grandchildren whose own parents had moved elsewhere. Agriculture was stagnant—fewer than 100 out of the 1,150 growers "could be called successful farmers in the sense that they are making a living for their families from the land and producing as much as $100 worth of cash crops." As in other southern communities, this was "largely due to the destruction of cotton as a money crop and the failure to find a substitute," but on St. Helena such problems were compounded by poor access to markets, overly subdivided holdings, high taxes, and meager grazing. The lack of decision-making experience among the freedmen farmers regarding planting, buying, and marketing hampered successive generations, so that the Penn School and its philanthropic supporters struggled to promote self-sufficiency: "On the whole the situation of the people of St. Helena leaves the very strong feeling in the minds of the investigators that the social experiment of the building of a self-sufficient Negro community on the Island has not been completed."[52]

The fabled biological and cultural homogeneity of the St. Helena islanders was also questioned—the original slave population was drawn from several parts of West Africa, and only half of the island's folk tales were of African origin; the rest were European. The one positive point that the investigators stressed was that the community was harmonious: any disputes were resolved "outside the court in the praise houses or lodges." The "remarkably low" crime rate of two serious cases a year, like the other sea islands, was attributed to home ownership, the Penn School, "the absence of irritations which occur when a large proportion of white people are present," and the fact that the community had "evolved its own system of social control."[53]

It is clear from Jack and Ethel Woofter's correspondence with the Penn School staff that they were smitten with life on St. Helena; during the 1930s he became one of the twenty-four trustees of the school. In May 1929, the Woofters bought farmland from a group of residents whose circumstances were highlighted in the report. A ten-acre tract on the large Tom Fripp plantation, where the Woofters lived during the research project, was sold to them by the grandchildren and great-grandchildren of the freedman granted the land after the Civil War, who died intestate around 1880. The oldest of these descendants, Abbie Holmes, a recently widowed farmer in her mid-sixties, had her own farm, but she struggled with the shortage of labor. Her daughters had departed, leaving her with three grandchildren to raise, and the land Woofter bought was probably more than the extended family could manage. He paid $250 for it, giving the seventeen interested parties named on the deed record less than $15 each. He may have bought the land for sentimental reasons or from altruism, or he may have considered it a good investment in view of the bridge construction, but he does not appear to have done much with it. In April 1945, he tried to dispose of it for $2,500, citing its "unique beauty, easy access to Beaufort, S. C., and ocean," but it apparently failed to attract a buyer.[54]

Woofter's assumption in 1927 that the bridge would change life on St. Helena was justified, but the Great Depression probably had just as much impact. In January 1937, Guy Johnson published a brief update on the island's black community, in which he concluded:

> The future of these Negroes is not bright. During the depression most of the white men who acted as bankers to the Negroes have failed. The large truck garden run by a white man is a possible threat to the economy of the Negroes. It is also possible that one of the beaches will be used for [the] building of a

Left to right: Jack and Ethel Woofter, Clyde V. Kiser (Columbia University), Jessie Alverson (UNC secretarial staff), Guy B. Johnson, Guion G. Johnson, and Guy (Ben) Johnson Jr., at Triuna Island, Lake George, near Saratoga, N.Y. As guests of George Foster Peabody and the Yaddo estate, they spent July and August 1929 on Triuna completing *Black Yeomanry,* a study of life on St. Helena Island, S.C. *Vol. 44, Triuna Island, Scrapbooks and Photograph Albums, Series V, Yaddo Records, 1870–1980, Manuscripts and Archives Division, New York Public Library, Astor, Lenox and Tilden Foundations.*

summer resort. The introduction of autos, radio, [and] telephones is making for change. Crimes are on the increase. A large number of Negroes are emigrating to the mainland and the North. Thus it is probable that the old culture of the community will gradually disintegrate.[55]

When the 1928 fieldwork was complete, Jack and Ethel Woofter and the main coauthors, including the Johnsons and their new son, repaired to a rather different island, Triuna, on Lake George, part of the Yaddo writers' retreat at Saratoga Springs, New York. Along with Thomas Jesse Jones and his family, they were guests of the island's owner, George Foster Peabody, whose late wife, Karen Trask, founded Yaddo with her first husband, the financier Spencer Trask.[56] The resulting book, *Black Yeomanry: Life on St. Helena Island,* was intended for a commercial publisher, rather than the University of North Carolina Press, in an attempt to tap into a perceived public demand for community studies. Woofter read Robert and Helen Lynd's *Middletown* and was "encouraged as to the popular reception which it has had. [Lynd's] material is organized very much like mine, with the exception, however, that he deals with a more typical segment of American life. On the other hand, St. Helena is naturally more picturesque."[57]

212 | Race Harmony and Black Progress

Jones wanted to place *Black Yeomanry* with Harcourt, but Odum persuaded Woofter that his own publisher, Henry Holt, would produce a more attractive volume and sell it effectively. *Black Yeomanry* appeared in 1930 with Woofter as sole author, but it represented a dozen people's work on St. Helena's history, economy, religious and family life, songs, language, and anthropology. Woofter wrote the opening and closing chapters, giving an overall verdict on the St. Helena experiment, a thin chapter on education, and a summary of data gathered by Clyde V. Kiser and Frank A. Ross on the effects of migration. Kiser compared the survey team's island census with the U.S. Census Bureau's data for Beaufort County to show that migration began after 1900 when the decline of phosphate dredging in the rivers removed one of the few sources of cash. Savannah was now home to 600 islanders, while New York had attracted another 480. A further 400 people from St. Helena were scattered in Philadelphia, Boston, Charleston, and other northern and southern cities. The clearest effects of this migration were a falling birth rate on St. Helena and an overwhelmingly female population.[58]

O. M. Johnson of the U.S. Department of Agriculture, William H. Mills of Clemson University, and the IRSS's tax expert, Clarence Heer, prepared sections on the island's economy, while material on the family, crime, and religion was gathered by the IRSS psychologist, Ernest R. Groves, and criminologist Roy M. Brown. A chapter on the islanders' health drew on research by psychologist Joseph Peterson of Peabody College in Nashville, Tennessee, and the Harvard anthropologist Earnest A. Hooton. Peterson, who insinuated himself into the project at the Dartmouth conference, was useful to Woofter, because of his connections with the SSRC, but black social scientists would have been unimpressed by his involvement. Speaking on intelligence tests at Dartmouth in the presence of Charles S. Johnson, Monroe N. Work, and Carter G. Woodson, Peterson, who was raised in Utah, stated that when variable social factors had been taken into account, white people were basically more intelligent than all others: "Some races, as the Negro for example, may have definite skewness toward low mentality that is not reflected in mere medians."[59]

At this stage of his UNC career, Woofter lacked the confidence to challenge such breathtaking offensiveness, but later, when he was about to join the federal government, he issued a sharp critique of the "enthusiasm for measurement in social science [of] . . . many mental and social traits which were formerly thought of in a qualitative rather than a quantitative way." He warned researchers about the numerous subjectivities involved: the problem of creating questions and scales that supposedly indicated intelligence, the problem of telling "native mental ability apart from things learned," the danger of comparing dissimilar samples of subject groups, and the "great difficulty if the concepts of superiority and inferiority are introduced into the picture." Any test could throw up differences, he argued, but, whereas social scientists had "progressed in the technique of measuring difference, we have made no scientific approach to determining the ethical value of such differences."[60] *Black Yeomanry* contained no such insights; had it done so, it might have attracted less criticism from black readers.[61]

The most thoroughly researched chapter in *Black Yeomanry* was a condensation of Guion Johnson's work on plantations, in which the slaves' living conditions were compared favorably with those of the freedmen; she spent over a year tracking down and transcribing previously unknown records. In his chapter on culture, Guy Johnson claimed that enslaved Africans could be glimpsed in the style and rhythm of the island's songs, but not in their content, and that the island's folklore and other customs, even the Gullah dialect, revealed "the predominance of the English culture over the African." He was surprised by this, and his findings caused much debate. To analyze the songs and stories, he recorded them on an Ediphone dictation machine, paying the islanders small sums for the privilege. Islands like St. Helena, wrote Guy Johnson, were "the reservoir *par excellence* of African culture traits. . . . But, at the same time, the sea island folk furnish us with about as good a replica of 17th and 18th century peasant English culture as could be found in this country." Both Guion Johnson and Guy Johnson produced substantial separate volumes on their sea island research with the UNC press.[62] *Black Yeomanry* was informative and well illustrated, but also sentimental and deliberately popular, despite Woofter's intention to make "picturesqueness a secondary consideration." With no index or bibliography, it was not the kind of work he normally produced, and in places it reads more like a tourist guide than a serious academic study; its wider conclusions about land tenure, southern agriculture, and African American culture are slight. The project's scientific basis might have been strengthened if Woofter had succeeded in his attempt to recruit the anthropologist Paul Radin, known for his important studies of American Indians, who was teaching at Fisk University.[63] Most of the illustrations showed the farming and communal life of the island, but Woofter included an image made by Indiana photographer Frank N. Hohenberger, as part of a commission for New York businesswoman Kate Gleason, who was building an artists' and writers' colony at Beaufort. It showed graves in the cemetery at Coffin Point on St. Helena, decorated with ornaments and household items, such as clocks and bowls; Woofter felt this captured the distinctiveness of the Gullah culture of the Sea Islands, but Guy Johnson noted this practice occurred in other parts of the South.[64]

Woofter depicted St. Helena as an idyllic, but remote island, where large plantations had seen various cash crops come and go—indigo, rice, Sea Island cotton—along with phosphate mining, as the markets fluctuated and infestations blew in. Here was "a test tube for the observation of the action of constructive forces on an isolated Negro group of as pure African descent as could be found in the country." There were around twenty voters on the island, but none were black. The old plantations still formed the basis of the different communities on St. Helena, although the white families whose names they bore were long gone. The linguistic influences of old England and early America lived on and aspects of slave culture were strong, as might be expected, but Woofter remarked: "There is astonishingly little from Africa which is of functional importance in the present day activities of this isolated Negro culture." The islanders were a tight-knit community, but "cultural contact with contemporary movements has been supplied by Penn School, which has brought to them the riches of ideas." Here, the missionary Methodist in Woofter emerged, and he sounded much like Thomas Jesse Jones in his eagerness to uplift the darker races "along fundamental and practical lines."[65]

In his published conclusions, Woofter was upbeat about the outcome of handing over the plantations to slaves described by a government agent during Reconstruction as "a herd of suspicious savages." In terms that grated with black critics, he speculated, "If progress can be made with such a group, then similar methods may be relied upon to show even greater results when applied to people who have had more advantages. Thus the experiment on St. Helena throws light upon the question as to what can be accomplished with a group of pure-blooded, isolated Negroes, when they are given the stimulus of intelligent paternalism."[66] He found the islanders comparatively healthy, their religious organization strong, and crime low, but because of isolation they had "not adapted themselves to American standards" in three main respects. The first was the "rather easy-going attitude toward life.... This is a survival of the standards of the slave street where less than twenty dollars a year sufficed to feed and clothe a slave." Under such conditions, "life is an Oriental pursuit of a calm, unhurried destiny, rather than a drive under the spur of ambition." The second weakness was "the failure of most of the families to accumulate that surplus which is essential to progress," although in this respect they were little different from cotton and tobacco farmers right across the South, "bound to a system in which the lean years consumed most of the surplus of the fat, and the purchase of a few comforts dissipated the balance." The third and starkest "aberration from American standards [was] the relative laxity of sex morals, evidenced by the high illegitimacy rate," although the rate of eventual marriage and the number of households headed by couples matched societal norms. "In short, the achievement on St. Helena has been an orderly community, a healthy community, one which is fairly stable, but in which bread winning is difficult."[67]

The statistical element of the book was poorly integrated, although it contained revealing data. In 1928, adult female islanders outnumbered men in all age groups, by a total of 1,231 to 952. The number of children born on the island, according to the 1910 census, showed that the largest single category of mothers were those who had already given birth at least twelve times; they also had the fewest surviving children. The death rate among black residents of St. Helena Township (1,902 per 100,000) was lower than that of urban blacks nationally (2,340 per 100,000) and rates of death from heart disease, tuberculosis, nephritis, pneumonia, birth defects, pregnancy, and accidents were markedly lower. The infant mortality rate was also lower than the average for whites and blacks nationally; the only cause of death with a raised incidence was malarial fever.[68]

Several sections of *Black Yeomanry* criticized the southern racial status quo, especially the chapters on government and education. In the former, Clarence Heer noted the islanders' sense of grievance that they were "required to contribute, out of their meagre incomes, toward the support of governmental activities which benefit sections of the [county] far wealthier than their own." Although annual per capita tax payments on the island were relatively low (just $3.77, compared to $10.58 in Beaufort County, a statewide average of $21.39, and a national average of $48.69), these taxes were burdensome in relation to the average family cash income on St. Helena of $270, at a time when average family income in South Carolina stood at $2,119 and in the United States as a whole, at $3,347. As Heer pointed out, "An income as small as this is required in its entirety for food and clothing; it cannot be taxed by as much as a dollar without entailing severe hardship." Much of the money raised in taxes on St. Helena was spent on "the illusory benefits of motor highways" elsewhere in Beaufort County, a situation Heer conceded "may seem in the highest degree unjust, [but] can scarcely be attacked as illegal. . . . The Island is simply the victim of its isolation, its poverty, and of the fact that it is tied to a county whose dominant economic interests are at variance with its own." This situation was found in other "backward" rural areas, but it was compounded, especially in "Negro communities, [by] the lack of consideration given to these communities because they have no voice in electing the officials." In this oblique manner, Heer was raising highly sensitive issues. St. Helena residents had been consulted on the new bridge and a new highway across the island, but their opposition had been outweighed by the views of white mainland residents who stood to benefit from tourism as soon as the beaches were accessible. Clearly, disfranchisement was a major handicap. Regarding education, Heer was more critical still. St. Helena's nine schools, only two of which had more than one teacher, received none of the additional state educational aid given to Beaufort County, although the islanders paid a total of $2,400 in state property taxes. The county's education expenditure on St. Helena in the 1927–28 sessions was a pitiful $3.36 per pupil; for the county as a whole it was $6.11 per black pupil, and $56 for each white pupil. There were fifty-seven children per teacher on St. Helena, compared to forty-six per teacher in black schools in the rest of the county and twenty-six per teacher in white schools. The island schools opened for only 100 days a year, for which a teacher was paid $185, compared to the 117 days of mainland black schools, where teachers received $258, and 178 days in the case of white schools, where teachers received $1,004. In effect, the county's expenditure on St. Helena schools equaled three-quarters of what the islanders paid in school-related taxes.

Heer concluded "that the taxpayers of St. Helena are being made to contribute toward the education of the children of the rest of the county." As a "victim of [interdistrict] discrimination," St. Helena was hardly unique, but white communities had "redress at the polls which [was] denied to Negro communities." Thus, Heer stated explicitly, problems such as the county's underspending on St. Helena would persist for as long as black disfranchisement existed. It was a small, but significant, statement by a white southern scholar, and one that Woofter could easily have removed if he wished.[69]

Instead, he included a rationalization for discriminatory spending that was at odds with Heer's argument. It was swiftly picked up by black commentators, and the consequent reevaluation of Woofter, personally, marked a turning point in his standing with black social scientists. He stated there was nothing especially remarkable about white people in the South, as the richer race, enjoying better public education than blacks. This probably seemed a reasonable and realistic remark in the context of Beaufort County and the known attitude of South Carolinian politicians, but he did not anticipate the reaction of black readers. The offending passage read:

> It is evident that the school authorities of Beaufort County do not consider that equality in the matter of school tax burdens necessarily involves the obligation to equalize educational opportunities. This point of view cannot be condemned off-hand, if equal educational opportunity is to be understood as meaning the establishment of common standards for Negro and white schools. The Negroes of Beaufort County do not possess enough taxable wealth to support their schools according to white standards. If such standards were to be maintained, the additional cost would have to be defrayed by the white taxpayers. Beaufort County is not overly wealthy, and it is having a difficult struggle to maintain even its white schools in accordance with acceptable standards. These standards would be jeopardized if equal money were expended on Negro schools. Equality of educational opportunity as between Negroes and whites would, therefore, require a degree of altruism on the part of the white population which it is scarcely practical to expect. Under the circumstances, probably all that can be asked on behalf of the Negroes is that they receive back in school services at least as much as they contribute in school taxes, and that no part of their tax monies be used for the support of the white schools.[70]

The whites were wealthier, he was saying, and expected their relative affluence to deliver certain advantages; and the poorer blacks realistically ought to expect less in life, including weaker schools. "Under the circumstances"—by which Woofter meant racism, disfranchisement, segregation, and white parsimony—it was pointless for blacks to demand equal educational provision if that meant taking funds away from white schools. Woofter was effectively repeating what the leading white Methodist bishop, Warren Akin Candler, had said thirty years earlier: black education should be supported, but the higher taxes generally paid by whites entitled them to a better education; it was "simple justice that the money thus raised should be so expended as to secure good teachers for [white taxpayers'] own children rather than to provide salaries for negro teachers above an amount necessary to secure competent instructors for negro schools."[71]

Otherwise, in his chapter on education, Woofter focused on philanthropic work, such as the planned program of Rosenwald Fund school construction, the appointment of a supervising teacher for the island, and the work of the Penn School, with a charitably funded annual budget of $44,000, an enrollment of 264 pupils, and its various farming, industrial, domestic, and social clubs with almost 900 members. Woofter was as ardent as Thomas Jesse Jones in his admiration for Rossa B. Cooley and Grace B. House and the "cooperative spirit" of the Penn School staff.[72] *Black Yeomanry* gave Woofter the chance to argue for better-funded black education, but it was typical of his tendency to write for white readers that he failed to put the case for radical change, leaving black readers to draw their own conclusions. As a result, the *Baltimore Afro-American* coined a new word—"Woofterism"—in an editorial that took him to task for accepting levels of school funding commensurate with black poverty. It claimed his views were "beclouded with race hate." The term "Woofterism" caught on and would be used repeatedly by black commentators to describe white liberal failures to condemn conditions that clearly arose from racial inequality and discrimination. (In his pioneering biography of W. E. B. Du Bois, Francis L. Broderick wrongly credited the *Crisis* editor with inventing the term "Woofterism," but aptly described it as meaning "a collection of facts, themselves accurate, which tells only part of the truth.") The *Afro-American* accused Woofter of implying that black people got the schools they more or less deserved, and denounced his claim that improving their funding would do unacceptable damage to white schools as a "pernicious doctrine." It argued that the entitlement of black children to an equal education was not only a matter of fairness; it was a right, due to a people whose rents and labor created the taxable wealth of white landowners. In this respect, the *Afro-American* overlooked the fact that Woofter was writing about a sea island community of landowning taxpayers, and not about tenants, but the newspaper was making a wider point. Quoting Woofter selectively, the *Afro-American* protested that a supposedly "enlightened white educator" was endorsing unequal school funding in America based on the ability to pay of segregated groups—"a theory ancient and un-Christian, unscientific and fallacious, impractical if extended and altogether subversive of the best interests of the state and the nation." Applauding the NAACP's legal challenges to racial discrimination in education, the *Afro-American* concluded, "The National Association will have the full support of thinking citizens in its war on Woofterism." Jack Woofter did not see the editorial, but other black newspapers reprinted it and he was sent a version from the *Savannah Tribune*. In response, he said the *Afro-American* had "misunderstood my point of view and classed me where I do not belong." He claimed he was only trying to explain the tax system as it applied to the St. Helena islanders and that he was personally in favor of "more and better schools of all kinds and a more just distribution of the public funds." He pointed to his statements to this effect in *The Basis of Racial Adjustment*, but said it was only realistic to acknowledge that more equal treatment "would require a degree of altruism which does not now exist in [black belt] counties. Mark you I do not say that it ought not exist." In the current racial climate, the best blacks could expect in school spending was the amount they paid in school-related taxes, although, he added, "Under other circumstances they might and ought to ask more." He signed off with a plea: "Please remove me from the ranks of the Bourbons. Yours for big red schoolhouses."[73] He was being sincere, but it was typical of him not to say forcefully what those "other circumstances" were, or spell out how civil rights progress might be achieved. In his eagerness not to offend white readers in *Black Yeomanry* and his refusal to endorse black demands for immediate reform, he exposed the interracial cooperation movement's fatal weakness.

W. E. B. Du Bois's reaction to *Black Yeomanry* showed that his patience with southern liberalism had finally run out. He was appalled—it was "another result of the recent school of white southerner investigation into the situation of the Southern Negro," in which negative aspects of black autonomy were stressed and the myriad failings of American democracy were skirted around. He trashed it in the November 1930 *Crisis:* "There is not a single word of really illuminating information. . . . Woofter's study is little less than a calamity. It is a glossing over of obvious facts and seeking to say that on the sea islands of Carolina we have a simple development in agricultural depression much like that elsewhere in the world and not particularly complicated by political disfranchisement, race prejudice, and enforced ignorance."[74]

As well as the perceived laziness of *Black Yeomanry*, Du Bois was troubled by the funding lavished on the project—over $16,000 provided by the SSRC—at a time when able black scholars struggled to get assistance.

> It is a shame that the Boards and Funds which are spending money for investigation in the South should continue to pursue this line of so-called sociological research. There is absolutely no need of it. The conclusions to which the Woofter school of investigation is coming are well-known and perfectly clear before they put pen to paper. They need no statistics nor investigation, or other scientific paraphernalia. Their reports are propaganda, pure and simple, and attempt to say to the world that whatever is wrong in the South is not due to the race question but to ordinary social difficulties which can be found everywhere.
>
> Why is it that Negro scholars, like Woodson, Frazier and Ira Reid, men who when they see obvious conclusions, have the common honesty to express them, can seldom get funds for work?[75]

What dismayed Du Bois about studies of racial issues was the casual manner with which white analysts offered data, tentative insights, and mild liberal critiques, before concluding that racial attitudes and barriers in the South were fixed, that only small adjustments could be made within existing structures and mores, and that basic discrimination would persist for the foreseeable future.[76] In 1928, while noting Melville Herskovits as an exception, Du Bois had remarked that "social science in America has so long been the football of 'nigger'-hating propaganda that we Negroes fail to get excited when a new scientist comes into the field . . . we assume he is going to come out exactly where he went in." During the 1930s, Du Bois would have repeated reason to lament the ease with which white-authored studies on race gained support. He longed to "restore to the American Negro his rightful hegemony of scientific investigation and guidance of the Negro problem" and believed that white liberals were incapable of telling the truth to each other, let alone to African Americans.[77]

In the case of *Black Yeomanry*, Du Bois was not entirely fair. In the chapters on government and education, Woofter and Heer delivered carefully worded critiques of the inequality endured by the black residents of St. Helena Island because of their skin color, but it was that very carefulness that was starting to exasperate the *Crisis* editor. On the research funding issue, Du Bois ignored the fact that Woofter's book was a commercial product of the St. Helena Island project and that the UNC Press had put out Guy Johnson's study of the Gullah dialect, folk songs, and folklore of St. Helena and Guion Johnson's social history of the Sea Islands, both paid for by the same grant as *Black Yeomanry* and containing sharply focused, revisionist analyses.[78] But Du Bois was right to complain that the research councils were gravy trains for white scholars and that important projects were closed off to black researchers.

Carter G. Woodson, writing in the *Journal of Negro History,* saw *Black Yeomanry* as proof that "in the final analysis the Negro must treat his own record scientifically." The main problem was the all-white research team. Although "the effort does point the right way," he wrote, the book was "a combination of almost all observations which white persons travelling in an isolated rural community in the South would publish as comments on the life of people of whom they have just begun to learn." It said nothing that black social scientists did not know, "but probably because Negroes cannot break bread with white men they were not required to cooperate." Woodson saw some hopeful signs in the work of "Woofter and others like him. . . . Some of these persons are really sincere in their efforts to employ science to improve interracial relations, although, until they take account of the Negro investigator . . . they can never perform such a task." Nevertheless, Woofter and his colleagues were an improvement on the generation of southerners who rewrote Reconstruction "in order to white-wash their ancestors who overthrew the only democratic governments the South ever had and reestablished slavery as peonage."[79]

In the *Journal of Negro Education,* Helen C. Harris, a black teacher, was dismayed by Woofter's comments on black education and aspiration: "One may question the philosophy which occasionally gives a characteristic tone to his interpretations, for example, his fatalism with respect to the possibilities of improvement in the distribution of school funds, or his apparent assumption, in the discussion of migration, that a long, quiet life is to be desired in preference to a less long but more varied existence." The black sociologist Ira De A. Reid, writing in the NUL journal, *Opportunity,* reacted similarly. He appreciated the "intelligent simplicity" of *Black Yeomanry,* calling it a "vivid recital of a lesser known phase of Negro life," and welcomed the project's other detailed studies, but he found it "unfortunate . . . that the book had to be patterned into our present unsettled scheme of race relations." Reid would have preferred Woofter to confront Beaufort County's unjust taxation system, instead of stating baldly that, in the absence of white altruism, poor black schooling for poor black people was a fact of life.[80]

In contrast, the white reviewers of *Black Yeomanry* were almost uniformly complimentary and oblivious to the glaring flaw that preoccupied black readers. Robert Redfield of the University of Chicago, writing in the *American Journal of Sociology,* was impressed by the book's "reliability and freedom from distortion." In the *New York Herald Tribune,* the playwright Paul Green, who studied folklore with Odum, recognized that *Black Yeomanry* was "a synopsis of the whole project written in a readable and nontechnical style" and called it "unique among the thousands of books concerned with the Negro in that it sets out to present a unified picture of a whole community and the factors that have made it what it is." He thought Guy Johnson's chapter on folklore was the best; "the rest of the volume, for all its information and interest, shows all the faults of sociologists— balky and uncertain writing." Columbia University linguist Allen W. Porterfield in the *Outlook* found the book "a glorious story of this out-of-way place."[81]

On his return to Chapel Hill, Woofter was made professor of statistics and population problems in the Department of Sociology and the IRSS, a post he held until 1935. He served the functions Odum had envisaged: teaching undergraduate and graduate students, advising research teams about statistical analysis, and liaising between the IRSS and various charities. The IRSS hit its stride from 1928 onward, with three professors, and a dozen research associates and assistants occupied on a range of local and regional projects and publications. Odum targeted the collection and analysis of data on southern women, state government, voting rights, the 1928 election, the Florida land boom, taxation, farming, industry, black history, "folk background and cultural patterns," the physical environment, diet, county studies, crime and justice, welfare, and music. The one area that was inadequately covered in Odum's plans was southern education.[82]

During the St. Helena project, Woofter undertook other work and was not shut away until Danville was forgotten. In February 1928, he attended a gathering of leading social scientists in Washington, D.C., one of three special conferences paid for by the LSRM and organized by the Division of Anthropology and Psychology of the NRC, on deafness, experimental psychology, and race. The race conference was run in collaboration with the SSRC and led to an agreement on future studies. The twenty leading scholars invited to participate included Franz Boas and W. I. Thomas (for their work on immigrants); Melville Herskovits (for work on social selection and physical types); Joseph Peterson (for work on testing African American intelligence); and Clark Wissler of the American Museum of Natural History. There were seven presentations, including Woofter's paper on "Negro Sociology."[83] Reviewing American race relations during 1928, Herskovits had Woofter in mind: "Interracial groups continue to function, and white southern writers seem to have reached a point where they attempt to portray the Negro as he actually lives and do not caricature him in the traditional manner."[84]

Another of Woofter's projects during the St. Helena period relied on three master's students, Thomas Holland, Roland B. Eutsler, and Robinson Newcomb, and concerned the farm population between 1920 and 1925. Published in *Social Forces* as "The Negro and the Farm Crisis," it described conditions in southeastern farming communities in the terms later associated with the Great Depression. Woofter argued that "the evils attending the farm tenant system and conditions in the courts" meant that for the poorest people in the South it was now class, rather than race, that caused disadvantage. His figures suggested otherwise, however: between 1920 and 1925, 84 percent of the 96,000 farmers in South Carolina, Georgia, Alabama, and Mississippi who left the land were black. Faced with bad weather, pests, debt, primitive methods, and limited markets, farm families were abandoning cotton and harvesting woodland instead, or moving to cities, so that in several central Georgia counties it was "possible to ride from one town to another without passing an occupied farm." The most prosperous states were North Carolina and Tennessee, which had diversified and reduced cotton acreage. Woofter implied that having a substantial black population in a community damaged its chances of economic recovery, since blacks were less resourceful: "The rural population of an area with a smaller proportion of colored people can handle the situation much better than could be done in such states as Mississippi and South Carolina which contained a majority of negroes up to 1910." He therefore welcomed the fact that in 1925 there were a million fewer black farmers than in 1910. Farming had once been the best way for a black family to become independent in the South, but by the late 1920s this was no longer true. Many of the black families seeking tenancies after World War I were former landowners who lost their farms, along with their animals and tools, in the crosscurrents of postwar depression, deflation, and cotton overproduction. From a peak of 161,000 in 1910, the number of southern black farm owners had fallen to 145,000 by 1925, and Woofter, for all that he re-

spected men like Asbury McClusky in Barrow County, Georgia, gave no indica-
tion that he wanted special measures to increase their ranks.[85]

The national academic engagement with race and interracial cooperation in
the 1920s peaked with the second National Interracial Conference in Washington, D.C., in 1928. George E. Haynes and Will Alexander used the impetus of the
Cincinnati interracial conference in 1925 to link sixteen organizations, led by the
NUL, the NAACP, the CIC, the Phelps-Stokes Fund, the YMCA, the YWCA,
and the Federal Council of Churches. In February 1926, they announced that the
"National Interracial Conference" organizing body, chaired by Mary van Kleeck,
would plan another event the following year around the theme of "race problems
in the United States in the light of research," but it proved impossible to final-
ize. Instead, in December 1927, Leonard Outhwaite of the LSRM created a small
Negro Problems Conference at Yale University along interracial cooperationist
lines. Twenty-two men, fourteen of them black, took part in frank, informal dis-
cussions about the future of American race relations. The black men included
John Hope and Robert Russa Moton of the CIC, Charles S. Johnson and Eugene
Kinckle Jones of the NUL, James Weldon Johnson of the NAACP, and A. Philip
Randolph of the Brotherhood of Sleeping Car Porters. The white men included
Will Alexander, Thomas Jesse Jones, and Edwin R. Embree of the Rosenwald
Fund.[86] By 1928, momentum for a National Interracial Conference was such that
Alexander, as chair of the SSRC's interracial relations committee, agreed to fund
"an attempt to bring together the leaders of the various organizations which are
working practically in the field of race relations—those persons who are actually
trying to improve the race situation in America."[87] It would also allow them to
highlight issues for the incoming federal administration.

Hosted by the Department of the Interior and Howard University in December 1928, and largely administered by the NUL, the second National Interracial
Conference invited several organizations and government agencies to share their
perspectives. The executive committee provided all participants in advance with
recent research on African American life, organized into a single volume by outgoing NUL research director Charles S. Johnson. When the conference actually
began, Johnson, who trained under Robert E. Park in Chicago, was chairman
of the department of social sciences at Fisk University. His work for the Chicago Commission on Race Relations and the NUL convinced him that assimilation of minorities in all walks of American life was imperative, whatever tensions
might be aroused, and he hoped the 1928 gathering would celebrate this principle.
Every delegate received a 300-page "data-book," edited and largely written by
Johnson and later reused in *The Negro in American Civilization* as "The Problem";
the second part, entitled "The Problem Discussed," would consist of the conference proceedings. *The Negro in American Civilization* proclaimed the capacity of

the social sciences to help solve problems such as ill health, poor education, and crime through "planning and engineering."[88] A 350-page issue of the *Annals of the American Academy of Political and Social Science* was also devoted to "The American Negro" (with an advisory editorial committee including Charles S. Johnson, James Weldon Johnson, and Mary van Kleeck), timed to coincide with the Washington conference.[89]

The 1925 and 1928 National Interracial Conferences differed markedly. The first event was explicitly interracial, but attracted an uneasy mix of community organizers, religious and secular do-gooders, civil rights activists, and social scientists. The 1928 conference was less religious, and its structure allowed fruitful interaction between activists, cooperationists, academics, and government officials. Moreover, by 1928, a decade's worth of postwar advances in social science research on racial matters could be displayed to the charities that paid for most of the work. The lives of African Americans were examined in relation to changes in health, education, housing, recreation, employment, migration, voting, and the courts, in the contexts of war, mass urbanization, and the Harlem Renaissance. The Washington conference thus gave two hundred delegates opportunities to challenge conventional thinking and identify areas for research. Black politicians and journalists were underrepresented, but Howard University's Alain Locke insisted the proceedings represented "the most comprehensive and authoritative analysis of the contemporary situation of the Negro in America anywhere available."[90]

The optimism of the interracial cooperation movement was evident in Washington—Will Alexander and Robert B. Eleazer arrived fresh from the tenth annual meeting of the CIC, having noted numerous "encouraging trends"—but southern liberals were outnumbered by radical delegates from the North, including A. Philip Randolph, an NAACP contingent of W. E. B. Du Bois, Walter White, James Weldon Johnson, Herbert J. Seligmann, Oswald Garrison Villard, and Arthur Spingarn, and NUL leaders Eugene Kinckle Jones and T. Arnold Hill. The main black Christian denominations were present with the YMCA and the YWCA and various smaller groups working for racial harmony, such as the progressive reforming group, the Inquiry, represented by John Hope and Bruno Lasker, and the Fellowship of Reconciliation, which sent the Congregationalist minister Howard Kester. The prominent white social worker Grace Abbott, who worked with Jane Addams in Chicago, attended on behalf of the U.S. Children's Bureau with Mary Anderson, first director of the Department of Labor's Women's Bureau. With one exception, the philanthropic bodies sent white men: Anson Phelps Stokes, Clark Foreman, and Thomas Jesse Jones represented the Phelps-Stokes Fund; Leo Favrot, the General Education Board; Graham R. Taylor, the Commonwealth Fund; Robert M. Lester, the Carnegie Foundation; and Beardsley Ruml, the LSRM. Edwin Embree attended for the Rosenwald Fund with the former Chicago YMCA official George R. Arthur, described by Embree's biographer as "probably the first person of African descent to work for any foundation in a professional capacity."[91]

Black women educators present included Nannie H. Burroughs and Mary McLeod Bethune, who had just completed four years as president of the National Association of Colored Women. Howard University sent Alain Locke, Kelly Miller, Abram Harris, Charles Wesley, and President Mordecai W. Johnson; Fisk University sent Horace Mann Bond, Charles S. Johnson, and President Thomas Elsa Jones; Hampton and Tuskegee Institutes sent their respective principals, James E. Gregg and Robert Russa Moton, who was accompanied by Monroe Work. Lorenzo Greene attended for the Association for the Study of Negro Life and History. White social scientists present included Robert Lynd of the SSRC, Broadus Mitchell and Raymond Pearl of Johns Hopkins University, the criminologist Thorsten Sellin of the University of Pennsylvania, Harold Gosnell of the University of Chicago, and Frank Porter Graham and Jack Woofter from UNC. The only significant figure to decline van Kleeck's invitation was the political scientist Charles E. Merriam.[92]

Woofter reported on the "alarming sanitary conditions and direct and indirect exploitation in housing" and violence that black families faced in parts of northern cities. He called on financiers to provide cheap mortgages and for loan associations and model housing schemes to replicate the work in New York of the Rockefeller Foundation and in Chicago of the Rosenwald Fund.[93] His optimistic tone was echoed by most speakers, especially Herbert A. Miller of Ohio State University, one of the few white academics who had also been present at Cincinnati. Miller claimed that immigration restriction made "the Negro question the dominating minority problem now before the country." "The Negro was inheriting the interest and the effective co-operation of that group of people who previously had been interested in [immigration]. In fact, something of the technique of the whole Americanization program in connection with the emigrant foreigner had transferred itself to a consideration, a rather constructive consideration, of the Negro and his problem." Consequently, argued Miller, a "rationalization of race antipathies and race prejudices" would gradually occur as black people disproved the lies told about them, so that by the 1950s, he predicted, they would have made more progress than any other group in American society.[94] W. E. B. Du Bois was a good deal less sanguine. He saw the failure to guarantee immediate rights of citizenship to blacks in all parts of the country as the fundamental problem: "I hold this truth to be self-evident, that a disfranchised working class in modern industrial civilization is worse than helpless. It is a menace, not simply to itself, but to every group in the community. It will be diseased; it will be criminal; it will be ignorant; it will be the plaything of mobs, and it will be insulted by caste restrictions."[95]

In contrast, Alain Locke's final review of the conference was deliberately upbeat. He commended the organizers for getting around segregationist practices in the District of Columbia: "As a result of tactful canvass by officers of the conference, four of the leading Washington hotels housed both the white and Negro members of the executive committee, thus opening up the civilized amenities of the national capital as an interracial conference center. This significant departure... removed the embarrassments of many previous Washington conferences." By the end, he claimed, the conference sessions had "reinforced much isolated and lonely liberalism with the realization that a rapidly accumulating body of sound facts and human precedent are on the side of progress." According to Locke, the race question had been elevated to a new plane of "non-sentimentality" and "mutuality of the group gain," making the conference "'unique' 'historic,'... 'epoch-making.'" He settled on "pentecostal," because people whose personalities and opinions normally clashed were united behind a "new scientific race thought."[96] Charles S. Johnson's report for the *American Journal of Sociology* also implied that interracial dialogue was permanently established; as a result, "the conference group, feeling that its task had been accomplished, voted to discontinue itself as a formal organization."[97] Walter White of the NAACP, writing in the *Nation,* called the conference "the most significant gesture ever made in these United States towards solution of the race problem," and Mary van Kleeck thought it left "an enlarged consciousness of the many phases of this process of attempting to create a composite civilization."[98] All of these assessments were excessively positive, but the 1928 conference affirmed the commitment of the Rosenwald Fund, the Phelps-Stokes Fund, the Carnegie Foundation and others, thereby enabling collaborative studies over the next decade that increased public appreciation of the complexity of American racial problems. The principle that Jack Woofter advocated throughout the 1920s—that for the good of all, whenever race was discussed, interracial cooperation should supplant old inhibitions—won out at Washington, and herein lay the conference's lasting importance. Nevertheless, as historian Leah Gordon has noted, the planning and discussions of the conference still rested on narrow questions about "Negro problems," rather than wider societal or political problems.[99]

Between 1929 and 1934, Woofter grew increasingly expert on farm problems and rural poverty at the IRSS and became a valued colleague, recalled by Arthur Raper as "quiet and discerning" and often amusing. He continued to serve with the white industrial psychologist Morris S. Viteles, and the black biologist Ernest E. Just, on the SSRC's interracial relations subcommittee, under Joseph Peterson's chairmanship, until it was dissolved in 1930.[100] Thereafter, he remained interested in black life—calling for studies of the "dominant" role of race in southern politics following the 1928 election, and writing about changes in African American demographics, migration, and agriculture, before branching out into analyses of other minority issues, the problems of tobacco production, and the southern regional studies fostered by Odum.[101]

In 1930, he was given a stark warning about the hazards of government-sponsored research and the frustration that black social scientists felt concerning white academic work on race. Seeking advice on the economic plight of black Americans, President Herbert Hoover established a commission consisting of Robert R. Moton, Secretary of Commerce Robert P. Lamont, Secretary of Agriculture Arthur M. Hyde, American Federation of Labor leader William Green, and Julius Rosenwald, who paid for the necessary research and meetings. Woofter was hired to write the commission's report, "A Study of the Economic Status of the Negro," completing it in June 1930. He proposed numerous federal, state, and private initiatives, including farm cooperatives, employment schemes under the Federal Board for Vocational Education, and black employment bureaus under the Department of Labor. The largest section was on agriculture, with smaller sections on population and industry. The key findings were released to the press in October, but several copies of the 120-page typescript, marked "Confidential," were already circulating. The Rosenwald Report, as it became known, was informative, succinct, and, in Woofter's eyes, hardly sensational: it acknowledged widespread discrimination, but it was primarily a survey in his usual, fact-filled, detached style. It offered a muted critique of racial discrimination in African American economic life, noting the exclusivity of white farmers' associations and labor unions and tensions over access to skilled work in areas such as carpentry. Arthur Raper's investigations in and around Greene County, Georgia, were mentioned in relation to farm desertion, but the report said nothing about the lynching problem that Raper exposed, focusing instead on the value of cooperatives. Hoover's failure to act on the report as the economic crisis worsened in the following months dismayed his remaining black supporters and added to what historian Donald Lisio has called an "impression of presidential neglect."[102]

For W. E. B. Du Bois, the Rosenwald Report was the last straw; his patience with well-funded white social scientists had run out and in the February 1931 *Crisis,* he promised readers a "frank and telling criticism of Woofterism."[103] The following month, in a three-page, tightly spaced article, entitled simply "Woofterism" (acknowledging the *Baltimore Afro-American*'s coinage), he flayed Woofter and his research assistants, including the black sociologist Ira De A. Reid, and T. Arnold Hill, director of the NUL's department of industrial relations. They had produced a report that was "neither candid, scientific nor conclusive," Du Bois wrote. "In fact, I regard it as a distinctly dangerous symptom. . . . When a Southern white man comes to the study of the race problem apparently with the idea of leaving out all 'controversial' matter, and nevertheless calls the results scientific, then something is being done that is not only wrong but vicious."

Du Bois recalled commending *The Basis of Racial Adjustment* in 1925, but Woofter's work had deteriorated—now he was a collector of facts, although "he does not give all the facts, while his conclusions are grossly inadequate and incomplete." Woofter's refusal to rock the boat was exasperating, and Du Bois was disgusted by the claim that poor black farmers were too ignorant and dull to seek credit and expert advice. Black people needed a fair chance to gain skills and equal pay, and an end to segregation, he wrote, "but in such a development of a new and self-respecting industry, Mr. Woofter is not interested. He is interested in the old 'darkey' servant, paid low wages, working under conditions of personal subjection, which the working people of the world and of all colors are trying to repudiate." Why else, he asked, would Woofter recommend industrial education and domestic science, and deny black children any hope of white-collar jobs?[104]

Du Bois had had enough. For a decade, he had watched liberal white researchers with few real qualms about Jim Crow or disfranchisement (and a handful of conservative black scholars) cornering philanthropic funds for "Negro problem" research in which fact-harvesting was prized more highly than critical analysis. In a society in urgent need of honesty about intentional inequality, the sight of academics from wealthy research centers sidestepping the issue, especially in the South, nauseated Du Bois, who decided to make Woofter the whipping-boy for a generation of white liberal social science.

Woofter never forgot the *Crisis* editor's jibes—Du Bois's condescension toward the CIC in the *Nation* in 1925, his attack on *Black Yeomanry,* and the "Woofterism" insults regarding the Rosenwald Report. Thirty years later Woofter wrote, "He was a brilliant writer but one whose pen was often dipped in vinegar and whose sarcasm was so sharp as to alienate Southern opinion rather than to win it over."[105]

If Woofter wanted revenge, an opportunity presented itself at the end of 1931 when Du Bois was belatedly invited to join the Phelps-Stokes Fund's projected "Encyclopedia of the Negro," an idea Du Bois had fostered for twenty years. An eminent interracial advisory panel was assembled, but Du Bois apparently felt that Jones and Woofter, who both sat on the executive committee, had tried initially to marginalize him. He told James H. Dillard that he "could not for a moment contemplate a Negro encyclopedia dominated and controlled by Thomas Jesse Jones and Mr. Woofter. I do not, of course, want to exclude them or what they represent," but the work had to be entrusted mainly to black writers and editors. He told the advisory panel that he had not "the slightest animus" against Jones or Woofter, who had "tried honestly to express their point of view and to carry out the measures which they personally think best for the colored people, nevertheless, there is no doubt but that a large number of American Negroes do not believe that anyone of these . . . men can adequately today express the point of view of the American Negro." It raised a fundamental question: "Have those people who have control of the philanthropic endowments and the scientific endowments yet reached the place where they are willing to finance such an effort of Negro scholarship without seeking to control it?" A few years earlier, Du Bois had complained, "Thomas Jesse Jones and the Phelps Stokes Fund are very much afraid of me and mine [.] . . . They belong to that group of Americans who propose to do things for the Negroes by means of white people and to allow the Negroes themselves to have no voice in it." Du Bois's biographer, David Levering Lewis, suspects Jones and Woofter did work against him. Certainly, Jones took an almost paternal interest in Woofter's career and well-being, and was known to harbor and act on grudges against critics, but there is no evidence that he or Woofter tried directly to impede Du Bois's hopes for the encyclopedia, unlike Melville Herskovits, who wrote several letters of opposition. Woofter attended planning meetings at Howard University along with Will Alexander, Benjamin Brawley, Jackson Davis, James Dillard, W. E. B. Du Bois, George E. Haynes, John Hope, Charles S. Johnson, Mordecai Johnson, James Weldon Johnson, Eugene Kinckle Jones, Thomas Elsa Jones, Thomas Jesse Jones, Alain Locke, Kelly Miller, Walter White, and Monroe Work. During the meetings, Woofter proposed that the emphasis should be on the American Negro and indicated, when the editorship was discussed, that, "of the two propositions, a joint [black and white] editorship or an all-Negro board, he favored the former but would not be displeased with the latter." The group voted for a mixed editorial board and agreed by a majority that the editors should be led by a black person, Du Bois being duly selected. Over the following decade, the project failed to secure additional funding from the SSRC, the Rosenwald Fund, the GEB, or the Carnegie Corporation. In the protracted wrangling over money and the scope of the "Encyclopedia of the Negro," Du Bois may have suspected that Thomas Jesse Jones and Woofter hampered the project because of things he had written about them, but they were not the only ones with doubts about his temperament. If Woofter and Jones affected the outcome at all, it was only indirectly. They may have colored the views of Dillard, Davis, and the GEB, which withheld its support, because, as Anson Phelps Stokes told Du Bois, there were "objections, which were apparently mainly based on the difficulty of assuring absolute objectivity." The subsequent unfavorable decision of the Carnegie Corporation followed an observation by its secretary, Robert M. Lester, a white educationist from Alabama, that relations between black and white participants at planning meetings were "tense," but there were also concerns about how long the seventy-three year-old Du Bois could remain active.[106]

By now, Woofter was fair game in the black press. Carter G. Woodson, who had been pushing his own "Encyclopedia Africana," took a swing at Woofter in an attempt to discredit Du Bois's project. Woodson had already trashed the charitable foundations' approach to race scholarship, calling *Black Yeomanry* an example of the "futile . . . efforts of numerous boards and groups which have organized to solve the Negro problem without consulting the Negro himself. They meet behind closed doors, work out their plans, and then have them accepted by certified Negroes, who know nothing about the problem at hand. That is what is now known as interracial cooperation."[107] In June 1932, in his *New York Age* column, Woodson commented, "Recently Negroes have cooperated with T. J. Woofter, who in his 'Race Adjustment' justified segregation and in his report on agricultural conditions makes a good case for peonage and slavery enforced on cotton and sugar plantations. If the Negroes keep up such co-operation, they will soon be 'co-operated' back to bondage."[108]

Mounting black criticism did not noticeably harm Jack Woofter's career, but it impressed on him that prejudice and discrimination could not be glossed over. His profile as an authority on race continued to grow, so that when Odum became assistant research director of the President's Research Committee on Social Trends, set up by Herbert Hoover with Rockefeller funding, Woofter was asked to contribute on racial and ethnic groups. The authors of the twenty-nine chapters assembled in June 1930 to be told by the chief editor, William F. Ogburn, of the University of Chicago, to be "as scientific as possible." Woofter's submission presented racial prejudice and violence, stemming from economic competition and social anxieties, as explicit causes of group differences in wealth, education, and health. These problems, he argued, would gradually lessen over time. According to historians Donald Lisio and Barry Karl, this stress on prejudice in American life so alarmed the research committee's secretary, the Columbia University-based economist and bureaucrat Edward Eyre Hunt, that he removed it from the interim release of Woofter's findings in 1932. When Woofter complained, Hunt told Odum, "If you think there is apt to be any sensitiveness at all on Mr. Woofter's part, won't you please grab him and hold his hand during the reading of the revision?" Odum protested that Woofter was not "stubborn. . . . It is simply his temperament, and Ogburn ought to understand this." In the end, despite Ogburn's aversion to opinions, Woofter's conclusions regarding "exploitation and prejudice" survived, not only in the two-volume report, *Recent Social Trends,* but also in his 250-page contribution to the committee's monograph series, also published in 1933 as *Races and Ethnic Groups in American Life.*[109]

In the monograph, Woofter wrote about the "progress of the Negro in the acquisition of American culture" and attacked white prejudice. He also covered the geographic distribution of different groups, their employment, education, health, assimilation, and social problems. He included a sparkling section by Guy Johnson on "Negro-White Relations," showing how African American progress and rising confidence were impeded by nationwide prejudice and southern segregation. Noting the militancy of northern black political thought, Johnson predicted, "the thinking of Negroes in the South will come to be more and more aggressive. . . .

Prejudice is a reality. The determination of Negroes to secure equality of status is also a reality. In the very nature of the case, the problem is dynamic, constantly calling for new thought, new methods, new adjustments."[110]

At the end of the book, Woofter introduced a personal note, as he considered the future of American race relations and the "Complexity of race adjustment." He affirmed his belief in interracial cooperation and the power of goodwill, and showed that, of his three great mentors—Thomas Jesse Jones, Will Alexander, and Howard Odum—it was the first who most influenced him still. In 1929, Jones had published *Essentials of Civilization,* in which he wrote, "Sound policy requires both the conservation of worth-while [racial] differences and also the stimulation of the identities necessary to cooperative relations of all races. Individual and racial differentiations thus become the basis of mutual respect, and identities serve to unite all in the tasks that are common to all."[111] Jack Woofter firmly believed this, and his analysis of American racial problems exhibited the same mixture of fatalism, liberalism, and racism to be found in Jones's work. Woofter's fatalism led him to write in *Races and Ethnic Groups in American Life* that as long as racial difference existed, prejudice would be a "a real and stubborn fact" and that, "little as one may sympathize with prejudice in its more unjust manifestations[,] it is well to recognize its inevitability as a social phenomenon and to deal with it as such." Woofter's liberalism lay in his parallel argument that progress depended on the achievement of "a double goal[:] . . . the elimination of un-useful differences through the processes of assimilation and the curbing of the inhuman and unjust manifestation of prejudice through the development of tolerance and the promotion of cooperation."[112] Woofter's racism lurked in the final sentence of the book, where he spelled out the conceivable degrees of assimilation and change in America. He was all for "healthy tolerance and efficient utilization of differences and the elimination of the undesirable manifestations of prejudice," but he was still haunted by the specters of "social equality" and "amalgamation." He remained convinced that, through non-ideological interracial cooperation, "a heterogeneous nation may safeguard its institutions and the race purity of the majority while granting to the minorities justice and opportunities for free self-development."[113] Here was the line in the sand that white interracial cooperationists like Woofter, Jones, and Alexander drew for African Americans (and especially African American men). The imaginary sign above that line read, "We respect you as faithful brethren in Christ; we believe in your constitutional rights as citizens; we want you to share in American prosperity; but do not seek intimacy with white people and do not aspire to govern."

In 1933 and 1934, Woofter undertook special studies for the Tennessee Valley Authority after Odum commended him to TVA director Arthur E. Morgan as "a very genuine spirit as well as a good social statistician."[114] In 1935, like dozens of other social scientists, Woofter was formally recruited by the federal government—

"the mad house which is Washington," as he called it—and became a civil servant until his retirement. His work for the New Deal involved issues of race, class, and poverty, but he never became part of what Jacquelyn Dowd Hall has identified as a radical intellectual "Southern Front."[115] The North Carolinian social economist Ellen Winston, Woofter's coauthor on *Seven Lean Years,* a survey of the rural impact of the Great Depression, recalled him as generous, "gentle and courteous. . . . Appearing older physically than his years, he was ever a highly professional sociologist in the best liberal tradition, dedicated to understanding and amelioration of basic social problems."[116] Woofter served successively as either director of research or economic advisor in the Federal Emergency Relief Administration, the Farm Security Administration, the Federal Security Agency, and the Central Intelligence Agency, publishing numerous lengthy studies and short articles that either influenced government policy or became standard summaries of its effects. He also briefed Gunnar Myrdal in detail concerning southern race relations during the latter's preparation of *An American Dilemma,* published in 1944.[117]

In 1957, Jack Woofter self-published his memoirs, *Southern Race Progress: The Wavering Color Line,* after failing to attract a commercial or university press for the first time in his career. It contained his experiences in the interracial cooperation movement and called on America to respond to the civil rights movement of the 1950s with gradual reform to win over moderate white southerners. The North Carolinian author and journalist Jonathan W. Daniels found it a "charming and challenging" autobiographical account of "this troubled South." Henry McGuinn, a coauthor of *Negro Problems in Cities* in 1928, called Woofter's memoirs "an eloquent expression of faith in the efficacy of voluntary cooperation [and] the product of a generous spirit," and Carl Holman, who would become deputy director of the Civil Rights Commission and president of the National Urban Coalition, called it "an outstanding scientist's painstaking retrospective."[118]

When Jack Woofter left federal government service in 1958, he and Ethel retired to Alabama to be near her relatives. He died in Montgomery in 1972, aged seventy-nine (she died a year later, aged eighty-five), having witnessed the kind of strife over civil rights that he deplored—and political changes that he could scarcely have imagined fifty years earlier, in the aftermath of the War for Democracy, when he was secretary of the Georgia State Committee on Race Relations during the heyday of the Klan.

Conclusion

THE CONVENTIONAL VIEW of the southern interracial cooperation movement of the 1910s and 1920s is that it was too conservative and, by implication, that it would have achieved more by challenging racial discrimination head-on. This is wrong on both counts. The movement was about as critical, far-reaching, and effective as the forbiddingly racist and violent context allowed, and the CIC, in particular, initiated face-to-face dialogue between the races, promoted the reform of education and social work, improved health care, encouraged responsible journalism, and accelerated the eradication of lynching. White southern liberals were not responsible for the fact that they were a tiny, beleaguered minority after World War I, or for the racism that affected their own upbringing as individuals. Jack Woofter's observation, that "all of us—white and colored, North and South—interpret race through the film of our environment and experience" is undeniable, and to argue that southern liberals ought to have openly attacked white supremacy and segregation before the Great Depression is unrealistic.[1] Southern white liberals were able to work to improve race relations and public knowledge *because* they were cautious.

The white members of the CIC were determined to live in the South and make a difference, but that meant slow, uneven progress, at best. Equivocation, so often the main charge against southern white liberals, was an essential tactic in the preservation of a network and creed of interracial cooperation that might otherwise have been destroyed by scorn. For a white person in the South, there was a price to pay for espousing interracial cooperation, in terms of one's social standing and peace of mind. The abuse heaped on Will Alexander and Robert Eleazer when they briefly questioned Jim Crow suggests they and others would have been pilloried into silence had they been as demonstrative on the race question as their successors after World War II. When Woofter wrote in his memoirs about the white "nonconformist on race . . . courting melancholia," he was recalling his own feelings and also, no doubt, those of his friend, Walter B. Hill, who became unstable a decade after clashing with reactionaries over the school-building program in Georgia. Shortly after Woofter completed his memoirs in 1957, the suicide of Juliette Hampton Morgan, an ostracized white librarian who supported civil rights protesters in Montgomery, Alabama, would have dismayed, but not surprised, him.[2]

Woofter understood why radical critics charged white liberals of his generation with cravenness, but he also vividly recalled the mentality that dominated the CIC's central office and its local committees:

[The] criticism which was lodged against the movement, with considerable justification, was that it was not bold enough, that it was too prone to implant the philosophy of cooperation without pushing for more spectacular actions. In any case this is a matter of judgment. The conscientious conviction of the members was that its modest gains would have been endangered by trying to push ahead too rapidly in the atmosphere of hostility which was encountered from considerable powers at that time.[3]

In the end, he believed, moderation was essential to ward off racist reaction and attract more white liberal support. He was certain that a "substantial part of the Southern support of the Commission was given because its philosophy was to adhere tacitly to the 'separate but equal' objective in race relations." He was right, except that the CIC's compliance with segregation was far from tacit.[4]

Most white supporters of interracial cooperation between 1910 and 1930 knew that a radical push for civil rights would come one day, but they were not inclined to support a premature struggle. For example, in 1912, James Hardy Dillard counseled like-minded southerners to concentrate on areas where improvement could be achieved in the short term, such as housing, education, and morality. Overambitious programs were to be avoided; "in the meanwhile there is enough at hand to engage our attention for a time." By the late 1920s, American society had undergone massive changes, but moderation still gripped liberals, who looked to future generations for fundamental change. In 1927, the University of South Carolina philosopher Josiah Morse, a cooperationist stalwart, predicted that new organizations would rise up to insist on "fair play." He foresaw a civil rights movement of "Klan-like" dedication, requiring "zealots and fanatics to initiate and forward it. Wars and crusades shape future history more in a year than the slower processes of education can in half a century, but we are not warriors or crusaders."[5]

If they were not warriors, Morse and his ilk were far from innocuous observers. As historian Adam Fairclough has remarked, there was a boldness in the mere advocacy of interracial cooperation in the era of World War I because it implied new relationships between blacks and whites: "Being civil to blacks as one might be civil to whites subverted segregation, because the caste system demanded an etiquette that made explicit, in *all* social interaction, the superiority of the white and the inferiority of the black."[6] In Will Alexander's eyes, those were precisely the terms in which the interracial cooperation movement deserved to be judged: had the work of the CIC positively affected attitudes and manners? He told the International Missionary Council in Jerusalem in 1928, "[T]he most important things are not what has actually been done, but the atmosphere that has been created. Race prejudices are not removed by a frontal attack. Goodwill is a by-product of contact and understanding. So the Church's policy must be one of 'persistent peaceful' penetration."[7] The black leader who most closely shared Alexander's vision, John Hope of Morehouse College, agreed that the movement's force lay in the essential questions it posed. He believed his generation was witnessing the start of white supremacy's destruction by its inherent contradictions. Hope predicted, "From now on injustice to Negroes may have a serious moral reaction on the white people even in their dealings with one another." A British missionary at Jerusalem found this a "luminous comment."[8]

Economic considerations also made interracial cooperation a timely strategy for southern progress after 1910. Many white businessmen, politicians, and journalists, alarmed at the preference for city life of two million or more black people, conceded the need for racial reconciliation within certain parameters, and African American leaders welcomed this effect. In 1928, Dean William S. Turner of Shaw University at Raleigh, North Carolina, concluded that a decade of migration wrought beneficial changes for blacks who remained in the South: "No one can travel, even through the remote provinces, without noting a growing civility on the part of white people toward Negroes. . . . The professional social equality bogey howler is losing his function in the changing South."[9] Partly out of self-interest and the fear of losing local labor, more white southerners were listening to arguments against discrimination.

Clearly, the mere existence of liberal white southerners in the Jim Crow era does not make them important; what is significant is that they formed a movement and made a difference. But how much difference, and how did the interracial cooperation movement contribute to the later civil rights movement? Ann Wells Ellis, the first historian to examine the CIC in any depth, offered the generous verdict that interracial cooperation "represented a beginning to a solution, not the solution itself, and as such was an important stepping-stone in the campaign for black rights."[10] More recently, the "long civil rights movement" thesis, in which protests of the 1950s and 1960s are traced to an alliance of labor-oriented black and white radicals responding to social ills during the Great Depression, has invited a new question: what did the activism of the 1930s owe to the interracial cooperation movement of the preceding two decades? The answer appears to be, not a great deal: ratcheting the civil rights movement narrative back into the 1920s in this way is unworkable, because only slight degrees of continuity existed between the interracial cooperation movement and the "Southern Front" of the 1930s. For one thing, the CIC and its supporters chipped away at different layers of white and black society from those that concerned the Southern Front writers and activists and the subsequent civil rights movement. And the prescriptions of the interracial cooperation movement and the civil rights movement for the amelioration of life in the South differed so much, ideologically and tactically, that the first movement can hardly be said to have given birth to the second.[11]

There is no reason to assume, therefore, that because white liberals operated in the South in the 1920s they must be the forerunners of whites who supported the Freedom Riders, or that Alexander's black collaborators must have laid organizational foundations for later grassroots black activism. White liberals after World War I sought to address certain legacies of southern history and resolve immediate problems. Whatever changes they may have hoped for as individuals, they were not collectively attempting to prepare the ground for a radical integrationist and mass democratic movement. Jack Woofter, writing in 1929 about the multiple effects of race on southern politics, anticipated merely "controversies which will undoubtedly rage before this agitated social situation is stabilized."[12] Later, in the era of the civil rights movement, activists tended to dismiss the interracial cooperation movement as unhelpful baggage. The writer Lillian Smith complained in 1957, a year after Alexander's death, that

> the very fact that the first interracial work in the South began in Georgia has proved recently to be a deterrent to progress. The old-timers are dogmatic; they stirred up a lot of dust in their day; all right, they say, that is the only way you can stir up dust, paw the ground the way we did. You can't move them. Some are dead now but their ghosts are still around. I appreciate what they did and what those still around are doing. But we need a fresh approach. Something younger, more vital, more risky, full of fun and ardor.[13]

In discussing the "long civil rights movement," Jacquelyn Dowd Hall cautions historians against "easy closure and satisfying upward and downward arcs."[14] Certainly, the history of the interracial cooperation movement offers tempting paradigms in which the CIC rises and the Ku Klux Klan and lynching fall, until the CIC gives way in the 1930s to more radical, energetic groups, such as the Fellowship of Southern Churchmen, the Southern Conference for Human Welfare, and the Southern Committee for People's Rights. Of course, the actuality was not so neat. At the end of the 1920s the southern liberal minority was not simply succeeded by a southern radical minority. For one thing, the interracial cooperation movement was not a static aggregation of people or ideas; for most of the men and women drawn to Atlanta in the 1920s to work for the CIC, it was a phase in their careers that propelled them on to other work elsewhere. This was certainly true for Clark Foreman, Arthur Raper, Jessie Daniel Ames, Jack Woofter, and even Will Alexander. The first two played a part in the "long civil rights movement," whereas the latter three did not, although their work impacted at times on race relations and government policy.[15] As federal officials in Washington, D.C., Woofter and Alexander remained largely committed to the ideals and methods of the CIC, but Foreman became more radical in the context of the New Deal. Tellingly, some white graduate students at UNC in the 1930s who participated in the "long civil rights movement" drew a distinction between their own radicalism and the "Will Alexander approach" of some of their professors.[16]

The interracial cooperation movement is best understood as an attempt to realize the objectives of late-nineteenth- and early-twentieth-century southern racial liberals, rather than the commencement of something that flowered thirty years later. The "Will Alexander approach" of avoiding unnecessary controversies that could incite extremists was learned in the face of the vigorous racist defense of disfranchisement and segregation that occurred after 1900. Southern writers, politicians, clergymen, and educators stressed the threat of amalgamation and the need for black subordination, and often forgave the passions that roused lynch mobs. The various organizations that called for interracial cooperation after 1910 represented the small number of white people who opposed the hardening of anti-Negro thought and were aware that black patience had limits. Jack Woofter was an instinctive conciliator, but Alexander instilled in him the resolve to challenge state underspending on black schools and health care, disfranchisement, aspects of segregation, injustice in the courts, and, above all, the violent tradition. Although he indulged in scientific racism in his own writing for the CIC, Woofter rejected the southern Herrenvolk ideal and was repelled by the vindictiveness of men like Dixon and Shufeldt.

During the two decades when race was a central part of his career, Woofter willingly occupied an uncomfortable position. Working in the direct or indirect employment of northern philanthropic bodies or the United States government, he was well aware that a white Georgian with northern friends and a record of championing black progress looked like a scallywag to many southerners. His CIC membership did not make him lose caste—he remained part of the Progressive middle class, with strong connections in church and education circles—but he knew the racial climate in Georgia could generate antipathy toward anyone advocating enlarged opportunities for the black population, even when the additional tax burden on whites was likely to be small. Merely by debating aspects of white supremacy, liberals invited the accusation that they were damaging a cornerstone of southern society. The editors of *Jumpin' Jim Crow* have noted that white supremacy was "a precarious balancing act, pulled in all directions by class, gender, and racial tensions," but to those who had the temerity to question it in the 1920s it must have seemed firmly entrenched.[17] By suggesting that many forms of segregation were pointless and that black education required massive investment, Jack Woofter was out of step with most white southern men and women of his class and generation, and he sensed their disapproval.

Woofter's analysis of southern problems often split readers along racial and ideological lines. Like so many southern liberals, he addressed the white reader, leaving black readers to follow the discussion at one remove, as part of the subject, rather than the audience. In publications sponsored by the Phelps-Stokes Fund, the Bureau of Education, the Bureau of Immigration, the CIC, the Rockefeller funds, the University of North Carolina, the state of Tennessee, and numerous New Deal agencies, he informed the white middle class about race problems, but revealed little that was new or meaningful to black people. When he referred to African Americans as "these belated people" and proceeded to describe their opinions and supposed qualities, the word "these" revealed even more than "belated"—as if he were indicating an exotic specimen to a botany class. There was also his fondness for supposedly humorous anecdotes about black life. His stories were gentle compared to his criticism of white people, but the stereotypes on which they rested negated his intended message so far as black readers were concerned. Most white liberal readers found his work farsighted and enlightened, whereas many blacks saw him as a plausible conservative, at best. The co-operationist sponsors of *Black Yeomanry* and the Rosenwald Report thought his work exemplary, whereas to W. E. B. Du Bois and Carter G. Woodson it revealed all that was wrong with southern liberalism. After working with civic leaguers in Atlanta in 1908, Du Bois was already skeptical about people who knew the racial status quo was immoral, but would not say so. In 1925, *The Basis of Racial Adjustment* fleetingly made him reconsider, but the more he saw of Woofter's work in the late 1920s and early 1930s, the more distasteful he found it. Woodson always harbored misgivings about Woofter and his associates in the interracial cooperation movement. He maintained a civil correspondence with Anson Phelps Stokes, who assisted the *Journal of Negro History,* but he despised Thomas Jesse Jones, regarding him as prejudiced and conspiratorial; he saw Jack Woofter as Jones's apprentice, and little better.

Woofter was a trained sociologist and statistician, but, apart from *Negro Migration,* his published work before he moved to Chapel Hill was influenced by whoever held the purse strings. The money keeping the interracial cooperation movement afloat came mostly from the North, in successive donations to the CIC from the YMCA, the Phelps-Stokes Fund, the Laura Spelman Rockefeller Memorial (LSRM), and the Rosenwald Fund. Rockefeller money, in particular, came with an expectation of scholarship on "the Negro problem"—hence Alexander's eagerness for Woofter to undertake research from 1924 to 1927—but it did not invite radical prescriptions for social change. Woofter's work contributed, therefore, to what John Stanfield has called "a race social science embedded in Jim Crow assumptions." Benefactors like Anson Phelps Stokes, John R. Mott, and Beardsley Ruml disbursed money to favored recipients like Charles S. Johnson, Jackson Davis, Jack Woofter, and Howard Odum, who duly fulfilled their obligations to their respective patrons.[18] That said, the work Woofter undertook clearly found an audience beyond the interracial cooperation movement and influenced scholarship. For several decades, *Negro Problems in Cities* was a starting point for black urban studies, and *The Basis of Racial Adjustment* was a standard college text in the South. His colleagues at UNC also drew on his expertise. Rupert B. Vance used Woofter's work on lynching for his study of cotton in southern culture, and Arthur F. Raper, who held Woofter's old job as CIC research director before returning to UNC, used his data indicating a correlation between cotton price fluctuation and the frequency of racial killing in *The Tragedy of Lynching,* an eloquent study sponsored by the CIC's offshoot, the Southern Commission on the Study of Lynching.[19]

Latterly, social scientists have cast Jack Woofter in the role of fact-gatherer for southern white liberalism—a technician, valuable to any venture with which he was connected, but far less important than those around him. There is some truth in this—while Woofter was eager to contribute to a new social order, he was not a leader. He was sincere and committed, but rarely made decisive judgments, tending to move in the directions he was nudged by Jones, Alexander, or Odum. Certainly, he never displayed the career-oriented drive and confidence of that trio, or the poise of Clark Foreman and Robert Eleazer, or the clear-eyed certainty of Willis D. Weatherford and Lily Hardy Hammond. Nevertheless, Woofter's career and publication record between 1917 and 1955 included groundbreaking practical applications of sociological method, statistical analysis, and demography, and his writings had intentional impact.

Further questions remain. Did supporters of the interracial cooperation movement in the 1920s lack courage and principle, compared to later white southern campaigners for civil rights such as Ira B. Harkey, Bob Zellner, and Claudia Thomas Sanders, who faced threats, beatings, shootings, cross-burnings, bombings, and false imprisonment?[20] Why did the CIC fail to reach the egalitarian positions adopted after 1934 by men and women such as Edwin Rogers Embree, Virginia and Clifford Durr, and James Dombrowski? Perhaps Jack Woofter's efforts, within narrow class confines during an era of inconclusive reform and undemonstrative protest, seem timid or inconsequential, but the wall of racial hatred was so solid—as the Sledd and Bassett cases proved—that it was almost impossible for a young white scholar to take an explicitly radical stand between 1910 and 1925, for fear of ridicule, ostracism, and loss of prospects. The next generation of white southern reformers began work when lynching and the Klan were in terminal decline and the political context was becoming kinder to those working for better race relations. In 1921, when Woofter joined the CIC, there were sixty lynchings in the South, and to be working in isolated rural parts where intense reaction was always a possibility, seeing at first hand the effects of racial violence, required considerable courage. He was spared the strain of constant peril endured by black farmers, but he knew that the Klan targeted white critics and that he was exposed.

Most southern white men of Jack Woofter's generation never queried the region's racial mores, whereas he remained a critic of white supremacy. In the 1950s, white men in late middle age—Woofter's peers—formed the backbone of local opposition to the civil rights movement. Woofter, however, welcomed the civil rights movement and denounced the White Citizens' Councils for their determination, as he put it, "to preserve the status quo, even if it impedes progress, and to do this by inflammatory appeals to fear and hatred of the Negro." Others of his ilk reacted differently. For example, the southern journalist, John Temple Graves II, only a few months older than Woofter, ended up firmly on the side of white supremacy after similar life experiences. Born in Rome, Georgia, in 1892, and educated in Georgia and at a northern university (Princeton), Graves served in France during World War I and worked in New York and Washington, before settling in Birmingham, Alabama. After showing liberal inclinations early in his career, he became steadily more conservative in the 1930s and 1940s, attacking the Southern Conference for Human Welfare and objecting to perceived northern interference in southern life. By the 1950s, Graves was an outspoken advocate of states' rights and a spokesman for the White Citizens' Councils.[21] Unlike Graves, Woofter approved of gradual school integration in the 1950s, so long as it was locally organized. As ever, he endorsed change at a pace dictated by "moderates ... [who were] deeply concerned with the day-to-day conduct of the affairs of their community in such a way as to promote orderly progress." He deplored "sensational reports in the national press [that] were rapidly creating the impression that moderation was almost dead in the South." At the age of sixty-four, as he prepared to retire, he celebrated southern reformers from the late-nineteenth-century pioneers of interracial cooperation to the "Southern moderates" of the 1950s who acknowledged the basic justice of African American demands for civil rights:

> It would be most salutary if we could get away from the heat of the immediate controversy and look back over the long road of progress travelled by such Southerners as [the North Carolinian universal education advocates] Alderman, Aycock, Page and Joyner and realize that, although slow, progress in adjusting race relations in the past has been real and has been brought about in large measure by the quiet determination of the moderates to do the right thing as early as feasable [sic].[22]

African American observers of the same age as Woofter remembered the interracial cooperation movement rather differently. Gordon Blaine Hancock, who as a child witnessed the murderous Phoenix Riot in 1898 in Greenwood County, South Carolina, began teaching sociology and economics at Virginia Union University at Richmond in 1921, just as the CIC was becoming established. In the interwar period, he put his faith in interracial cooperation, remarking in 1929 that, while charitable donors like the Duke family were very generous, they

> were by no means the chief exponents of fair play to Negroes. There are hundreds of whites scattered thruout the South who have not money to give Negroes, but they have what is just as essential to the Negro's future—good will and sympathy. When we are tempted to say mean things about the white people let's not lump them! There are some whites in the South who are making desperate efforts to redeem the South. These are the hope of the South![23]

In the 1940s, Hancock still believed in the value of cooperation, insisting, "The interracialist has been misunderstood and often maligned, [but] the principle underlying interracialism is fundamentally sound. . . . Interracialism is a bridge over the chasm that segregation creates, and although it lacks the glamorous and the spectacular, it has played a substantial part in the advance of the Negro." By 1960, however, when thirty-four Virginia Union students were arrested during a sit-in at a Richmond restaurant, Hancock had revised his view of the interracial cooperation movement of the 1920s and 1930s. He recalled the bitter disappointment of black Americans at the violence that followed World War I and the way in which interracial committees sprang up across the South with the aim of "lessening the impact which the great disillusionment brought with it." In the short term, cooperation had "served a worthy purpose. But through the subsequent years the committees on interracial cooperation lost their appeal; for it became apparent that they were designed primarily to keep the Negro illusioned about his station as an American citizen." The CIC, he concluded, was basically "paternalistic in its outlook and purpose [and was] designed to camouflage the fact that the South's 'not now' was a smooth way of saying 'no never.'" Hancock rejoiced that the coming of the civil rights movement meant white and black Americans could at last be "brutally frank" with each other:

> The current picture of Negro students protesting against segregation and the evils thereof and whites sworn to opposition is a much truer picture than that of whites and Negroes sitting around a discussion table forty years ago. . . . As ugly as the picture currently is, it offers a more fruitful basis of interracial adjustment. . . . The white man knows what the Negro wants; the Negro knows how determined the white man is that he will not get it. But such is interracial understanding.

What the CIC had offered, Hancock now saw, was deliberate "interracial misunderstanding." (He was saying here more or less what Martin Luther King Jr. would say in his *Letter from a Birmingham City Jail* three years later: "Shallow understanding from people of good will is more frustrating than absolute misunderstanding from people of ill will.") Nevertheless, Hancock insisted it had been right for people like Robert Russa Moton, Charlotte Hawkins Brown, and himself to at least *try* to work for peace by engaging with elements of the white South that were willing to talk: "What those Negroes did forty years ago makes possible what the young Negroes of today are doing."[24]

The achievements of the interracial cooperation movement before the Great Depression were certainly patchy. The movement encouraged the passage of new state laws and the enforcement of existing laws, but it inspired no federal legislation and no institutions of lasting note. It emboldened numerous speakers and writers on the need for tolerance, but it did not produce any towering political figures or literary milestones. It made a difference in terms of the relations be-tween middle-class blacks and whites locally; it sustained the flow of northern philanthropic money; it improved the fabric and reach of black education; it se-verely damaged the reputation of the Ku Klux Klan; it made governors, judges, churches, and editors more resolute in their opposition to racial violence; and it thereby reduced the degree of oppression. Crucially, it contributed to the steady decline of lynching, but it never developed, or intended to develop, a full-blown critique of white supremacy; for that reason, rather than inspiring a black cam-paign for equal rights, it drove conservative black leaders and radical black activ-ists further apart.

The biggest mistake the CIC made was probably its failure even to contemplate a focus on the vote during the 1920s. In certain places—such as Augusta and Sa-vannah in Georgia, Jacksonville in Florida, and Durham in North Carolina—the registration of a few hundred more black people could have altered the outcome of elections and made the relatively high levels of black political participation in San Antonio and Memphis seem less exceptional. Perhaps the CIC was scared of provoking strife of the kind that surrounded voter registration and elections in Florida in 1919 and 1920, but if a registration strategy had been followed success-fully, the attitude of many African Americans, particularly northern observers like W. E. B. Du Bois, toward the interracial cooperation movement would have been much more positive.[25]

That is not to say that the interracial cooperation movement lacked strategies, or that those it pursued were all ineffectual. In the bloody aftermath of World War I, faith in the power of Christian goodwill clearly affected southern race re-lations, influencing individual and community behavior and convincing public figures that the time was right for clear statements on racial discrimination. By persuading Governor Hugh M. Dorsey to denounce overt injustice in 1921, the CIC caused a sensation and altered the tone of public debate. Thereafter, Will Alexander and Jack Woofter had good reason to believe that, by inspiring people of goodwill to stand up to the Klan and forcing Klansmen to appear in court to hear their crimes described, the CIC could contribute to its eventual demise. For example, in December 1926, masked men kidnapped and whipped Wimberly E. Brown, a white attorney who assisted the unsuccessful prosecution of five Klans-men for the lynching of a black man near Lyons, in Toombs County. Brown stated that men dressed in full Klan regalia then ordered him to leave Lyons; the Klan claimed he was attacked by unknown men wearing flour sacks. Indictments were brought in against Brown's assailants, and although no convictions were secured, the Klan's local reign of terror attracted national attention, and something akin to an apology, to protect the state's reputation, was forced from the normally pro-Klan governor, Clifford Walker. Wimberly Brown remained in Lyons, practicing criminal law for another ten years.[26]

Thus, the CIC's antilynching campaign helped to create a new public and judicial mood regarding mob violence across the South, before the formation of the Association of Southern Women for the Prevention of Lynching by Jessie Daniel Ames and other white women in 1930. In 1927, lynchings decreased to sixteen in the South, and there were none in Alabama and Georgia. In 1928, ten black people were lynched, and for the second year in succession there were none in Georgia.[27] Changes in the frequency of lynching were not uniform—it disappeared more quickly from some states than others and certain counties remained prone to outbreaks, but these figures represented a dramatic fall from the prewar years (between 1905 and 1915, ninety-eight black people were lynched in Georgia alone). There was a brief increase in lynching during the first years of the Great Depression, but the habit had been essentially broken during the 1920s by a combination of factors: the threat of federal legislation, black migration, southern urbanization, improved communications, international scrutiny, and an increased black determination to resist the mob. Further causes of the decline in lynching included the improvement of local law enforcement, which the CIC and its committees actively supported in first half of the 1920s, and the investigations and court cases that CIC's attorneys pursued. Between 1921 and 1925, therefore, the CIC worked out a legal, political, religious, and above all, southern, formula for making lynching indefensible. Ann Wells Ellis has argued that this "made it socially unacceptable to use violence and intimidation against blacks seeking to improve their status. . . . Without this change in attitude the civil rights movement would have been stifled at the outset."[28] That is a bold conclusion, but it is probably just as tenable as Diana Selig's suggestion that the subsequent educational programs of the CIC "could provide a distraction that subverted the work of civil rights."[29]

Even as the Great Depression began to bite, many white social scientists retained their faith in the power of interracial cooperation and its value as part of the national spirit. In March 1930, Mary van Kleeck of the Russell Sage Foundation, who chaired the National Interracial Conference, measured American social justice in terms of the unhindered entitlement of groups or individuals to enjoy their lives and opportunities—to do one's "own work," as she put it. Much had changed in recent years, and she was certain even greater changes were to come, but it remained the case, she wrote, that the "power of the Negro in the United States to do his own work is still hindered at many points"—including education, living conditions, the vote, and the courts. She concluded, "All these are limiting factors in American civilization. Their limitation is not only upon the doing of justice to the Negro, but also upon the quality of justice in the nation. That this quality of justice in the nation may be achieved through interracial cooperation is a hope for which the findings of social research . . . give substantial support."[30]

Although interracial cooperation made little difference to the constitutional rights of African Americans in the southern states after World War I, the movement's tangible achievements included the diminished threat of violence, better schooling and health care, and an emerging consensus on the benefits of dialogue and improved race relations. A significant proportion of the white population—especially the conservative rural folk studied by Howard Odum—would remain rigidly ill-disposed toward black people, but the CIC successfully targeted southern middle-class whites, and particularly women. It made little attempt to persuade them that Jim Crow laws and disfranchisement might be wrong, but it convinced them that black economic progress would bring local and regional benefits and pricked their consciences about lynching and the Klan. Moreover, the interracial meetings of the CIC forced white participants to acknowledge the human needs of their black neighbors.

The lasting impact of the interracial cooperation movement was twofold, therefore. First, through its literature, summer schools, visiting professors, and student groups, it succeeded in showing thousands of young white people in the South that their interests and those of black people were often identical and intertwined. A few young white people became activists; many more became less prejudiced, and this opened new possibilities. Second, the CIC's success in the 1920s in challenging mob violence where it was occurring—in the South—meant that, although the civil rights movement after World War II suffered vigilantism on a shocking scale, including forty deaths between 1954 and 1968, African Americans could protest against discrimination in the knowledge that lynching itself was almost entirely a thing of the past. The memories and testimony of a century of racial violence since emancipation now inspired new forms of black resistance and white expiation. This would not have been the case without the efforts of Jack Woofter, James M. Bond, and other state secretaries of the CIC in their "citizen's fight" against lynching.[31] Woofter understood that lynching's significance went beyond the rituals of public murder—that it was one of the pillars of the caste system, producing despair among African Americans because of the immunity enjoyed by mobs. He also believed that lynching would decline only when influential southern white people were determined that it must. The CIC's press campaign, lobbying, and work through the courts meant that participants in lynchings incurred unprecedented levels of public censure and new risks of prosecution, even though actual convictions were rare. It meant that, although racial conflict was still widespread in 1950, the spectacular carnivals of torture and mayhem that stained the South and strengthened white supremacy after 1890 were over. If this change in attitude toward lynching had not occurred when it did and if southern white mobs had killed fifty black people annually during the interwar period (in 1918–1922, the annual average was sixty), then the task of mounting a civil rights struggle after World War II would have been even more daunting, more sanguinary, and more enduringly divisive. In that important respect, the interracial cooperation movement changed fundamentally the landscape through which African Americans marched on the long road to democracy and civil rights.

Notes

Introduction

1. Woofter, *The Basis of Racial Adjustment*, 23.
2. Moton, *What the Negro Thinks*, 260–61.
3. Dykeman and Stokely, *Seeds of Southern Change*; Dykeman, *Prophet of Plenty*; Brazil, *Howard W. Odum*; Salmond, *Southern Rebel*; Salmond, *Miss Lucy of the CIO*; Elna C. Green, "Introduction," in Hammond, *In Black and White*, vii–liii; Fitzpatrick, *Gerald W. Johnson*; Leidholdt, *Editor for Justice*.
4. McKee, *Sociology and the Race Problem*, 131. See also Rees, *Shades of Difference*, 91–92, and Roediger, *Working toward Whiteness*, 23–24.
5. Samuel C. Mitchell, "The Nationalization of Southern Sentiment," 109, 112. Dennis, *Lessons in Progress*, 44, 161–91, 192–216. Thomas Pearce Bailey, *Race Orthodoxy in the South*.
6. Stanfield, "The 'Negro Problem' within and beyond the Institutional Nexus of Pre–World War I Sociology," 195–96.
7. Grantham, *South in Modern America*, 147. See also Grantham, "Regional Imagination," 3–32. For examples of citations of Woofter, see Wiese, "Blacks in the Suburban and Rural Fringe," 158, 166–70; Badger, *Prosperity Road*, 240; Brundage, *Under Sentence of Death*, 7; Killian, *White Southerners*, 93–94; Lowry, "Population and Race in Mississippi," 576, 588. During and after World War II, Woofter's demographic studies helped develop federal welfare provision and planning for the postwar baby boom. In the 1950s, he undertook population studies for the Central Intelligence Agency. See Ellen Winston, "Thomas Jackson Woofter," 6.
8. Aiken, *William Faulkner and the Southern Landscape*, 225. See also Aiken, *Cotton Plantation South Since the Civil War*, 35–39, 52–53. Aiken describes Woofter's work as "the apogee of a genre of technical plantation studies."
9. Woofter, *Negro Migration*, 8.
10. Platt, *History of Sociological Research Methods in America*, 32, 76–77. See also Turner, "Does Funding Produce Its Effects?," 213–26.
11. Singal, *The War Within*, 112.
12. Woofter, *The Basis of Racial Adjustment*, 13.
13. Moton, *What the Negro Thinks*, 266.
14. Stanfield, *Philanthropy and Jim Crow*, 9–10.
15. Brewer, Review of *Southern Race Progress*, 161–63.
16. Howard W. Odum to Leonard Outhwaite, Oct. 27, 1927, box 62, Laura Spelman Rockefeller Memorial Collection (LSRM), Rockefeller Archive Center (RAC), Sleepy Hollow, N.Y. Myrdal, *An American Dilemma*, 456, 466, 1441–83.
17. Gruening, *These United States*, 322–45. Du Bois, "Georgia: Invisible Empire State," 66. Godshalk, *Veiled Visions*, 157–61.
18. Morton Sosna defined liberals as "white Southerners who perceived that there was a serious maladjustment of race relations in the South, who recognized that the existing system resulted in grave injustices for blacks, and who either actively endorsed or engaged in programs to aid Southern blacks in their fight against lynching, disfranchisement, segregation, and blatant discrimination in such areas as education, employment, and law enforcement." Sosna, *In*

Search of the Silent South, viii. Notable white liberals included Will W. Alexander, Willis D. Weatherford, John J. Eagan, Thomas Jesse Jones, Anson Phelps Stokes, James Hardy Dillard, George Foster Peabody, Howard Odum, and Thomas Jackson Woofter Jr. Black associates included Robert Russa Moton, John Hope, Isaac Fisher, George E. Haynes, and Forrester B. Washington.

19. On the "tendential unity" of social movements, see Barker et al., "Leadership Matters: An Introduction," in *Leadership and Social Movements,* 4.

20. Thomas Jesse Jones to R. R. Moton, March 25, 1920, box 14, Moton Family Papers, Manuscript Division, Library of Congress (LC), Washington, D.C.; Edward T. Ware to T. J. Woofter, Nov. 15, 1921, box 6, series VII, Atlanta University Collection, Auburn Avenue Research Library of African American Culture and History, Atlanta, Ga.

21. Tindall, "Southern Negroes since Reconstruction,"341.

22. Tindall, *Emergence of the New South,* 175.

23. White, *Liberty and Justice for All,* xiii. See also Goodstein, "Rare Alliance," 245.

24. See Judson, "Solving the Girl Problem," 152–73; Dowden-White, "To See Past the Differences to the Fundamentals," 174–203; Robertson, *Christian Sisterhood, Race Relations, and the YWCA;* Frystak, *Our Minds on Our Freedom,* 33–37; Greenwood, *Bittersweet Legacy;* Joan Marie Johnson, "The Shape of the Movement to Come," 201–23; Higginbotham, *Righteous Discontent,* passim.

25. Jacquelyn Dowd Hall, *Revolt against Chivalry,* 59.

26. Gilmore, *Gender and Jim Crow,* xix, 45–59. Brooks,"Unlikely Allies," 120–52.

27. Montgomery, *Politics of Education in the New South,* 61.

28. Hammond, *In Black and White,* 28.

29. Montgomery, *Politics of Education in the New South,* 129, 232. See also Kuhn et al., *Living Atlanta,* 249–51.

30. Murphy, *Problems of the Present South,* 233. Hugh C. Bailey, *Liberalism in the New South,* 121–30; Fredrickson, *Black Image in the White Mind,* 284–97, 300–302, 310–11. See also Chappell, *Inside Agitators,* 3–25.

31. Murphy, *Problems of the Present South,* 167–71; Murphy, *Basis of Ascendancy,* 5, 51, 73–94.

32. Sosna, *In Search of the Silent South,* 1–7; Williamson, *Rage for Order,* 72–86. See also Berry, "Repression of Blacks in the South 1890–1945," 29–43.

33. Gossett, *Race,* 174–75, 177. See also Green, "Introduction" in Hammond, *In Black and White,* xiv–xxii, xlvi–xlvii. Lewis, *W. E. B. Du Bois, 1868–1919,* 224–25, 294.

34. White and Hopkins, *Social Gospel,* xviii–xix, 82–86.

35. See Ellis, "A Crusade against 'Wretched Attitudes,'" 21–44; Ellis, "Commission on Interracial Cooperation." McDonough, "Men and Women of Good Will." Pilkington, "Trials of Brotherhood," 55–80.

36. Selig, *Americans All,* 151, 151–82. Johnson, *Reforming Jim Crow,* 9, 21–22.

37. Fredrickson, *Black Image in the White Mind* (1971), 283–84.

38. Fredrickson, *Black Image in the White Mind* (1987), x–xii.

39. Sosna, *In Search of the Silent South;* Eagles, *Jonathan Daniels and Race Relations;* Singal, *War Within;* Kneebone, *Southern Liberal Journalists and the Issue of Race;* Loveland, *Lillian Smith;* Martin, *Howard Kester and the Struggle for Social Justice;* Matthews, "Virginius Dabney, John Temple Graves," 405–20; Hall, *Revolt against Chivalry;* Egerton, *Speak Now against the Day;* Chappell, *Inside Agitators;* Sullivan, *Days of Hope;* Sullivan, *Lift Every Voice;* Clayton, *W. J. Cash: A Life;* Teel, *Ralph Emerson McGill;* Chappell, *A Stone of Hope;* Mazzari, *Southern Modernist;* Gilmore, *Defying Dixie.*

40. McGill, *South and the Southerner,* 159.

41. Chappell, *Inside Agitators,* 36.

42. Janken, *White*, 34–35, 206–207.

43. Sosna, *In Search of the Silent South*, 20–41.

44. Waldrep, *Many Faces of Judge Lynch*, 132.

45. Harvey, *Freedom's Coming*, 64–65, 67, 78–79.

46. Stanfield, "Northern Money and Southern Bogus Elitism," 1–22.

47. J. Douglas Smith, *Managing White Supremacy*, 46–47, 56, 155–88.

48. Link, *Paradox of Southern Progressivism*, 248–67.

49. Grantham, *South in Modern America*, 97.

50. Brundage, *Lynching in the New South*, 215–25, 244.

51. Sullivan, *Days of Hope*, 32.

52. Egerton, *Speak Now against the Day*, 48–50.

53. Godshalk, *Veiled Visions*, 263–67.

54. Kneebone, *Southern Liberal Journalists*, 24–25, 79–80. Davis, *Clashing of the Soul*, 260, 262–64, 273–74.

55. Williamson, *Rage for Order*, 259–61. Williamson makes some errors over names, including calling Thomas Jackson Woofter Jr. "John A. Wooster."

56. Hall, *Revolt against Chivalry*, 63–65, 95–106.

57. Fairclough, *Race and Democracy*, 11–13.

58. Green, "Introduction" in Hammond, *In Black and White*, xxxviii, xliii.

59. Singal, *War Within*, 303, 316. Singal writes, "The safest and most comfortable course by far, almost everyone concluded, was to agree that the matter of segregation was closed and that any discussion of southern racial mores was fruitless." He adds (316):

> Under the rules of this tacit consensus, liberals could concern themselves with social problems like poverty, poor schools, or disease among blacks if they wished, but never in the specific context of racial oppression. There could be no openly acknowledged "race problem" in the South, only a "task" of "adjustment" that could be readily met through "cooperation" of leaders of both races. This philosophy guided the Commission on Interracial Cooperation in the early 1920s and informed the writings of those few southern social scientists of the era like Thomas J. Woofter, Jr., who wrote directly on race. The handful of black writers within the region likewise abided by this consensus.

60. Gilmore, *Defying Dixie*, 7, 19, 234–36.

61. Singal, *War Within*, 111–13.

1. Jack Woofter

1. *Who Was Who in America*, vol. 1: *1897–1942* (1943), 1381, cf. "Woofter, Thomas Jackson." The Woofters were descended from early-eighteenth-century English settlers; the name was a corruption of Wooster, itself a variant of Worcester. J. F. Sellers, "Thomas Jackson Woofter," in Northen, *Men of Mark in Georgia*, 218–21. Woofter Sr., *Teaching in Rural Schools;* Reed, *History of the University of Georgia*, 2199–2204, 2207. See also Board Minutes, June 19, 1911; June 15, 1912; and June 13, 1918, in Transcript of the Minutes of the University of Georgia Board of Trustees, 1786–1932 (MUGAB), http://www.libs.uga.edu/hargrett/archives/trustees/index.html.

2. T. J. Woofter Sr. to Walter Barnard Hill, Dec. 14, 1904, cited in Dennis, *Lessons in Progress*, 137.

3. Woofter, *Basis of Racial Adjustment*, frontis.

4. U.S. Census, 1860, Slave Schedule, Lowndes County, Miss., 136–37, at ancestry.com; U.S.

Census, 1860, Lowndes County, Miss., roll M653_586, 718; U.S. Census, 1870, Township 17, Lowndes County, Miss., roll M593_783, 388–90.

5. Woofter, *Southern Race Progress*, 28, 46–47. Woofter's uncle, Harvie Jordan, was a leading cotton growers' spokesman. See Jordan, "Cotton in the Southern Agricultural Economy," 1–7.

6. See Minutes of Athens Woman's Club, 1912–1920, at http://dig.galileo.usg.edu /athenswomansclub/awc002.php. Woofter's father produced guides for the Georgia Federation of Women's Clubs. See T. J. Woofter, "Studies in Citizenship."

7. Woofter, *Southern Race Progress*, 2, 4–5.

8. Ibid., 7, 46, 133.

9. Bohannon, "These Few Gray-Haired, Battle-Scarred Veterans," 89–109.

10. Dennis, *Lessons in Progress*, 150. The BA covered English, math, history, French, German, sociology, and psychology. In 1901, UGA enrolled 331 students; in 1908, 500; and in 1920, 1,262. Reed, *History of the University of Georgia*, 1861–2528.

11. In Brooks, *Georgia Studies:* Gregor Sebba, "Introduction," 10–11; Brooks, "Race Relations in the Eastern Georgia Piedmont," 27–49; Brooks, "The Agrarian Revolution in Georgia, 1865–1912," 50–122. Brooks, "Economic and Social Aspects of Slavery," 211–15.

12. Woofter, *Southern Race Progress*, 20–21.

13. Ibid., 21–23. Du Bois, "Georgia: Invisible Empire State," 65.

14. Thomas Nelson Page, *The Negro* (1908), extract in Joshi, *Documents of American Prejudice* 315–18. Ross, "Causes of Race Superiority," 67–89.

15. William Benjamin Smith, *Color Line*, xiv, 3, 7, 12–15, 111.

16. R. W. Shufeldt, *The Negro* (1907), extract in Joshi, ed., *Documents of American Prejudice*, 326–28. See also Shufeldt, *America's Greatest Problem*.

17. See White, *Liberty and Justice for All*, 41–90; Luker, *Social Gospel in Black and White*, 61–79, 114–22, 144–51, 282–89. Bailey, *Race Orthodoxy in the South*, 88–89.

18. Hovenkamp, "Social Science and Segregation before *Brown*," 624–72.

19. Tindall, *Emergence of the New South*, 175–76. Brough, "Work of the Commission of Southern Universities on the Race Question," 47–57. Morse, "The University Commission on Southern Race Questions," 302–10. Dennis, "Skillful Use of Higher Education to Protect White Supremacy," 115–23.

20. Reed, *History of University of Georgia*, 2271.

21. Minutes of Nov. 15, 1911 (appendix), Trustees of the Phelps-Stokes Fund, box 2, Papers of the Phelps-Stokes Fund (PSF), Schomburg Centre for Research in Black Culture, New York Public Library (SC). Yellin, "The (White) Search for (Black) Order," 319–52. Karl and Katz, "American Private Philanthropic Foundation and the Public Sphere," 236–70.

22. David C. Barrow to Anson Phelps Stokes, Oct. 5, 1912, box 42, PSF, SC. Minutes of June 15, 1912, MUGAB. Thomas Jesse Jones, *Educational Adaptations*, 21–22, 67–70.

23. Stanfield, *Philanthropy and Jim Crow*, 28.

24. Du Bois, *Philadelphia Negro*; Du Bois, *Negroes of Farmville, Virginia*; Lange, "W. E. B. Du Bois and the First Scientific Study of Afro-America," 135–46.

25. *Minutes of the University Commission on Southern Race Questions*, 6–13. On the work of the UCSRQ, see Jones, *Educational Adaptations*, 76–79. Bernard, "Southern Sociological Congress," 91–93.

26. Thomas Jesse Jones to Anson Phelps Stokes, May 5, 1913, box 44, PSF, SC.

27. Woofter, "Negroes of Athens," 4.

28. Ibid., 7, 10–20.

29. Ibid., 20–22. Woofter may have been influenced by Thomas Jesse Jones, "Alley Homes of Washington," 67–71. See also Mark M. Smith, *How Race Is Made*, 63–65.

30. Woofter, "Negroes of Athens," 28, 33.

31. Ibid., 33–49.

32. Ibid., 51, 54–55. UGA chancellor David C. Barrow was especially taken with a table (51) "showing the comparative thrift of the Saxon laborer and the Negro." David C. Barrow to Anson Phelps Stokes, Jan. 24, 1914, box 15, PSF, SC.

33. Woofter, *Southern Race Progress*, 10. Bulmer, "Social Survey Movement," 15–34.

34. Historical Census Browser at http://mapserver.lib.virginia.edu/php. Woodson, *Negro in Our History*, 502.

35. See White, *Liberty and Justice for All*, xviii.

36. Woofter, *Southern Race Progress*, 24.

37. Cited in Joan Marie Johnson, "The Shape of the Movement to Come," 204.

38. Moton, *What the Negro Thinks*, 254–55.

39. Newby, *Jim Crow's Defense*, 142. Carlton and Coclanis, eds., *Confronting Southern Poverty*, 3. Egerton, *Speak Now against the Day*, 76.

40. Sledd, "The Negro: Another View," 65–73. Warnock, "Andrew Sledd, Southern Methodists, and the Negro," 251–71; *Atlanta Constitution*, Aug. 3, 1902, B4; ibid., Aug. 5, 1902, 6; ibid., Aug. 7, 1902, 4. Arnold, "*What Virtue There Is in Fire,*" 173–77. After gaining a PhD at Yale in less than a year, Sledd became president of the University of Florida in 1904 and returned to Emory in 1914.

41. "John Spencer Bassett, 1867–1928," in William S. Powell, ed., *Dictionary of North Carolina Biography,* reproduced at *Documenting the American South,* University of North Carolina Library, Chapel Hill, 2004, http://docsouth.unc.edu/nc/bassettnc/bio.html. Bassett, "Stirring Up the Fires of Race Antipathy," 297–305. On Josephus Daniels's racism, see Gilmore, *Gender and Jim Crow,* 82–89, 102–103, and Leidholdt, *Editor for Justice,* 46–54.

42. Link, *Paradox of Southern Progressivism,* 64–65. Dittmer, *Black Georgia in the Progressive Era,* 142–43. Gilmore, *Gender and Jim Crow,* 159–60. "Negro Education," *Bulletin of Atlanta University* 191 (May 1909): 3–4. *Atlanta Constitution,* April 17, 1909, 4.

43. Bauman, "Race and Mastery," 181–94. See also Wynes, *Forgotten Voices.*

44. Sledd, "The Negro: Another View," 71, 72.

45. Fish, "Southern Methodism and Accommodation of the Negro," 207. Bailey, *Liberalism in the New South,* 56; Chappell, *Inside Agitators,* 25–32.

46. Kelly Miller, "Social Equality," in *Race Adjustment,* 112–13.

47. *Atlanta Constitution,* July 3, 1905, 5.

48. Booker T. Washington to Oswald Garrison Villard, July 10, 1905, in *Booker T. Washington Papers,* 8:322–23.

49. *Atlanta Constitution,* July 11, 1905, 3.

50. *Atlanta Constitution,* Sept. 26, 1905, 7; ibid., Nov. 26, 1905, C1. Alderman and Harris, *Library of Southern Literature,* pt. 15, 47–48.

51. *Christian Advocate,* Sept. 11, 1908, cited in Fish, "Southern Methodism and Accommodation of the Negro," 209.

52. Dennis, *Lessons in Progress,* 192–216.

53. T. J. Woofter Jr. to Anson Phelps Stokes, June 7, 1913, box 15, PSF, SC.

54. Anderson, "Northern Foundations and the Shaping of Southern Black Rural Education," 371–96. Anderson and Moss, *Dangerous Donations,* 39–108. Fish, "Southern Methodism and Accommodation of the Negro," 202–203, 211. Bond, *Negro Education in Alabama,* 262–86. Ellison, "*An American Dilemma: A Review,*" in *Shadow and Act,* 303–17. On the GEB, see Davis, "Stimulation, Sustenance, Subversion," 313–22.

55. Fairclough, *Class of Their Own,* 469n49. Dennis, *Lessons in Progress,* 8–10.

56. Miller, "Education for Manhood" (April 1913), in Dunbar, ed., *Masterpieces of Negro Eloquence*, 445–54.

57. Jones, *Negro Education*, 1:36–37, 41–43.

58. Walter A. Jackson, *Gunnar Myrdal and America's Conscience*, 23.

59. Anderson, *The Education of Blacks in the South*, 97. Harlan, *Separate and Unequal*, 102.

60. Cited in Carl V. Harris, *Political Power in Birmingham*, 173.

61. William Anthony Aery, "Loosening Up Louisiana," *Survey* 34 (June 19, 1915): 266–69, in *Booker T. Washington Papers*, 13:321–30.

62. Thomas, "Mr. B. T. Washington in Louisiana," 145.

63. Booker T. Washington to Anson Phelps Stokes, Nov. 1, 1912, in *Booker T. Washington Papers*, 12:44–45. Jones, *Educational Adaptations*, 17–19. Ware, "Higher Education of Negroes in the United States," 209–18. W. T. B. Williams, *Report on Negro Universities in the South*. Williams reported again in 1922, when he found thirty-three institutions doing college-grade work. See Williams, *Report on Negro Universities and Colleges*.

64. Board Minutes, Nov. 20, 1912, box 2, PSF, SC. J. H. Dillard to Anson Phelps Stokes, Nov. 15, 1912, box 15, ibid. Edwin A. Alderman, to Anson Phelps Stokes, Nov. 15, 1912, ibid. Booker T. Washington to Robert Ezra Park, Oct. 6, 1912, in *Booker T. Washington Papers*, 12:39–41; Anson Phelps Stokes to Washington, Nov. 6, 1912, ibid., 47–48; Washington to Anson Phelps Stokes, Nov. 1, Nov. 9, 1912, ibid., 44–45, 52–53.

65. Anson Phelps Stokes to Washington, Nov 12, 1912, ibid., 53–54. Woofter, *Southern Race Progress*, 23. At a meeting in 1919, Jones said, "I am a white man, but thank God, I am not an Anglo-Saxon." Enclosure with W. E. B. Du Bois to R. R. Moton, Jan. 26 1926, W. E. B. Du Bois Papers (MS 312), Special Collections, University of Massachusetts Amherst Libraries (UMAL).

66. Park to Washington, Dec. 3, 1912; March 1, May 19, 1913, in *Booker T. Washington Papers*, 12:82, 129–30, 190–93.

67. Jones, *Social Studies in the Hampton Curriculum*. Jones, *Educational Adaptations*, 64. Johnson, "W. E. B. Du Bois, Thomas Jesse Jones and the Struggle for Social Education," 71–95. Johnson calls Jones "the founder of the field of Social Studies" (pp. 77–81). Yellin, "The (White) Search for (Black) Order," 326–51. Odum, *American Sociology*, 15. See also Gossett, *Race*, 160–75, Anderson, *Education of Blacks in the South*, 51–53; Stanfield, "'Negro Problem,'"196–99; Patti McGill Peterson, "Colonialism and Education," 146–57. L. Hollingsworth Wood, "The Phelps-Stokes Fund," reprint from *Opportunity* (Oct. 1932), box 1, PSF, SC. Woofter, *Southern Race Progress*, 23. For Jones's urban studies background, see Jones, *Sociology of a New York City Block*. See also Giddings, *Inductive Sociology: A Syllabus of Methods, Analyses and Classifications, and Provisionally Formulated Laws* (New York: Macmillan, 1901) and *Readings in Descriptive and Historical Sociology* (New York: Macmillan, 1906).

68. Jones, *Educational Adaptations*, 66.

69. Webster, "The Bureau of Education's Suppressed Rating of Colleges," 499–511. Evans, "International Conference on the Negro," 425.

70. Anderson, *Education of Blacks in the South*, 247–49, 250.

71. Jones, *Educational Adaptations*, 26.

72. Donald Johnson, "W. E. B. Du Bois, Thomas Jesse Jones and the Struggle for Social Education," 84–89. Robert Russa Moton, "Some Elements Necessary to Race Development," Tuskegee Commencement address, May 1912, in Dunbar, ed., *Masterpieces of Negro Eloquence*, 367–78. On Jones's work and influence, see Phelps Stokes, *Negro Status and Race Relations*, 18–22, 93–115, 191–94; King, *Pan-Africanism and Education*; Berman, "American Influence on African Education," 132–45; Watkins, *White Architects of Black Education*, 98–117. Correia, "For Their Own Good."

2. Thomas Jesse Jones and *Negro Education*

1. Dennis, "Schooling along the Color Line," 142–56. See also, Dennis, *Lessons in Progress,* 43–66.

2. Philander P. Claxton to Anson Phelps Stokes, Nov. 12, 13, 1912, box 44, PSF, SC. Thomas Jesse Jones to Phelps Stokes, Nov. 14, 1912, ibid. "Report on Schools for Colored People: Outline of Work," n.d., ibid. Jones, *Negro Education,* 2:2–3, 15.

3. Jones, *Educational Adaptations,* 38–6, 48, 49–52.

4. Cited in Fish, "Southern Methodism and Accommodation of the Negro," 203. Fish claims that Methodists promoted black education to encourage black workers to stay in the South and to deter Catholic immigrant labor from the North.

5. Jones, *Negro Education,* 2:1.

6. Jones to Anson Phelps Stokes, Jan. 31, Feb. 9, April 19, 1913, box 15, PSF, SC. *Indianapolis Freeman,* April 16, 1910, 1; ibid., June 4, 1910, 11. *Baltimore Afro-American,* Aug. 12, 1911, 7. *Washington Star,* Dec. 15, 1911, in *Booker T. Washington Papers,* 11:419–20. *Washington Post,* Dec. 17, 1911, 15; ibid., April 15, 1912, 12; ibid., Feb. 11, 1913, 14. Ocea Taylor was described in the 1910 census as a "mulatto." 1910 Census Roll T624_153, p3A, Washington, D.C., at ancestry.com. The Library of Congress holds five issues of the *Washington American* from 1911. Its irreverent reports on the capital's black community led to criticism of Taylor and Randolph. See *Washington Bee,* Oct 30, 1909, 8. Jones, *Negro Education,* 1:xiii–xiv.

7. Jones to Anson Phelps Stokes, Feb. 14, 1913, box 44, PSF, SC. On segregation in the civil service, see Patler, *Jim Crow and the Wilson Administration.*

8. Jones to Anson Phelps Stokes, Feb. 9, 1913, box 15, PSF, SC. W. D. Weatherford to Richard C. Morse, March 2, 1913, ibid.; Wickliffe Rose to Anson Phelps Stokes, May 1, 1913, ibid.

9. Thomas Jesse Jones to Anson Phelps Stokes, May 5, 1913, official personnel folder, Thomas Jackson Woofter Jr., d.o.b. 6/18/93, Civilian Personnel Records, National Personnel Records Center, St. Louis, Mo.

10. Jones to Claxton, May 6, 1913, ibid.; Claxton to Jones, May 9, 1913, ibid.; Claxton memorandum, Sept. 26, 1913, ibid.; James I. Park memorandum, Sept. 27, 1913, ibid.; Woofter to chief clerk, Dept. of Interior, Sept. 27, 1913, ibid.; acting chief clerk to Woofter, Oct. 3 1913, ibid.; Woofter, oath of office, Oct. 8, 1913, ibid. Woofter to Anson Phelps Stokes, June 7, 1913, box 15, PSF, SC.

11. Brewer, Review of *Southern Race Progress,* 161–63.

12. Woofter, *Southern Race Progress,* 23.

13. Jones to Anson Phelps Stokes, May 5, 1913, box 44, PSF, SC. Jones to Olivia Stokes, May 9, 1913, box 15, ibid. *New York Times,* June 19, 1917, 6. Fairclough, "Being in the Field of Education and also Being a Negro," 71–72. Jones, *Negro Education,* 1:13–14, 2:167, 268–69, 415, 417. Jones, *Educational Adaptations,* 52–56.

14. Jones to Anson Phelps Stokes, Nov. 29, 1913, box 15, PSF, SC. For Jones's views on particular schools, see "Recommendations to the Trustees of the Phelps Stokes Fund," April, 1914, ibid.; M. W. Reddick to Anson Phelps Stokes, Dec. 18, 1914, ibid.; Jones to Anson Phelps Stokes, April, 1916, box 16, ibid. Jones, *Negro Education,* 1:6–7, 17; 2:50–52, 58–60, 483–85. Jones, *Educational Adaptations,* 52.

15. Jones to Anson Phelps Stokes, Oct. 21, 1913, box 44, PSF, SC. "Itinerary and Plans for December, 1913 and January, February, 1914," ibid. Claxton to Anson Phelps Stokes, Nov. 18, 1913, box 69, Records of the Office of the Commissioner of Education, Historical File, 1870–1950, entry 6, Record Group (RG) 12, National Archives and Records Administration (NARA), College Park, Md.

16. "Itinerary and Plans for December, 1913 and January, February, 1914," box 44, P-SF, SC. Jones, *Negro Education,* 2:4. The Phelps-Stokes trustees increased Jones's budget for 1914 from

$8,000 to $12,000, believing it would "pay for itself ten times over in a short period by increasing gifts and grants to the most deserving schools." Jones's pay rose by $500 to $4,000; Taylor and Woofter were given $1,600 and $1,200, respectively, well over the $1,000 average for native-born white-collar workers. Their travel expenses reflected their segregated travel and accommodation: Jones got a year's expenses of $1,400; Taylor, $900 for eight months; and Woofter, $1,000 for eight months. See Executive Committee Minutes, Nov. 19, 1913, box 1, PSF, SC.

17. Jones to Anson Phelps Stokes, June 19, 1914, box 44, PSF, SC. Jones to Walter B. Hill, June 19, 1915, ibid.

18. Hill, "Negro Education in the South," 76–85. The author of the latter article was the father of the Walter B. Hill who worked with Thomas Jesse Jones. Chirhart, *Torches of Light*, 80–82. Montgomery, *Politics of Education in the New South*, 73–86, 95–96. Hill, "A Rural Survey of Clarke County, Georgia." Walter B. Hill to Anson Phelps Stokes, Oct. 28, 1914, box 44, 1914, PSF, SC. Hill to Anson Phelps Stokes, Jan. 14, 1915, ibid.

19. Jones to Anson Phelps Stokes, Sept. 1, Oct. 4, Dec. 15, 1914, PSF, SC. "Tentative Report of Negro Schools" (Georgia), ibid. Jones to Anson Phelps Stokes, Jan. 13, 1915, ibid. Woofter to Anson Phelps Stokes, Jan. 30, 1915, box 15, ibid.

20. Woofter to Helen Stokes, April 17, 1914, ibid. Woofter to Anson Phelps Stokes, April 29, 1914, ibid. *Washington Post,* March 8, 1914, 10. Jones, *Negro Education,* 2:134–38.

21. Jones, *Negro Education,* 2:423. *Crisis* 8 (May 1914): 11. Jones to Anson Phelps Stokes, April 23, April 30, May 22, Aug. 26, 1914, box 44, P-SF, SC. Jones, "Recommendations and Report on Parmele Industrial Institute," June 3, 1914, ibid.; N. C. Newbold to Woofter, June 2, 1914, ibid. Leloudis, *Schooling in the New South,* 194–99. The U.S. Supreme Court ruled on a suit initiated by Chance concerning interstate travel in 1948. *Time,* Nov. 24, 1952.

22. Jones, *Negro Education,* 2:255. Woofter, *Southern Race Progress,* 15. Woofter, *Negroes of Athens,* 27–28.

23. Odum, "Negro Children in the Public Schools of Philadelphia," 186–208.

24. Anderson, *Education of Blacks in the South,* 256–59.

25. Booker T. Washington to Oswald Garrison Villard, Feb. 27, March 21, 1913, in *Booker T. Washington Papers,* 12:127–28, 144–45; Washington to Emmett Jay Scott, March 21, 1913, ibid., 145. *Crisis* 6 (Sept. 1913): 217–18; *Crisis* 7 (Dec. 1913): 60; *Crisis* 7 (March 1914): 242–44; *Indianapolis Freeman,* April 25, 1914, 1.

26. Villard to Washington, May 21, June 3, 1914, in *Booker T. Washington Papers,* 13:27–28, 41–42; Leslie P. Hill to Washington, May 21, 1914, ibid., 28–30. Abraham Flexner to Villard, Dec. 1, 1914, cited in Anderson, *Education of Blacks in the South,* 257.

27. Washington to Villard, May 27, 1914, in *Booker T. Washington Papers,* 13:36–38; Washington to Jones, March 6, 1915, ibid., 250–51. Washington told New York donors that ANISS was unnecessary. See Washington to Alfred Tredway White, June 1, 1915, ibid., 314–16.

28. Ocea Taylor to Anson Phelps Stokes, April 10, 1915, box 15, PSF, SC. Franklin K. Lane to Claxton, May 29, 1915, ibid.; Jones to Anson Phelps Stokes, June 31, 1915, ibid. Jones's hostility toward the National Religious Training School at Durham, N.C., caused protests to the Phelps-Stokes Fund and Bureau of Education. See Julian S. Carr to Anson Phelps Stokes, March 23, March 25, March 29, 1915, ibid.; Carr to Claxton, March 23, 1915, ibid.; Claxton to Anson Phelps Stokes, March 31, 1915, ibid.; and Edward W. Sheldon to Anson Phelps Stokes, Jan. 8, 1917, box 16, ibid.

29. Arthur R. Burnet to Anson Phelps Stokes, Aug. 3, 1915, box 15, ibid.

30. Anson Phelps Stokes memo, March 11, 1915, ibid. Jones to Anson Phelps Stokes, April 27, 1915, box 44, ibid. Ocea Taylor to Anson Phelps Stokes, May 4, 1915, box 15, ibid.

31. Woofter to Anson Phelps Stokes, May 2, 1915, ibid. Jones, *Negro Education,* 2:695.

32. Hill to Anson Phelps Stokes, Nov. 24, 1915, box 15, PSF, SC. Woofter to Anson Phelps Stokes, Nov. 19, 1915, ibid. Executive Committee minutes, Nov. 3, 1915, box 1, ibid.

33. Executive Committee minutes, Nov. 2, 1916, ibid. Hill to Anson Phelps Stokes, Jan. 20, 1917, box 16, ibid. Jones to George Foster Peabody, Feb. 19, 1917, ibid. Hollis B. Frissell to Anson Phelps Stokes, March 23, 1917, ibid.; Claxton to Anson Phelps Stokes, March 28, April 21, 1917, ibid.; W. Ryan Carson Jr. to Anson Phelps Stokes, July 14, 1917, ibid. *New York Times*, June 19, 1917, 6. Eventually, 12,500 copies of each volume were printed, and several hundred chapter reprints. Jones, *Educational Adaptations,* 31.

34. Jones, *Negro Education,* 1:xiii–xiv.

35. *Minutes of the University Commission on Southern Race Questions,* 41–43, re. Meeting of Aug. 29, 30, 31, 1917.

36. Jones, *Negro Education,* 2:2, 13. On W. E. B. Du Bois's reservations about educational philanthropy, see Gasman, "W. E. B. Du Bois and Charles S. Johnson," 493–516.

37. Anderson and Moss, *Dangerous Donations,* 202–13.

38. Jones, *Negro Education,* vol. 1, passim. On the political economy of race and education, see Anderson, "On the Meaning of Reform," 263–84.

39. Bureau of Education, press release for Jones, *Negro Education,* n.d., box 69, entry 6, RG 12, NARA. Jones, *Negro Education,*1:7. See also Thomas Jesse Jones, *Four Essentials of Education.*

40. Jones, *Negro Education,* 2:7.

41. Ibid., 23. The report led to increased aid to Fisk University; Jones joined the Fisk executive committee and became executive secretary of the board of trustees. See Anderson, *Education of Blacks in the South,* 263–71. On the contortions that principals of private black schools engaged in to keep afloat financially, see O'Brien, "Perils of Accommodation," 806–52.

42. Woofter, *Southern Race Progress,* 115–20. Jones, *Educational Adaptations,* 29–31. Bailey, *Liberalism in the New South,* 54. Harlan, *Separate and Unequal,* 235–36, 248–52, 259–61.

43. Harris, "Stability and Change in Discrimination against Black Public Schools," 375–416. Feldman, *Disfranchisement Myth,* 161–65.

44. Montgomery, *Politics of Education in the New South,* 64–65, 71–72, 100; Bond, *Negro Education in Alabama,* 178–94, 247–54.

45. Ng, "Wealth Redistribution, Race, and Southern Public Schools, 1880–1910." Bailey, *Liberalism in the New South,* 48. Toppin, "Walter White and the Atlanta NAACP's Fight for Equal Schools," 5–6. Margo, "Teacher Salaries in Black and White," 306–26. See also Sims, "School Statistics from Mississippi," 4. Anderson, *Education of Blacks in the South,* 156, 178–85.

46. Jones, *Negro Education,* 2:471–526.

47. Ibid., 2:247–50, 312, 328, 376, 416–17, 451–56, 515–22, 652–53, 660.

48. Steffes, "Solving the 'Rural School Problem'," 181–220. Du Bois, "Education," 132–36.

49. Du Bois, "Negro Education," 173–78. In 1900 and 1910, Du Bois found thirty effective colleges, and ten especially good ones, including Howard, Fisk, Atlanta, Morehouse, and Virginia Union. He argued that they could coexist with industrial education. See Du Bois, *College-Bred Negro;* Du Bois, "Training of Negroes for Social Power," 409–14. Du Bois and Augustus G. Dill, *College-Bred Negro American.*

50. Du Bois, "Negro Education," 177. See also Du Bois, "Thomas Jesse Jones," 252–56. Watkins, *White Architects,* 114–16; Tindall, *Emergence of the New South,* 268–69, 274.

51. Woodson, *Negro in Our History,* 503–505. Woodson, *Mis-Education of the Negro,* 29–30. Woodson, "Thomas Jesse Jones," 107–109. Hine, "Carter G. Woodson," 405–25. Scally, "Phelps-Stokes Confidential Memorandum," 48–60. Goggin, *Carter G. Woodson,* 81–83.

52. Jones, *Educational Adaptations,* 33–36.

53. Ibid., 31.

54. Mitchell, Review of *Negro Education,* 246–48. Broadus Mitchell's dissertation was published as *The Rise of the Cotton Mills in the South* (1921). His father was former University of South Carolina President Samuel Chiles Mitchell. Hall, "Broadus Mitchell," 25–31.

55. Jones, *Educational Adaptations*, 22–24.

56. Jones, *Negro Education*, 2:3. On targeted funding, see Slater Fund, *Proceedings and Reports for Year Ending September 30, 1919* 9, 11–40. Tuskegee and Hampton Institutes received $6,000 each from the Slater Fund; a further twenty-two colleges in nine states received between $450 and $2,000, including Fisk University ($2,000), Atlanta University ($1,500), Spelman College ($1,500), Shaw University ($1,500), Morehouse College ($1,200) and Claflin College ($1,200). See also Thuesen, "The General Education Board and the Racial Leadership of Black Education."

57. Lane, "Legal Trend toward Increased Provisions for Negro Education," 396–99. Anderson and Moss, *Dangerous Donations*, 211–13.

58. Woofter, *Southern Race Progress*, 115–20. On the "colonial economy" thesis, see Carlton and Coclanis, *Confronting Southern Poverty*, 34–36.

59. Evans, "International Conference on the Negro," 416–29; Berman, "American Influence on African Education," passim. See also African Education Commission, *Education in Africa* (1922) and *Education in East Africa* (1925). On similarities between benevolent imperialism and interracial cooperation, see Fredrickson, *Black Image in the White Mind* (1987), 308–311.

60. Hill to Anson Phelps Stokes, Dec. 6, 1917, box 16, PSF, SC. Scott, *American Negro in the World War*, 328–33. James, "Robert Russa Moton and the Whispering Gallery after World War I," 235–42. Ellis, *Race, War, and Surveillance*, 122–23, 176, 187, 208–209.

61. *Washington Bee*, clipping, May 17, 1919, box 44, PSF, SC. Walter B. Hill to Jackson Davis, May 7, 1919, box 292, GEB Records, RAC. See Du Bois, "Robert R. Moton," 9–10. Jones claimed, "The reception of the report by the public was most satisfactory. Adverse criticism was limited to schools unfavorably described and to a few Negroes who feared that the report did not give sufficient recognition to college education." Jones, *Educational Adaptations*, 31.

62. Claxton to Anson Phelps Stokes, Oct. 26, Dec, 7, 1917, box 16, PSF, SC; Hill to R. M. Chatfield, April 30, 1918, ibid.; Hill to Anson Phelps Stokes, Nov. 30, Dec. 6, 1918, ibid.; Hill to Anson Phelps Stokes, Feb. 25, 1919, ibid.; Hill to Anson Phelps Stokes, July 5, 1919, ibid.; Board minutes, Nov. 20, 1918, box 1, ibid Executive Committee minutes, Nov -?, 1917, box 1, ibid. Jones, *Educational Adaptations*, 71, 88. Hill claimed a Class 5 draft deferral on the grounds of federal government employment. See "Walter Barnard Hill," Clarke County registration card 1145, June 5, 1917, at ancestry.com.

63. Taylor to Anson Phelps Stokes, Nov. 5, 16, 1917, box 16, PSF, SC. Executive Committee minutes, Nov. -?, 1917, box 1, ibid. Jones, *Educational Adaptations*, 58.

64. *Washington Post*, Aug. 16, 1919, 7; ibid., Aug. 29, 1919, 13.

65. Woofter to Jones, Oct. 12, 1937, and index to *Education for Life*, 13, 185, in Papers of Thomas Jesse Jones, Special Collections, Milbank Memorial Library, Teachers College, Columbia University, New York.

66. Woofter, *Southern Race Progress*, 115.

67. Woofter, Review of *In Freedom's Birthplace*, 494–95.

3. Migration and War

1. Woofter to Claxton, March 30, 1916, Jan. 12, 1917 (twice), official personnel folder (OPF), Thomas Jackson Woofter Jr., d.o.b. 6/18/93, Civilian Personnel Records, National Personnel Records Center (NPRC), St. Louis, Mo. Claxton to Woofter April 4, 1916, Jan. 18, 1917, ibid.; Claxton to Dr. Collier, April 4, 1916, ibid.; Claxton to Committee on Fellowships, Columbia University, Jan. 18, 1917, ibid. "Fourteenth List of Doctoral Dissertations in Political Economy in Progress at American Universities and Colleges," *American Economic Review* 7 (June 1917): 489. Woof-

ter, *Southern Race Progress,* 19. Camic and Xie, "Statistical Turn in American Social Science," 773–805.

2. Giddings, "Social Self Control," 569–88. See also Giddings, *Studies in the Theory of Human Society* (1922) and *Scientific Study of Human Society* (1924). McFarland, "Adding Machines and Logarithms," 249–55.

3. Giddings, "Social Self Control," 575, 578. Many writers, including William Graham Sumner, Edgar Gardner Murphy, Edward A. Ross, Charles H. Cooley, W. I. Thomas, Charles A. Ellwood, Alfred H. Stone, and Robert E. Park, saw race prejudice as natural.

4. Giddings, *Elements of Sociology,* 66. Fredrickson, *Black Image in the White Mind,* 2nd ed., 312–19.

5. Camic and Xie, "Statistical Turn in American Social Science," 791–94. Phelps-Stokes Fund, *Education for Life,* 185.

6. Woofter to Claxton, Jan. 17, 1917, Woofter OPF, NPRC; Anthony Caminetti to Louis F. Post, June 6, 1917, ibid.; Chief Clerk, Dept. of Labor, to Woofter, June 9, 1917, ibid.; Oath of Office, Thomas Jackson Woofter Jr., June 16, 1917, ibid.

7. *Negro Migration in 1916–17,* 5–8, 10. "William Taylor Burwell Williams," 202.

8. *Historical Statistics of the United States* (1975), 22–23.

9. Dillard, "Introduction" (1914), in Hammond, *In Black and White,* 4–5.

10. *Negro Migration in 1916–17,* 9–13, 75–86. Shenk, "Race, Manhood, and Manpower," 622–62. Shenk found few Georgia counties lost more than 1% of their farm labor. On migration and oppression, see Palmer, "Moving North," 52–62.

11. See, for example, Seligmann, *Negro Faces America,* 271. On black discussion of migration, see Trotter and Lewis, *African Americans in the Industrial Age,* 5–104.

12. *Negro Migration in 1916–17,* 86–91. Woofter included a few pages on South Carolina. Tolnay and Beck, "Racial Violence and Black Migration," 103–116.

13. Registration Card 1374, "Thomas Jackson Woofter, Jr.," Clarke County, Ga., June 5, 1917, *World War I Selective Service System Draft Registration Cards, 1917–18,* at ancestry.com. Woofter to Post, Sept. 18, 1917, Woofter OPF, NPRC; Woofter application to Council of National Defense (CND), Sept. 18, 1917, ibid.; Woofter oath of office, Sept. 19, 1917, ibid.; Woofter to Walter S. Gifford, Oct. 5, 1917, ibid.; Leonard P. Ayres to Gifford, Oct. 6, 1917, ibid. Woofter commission, Sept. 20, 1917, Adjutant General's Office Records, Record Group (RG) 407, National Archives (NA), College Park, Md. *Washington Post,* Oct. 10, 1917, 6. Breen, "Foundations, Statistics, and State-Building," 451–82. Woofter joined the CND on the day it enlarged Ayres's group; in 1918 Ayres took over the Statistics Branch of the General Staff. On his work in World War I, see reports in boxes 4, 5, and 6, Papers of Leonard Porter Ayres, LC, and *War with Germany.* See also Cuff, "Creating Control Systems," 588–613.

14. Woofter to Anson Phelps Stokes, Dec. 19, 1917, box 16, PSF, SC. Files of Records of Statistical Division, Adjutant General's Department, G1, GHQ, AEF, entries 6, 554, 555, 556, 558, 559, 560, 564, 566, Record Group 120, NA. On the transfer of skilled men to AEF HQ in 1918, see file 10874-A, boxes 338 and 339, entry 6, ibid.

15. For Woofter's work, see "Losses" folder 114, box 3890, entry 556, RG 120, NA; "Memorandums from GHQ Statistical Division," box 1, entry 558, ibid.; "Station Lists," "Roster of Officers," "Daily Station Changes," "Troop Movements," "Daily Troop Movements," in Miscellaneous Records File, 1917–1918, box 4995, entry 559, ibid.; Miscellaneous Correspondence File, box 2284, entry 560, ibid.; "Reports of Divisional Changes," box 3953, entry 564, ibid.; "Reports of Daily Station Changes, 1918–1919," boxes 2003, 2004, 2005, 3891, entry 566, ibid.

16. T. J. Woofter Jr., memorandum on graphs, n.d., file 050 ("Graphs"), box 3591, entry 554, ibid. He requisitioned an adding machine from an officer in the rearguard at Blois. Record of telephone call, Maj. Hambleton, June 16, 1918, index to file 10874-A, microfilm roll 258, entry

6, ibid. On Statistical Division dissemination, see, for example, Gen. John J. Pershing to commanding general, Services of Supply, June 25, 1918; Gen. Tasker H. Bliss to Pershing, May 19, Sept. 11, 1918, file 16139, box 652, entry 6, ibid.

17. See reports and memorandums in file 16139-A, box 652, entry 6, ibid.; W. Ball to chief clerk, Adjutant General's Office, April 28, 1919, file 24249-A-76, box 1023, ibid. On AEF filing systems, see Ryan, "Disposition of AEF Records of World War I," 212–19. Pershing believed accurate casualty and supply figures were crucial. Huelfer, *The "Casualty Issue" in American Military Practice,* 57–79.

18. Woofter's misconduct file is missing, but the index shows what occurred. Index to Correspondence of the C-I-C, AEF, 1917–19, RG 120, NA, and files 14796A-601–625, box 590, entry 6, ibid. Discharge card, Oct. 13, 1919, Woofter, T. J., Adjutant General's Office Records, RG 407, NA. Pershing and his staff left France on September 1, 1919. One of Woofter's UGA classmates died in the AEF; another was killed by gas while serving as a British army medic. Reed, *History of the University of Georgia,* 2409.

19. "Students' Dissertations in Sociology," *American Journal of Sociology* 25 (July 1919): 66; *American Journal of Sociology* 26 (July 1920): 99.

20. Woofter, *Negro Migration,* 7–8. Scott, *Negro Migration during the War*; Donald, *Negro Migration of 1916–1918*; Duncan, *Changing Race Relationship in the Border and Northern States.* See also "The Exodus during the War," in Woodson, *Century of Negro Migration,* 167–92. Odum, *American Sociology,* 347–50. Odum overlooked the work of Walter Wilcox at Cornell University. See Aldrich, "Progressive Economics and Scientific Racism," 1–14.

21. Woofter, *Negro Migration,* 181–83.

22. Ibid., 187.

23. Ibid., 188–95. Noting that "the application of statistics to social problems is in its infancy," he outlined "the practical use of correlation in measuring social relationships."

24. *Negro Population in the United States, 1790–1915.* See also Thomas Jesse Jones, *Negroes and the Census of 1910* and "Negro Population in the United States," 1–9. Odum, *American Sociology,* 325–32.

25. Woofter, *Negro Migration,* 26

26. Ibid., 53–91, 157. See Kyriakoudes, "Southern Black Rural-Urban Migration," 341–51.

27. Woofter, *Negro Migration,* 99–147, 172. Ginzburg, *100 Years of Lynchings,* 98–99.

28. Woofter, *Negro Migration,* 149–56, 171. See Boas, *The Mind of Primitive Man.*

29. Woofter, *Negro Migration,* 166, 169–72.

30. Ibid., 157–62.

31. Ibid., 172–80.

32. Miller, Review of *Negro Migration,* 256–58.

33. Kelsey, Review of *Negro Migration,* 216. "H.J.S.," Review of *Negro Migration,* 141–42. Sydney D. Frissell, "Cause, Effect and Remedy for Negro Migration," *Atlanta Constitution,* Dec. 27, 1920, 4. Frissell also published a review in the *Springfield Republican,* July 19, 1921, 6. Frissell's life contained many parallels with Woofter's. He served with the Hampton Institute artillery corps on the Mexican border in 1916 and as an officer with the Ninety-second Division on three fronts in France. Obituary of Sydney D. Frissell, *Newport News Daily Press,* Jan. 19, 1966, 3, 10.

34. Woofter, *Negro Migration,* 27–28. Washington, *My Larger Education,* 118.

35. Jones, *Educational Adaptations,* 70–75. Reed, *Negro Illegitimacy in New York City.* David C. Barrow to Anson Phelps Stokes, Oct. 16, 1914, box 15, PSF, SC. Barrow to Anson Phelps Stokes, Feb. 4, 1914, ibid. Woofter to Anson Phelps Stokes, Jan. 13, 30, 1915, ibid. Woofter to Anson Phelps Stokes, Nov. 8, 19, 1915, ibid. Woofter provided Anson Phelps Stokes with updates on the fellowships.

36. E. Alderman to Anson Phelps Stokes, Feb. 16, 1915, box 15, PSF, SC. The lectures published in 1915 included contributions from Alfred Holt Stone, James Hardy Dillard, Ulrich B. Phillips, Clarence H. Poe, and William O. Scroggs, appealing for better treatment of blacks within a segregated society. By 1931, Phelps-Stokes fellows had completed twenty reports, ten at the University of Georgia and ten at the University of Virginia. See Thomas Jesse Jones to Anson Phelps Stokes, March 25, 1932, box 17, ibid.

37. Walter B. Hill to Thomas Jesse Jones, Nov. 24, 1919, box 42, ibid. Jones, *Educational Adaptations*, 75–76.

38. Walter B. Hill to Woofter, Oct. 28, 1920, box 42, PSF, SC; Woofter to E. C. Sage, n.d., ibid.; Anson Phelps Stokes to Woofter, Nov. 18, Dec. 1, 1920, ibid.; Howard W. Odum to Woofter, Dec. 1, 1920, ibid.; Wallace Buttrick to Woofter, Dec. 22, 1920, ibid. *New York Times*, March 2, 1921, 15. During the 1920s, the Phelps-Stokes Fund tracked the fellows' careers, to gauge the program's impact, and Woofter gave them advice. See Carl Foreman to Phelps-Stokes fellows, Sept. 23, 1926, box 42, PSF, SC; Graham F. Campbell to Foreman, Nov. 17, 1926, ibid.

39. Minutes of Executive Committee, March 16, 1920, box 1, ibid. African Education Commission, *Education in Africa*, xiv–xx. Jones led another African tour between January and August 1924. W. E. B. Du Bois dubbed the subsequent report, "making Africa safe for white folks." Du Bois, *Education in Africa*, 86–89.

40. T. J. Woofter, "Observations on Interracial Work," typescript, Feb. 1921, box 16, PSF, SC. Woofter to W. R. Connors, Jan. 14, 1921, ibid.; Connors to Woofter, Jan. 19, 1921, ibid. Booker T. Washington considered Cincinnati's blacks especially deprived; it was "the dumping ground for a class of Negroes who desire to get out of the South, but have not the money or the energy to go further than the Ohio River." Washington to Jacob Godfrey Schmidlapp, Jan. 12, 1910, in *Booker T. Washington Papers*, 10:260–61.

41. Woofter, "Negro and Industrial Peace," 420–21, and Woofter, "Square Deal for Negroes at the American Rolling Mill Company's Plant," 209–16.

42. Woofter to George Foster Peabody, n.d., box C-319, Papers of the NAACP, LC. See also Gudza, "Labor Department's First Program to Assist Black Workers," 39–44, Stewart, "George Edmund Haynes and the Office of Negro Economics," 213–29, and Wilson, *Segregated Scholars*, 127–35.

43. "Southland College Papers," Special Collections, University of Arkansas Libraries, http://libinfo.uark.edu/SpecialCollections/findingaids/southland/southlandaid.html#contents (August 6, 2006); Kennedy, "Southland College," 207–24. Jones, *Negro Education*, 2:125–26. Weatherford, *Interracial Cooperation*, 49–50. On the Phillips County riot, see Stockley, *Blood in Their Eyes*.

44. On Jackson Davis, see Anderson, *Education of Blacks in the South*, 136–44. Davis took several photographs of Southland's campus, workshops, and 170 acres of farmland. Negatives 1929–30, 2307, Jackson Davis Collection of African American Educational Photographs, University of Virginia Library, http://www.lib.virginia.edu/small/collections/jdavis/.

45. Kennedy, "Last Days at Southland," 1–19; Kennedy, "Southland College," 225–34. The Rosenwald Fund built a new county school. S. L. Smith, *Builders of Goodwill*, 132–38.

46. Simms, "Four Days at Southland Institute," 165–66.

4. Will Alexander and the Commission on Interracial Cooperation

1. On Alexander, see Dykeman and Stokely, *Seeds of Southern Change*.

2. Grant, *The Way It Was In the South*, 294.

3. Dittmer, *Black Georgia in the Progressive Era*, 210.

4. James O. Dobson, "Account of the Discussion," in *Christian Mission in the Light of Race Conflict,* 230–31.

5. John Hope, "The Negro in the United States of America," in *Christian Mission in the Light of Race Conflict,* 16, 22.

6. Woofter, "Agencies for Inter-Racial Co-Operation in the United States," in *Christian Mission in the Light of Race Conflict,* 83–84.

7. *Montgomery Emancipator,* March 1, 1919, 2, cited in Bristow, *Making Men Moral,* 283n151.

8. W. D. Weatherford to Cleveland H. Dodge, July 21, 1919, box 16, PSF, SC. Weatherford to Anson Phelps Stokes, July 23, 1919, ibid. See also Weatherford to Anson Phelps Stokes, Dec. 20, 1920; April 4, 1921; and April 27, 1921, ibid. Mjagkij, *Light in the Darkness,* 102–106. Katherine Kuntz Dill, "Negro Christian Student Conference," in Mjagkij, *Organizing Black America,* 499–500. White, *Liberty and Justice for All,* 187–207. Weatherford, *Interracial Cooperation,* 82. Blue Ridge Assembly was a large complex by the mid-1920s, often used by the YMCA.

9. Woofter, *Progress in Race Relations in Georgia,* 4–10, 14–15; Dykeman and Stokely, *Seeds of Southern Change,* 100–109; Woofter, *Southern Race Progress,* 31–37. Streitmatter, "Defying the Klan."

10. Ellis, *Race, War, and Surveillance,* 187, 199, 203–209. Wolters, *Du Bois and His Rivals,* 131–42.

11. McDonough, "Men and Women of Good Will," 38–46. Godshalk, *Veiled Visions,* 264.

12. Minutes of meeting on After the War Cooperation, March 17, 1919, box 16, PSF, SC. White, *Liberty and Justice for All,* 59. Jones, *Educational Adaptations,* 90–92.

13. Shivers, "Twentieth Century South-wide Civic and Lay Organizations for Human Welfare," 187–88.

14. Newman and Crunk, "Religious Leaders in the Aftermath of Atlanta's 1906 Race Riot," 460–85. Link, *Paradox of Southern Progressivism,* 248–51. Tindall, *Emergence of the New South,* 178. Seligmann, *Negro Faces America,* 58. McMillen, *Dark Journey,* 304–306. Godshalk, *Veiled Visions,* 161–70. Mikkelsen, "Coming from Battle to Face a War." Davis, *Clashing of the Soul,* 260–64. Dykeman, *Prophet of Plenty,* 138–44. See also Brundage, *Lynching in the New South,* 212–15; Pilkington, "Trials of Brotherhood," 55–80.

15. White, *Liberty and Justice for All,* 238.

16. Weatherford, *Interracial Cooperation,* 25–26. Ellis, *Race, War, and Surveillance,* 128–29. Bolton Smith, "Negro in War-Time," 1110–13. Bolton Smith to Fred R. Moore, June 17, 1922, box 6, Moton Family Papers, LC.

17. Hammond, *Southern Women and Racial Adjustment,* 3.

18. Weatherford, *Interracial Cooperation,* 25; Palmer, "Moving North," 60. On Hilbun, see Smith, *Builders of Goodwill,* 29–32. Hubbard, "Are There Any Blind Black Babies?," 92–94.

19. Weatherford, *Interracial Cooperation,* 58–73.

20. J. H. Dillard to Anson Phelps Stokes, April 27, 1919, box 16, PSF, SC; W. M. Hunley to Anson Phelps Stokes, May 3, 15, 1919, ibid. "A New Reconstruction" (April 26, 1919), in *Five Letters of the University Commission on Southern Race Questions,* 12–14.

21. Jones, *Educational Adaptations,* 79–86. Executive Committee minutes, March 16, 1920, box 1, PSF, SC. Walter B. Hill to L. H. Hammond, Nov. 27, 1917, box 16, ibid. Hammond to Anson Phelps Stokes, Nov. 28, 1917, ibid.; Anson Phelps Stokes to Hammond, Dec. 4, 1917, ibid.; Hammond to Anson Phelps Stokes, Dec. 2, 1918, ibid.; Hammond to Anson Phelps Stokes, Jan. 8, 1921, ibid.; Southern Publicity Committee press releases, n.d., box 33, ibid.

22. *New York Times,* June 8, 1919, 36.

23. Brundage, *Lynching in the New South,* 77.

24. McCulloch, *"Distinguished Service" Citizenship,* 106, 110–11, 113–19. The Knoxville meet-

ing of the SSC was followed by its last, in Washington, D.C., in 1920. See also J. H. Dillard, "Introductory Address," in *Five Letters of the University Commission*, 17–20. See also J. L. Kesler, "In Justice to Waco" (letter), *Nation* 103 (Dec. 28, 1916): 609. Kesler wrote: "Waco has a conscience, but it happens here as elsewhere that the criminal minority takes us unawares; and here as elsewhere there is an irresponsible element that misrepresents the community."

25. *Booker T. Washington Papers*, 4:198.

26. Speech to Augusta Exposition, Nov. 1887, in Harris, *Life of Henry W. Grady*, 131–32.

27. McCulloch, *"Distinguished Service,"* 122–28.

28. Minutes of Interracial Committee, July 17, 1919, cited in McDonough, "Men and Women of Good Will," 46. On "Negro subversion," see Ellis, *Race, War, and Surveillance,* passim.

29. *Proceedings of the Eleventh Meeting of the Governors*, 102–108. McCulloch, *"Distinguished Service,"* 107–109.

30. Dykeman and Stokely, *Seeds of Southern Change*, 65–67.

31. Sidney [sic] D. Frissell, "Meeting the Negro Problem," *New York Times*, Dec. 14 1919, X10.

32. McDonough, "Men and Women of Good Will," 51. "Inter-racial Committees," 4–5. Tindall, *Emergence of the New South*, 181.

33. Thomas Jesse Jones to Robert R. Moton, March 25, 1920, enclosing a copy of his letter to R. H. King, March 25, 1920, box 14, Moton Family Papers, LC. The other African American bishop elected in 1920, Matthew W. Clair, was assigned to Monrovia. Robert Elijah Jones had been a contender for election at previous conferences. See *New York Times*, May 18, 1916, 7; ibid., May 24, 1920, 7; ibid., May 26, 1920, 17.

34. Ellis, "Commission on Interracial Cooperation," 368.

35. "General Survey of the Work of the Commission on Interracial Cooperation for 1921–23," box 96, Laura Spelman Rockefeller Memorial Collection (LSRM), Rockefeller Archive Center (RAC), Sleepy Hollow, N.Y. Woofter lived at the famous Ansley Hotel.

36. Woofter, *Southern Race Progress*, 164. McDonough, "Men and Women of Good Will," 66. Edith Armstrong Talbot, "Inter-Racial Co-Operation in South Commission's Aim," *Christian Science Monitor*, Aug. 1, 1922, 3. Pearson, "Race Relations in North Carolina," 1–9.

37. *An Appeal to the Christian People of the South* (n.p., 1920), at http://www.archive.org /details/appealtochristiaoochri

38. *Atlanta Constitution*, June 3, 1920, 9. Dittmer, *Black Georgia*, 206–207. NAACP, *Eleventh Annual Report* (1921), 67–72. Sullivan, *Lift Every Voice*, 89–93. Wilmer sought fair treatment of Leo Frank and described Imperial Wizard W. J. Simmons as "one of the most skillful performers on the organ of Southern prejudices that I have ever listened to." Ellis, "A Crusade against 'Wretched Attitudes,'" 23.

39. Josiah Morse to Samuel C. Mitchell, Aug. 31, 1919, cited in Ellis, "Commission on Interracial Cooperation," 370. Morse changed his name from Moses to overcome prejudice.

40. Walter F. White to James Weldon Johnson, Dec. 4, 1923, "CIC 1921–23" folder, box L13, group II, NAACP Papers, LC. Dittmer, *Black Georgia in the Progressive Era*, 206–207. Brundage, *Lynching in the New South*, 215–25.

41. Rolinson, *Grassroots Garveyism*, 161–82. The UNIA also grew in Florida, the Arkansas Delta, and the Yazoo-Mississippi Delta. Out of 45 NAACP branches formed in 1921, only six were southern. See NAACP, *Eleventh Annual Report*, 64–66.

42. *Cleveland Advocate*, Sept. 25, 1920, 1.

43. National Interracial Conference, *Toward Interracial Cooperation*, 71–73.

44. McDonough, "Men and Women of Good Will," 99–112, 117–21.

45. Hammond, *In Black and White*, 37. Janken, *White*, 34–35.

46. Robertson, *Christian Sisterhood, Race Relations, and the YWCA*, 45–91. Hall, *Revolt*

against Chivalry, 77–86. In December 1920, at the YWCA national headquarters in New York, twenty African American delegates led by Mary McLeod Bethune called on black and white women to work more closely together. *Cleveland Advocate,* Dec. 18, 1920, 4.

47. *Southern Women and Race Cooperation,* 5–6, at http://docsouth.unc.edu/nc/racecoop /racecoop.html. Gilmore, *Gender and Jim Crow,* 149–50, 192–95. Dykeman and Stokely, *Seeds of Southern Change,* 88–90. McDonough, "Men and Women of Good Will," 112–16. Hall, *Revolt against Chivalry,* 65–77, 86–90. Harvey, *Freedom's Coming,* 67–77.

48. Cited in Ellis, "Commission on Interracial Cooperation," 30–31. Palmer Memorial Institute, a rural elementary school, was commended in *Negro Education,* 2:419. On Brown, see Gilmore, *Gender and Jim Crow,* 178–90, 199–202. In 1919 and 1920, black and white women voters in Tennessee jointly supported reform candidates. See Goodstein, "A Rare Alliance," 219–46.

49. Address by Mrs. Charlotte Hawkins Brown, Women's Interracial Conference, Memphis, Tenn., Oct. 8, 1920, frames 932–39, microfilm reel 20, Papers of the Commission on Interracial Cooperation (CIC), Robert W. Woodruff Library, Atlanta University Center (AUC), Atlanta, Ga. See also Brown, *Eradicating This Evil,* 133–34; Hall, *Revolt against Chivalry,* 86–95. Dykeman and Stokely, *Seeds of Southern Change,* 91–96.

50. Hall, *Revolt against Chivalry,* 95–98.

51. Gilmore, *Gender and Jim Crow,* 216–18. Bickett chaired the CIC's North Carolina women's committee; Charlotte Hawkins Brown was a member. "Southern Negro Women and Race Co-operation," in McCluskey and Smith, *Mary McLeod Bethune,* 145–49.

52. "Minutes of Joint Meeting, Woman's General Committee of the Commission on Interracial Cooperation and the Interracial Committee of the Southeastern Federation of Colored Women's Clubs," ibid., 149–54.

53. Hall, *Revolt against Chivalry,* 102–105. Joan Marie Johnson, "Shape of the Movement to Come," 201–23. Ellis, "Commission on Interracial Cooperation," 23–34. Link, *Paradox of Southern Progressivism,* 254–56.

54. "Constructive Measure Recommended by Southern White Women," 35–37. *Christian Science Monitor,* Aug. 1, 1922, 3.

55. *Cleveland Advocate,* Aug. 31, 1920, 1, 6; ibid., Sept. 11, 1920, 8. *Atlanta Independent,* Feb. 10, 1921, 1. Brown, *Eradicating This Evil,* 132–33. Blacks sought Harding's views on voting, desegregation, antilynching legislation, and education. "Memorandum to Dr. Du Bois," n.d., in Aptheker, *Documentary History of the Negro People,* 2:303.

56. Oral History interview with Will Winton Alexander, 1952, Columbia University Center for Oral History Collection (CUCOHC), New York, 304–307. Woofter attributed the "stutter" comment to another delegate, M. Ashby Jones. See Woofter, *Southern Race Progress,* 125. On Harding and race, see Sherman, *Republican Party and Black America,* 134–99, and Palmer, *Twenties in America,* 46–47. Other special interest delegations, such as a German-American group, found Harding's attitude at this time "unimpeachable in its courtesy and kindness." *New York Times,* Feb. 20, 1921, 2.

57. T. J. Woofter to Anson Phelps Stokes, Feb. 19, 1921, box 16, PSF, SC.

58. *New York Times,* April 13, 1921, 7.

59. *Atlanta Independent,* Jan. 27, 1921, 1.

60. *New York Times,* Oct. 27, 1921, 1, 11; ibid., Nov. 7, 1921, 13. *Atlanta Constitution,* Oct. 27, 1921, 2; ibid.; Oct. 30, C2. *Crisis* 23 (Jan. 1922): 127–32; *Crisis* 23 (Feb. 1922): 151–52; *Crisis* 23 (April 1922): 211. "The Negro's Status Declared by the President," 7–9. Harding gave five speeches in Birmingham, mentioning race in one. In a speech in Atlanta the next day, he made no reference to race, preferring to praise southern heritage. *Atlanta Constitution,* Oct. 28, 1921, 1.

61. *Atlanta Independent,* May 26, 1921, 3; ibid., Sept. 8, 1921, 1. Initially, the Associated Ne-

gro Press reported that all segregation signs in government departments in Washington had been removed. Ibid., March 10, 1921, 1.

62. Woofter memorandum to Anson Phelps Stokes, March 9, 1921, box 16, PSF, SC. Sherman, *Republican Party and Black America*, 146–73. Daniel, "Black Power in the 1920s," 368–88. Dykeman and Stokely, *Seeds of Southern Change*, 159–62. Ellis, "Commission on Interracial Cooperation," 96–99.

63. John J. Eagan to the Laura Spelman Rockefeller Memorial, Oct. 1, 1921, box 96, LSRM, RAC; Will W. Alexander to James H. Dillard, Oct. 1, 1921, ibid.; Eagan to Raymond B. Fosdick, Dec. 31, 1921, ibid. See also Ellis, "Commission on Interracial Cooperation," 1–38. For contemporary accounts of the CIC and "racial cooperation," see Dowd, *Negro in American Society*, 547–65, and Paul E. Baker, *Negro-White Adjustment*, passim. Woofter, *Southern Race Progress*, 171.

64. Hall, *William Louis Poteat*, 93–94. Gilmore, *Gender and Jim Crow*, 165–74. On the intentions of the North Carolina committee, see Odum, "Fundamental Principles Underlying Inter-Racial Cooperation," 282–85. Interview with Guy B. Johnson, Dec. 16, 1974 (B-0006), Southern Oral History Program Collection (#4007), at Documenting the American South, http://docsouth.unc.edu/sohp/B-0006/B-0006.html. See also Miles, "The North Carolina Inter-Racial Committee," 154–55.

65. Cited in Hall, *William Louis Poteat*, 94–95. Harvey, *Freedom's Coming*, 54–55.

66. On Foreman, see Sullivan, *Days of Hope*, passim. On Raper and the CIC, see Mazzari, *Southern Modernist*, 51–76.

67. McDonough, "Men and Women of Good Will," 82–84. *Christian Science Monitor*, Aug. 1, 1922, 3. Fairclough, *Race and Democracy*, 12–13.

68. *Booker T. Washington Papers*, 4:478. Isaac Fisher, "A College President's Story," in Washington, *Tuskegee and Its People*, 101–10. *Crisis* 9 (Dec. 1914): 65–66; *Crisis* 22 (May 1921), 6–7. Wheeler, "Isaac Fisher," 3–50.

69. "Ninth Meeting, University Commission on Southern Racial Questions, Nashville, Tennessee, April 25–26, 1919," cited in Fairclough, *Class of Their Own*, 326.

70. Minutes of the CIC, March 29, 1921, cited in McDonough, "Men and Women of Good Will," 58.

71. Isaac Fisher to John J. Eagan, Sept. 16, 1921, cited in Pilkington, "The Trials of Brotherhood," 55.

72. Will W. Alexander to Isaac Fisher, April 20, 1927, box 1, Isaac Fisher Papers, Tuskegee University Archives (TUA), Tuskegee, Ala. E. S. Lotspeich to Isaac Fisher, May 7, 1927, box 1, ibid. Alexander to Fisher, May 17, 1921, box 002.072, Moton Collection, TUA. Leonard Outhwaite, "Southern Trip," Nov.–Dec. 1925, cited in Stanfield, *Philanthropy and Jim Crow*, 73.

73. Woofter and Fisher, *Cooperation in Southern Communities*, 7.

74. Ibid., 7, 9–11

75. Ibid., 13–18.

76. Ibid., 19.

77. Ibid., 30–32.

78. Ibid., 33–40.

79. Ibid., 54–56.

80. Ibid., 23–26.

81. Ibid., 27–29. *New York Times*, April 19, 1914, 6. *Atlanta Constitution*, May 18, 1921, 10. Under Nevin's editorship (1910–31), the *Georgian* was the first major Atlanta paper to demand a retrial for Leo Frank; it defended the city's Jewish community. It sold less than the *Atlanta Constitution* and the *Atlanta Journal*. On the black press, he relied on Robert Kerlin's collection of radical journalism from 1919, *The Voice of the Negro*.

82. Miles, "The Virginia Inter-Racial Committee," 153–54, and Miles, "The South Carolina Inter-Racial Committee," 155.

83. Woofter and Fisher, *Cooperation in Southern Communities*, 21–23.

84. Ibid., 50–65.

85. Ibid., 45–49. The weakest contribution consisted of some thoughts on health and housing by Howard Odum, which completely evaded the question of race (41–44).

86. "Inter-Racial Commission in Annual Meeting Emphasizes Anti-Lynching Crusade," 712–13. Link, *Paradox of Southern Progressivism*, 254.

87. *Atlanta Constitution*, Nov. 14, 1921, 6. Ellis, "Commission on Interracial Cooperation," 22.

88. Woofter, *Southern Race Progress*, 164.

89. Ibid., 164–67. Woofter, *Races and Ethnic Groups in American Life*, 239.

90. Alexander, "Negro in the New South," 151.

91. Woofter, *Races and Ethnic Groups in American Life*, 238–39.

92. Mjagkij, *Light in the Darkness*, 106.

93. Woofter, *Races and Ethnic Groups in American Life*, 237.

94. Woofter, *Southern Race Progress*, 166.

95. Martin, "Race Cooperation." Pilkington, "Trials of Brotherhood," 75. Secretary's report to annual state meeting, Atlanta, Oct. 28, 1925, frames 46–52, microfilm reel 50, file 122, series I, CIC Papers, AUC. Ellis, "Commission on Interracial Cooperation," 156–58. *Washington Post*, March 27, 1927, 17. On the work of local interracial committees in Virginia, see J. Douglas Smith, *Managing White Supremacy*, 46–51.

96. R. W. Miles to J. D. Grimes, July 21, 1923, box 3, Junius D. Grimes Papers, Collection 571, East Carolina Manuscript Collection, J. Y. Joyner Library, East Carolina University, Greenville, N.C. Miles to Grimes, Nov. 17, 1923, box 3, ibid. Miles to Grimes, March 24, 1926, box 4, ibid. Robert B. Eleazer, *An Adventure in Good Will: The Interracial Commission, It's* [sic] *Origin and Work*, n.p., n.d., box 3, ibid. Robert B. Eleazer edited the Methodist journal, *Missionary Voice*, which carried a short piece by Woofter on how interracial committees might address grievances that caused black migration. See also Miles, "The Virginia Inter-Racial Committee," 153–54; Miles, "The North Carolina Inter-Racial Committee," 154–55; Miles, "The South Carolina Inter-Racial Committee," 155. Woofter, "Negro Migration," 88.

97. Will W. Alexander, "A Usable Piece of Community Machinery," 41–42.

98. R. L. Duffus, "South Solving Its Own Problems," *New York Times*, April 6, 1930, arts sect., 134.

5. Dorsey, Dyer, and Lynching

1. Dykeman and Stokely, *Seeds of Southern Change*, 112.

2. Woofter, "Southern Backfires against Lynch Law," 99–100.

3. Woofter, *Southern Race Progress*, 14.

4. Ibid., 25–26.

5. *Atlanta Constitution*, June 30, 1905, 1–2; ibid., July 1, 1905, 3; ibid., July 2, 1905, D3; ibid., July 4, 1905, 2; July 11, 1905, 3. *New York Times*, June 30, 1905, 6; ibid., Dec. 30, 1889, 1; ibid., June 23, 1908, 1. *Chicago Tribune*, June 30, 1905, 4. See also "Southern Press on the Georgia Lynching," *Literary Digest* 31 (July 15, 1905): 71–72. On forces underlying lynching in Georgia at the end of the nineteenth century, see Soule, "Populism and Black Lynching in Georgia," 431–49.

6. Woofter, *Negro Migration*, 109.

7. White, *Liberty and Justice for All*, xvii–xviii.

8. Hammond, *In Black and White*, 29.

9. Ibid., 27–28.

10. Baker, *This Mob Will Surely Take My Life*, 153–55. Kate Trawick was married to the older brother of Weatherford's deceased first wife, Lula Belle Trawick.

11. Cited in Montgomery, *Politics of Education in the New South*, 96.

12. Commission on Interracial Cooperation, *Southern Women and Race Cooperation*, 8.

13. *Atlanta Constitution*, Sept. 11, 1921, E1. *New York Times*, Sept. 11, 1921, 10.

14. *Atlanta Constitution*, Feb. 3, 1922, 7. The meeting was also attended by GEB agent Louis Favrot and Rosenwald Fund official S. L. Smith.

15. Statements by women members of North Carolina and Texas state committees, 1922, "CIC 1921–23" folder, box L13, group II, NAACP Papers, LC. Resolutions adopted by Florida State Federation of Women's Clubs, Sept. 5, 1922, ibid.

16. McDonough, "Men and Women of Good Will," 80–81. Georgia Committee on Race Relations minutes, Nov. 2, 1922, frame 1655–56, file 37, series VII, microfilm reel 45, CIC Papers, AUC. *Atlanta Constitution*, Nov. 3, 1922, 1; ibid., Dec. 8, 1922, 12; ibid., Aug. 3, 1923, 16.

17. Steelman, "Study of Mob Action in the South," 12. On Ames, see Hall, *Revolt against Chivalry*, passim.

18. Pickens, *New Negro*, 193.

19. M. Ashby Jones, "Approach to the South's Race Question," 40–41.

20. *New York Times*, Sept. 13, 1916, 1. *Crisis* 13 (Nov. 1916): 25. On the Frank case, see Oney, *And the Dead Shall Rise*, and Dinnerstein, *Leo Frank Case*.

21. Steelman, "Study of Mob Action in the South," 296–301. Walter White, "The Work of a Mob," *Crisis* 16 (Sept. 1918): 221–23. *Augusta Chronicle*, May 25, 1918, reprinted in Waldrep, *Lynching in America*, 198–99.

22. *Atlanta Constitution*, July 29, 1919, 8, 9. *Cleveland Advocate*, May 17, 1919, 1; ibid., Feb. 14, 1920, 8; ibid., Feb 28, 1920, 2.; ibid., March 13, 1920, 1; ibid., April 17, 1920, 1; ibid., Jan. 1, 1920, 1. Moton, "The South and the Lynching Evil," 191–96. NAACP, *Eleventh Annual Report*, 42–44.

23. NAACP, *Eleventh Annual Report*, 22–23.

24. *Atlanta Constitution*, Jan. 10, 1921, 5; ibid., Jan. 12, 1921, 3; ibid., Jan. 13, 1921, 9; ibid., Jan.14, 1921, 4; ibid., Jan.16, 1921, 1; ibid., Jan. 24, 1921, 7. Daniel, *Shadow of Slavery*, 134–35.

25. *Atlanta Constitution*, Feb. 18, 1921, 8; ibid., Feb. 20, 1921, 1; ibid., Feb. 22, 1921, 12.

26. Daniel, *Shadow of Slavery*, 110–31. *Atlanta Constitution*, March 26, 1921, 1; ibid., April 11, 1921, 1; ibid., Nov. 9, 1921, 1; ibid., Jan. 13, 1922, 6. *New York Times*, March 25, 1921, 3; ibid., March 29, 1921, 1; April 4, 1921, 6; ibid., April 7, 1921, 1; April 10, 1921, 1; ibid., April 13, 1921, 6. Dorsey offered a $500 reward for the arrest of each of Williams's sons, who fled to Florida. They surrendered in 1927, but were not tried. Manning and Williams died in prison; the former of tuberculosis in 1927, the latter in a riot in 1931. Dykeman and Stokely, *Seeds of Southern Change*, 128–30. See also Myers, *Race, Labor, and Punishment in the New South*.

27. Daniel, *Shadow of Slavery*, 132–40. *New York Times*, April 13, 1921, 6. The Georgia peonage cases were discussed at the 12th annual NAACP conference. *Crisis* 22 (Aug. 1921): 160–64; "Georgia's Death Farm," 13–14; "Georgia Declares War on Peonage," 17–18. *Freeman*, 3 (April 20, 1921): 123.

28. *A Statement from Governor Hugh M. Dorsey as to the Negro in Georgia*, April 22, 1921, http://www.archive.org/stream/statementfromgovoogeorrich.

Pitts, "Hugh M. Dorsey and 'The Negro in Georgia,'" 185–212. *Atlanta Constitution*, April 23, 1921, 7; ibid., April 24, 1921, 1. *Chicago Tribune*, April 26, 1921, 3; ibid., April 28, 1921, 6. *New York Times*, April 29, 1921, 26; ibid., May 1, 1921, editorial sect., 25; "Georgia's Indictment," 183,

190; "Governor Dorsey Stirs Up Georgia," 19. CIC supporters present included M. Ashby Jones, John J. Eagan, Will Alexander, Plato Durham, and Andrew J. Cobb. The latter, a former state supreme court justice, had called on Governor Slaton to commute Leo Frank's death sentence.

29. Dittmer, *Black Georgia*, 208–209. George Brown Tindall put it too strongly when he wrote that the CIC "induced" Dorsey to issue the statement. Tindall, *Emergence of the New South*, 181.

30. Pitts, "Hugh M. Dorsey," 198–207. Daniel, *Shadow of Slavery*, 127–28. MacLean, *Behind the Mask of Chivalry*, 17–18, 125–28. *Atlanta Constitution*, May 15, 1921, 1; ibid., May 18, 1921, 10; ibid., May 23, 1921, 3; ibid., May 24, 1921, 13, 16. *New York Times*, May 13, 1921, 17; ibid., May 16, 1921, 15. "Governor Dorsey Stirs Up Georgia," 19.

31. H. A. Hunt to W. E. B. Du Bois, June 1, 1921, W. E. B. Du Bois Papers, Special Collections and University Archives, University of Massachusetts Amherst Libraries (UMAL). *Atlanta Constitution*, April 25, 1921, 1; ibid., April 26, 1921, 1; ibid., April 28, 1921, 1; ibid., April 29, 1921, 1; ibid., May 27, 1921, 1. *New York Times*, April 29, 1921, 26; ibid., May 13, 1921, 17; ibid., May 19, 1921, 19. *Chicago Tribune*, April 26, 1921, 3. Historical Census Browser, University of Virginia Library, http://mapserverlib.virginia.edu.

32. *Atlanta Constitution*, May 22, 1921, E2; ibid., May 26, 1921, 1.

33. *Atlanta Constitution*, June 19, 1921, A8. *Baltimore Afro-American*, June 24, 1921, reprinted in Ginzburg, *100 Years of Lynchings*, 151–52; *Washington Eagle*, July 16, 1921, in Ginzburg, *100 Years of Lynchings*, 152–53.

34. Williamson, *Rage for Order*, 125. Giddings, *Ida*, 406–407. On Northen, see David F. Godshalk, "William J. Northen's Public and Personal Struggles against Lynching," in Dailey et al., eds, *Jumpin' Jim Crow*, 140–61. Candler, the last Confederate veteran elected governor of Georgia, ordered that Hose be held in prison in Atlanta, but when this was ignored he did nothing to prevent the lynching. Wells-Barnett, *Lynch Law in Georgia*, 7–10, 13–17.

35. *New York Times*, June 26, 1921, editorial sect., 1, 12. *Atlanta Constitution*, June 14, 1921, A7; ibid., June 16, 1921, 4; ibid., June 19, 1921, A8.

36. *Atlanta Constitution*, Aug. 7, 1921, 6. Grantham, *Hoke Smith and the Politics of the New South*, 176–78, 213. Hardwick had some reforming instincts; T. J. Woofter Sr. backed his education proposals. *Atlanta Constitution*, July 16, 1921, 6.

37. Burns, "Without Due Process," 233–52.

38. *Atlanta Constitution*, Jan. 27, 1922, 1. Levy, *James Weldon Johnson*, 249–51. On the Dyer bill's progress in 1922, see also *Atlanta Constitution*, Jan. 22, 1922, 1; ibid., Dec. 3, 1922, 1; ibid., Dec. 6, 1922, 6; ibid., Dec. 8, 1922, 12. On the early debates in the Senate, see *New York Times*, March 5, 1922, arts sect., 79. "Mob Violence a Federal Offense," 285–86. "The Dyer Bill," *Crisis* 23 (Jan. 1922): 114; *Crisis* 23 (March 1922): 211–12, 228; *Crisis* 23 (April 1922): 248, 262–63, 276–77; *Crisis* 24 (May 1922): 25; *Crisis* 25 (Nov. 1922): 23–27. Zangrando, *NAACP Crusade against Lynching*, 43–44, 54–61, 61–69; Sherman, *Republican Party and Black America*, 179–99; Sullivan, *Lift Every Voice*, 105–10, 194–97, 203–204. Ferrell, *Nightmare and Dream*, passim.

39. *Atlanta Constitution*, Jan. 22, 1919, 6. Burns, "Without Due Process," 239.

40. *New York Times*, March 9, 1919, 35. See also NAACP, *Burning at Stake in the United States*, 11–12.

41. *Atlanta Constitution*, May 18, 1919, D4.

42. *Hartford Republican*, May 16, 1902, 2. *Crisis* 19 (Jan. 1920): 141–42.

43. *Atlanta Constitution*, Feb. 1, 1922, 6. The *Constitution* was referring to three white men convicted in Oklahoma City after the lynching of Jake Brooks, a black packing-house worker. The *Crisis*, however, noted that two other men, both black, were also sentenced to life imprisonment for their part in the same lynching. *Crisis* 23 (April 1922): 271.

44. Dykeman and Stokely, *Seeds of Southern Change*, 46.

45. Sarah L. Silkey, "Redirecting the Tide of White Imperialism: The Impact of Ida B. Wells's Transatlantic Antilynching Campaign on British Conceptions of American Race Relations," in Boswell and McArthur, *Women Shaping the South*, 97–119.

46. *Daily Mirror*, Nov. 29, 1903, 1; ibid., Aug. 18, 1904, 3; ibid., Sept. 4, 1904, 3.

47. *New York Times*, March 8, 1913, 19.

48. Graham, *Children of the Slaves*, 160–62, 193, 196–214, 216–17, 226–27, 243–47, 257–60, 263–65, 291–92, 304.

49. Edwin Mims, "The Call of the South to Prevent Lynching," in McCulloch, "*Distinguished Service*," 135–36. On foreign comment, see also Steelman, "Study of Mob Action in the South," 3–7.

50. *Atlanta Constitution*, Feb. 5, 1922, D2. In February 1922, the secretary of the Southern Sociological Congress (SSC), J. E. McCulloch, told former governor of Arkansas (and SSC member) Charles H. Brough: "If the Republican Senators should force the bill through and the President sign it, they could not elect a Republican even to the office of 'dog-pelter' in the South for ten years to come." Cited in Grantham, *South in Modern America*, 89. See also "Would the Dyer Bill Halt Lynching?," 14. Brundage, *Lynching in the New South*, 220.

51. Cited in Fairclough, *Teaching Equality*, 28–29. On Moton's habitual diplomacy, see also Fairclough, "Tuskegee's Robert R. Moton," 94–105.

52. *Crisis* 22 (May 1921): 6–7. *Christian Science Monitor*, Jan. 11, 1922, 11.

53. *Atlanta Constitution*, June 4, 1922, D2. On the lynching of Charlie Atkins, see ibid., May 19, 1922, 20; ibid., May 20, 1922, 18. Williams, *They Left Great Marks on Me*, 213–14.

54. *Atlanta Constitution*, Dec. 10, 1922, C4. See also E. E. Miller, "What Southerners Think of the Dyer Bill," 598–99; "The Shame of a Nation," *Crisis* 25 (Jan. 1923): 132–33. On lynching in Georgia, see Brundage, *Lynching in the New South*, passim; Tolnay and Beck, *Festival of Violence*, 27, 168, 209–11, 219.

55. *Atlanta Constitution*, Jan. 3, 1923, 6. See also ibid., Sept. 16, 1922, 6, and Oct. 8, 1922, 6.

56. CIC Press Release, "It's Up to Us," CIC 1921–23 folder, box L13, series L, group II, NAACP Papers, LC.

57. *Atlanta Constitution*, Dec. 15, 1922, 4.

58. Levy, *James Weldon Johnson*, 263–64.

59. Rolinson, *Grassroots Garveyism*, 141–50. Marcus Garvey speech, Dec. 11, 1922, in Hill, ed., *Marcus Garvey and Universal Negro Improvement Association Papers*, 5:155–60.

60. *Atlanta Independent*, Jan. 26, 1922, 6. Rameau also presided at various times over the Southern Racial Welfare Social Uplift Association and the Southern Federation of Afro-American Industrial Brotherhood.

61. *Atlanta Constitution*, July 29, 1925, 2. "Col. Lawton on Mob Action," 589–90.

62. Douglas Smith, "Antilynching Law of 1928," in *Encyclopedia Virginia*, ed. Brendan Wolfe, http://www.EncyclopediaVirginia.org/Antilynching_Law_of_1928.

According to the *Cleveland Advocate*, a black weekly newspaper, lynching in southern Indiana ceased after the state passed a law in 1899 providing for the removal of any sheriff who allowed a mob to take a prisoner. *Cleveland Advocate*, Nov. 11, 1916, 1. Baker, *This Mob Will Surely Take My Life*, 166–68.

63. See White to Woofter, March 15, 1923, CIC 1921–23 folder, box L13, series L, group II, NAACP Papers, LC.

64. Woofter, "Southern Backfires against Lynch Law," 99–100. That a federal antilynching law was unenforceable is suggested by the conviction rate in peonage cases. Apart from the Williams "murder farm" case, some prosecutions in Georgia in 1921, a Florida case in 1925, and a Texas case in 1927, U.S. attorneys found indictments could be secured, but juries refused to convict white men on a federal peonage counts. Daniel, *Shadow of Slavery*, 133–34. In Georgia,

three white farmers were convicted. See *Atlanta Constitution,* Nov. 5, 1921, 1. In Florida, five white men were convicted of offenses in Calhoun County. See *New York Times,* May 24, 1925, 1; ibid., May 31, 1927, 20. In a Texas case, five whites, including a sheriff, were convicted in Willacy County. See ibid., Feb. 3, 1927, 33; ibid., Feb. 6, 1927, 18. For acquittals in federal courts on peonage charges in the 1920s, see *Atlanta Constitution,* Oct. 6, 1921, 4; ibid., Oct. 11, 1922, 6; ibid., Nov. 19, 1922, 1; ibid., Nov. 21, 1922, 2; ibid., Nov. 22, 1924, 24; ibid., June 9, 1927, 18; ibid., July 6, 1929, 1. Jerrell H. Shofner, "Postscript to the Martin Tabert Case," 161–73.

65. Woofter, "Southern Backfires against Lynch Law," 100.

66. *Survey* 51 (Jan. 15, 1924): 382. The CIC and its local work on education and lynching were noted in Britain. See, for example, "The Negro Problem in the United States," *Anti-Slavery Reporter and Aborigines' Friend* 13 (April 1923): 23–24.

67. "Federal Power to End Lynching?," 232–33.

68. Woofter, *Basis of Racial Adjustment,* 5. See James Weldon Johnson, "Lynching—America's National Disgrace," 596–601. In *The Negro Faces America,* 278, 300–301, 304–305, Seligmann was critical of the work of the Southern Sociological Congress and the University Commission on Southern Race Questions and the slow formation of local interracial committees in the South.

69. On White's investigations, see Janken, *White,* 29–43, 58–59.

70. Ross, "Where Lynching Is a Habit," 627. Sherman, *Republican Party and Black America,* 201–202, 213–16. "An Adventure in Good Will," 254. The last version of Dyer's bill was introduced in May 1929. See also, Sullivan, *Lift Every Voice,* 105–109, 194–97, 203–204. Rable, "The South and the Politics of Antilynching Legislation," 201–220. Dray, *At the Hands of Persons Unknown,* 259–82, 336, 341–62. Brown, *Eradicating This Evil,* 127–70, 172–209; 223–60. On the CIC's efforts regarding state laws and the idea of a separate body to examine lynching, see Southern Commission on the Study of Lynching, *Lynchings and What They Mean* (1931), and Milton, "Impeachment of Judge Lynch," 247–56. Milton chaired the commission.

71. James Bond to W. E. B. Du Bois, Feb. 16, 1925, W. E. B. Du Bois Papers, UMAL.

72. Woofter, *Southern Race Progress,* 28.

73. Ibid., 27–29.

74. National Interracial Conference, *Toward Interracial Cooperation,* 14. On the Georgia press and race questions in the 1920s, see Kneebone, *Southern Liberal Journalists and the Issue of Race.* Alexander interview, 1952, CUCOHC, 204–206.

75. Commission on Interracial Cooperation report, 1923, 14–16, box 96, LSRM, RAC.

76. Woofter, *Progress in Race Relations in Georgia;* Woofter, "Southern Backfires against Lynch Law," 99–100; *Atlanta Constitution,* Nov. 3, 1922, 1.

77. Steelman, "Study of Mob Action in the South," 279. Brundage, *Lynching in the New South,* 242. The last lynching in Georgia occurred in 1946. Ibid., 243.

78. *New York Times,* March 16, 1924, E1. Statistics gathered by Tuskegee Institute Archives, 1979, in Charles Chesnutt Digital Archive, Berea College, http://faculty.berea.edu/browners/chesnutt/classroom/lynching_table_year.html.

79. *Crisis* 33 (Feb. 1927): 180, 212–13. Shofner, "Judge Herbert Rider and the Lynching at Labelle," 292–306.

80. Brundage, *Lynching in the New South,* 95, 241. The white victim, Dave Wright, was accused of murdering a white woman who testified against him in a moonshine case in Coffee County. Wright was killed when a mob "overpowered" the sheriff; of the eleven white men arrested and tried for his murder, two were given a life sentences and seven got between four and seven years imprisonment. Steelman, "Study of Mob Action in the South," 275, 279. See also "Georgia's Body-Blow at Mob Murder," 10.

81. *Atlanta Constitution,* June 28, 1911, 1; ibid., June 29, 1911, 5; ibid., Aug. 9, 1911, 7. *Cleveland Advocate,* Feb. 8, 1919, 1; ibid., Sept 13, 1919, 1; ibid., Nov. 13, 1920, 1. *Washington Post,* Jan. 18, 1926, 17. Ellis, "Commission on Interracial Cooperation," 67–69. Rable notes that Vardaman was rhetorically in favor of vigilantism and opposed to federal legislation, but took action to prevent at least nine lynchings while he was governor of Mississippi. See Rable, "South and the Politics of Antilynching Legislation," 203. Also, Ben Tillman of South Carolina, an outspoken racist, proposed an antilynching law in 1890. Crowe, "Racial Violence and Social Reform," 242.

82. *New York Times,* Aug. 28, 1904, FS4.

83. Woofter, *Southern Race Progress,* 163.

84. "Growing Sentiment against Mob Action," 589; Eleazer, "Constructive Force in Race Relations," 302–307; George B. Logan, "Guides to Periodical Reading," *Journal of Social Forces,* 3 (Nov. 1924), 137; "Inter-Racial Commission in Annual Meeting Emphasizes Anti-Lynching Crusade," 712–13; "The South's Fight against Mob Murders," 30–31; "Lynching Decreasing," 30.

85. *Atlanta Constitution,* Dec. 8, 1921, 1; ibid., Jan. 26, 1922, 1, 11; ibid., Feb. 4, 1922, 2.

86. *Atlanta Constitution,* March 9, 1922, 4; ibid., June 4, 1922, 4; ibid., July 3, 1923, 16; ibid., Sept. 23, 1922, 1. *New York Times,* Dec. 6, 1921, 13; ibid., Sept. 23, 1922, 30. Woofter to Roger N. Baldwin, June 30, 1922, CIC 1921–23 folder, box L13, series L, group II, NAACP Papers, LC. Woofter to White, July 14, 1922, ibid. Affidavits of Odessa and Willie Peters, Aug.—, 1922, frames 1627–31, file 36, series 7, microfilm reel 45, CIC Papers, AUC.

87. Woofter to Alexander, Aug. 11, 1922, frames 1199–1206, file 60, series 7, CIC Papers, AUC.

88. Ibid.

89. T. J. Woofter, "Better Race Relations in Georgia," CIC 1921–23 folder, box L13, series L, group II, NAACP Papers, LC.

90. Minutes of the Georgia State Committee on Race Relations (GSCRR), Nov. 2, 1922, file 37, series 7, frames 1655–56, reel 45, CIC Papers, AUC. *Atlanta Constitution,* Nov. 3, 1922, 1. See also ibid., Oct. 29, 1922, C8; ibid., Nov. 18, 1922, 6.

91. Hale, *Making Whiteness,* 199–239. See also, Johnson, *Reforming Jim Crow,* 43–65.

6. The Limits of Interracial Cooperation

1. Du Bois, " Newer South," 163–65.

2. *Asheville Citizen,* July 22, 1922, clipping, file 39, series 4, frame 1638, microfilm reel 28, CIC Papers, AUC. *Christian Science Monitor,* Aug. 1, 1922, 3. Eleazer, "Broadcasting Good Will," 302–307. McDonough, "Men and Women of Good Will," 71–75, 84–85. On southern journalism, see Kneebone, *Southern Liberal Journalists and the Issue of Race,* 21–55.

3. Leonard Outhwaite, "Southern Trip," Nov.–Dec., 1925, cited in Stanfield, *Philanthropy and Jim Crow,* 73. Woofter, *Southern Race Progress,* 171.

4. Commission on Interracial Cooperation, report for 1923, 1–3, box 96, LSRM, RAC. John J. Eagan to Laura Spelman Rockefeller Memorial, Oct. 1, 1921, ibid. Will Alexander to James H. Dillard, Oct. 1, 1921, ibid. "Appropriations for Social Science and Social Technology up to December 1, 1927," box 63, ibid. The LSRM gave the National Urban League $71,500 in this period. See also "Financial Statement of Commission on Interracial Cooperation," 1925, in W. E. B. Du Bois Papers, UMAL.

5. GSCRR minutes, Jan. 25, 1923, file 38, series 7, frame 1659–64, microfilm reel 45, CIC Papers, AUC. *Atlanta Constitution,* Feb. 3, 1924, A8.

6. Will W. Alexander to James Weldon Johnson, Oct. 22, 1923, CIC 1921–23 folder, box L13, series L, group II, NAACP Papers, LC. See also J. H. Watson to NAACP, Oct. 15, 1923, ibid.;

Peter J. Fowles to Watson, n.d., ibid.; Alexander to Walter White, Dec. 3, 1923, ibid.; T. J. Woofter, Jr., Memo, in re: case of James Fowler, Tifton, Ga., n.d., ibid. The CIC did not resume significant legal casework until the 1930s. See Ellis, "Commission on Interracial Cooperation," 113–44.

7. See Henderson, "Heman E. Perry and Black Enterprise in Atlanta," 216–42.

8. GSCRR minutes, March 22, 1922, file 37, series 7, frames 1655–56, microfilm reel 45, CIC Papers, AUC; GSCRR minutes, Jan. 25, 1923, file 38, series 7, frames 1659–64, microfilm reel 45, ibid.; GSCRR minutes, Nov. 26, 1924, file 39, series 7, frame 1665–66, microfilm reel 45, ibid.; GSCRR minutes, Feb. 24, 1925, file 40, series 7, frame 1667–71, microfilm reel 45, ibid. *Atlanta Constitution*, Dec. 4, 1923, 19. Woofter, *Southern Race Progress*, 169–70.

9. *Atlanta Constitution*, May 18, 1923, 3. "Georgia Women Inaugurate Important Health Work," 494. Montgomery, *Politics of Education in the New South*, 234–35. Bauman and Kalin, eds., *Quiet Voices*, 3. Bauman and Kalin state that "Kaufman was forced to resign her position as head of the state welfare department later in the decade in response to Klan pressure." Ibid., 342. T. J. Woofter to Anson Phelps Stokes, Jan. 11, 1924, box 27, PSF, SC. Kaufman's request was met by the Rosenwald Fund. On Kaufman, see Patricia E. Smith, "Rhoda Kaufman," 43–50. On the Georgia Council of Social Agencies, see Blackburn, "Forward Move in Georgia," 261–64. On the CIC and health work, see also Ellis, "Commission on Interracial Cooperation," 147–56.

10. *Atlanta Constitution*, Feb. 8, 1922, 4.

11. Ibid., Feb. 3, 1924, A8.

12. *Chicago Daily News*, April 26, 1925, clipping, file 39, series 4, frame 1649, microfilm reel 28, CIC, AUC. Kenneth T. Jackson, *Ku Klux Klan in the City*, 35. Dykeman and Stokely, *Seeds of Southern Change*, 109, 165. Ellis, "Crusade against 'Wretched Attitudes,'" 23.

13. J. Douglas Smith, *Managing White Supremacy*, 55.

14. Du Bois, "Georgia: Invisible Empire State," 66.

15. *New York Times*, Jan. 23, 1906, 1–2. Choate held a reception in 1899 for Washington in London. Dixon may have had a mixed-race half-brother in New York; his sister, Delia Dixon-Carroll, a physician, supported interracial cooperation in North Carolina. She was against black women voting. See Gilmore, *Gender and Jim Crow*, 68, 191, 216–18.

16. *New York Times*, Jan. 29, 1906, 4.

17. Kelly Miller, "Social Equality," in *Race Adjustment*, 109–18. Degler, *Other South*, 353–57.

18. Work, "Race Problem in Cross Section," 251.

19. Cited in Foley, "Jean Toomer's Sparta," 747–75.

20. Davis, *Clashing of the Soul*, 272–74, 288.

21. Mays, *Born to Rebel*, 71–72, 96. Mays called W. D. Weatherford a "Jim Crow Liberal." Ibid., 126. On segregation on trains, see Hale, *Making Whiteness*, 125–38.

22. George C. Wright, *Life behind a Veil*, 206–209, 230–82. James Bond was succeeded as Kentucky secretary by his son, Max, later president of the University of Liberia. Another son, Horace Mann Bond, became president of Lincoln University.

23. Report to annual GSCRR meeting, Oct. 28, 1925, file 122, frames 46–52, microfilm reel 50, series 7, CIC Papers, AUC; Robert B. Eleazer, "From Slave Cabin to the Halls of Fame: The Remarkable Story of Roland Hayes, Interpreter of His Race," CIC press release, Feb. 28, 1926, file 249, series 1, frame 430, reel 12, ibid. Dykeman and Stokely, *Seeds of Southern Change*, 158–59. Northern mixed audiences for artists like Hayes and Ada Crogman sat together. See National Interracial Conference, *Toward Interracial Cooperation*, 76. On CIC activity in 1925, see *Social Forces* 3 (May 1925): 712–13. Woofter, "Negro on a Strike," 84–88. *Atlanta Constitution*, Dec. 18, 1925, 12; ibid., Dec. 19, 1925, 20; ibid., Dec. 27, 1925, 10.

24. Moton, *What the Negro Thinks*, 99.

25. Du Bois, Review of *What the Negro Thinks, 196*.

26. Link, *Paradox of Southern Progressivism*, 253.

27. Egerton, *Speak Now against the Day*, 48; McDonough, "Men and Women of Good Will," 85; Sosna, *In Search of the Silent South*, 25–26. Ellis, "Commission on Interracial Cooperation," 40.

28. *Chicago Daily News*, April 25, 1925, clipping, file 39, series 4, frame 1649, microfilm reel 28 CIC Papers. For Ashby Jones's and the CIC's outlook, see Jones, "Approach to the South's Race Questions," 40–41. He endorsed segregation for the sake of "purity."

29. Brundage, *Lynching in the New South*, 220.

30. McDonough, "Men and Women of Good Will," 85n73, 88. In 1929, Eleazer congratulated Atlanta mayor I. N. Ragsdale for his veto of a new segregation order. *Atlanta Constitution*, May 24, 1929, 3.

31. Egerton, *Speak Now against the Day*, 314–15. Harvey, *Freedom's Coming*, 79.

32. Sullivan, *Days of Hope*, 164. Sullivan (156) attributes the "dreamworld" analogy itself to Williamson, *Crucible of Race*, 475–82.

33. Robertson, *Christian Sisterhood, Race Relations, and the YWCA*, 97–127.

34. Trawick, "Good and Bad of Race Prejudice," 243–58. White, *Liberty and Justice for All*, 201–206. The president of Wofford College, Henry Nelson Snyder, was a member of the CIC's central committee.

35. Jones, "Approach to the South's Race Question," 40–41.

36. Cited in Joan Marie Johnson, "Shape of the Movement to Come," 204–205.

37. Harvey, *Freedom's Coming*, 53–77.

38. Oral history interview with Broadus Mitchell, Aug. 14 and 15, 1977. Interview B-0024, Southern Oral History Program Collection, http://docsouth.unc.edu/sohp/B-0024/excerpts /excerpt_3953.html. In 1931, Mitchell's foreword to an American Civil Liberties Union booklet on racial discrimination in the South was far more outspoken than anything produced by the CIC. See *Black Justice*, 5–7.

39. Hale, *Making Whiteness*, 255–56. Jacquelyn Dowd Hall makes a similar point regarding young women of both races. Hall, *Revolt against Chivalry*, 102–104. See also Kuhn et al., *Living Atlanta*, 166–67.

40. William Howard Taft et al., to Howard W. Odum, May 10, 1925, box 5, Howard W. Odum Papers, SHC.

41. Edwin A. Alderman to Taft, March 30, 1925, ibid.

42. Woofter, "Georgia's Choice—Ignorance or Progress," *Home, School and Community*, June 1925, 12–24, reprinted in Georgia Citizen's Education Movement, *Georgia's Educational Crisis*, n.p., n.d. Jones was reelected CIC chairman in 1927, although he retired as a minister and left Atlanta. His place as GSCRR chairman was taken by Bishop F. F. Reese of Savannah. *Atlanta Constitution*, Nov. 27, 1924, 15.

43. "Better Race Relations in Georgia," CIC 1921–23 folder, box L13, series L, group II, NAACP Papers, LC. Robert Preston Brooks, "A Local Study of the Race Problem," *Political Science Quarterly* 26 (June 1911): 193–221, abridged in Brooks, *Georgia Studies*, 27–49.

44. Fisher, "Multiplying Dollars for Negro Education," 149–53.

45. Newbold, "Common Schools for Negroes in the South," 209–223. Beale, *Are American Teachers Free?* 442–44. Ellis, "Commission on Interracial Cooperation," 210–21. Bond, *Negro Education in Alabama*, 255–61. See also Johnson, *Reforming Jim Crow*, 128–39.

46. Dykeman and Stokely, *Seeds of Southern Change*, 112–13.

47. National Interracial Conference, *Toward Interracial Cooperation*, 19. On Eleazer and the

CIC education program, see Selig, *Americans All*, 151–82. See also Ellis, "Commission on Interracial Cooperation," 257–67.

48. Woofter, "Teaching of Sociology in the South," 71–72. Woofter, *Negro Migration*, 183. Weatherford, *Negro Life in the South*, v–vi, 23–24, 78–79, 168; Weatherford, *Present Forces in the Uplift of the Negro*. See also, Weatherford, "Amazing Progress of the Negro Race," 510–20.

49. Weatherford, *Negro from Africa to America*. Guterl, *Color of Race in America*, 51–57, 127–46. Frazier panned Weatherford in his review of Woofter's *The Basis of Racial Adjustment* in *Social Forces* 4 (Dec. 1925): 442. Du Bois, Review of *The Negro from Africa to America*, *Nation* 119 (Sept. 10, 1924): 267, cited in Johnson, "Recent Literature on the Negro," 316. Woodson review in *Journal of Negro History* 9 (Oct. 1924): 575, cited ibid. Woodson review of *In the Vanguard of a Race*, *Journal of Negro History* 8 (Jan. 1923): 111–12.

50. Woofter, *Southern Race Progress*, 167.

51. Woofter, *Basis of Racial Adjustment*.

52. Ibid., 167–68. Tindall stated that *The Basis of Racial Adjustment* "supplanted" Weatherford's books. See Tindall, "Southern Negroes since Reconstruction," 341n16. See Hammond, *Southern Women and Racial Adjustment*; Green, "Introduction" to Hammond, *In Black and White*. Miller, *Race Adjustment*, passim. Miller, "Harvest of Race Prejudice," 711; Young, "Contribution of the Press in the Adjustment of Race Relations," 147–54; Baker, *Negro-White Adjustment*.

53. Work, "Race Problem in Cross Section," 250–52.

54. Alexander interview, 1952, CUCOHC, 220–21. Woofter's title mimics Edgar Gardner Murphy's *Basis of Ascendancy* (1909). Tindall, "Southern Negroes since Reconstruction," 341. Odum noted "the urgent need for study plans which will meet the needs of the undergraduate student, who in our region at least has been neglected." Odum to Beardsley Ruml, 29 Sept. 1926, box 62, LSRM, RAC.

55. *Chicago Daily News*, April 25, 1925, clipping, file 39, series IV, frame 1649, microfilm reel 28, CIC Papers, AUC.

56. Sosna, *In Search of the Silent South*, 176.

57. Ross, review of *The Basis of Racial Adjustment*, 638–39.

58. Woofter, *Basis of Racial Adjustment*, 167–68. See, for example, Dowd, *Negro in American Life*; Hankins, *Racial Basis of Civilization*; Herskovits, *The American Negro*; Reuter, *American Race Problem*; Lasker, *Race Attitudes in Children*; Melville Herskovits, "Preliminary Memorandum on the Problem of African Survivals," (1940) cited in Gershenhorn, *Melville Herskovits and the Racial Politics of Knowledge*, 105. Reuter, whose book was longer and less prescriptive than Woofter's, was taught by Robert E. Park, whom Gunnar Myrdal described as "bound . . . by fatalism"—a belief that certain "natural" forces determined race relations—a "fatalistic philosophy [that] has been transmitted to some of his students who have been working on the Negro problem." Myrdal, *American Dilemma*, 1049, 1051.

59. On social sciences and race (Woofter is overlooked), see John P. Jackson Jr., *Social Scientists for Social Justice*, 6–8, 17–42. Lewis, *W. E. B. Du Bois: 1919–1963*, 442–43. McDonough, "Men and Women of Good Will," 83. See also Alexander, "Southern White Schools Study Race Questions," 140. Whites in Ohio were found to be better disposed toward blacks after studying "the Negro." See Droba, "Education and Negro Attitudes," 137–41.

60. Woofter, *Basis of Racial Adjustment*, 167.

61. Ibid., 7–18.

62. Ibid., 25–36. Woofter cited Boas on changes in the cranial size of immigrant children.

63. Ibid., vi. See Gossett, *Race*, 176–78.

64. Kelly Miller, "Education for Manhood," 452.

65. Woofter, *Basis of Racial Adjustment*, 58–63. On Hoffman's influence, see Fredrickson, *Black Image in the White Mind*, 249–52; Wolff, "Myth of the Actuary," 84–91.

66. Woofter, *Basis of Racial Adjustment*, 87–95, 99–104, 105–18.

67. Myrdal, *American Dilemma*, 1337.

68. Woofter, *Basis of Racial Adjustment*, 125–38, 139–47. Woofter reused part of his October 1923 *Survey* article on lynching.

69. Woofter, *Basis of Racial Adjustment*, 156–61, 205, 227–28. Woofter, *Southern Race Progress*, 98–99.

70. Woofter, *Basis of Racial Adjustment*, 151, 154–55.

71. Ibid., 162–67. In the 1890s, sociologists Albion Small and George Vincent asked "whether widely different races can be amalgamated in a single civilization" and foresaw "the reduction of [blacks] to a state of servitude." *An Introduction to the Study of Sociology* (1894), 179, cited in Stanfield, "'Negro Problem,'" 190.

72. Woofter, *Basis of Racial Adjustment*, 155–56, 169–89.

73. Ibid., 235–37.

74. Ibid., 241. Park, "Concept of Social Distance," 339–44. See also Park, "Bases of Race Prejudice," 11–20, and Bogardus (Park's student), "Social Distance and Its Origins," 216–26. Abram L. Harris attacked the Giddings-Park-Bogardus "apologetic school of American race relations [that] considers the social distance between white and black Americans as conforming to a natural order" in "Economic Foundations of American Race Division," *Social Forces* 5 (March 1927): 468–78.

75. Woofter, *Basis of Racial Adjustment*, 26–27. Woofter, *Southern Race Progress*, 134, 141–42. Parts of *Southern Race Progress* appeared in Woofter, "Segregation—Voluntary and Involuntary," *Crisis* 64 (March 1957): 133–38, 190. By implying that social separation was a choice, Woofter ignored several state laws barring and nullifying interracial marriages in the wake of Virginia's 1924 Racial Integrity Act.

76. Woofter, "Teaching of Sociology in the South," 71–72.

77. Extracts from *Book Review Digest*, 1925, cf. "Woofter, Thomas Jackson." Ross, review of *Basis of Racial Adjustment*, 639. Review of T. J. Woofter, *Basis of Racial Adjustment*, *American Journal of Sociology* 31 (May 1926): 839.

78. *Atlanta Constitution*, June 7, 1925, B8. See also ibid., May 3, 1925, C6.

79. James Hardy Dillard, "Preface" (July 1927), in *Five Letters of the University Commission on Southern Race Questions*, 3–4.

80. *Survey* 55 (Nov. 15, 1925): 257.

81. *Baltimore Afro-American*, Jan. 30, 1926, 1. Ovington admired Will Alexander, calling him "a humane, fair-minded man, without cant and without prejudice." Ovington, "Revisiting the South," 43.

82. Du Bois, review of *Basis of Racial Adjustment*, *Crisis* 31 (Nov. 1925): 31–32.

83. Will Alexander to W. E. B. Du Bois, Nov. 7, 1925, W. E. B. Du Bois Papers, UMAL.

84. Du Bois, "Social Equality of Whites and Blacks," 16.

85. "Inter-Racial Activities in the South," 249–50; Du Bois, "Inter-Racial Comity," 6–7; Du Bois, "Mixed Schools." 150–51, 163. "Kerlin Case," 529–32. "Robert Thomas Kerlin," 230–32; Smith, *Managing White Supremacy*, 51–57.

86. Du Bois, "Georgia: Invisible Empire State," 64.

87. W. E. B. Du Bois to T. J. Woofter, Oct. 28, 1925, frame 746, microfilm reel 17, W. E. B. Du Bois Papers, UMAL.

88. Review of *Basis of Racial Adjustment*, *Journal of Negro History* 10 (July 1925): 572–73.

89. Review of *Basis of Racial Adjustment*, *Opportunity* 3 (Nov. 1925): 342–43.

90. Gilpin and Gasman, *Charles S. Johnson;* Robbins, *Sidelines Activist.* See also Holloway, *Confronting the Veil,* 136–46; Platt, *E. Franklin Frazier Reconsidered;* and Saint-Arnaud and Feldstein, *African-American Pioneers of Sociology,* 157–67, 204–21.

91. Frank H. Hankins to Odum, May 1, 1925, box 5, Odum Papers, SHC; Odum to Hankins, May 5, 1925, ibid.

92. Platt, *E. Franklin Frazier Reconsidered.* 69–75. Woofter, *Basis of Racial Adjustment,* 207. According to Horace Mann Bond, Frazier exemplified "the novel attitude adopted by the younger generation of Negro writers and publicists. It is a spirit that frees itself from a provincial and subjective view of race and its problems. Racial oppression, accordingly, comes to be a phenomenon to be studied and even laughed at, rather than a monstrous imposition calculated to stir one's soul to bitter anger." Bond, "Self-Respect as a Factor in Racial Advancement," 24.

93. E. Franklin Frazier to Frank Hankins, July 20, 1925, cited in Platt, *E. Franklin Frazier Reconsidered,* 233.

94. Frazier, review of *Basis of Racial Adjustment, Social Forces* 4 (Dec. 1925): 442–44. Frazier, "Negro and Non-Resistance," 213–14.

95. Platt, *E. Franklin Frazier Reconsidered,* 75–81, 82–85. Holloway, *Confronting the Veil,* 144. Stanfield, *Philanthropy and Jim Crow,* 86. Kuhn et al., *Living Atlanta,* 339. See also E. Franklin Frazier to W. E. B. Du Bois, March -?, 1927, W. E. B. Du Bois Papers, UMAL. Frazier, "My Relation with the Atlanta School of Social Work," n.d., ibid. Du Bois to Thomas Elsa Jones, March 30, 1927, ibid. Jones to Du Bois, April 11, 1927, ibid. Frazier to Du Bois, April 28, 1927, ibid.

96. Frazier, "Pathology of Race Prejudice," 856–62. See also discussion in *Forum* 78 (Sept. 1927): 458–60. Forrester B. Washington succeeded Frazier as director of the Atlanta School of Social Work.

97. R. B. Eleazer to W. E. B. Du Bois, Feb. 23, 1926, W. E. B. Du Bois Papers, UMAL. Du Bois to Eleazer, March 12, 1926, ibid.

98. E. Franklin Frazier to W. E. B. Du Bois, Nov. 7, 1936, ibid.

7. Northern Money and Race Studies

1. National Interracial Conference, *Toward Interracial Cooperation,* 183–89. *Washington Post,* March 27, 1925, 4. On Haynes, see White, *Liberty and Justice for All,* 250–60. Inspired by the FCC's Committee on the Welfare of Negro Troops, the CCRR was founded in 1921 with Alexander as its white secretary and Haynes as its black secretary and director. Haynes, who had degrees from Fisk, Yale, and Columbia, was the first director of the National Urban League (NUL) in 1910. During World War I, he assisted U.S. secretary of labor William B. Wilson and set up Negro Workers' Advisory Committees in states with migrant populations.

2. National Interracial Conference, *Toward Interracial Cooperation,* 183–89. Haynes held other "interracial" conferences on labor and migration. See *Christian Science Monitor,* May 8, 1923, 3. The Interracial Conference of New York was concerned with immigration. See *New York Times,* May 7, 1921, 12. David D. Jones worked for the St. Louis YMCA before joining the CIC in 1924. He was a CIC board member in the 1930s and from 1926 to 1955 was president of Bennett College for Women in Greensboro, N.C. On Jesse O. Thomas, see Thomas, *My Story in Black and White.* Forrester Washington worked in the Division of Negro Economics office in Chicago during World War I; he joined the Atlanta School of Social Work in 1926 and was director of Negro Work for the FERA in 1934–35, before resigning and returning to Atlanta. Earle Eubank gained his sociology PhD at the University of Chicago and worked for the YMCA's War Work Council during World War I. William H. Jernagin attended the Paris peace conference on behalf of the FCC (one of the few African Americans to secure a passport for this purpose)

and was an active national Baptist leader until his death in 1958. Ellis, *Race, War, and Surveillance*, 193–99.

3. National Interracial Conference, *Toward Interracial Cooperation*, 7. Alexander later stated: "Research [on race] as done by scientists is in danger of becoming an end in itself. It must be related to some dynamic force." See *Christian Mission in the Light of Race Conflict*, 231.

4. National Interracial Conference, *Toward Interracial Cooperation*, 74.

5. Ibid., 24–45. Kneebone, *Southern Liberal Journalists and the Issue of Race*, 95.

6. National Interracial Conference, *Toward Interracial Cooperation*, 44–61. W. E. B. Du Bois also named Durham as a southern city that allowed black progress. Du Bois, "Upbuilding of Black Durham," 334–38. See also E. Franklin Frazier, "Durham: Capital of the Black Middle Class," in Locke, ed. *New Negro*, 333–40, hailing an "outstanding group of colored capitalists" and calling the North Carolina Mutual Life Insurance Co. "the greatest monument to Negroes' business enterprise in America" (334–35).

7. National Interracial Conference, *Toward Interracial Cooperation*, 80–91. See Frazier, "Training Colored Social Workers," 445–46; and Frazier, "Social Work in Race Relations," 252–54; Frazier, "Social Equality and the Negro," 165–68; Platt and Chandler, "Constant Struggle," 293–97.

8. National Interracial Conference, *Toward Interracial Cooperation*, 92–103.

9. Ibid., 104–34.

10. Ibid., 135. See Phillips, *From the Farm to the Bishopric*.

11. National Interracial Conference, *Toward Interracial Cooperation*, 137–49.

12. Ibid., 164–68.

13. Ibid., 178–79. By 1929, the FCC was becoming more radical on race. Its president, Bishop Francis J. McConnell of the Methodist Episcopal Church, an Ohioan with missionary experience in India, rejected "assumptions of superiority of the white man, which have no basis whatever in fact." *New York Times*, Oct. 31, 1929, radio sect., 36.

14. National Interracial Conference, *Toward Interracial Cooperation*, 167. *Washington Post*, Jan. 18, 1926, 17. Woofter, *Negro Problems in Cities*. Zane L. Miller, review of *Negro Problems in Cities*, 1157–59. Caccamo, *Back To Middletown*, 38. Dykeman, *Prophet of Plenty*, 138, 143. Dykeman and Stokely, *Seeds of Southern Change*, 45–46.

15. Will Alexander to Leonard Outhwaite, Jan. 30, 1926, box 96, LSRM, RAC.

16. Sealander, *Private Wealth and Public Life*, 2–5, 12. Perkins, *Edwin Rogers Embree*, 48–61. By 1928, John D. Rockefeller Sr. and his son had donated over $600 million.

17. Turner, "Does Funding Produce Its Effects?," 213–26. See also Judith Sealander, "Curing Evils at Their Source: The Arrival of Scientific Giving," in Friedman and McGarvie, *Charity, Philanthropy, and Civility in American History*, 217–40, and Stanfield, *Philanthropy and Jim Crow*, 185–87. The SSRC consisted of twenty-one academics: three from each of the national associations representing economics, political science, sociology, statistics, psychology, anthropology, and history.

18. Interview with Clark Foreman, Nov. 16, 1974, interview B-0003, SHC, UNC, http://docsouth.unc.edu/sohp/B-0003/B-0003.html. Sullivan, *Days of Hope*, 25–35.

19. Sullivan, *Days of Hope*, 35–40, 152–58. Alexander interview, 1952, CUCOHC, 221–23. W. E. B. Du Bois, noting his CIC connections, criticized Foreman's recruitment by Ickes: "Mr Foreman does not understand the difficulties of American Negroes, and it is an outrage that we again, through the efforts of some of our best friends, should be compelled to have our wants and aspirations interpreted by one who does not know them and our ideals and ambitions expressed by a person who cannot understand them." Du Bois, "N.R.A. and Appointments," 237.

20. Will W. Alexander to R. R. Moton, March 12, 1930, box 9, R. R. Moton Papers (in Moton Family Papers), LC.

21. Stanfield, *Philanthropy and Jim Crow,* 70–71. "Report of the Representatives on the Social Science Research Council," *American Economic Review* 16 (March 1926): annual meeting supplement, 345; "Report of the Representatives on the Social Science Research Council," *American Economic Review* 17 (March 1927): annual meeting supplement, 206. Will Alexander to Thomas Jesse Jones, Feb. 24, 1927, box 27, PSF, SC. Commission on Interracial Cooperation, "Brief Statement of Work for 1927 and Brief Suggestions for 1928," box 27, PSF, SC.

22. "Members Added since December 1926," *Journal of the American Statistical Association,* 22 (March 1927), 86–88.

23. CIC, "Summary of Work for 1925–26," 2, LSRM, RAC. Woofter and Priest, *Negro Housing in Philadelphia.* Northern cities studied were Buffalo; Chicago; Dayton, Ohio; Gary, Ind.; Indianapolis; New York; and Philadelphia. Southern cities were Charleston, S. C.; Knoxville, Tenn.; Lexington, Ky.; Louisville, Ky.; Lynchburg, Va.; Memphis; New Orleans; Richmond; and Winston-Salem, N. C.. Data was also used from Cincinnati; Baltimore; Dallas; Charlottesville, Va.; Gainesville, Fla.; and Conway, Ark..

24. Woofter, *Negro Problems in Cities,* 17–20.

25. Ibid., 18–19.

26. Ibid., 39. Meyer, *As Long as They Don't Move Next Door,* 6.

27. Woofter, *Negro Problems in Cities,* 26–77. In *Buchanan v. Warley* [245 US 60], the Supreme Court found a Louisville, Ky., segregation law breached the Fourteenth Amendment.

28. Woofter, *Negro Problems in Cities,* 68, 78–95. Residential density in black neighborhoods of New York City was 336 persons per acre across 441 acres; white New Yorkers occupied 8,644 acres at a rate of 223 per acre. In Philadelphia, the density rates were 111 per acre for blacks and 28 for whites; in Chicago, they were 67 per acre for blacks and 31 for whites. The most evenly matched northern city was Indianapolis, with 21 people per acre in black areas and 15 people per acre in white areas. In the South, the biggest difference was in Charleston, where black and white populations of almost equal size showed residential densities of 57 and 19 per acre, respectively; the least difference was in Winston-Salem, with figures of 20 black and 19 white residents per acre. Ibid., 79.

29. Ibid., 19–21, 37–39, 96–111.

30. Ibid., 115–51. The weekly rent on apartments in the model Phipps tenements in Columbus Hill in New York rose 33% between 1919 and 1923.

31. Ibid., 152–70.

32. Ibid., 173–90. The segregation issue in Philadelphia and Indianapolis had been brewing for several years. See Du Bois, "Education," 136, and Du Bois, "Mixed Schools," 150–51. Indianapolis had fifteen separate elementary schools for blacks, twenty-one mixed schools with a few black children, and forty-six all-white schools. Herskovits, "Race Relations," 1129–39; Thornbrough, "Segregation in Indiana," 594–618; Logan, "Educational Segregation in the North," 65–67.

33. Woofter, *Negro Problems in Cities,* 180–81, 190.

34. Ibid., 201–24. There were forty kindergartens for white children in Atlanta, forty-six in New Orleans, forty-two in Louisville, and twenty-one in Richmond. Of those cities, only Louisville had any kindergartens for black children, with seven.

35. Ibid., 227–57. Attwell, "Recreation for Colored America," 162–65. Pilz, "The Beginnings of Organized Play for Black America," 59–72.

36. Woofter, *Negro Problems in Cities,* 258–81.

37. Kincheloe, review of *Negro Problems in Cities,* 150–51.

38. Muntz, review of *Negro Problems in Cities,* 115–17. See also, Muntz, *Race Contact.*

39. Herskovits, review of *Negro Problems in Cities,* 352–54.

40. Frazier, review of Woofter, *Negro Problems in Cities*, 737–38. See also Frazier, "Three Scourges of the Negro Family," 210–11, 234; Frazier, "Is the Negro Family a Unique Sociological Unit?," 165–68; Frazier, "The Negro Family," 21–25.

41. Woodson, Review of *Negro Problems in Cities*, 395–96. Ira De A. Reid, Review of *Negro Problems in Cities*, 277. R. W. Bagnall, Review of *Negro Problems in Cities*, in *Nation* 126 (April 25, 1928): 491.

42. *Negro Housing*, 6–7, 78–80, 117–18. Johnson also used *Negro Problems in Cities* in his summary of the 1928 National Interracial Conference. See Johnson et al., *Negro in American Civilization*, 202, 208, 213, 218, 333. The first scholarly work using Woofter's findings was Burgess, "Residential Segregation in American Cities," 105–15.

43. Taeuber and Taeuber, *Negroes in Cities*, 196, 198.

44. "Negro Education, Coahoma County," memorandum and questionnaires by T. J. Woofter Jr., ca. 1925, box 102, LSRM, RAC. Built in 1924, Coahoma County Agricultural High School was the first rural high school for blacks in Mississippi. On "Pete" Williams and Coahoma County, see S. L. Smith, *Builders of Goodwill*, 126–32. See also Williams, "South's Changing Attitude toward Negro Education," 398–400; Moton, *What the Negro Thinks*, 246–47.

45. Leo Favrot to Beardsley Ruml, May 5, 1925, box 102, LSRM, RAC. Favrot, T. J. Woofter Jr., and C. H. Lane, "Proposed Social Survey of Bi-Racial Southern Counties," May 5, 1925, ibid.; Favrot to Leonard Outhwaite, May 9, 1925, ibid.; W. T. B. Williams to Ruml, May 24, 1925, ibid.; Joseph Peterson to Ruml, May 25, 1925, ibid.; Josiah Morse to Ruml, May 25, 1925, ibid.; Frank A. Ross to Woofter, June 16, 1925, ibid.; Outhwaite to W. S. Richardson, June 17, 1925, ibid. Harris, *Deep Souths*, 122. Perkins, *Edwin Rogers Embree*, 57.

46. Woofter, Favrot, and Lane to LSRM, June 26, 1925, box 102, LSRM, RAC. Woofter to Outhwaite, June 26, 1925, ibid.; Outhwaite to Woofter, July 25, 1925, ibid.; Woofter to Outhwaite, Aug. 7, 1925, ibid.; Burra Hilbun to LSRM, Aug. 13, 1925, ibid.; Outhwaite to Woofter, Aug. 18, 1925, ibid.; Outhwaite to Woofter, Dec. 16, 1925, ibid.; Woofter to Outhwaite, dec. 18, 1925, ibid.; Outhwaite to Woofter, Dec. 22, 1925, ibid.; Woofter to Outhwaite, Dec. 26, 1925, ibid.; Memorandum of interviews between Outhwaite and Favrot, Feb. 26, 1926, and May 4, 1926, ibid.; W. F. Bond, to LSRM, May 11, 1926, ibid.; Outhwaite to Bond, May 18, 1926, ibid.

47. Harris, *Deep Souths*, 289.

48. See, for example, Blackwell, "Rural Relief in the South," 390–97.

49. Dykeman and Stokely, *Seeds of Southern Change*, 167–69. *Atlanta Constitution*, Feb. 24, 1928, 7. See also Davis, *A Clashing of the Soul*, 290–93.

50. John R. Mott to W. W. Alexander, Jan. 7, 1927, file 123, frame 162, microfilm reel 7, series I, CIC Papers, AUC. Alexander to Mott, Jan. 20, 1927, frame 160, ibid. *Atlanta Journal*, Feb. 24, 1928, clipping, ibid. Woofter, "Agencies for Inter-Racial Co-Operation in the United States," in *Christian Mission in the Light of Race Conflict*, 4:23–92. Over thirty Americans were present in Jerusalem, mostly from northern cities.

51. Woofter, "Agencies for Inter-Racial Co-Operation in the United States," 23–24.

52. Ibid., 27–29.

53. Ibid., 30, 33–41.

54. Ibid., 41–80. Kuhn et al., *Living Atlanta*, 37.

55. Woofter, "Agencies for Inter-Racial Co-Operation," 80–82.

56. Ibid., 82–92.

57. Woofter, *Southern Race Progress*, 172.

58. Ibid., 165.

59. Commission on Interracial Cooperation, "Brief Statement of Work for 1927 and Brief Suggestions for 1928," folder 4, box 27, PSF, SC. On state committees, see Ann Wells Ellis, "Com-

mission on Interracial Cooperation," 37–42. On the CIC essay competitions, textbooks, and other classroom experiments, see Selig, *Americans All*, 157–75. Woyshner, "No Unfavorable Comments from Any Quarter."

60. CIC, "Brief Statement of Work for 1927 and Brief Suggestions for 1928." McDonough, "Men and Women of Good Will," 89–91. See Eleazer, *Adventure in Faith* (1929), and *America's Tenth Man*. Moton noted, "As a class, white ministers appear to have fewer contacts with Negroes than any group of their race." Moton, *What the Negro Thinks*, 253.

8. Howard Odum and the Institute for Research in Social Science

1. On Odum's changing views on race, see Sanders, *Howard Odum's Folklore Odyssey*; Thomas, "Howard W. Odum's Social Theories in Transition," 25–34. His psychology PhD at Clark University used black folk songs from Mississippi; his second PhD, in sociology, completed at Columbia University in 1910 under Franklin Giddings's supervision, referred to "the onrush of [the African American's] animal nature which leads him to neglect and abuse himself, his home and his family" and "the frequent instances in which the weakness of the black race is accorded patience by the stronger race." Read widely, it was published as *Social and Mental Traits of the Negro* (New York: Columbia University Press, 1910). In 1920, Woofter called it, "A scholarly treatment of several phases of the Negro problem, especially psychology and folk-lore." Woofter, *Negro Migration*, 183.

2. Odum, *Southern Pioneers in Social Interpretation*; Odum and Willard, *State Systems of Public Welfare*; Odum and Johnson, *Negro and His Songs*; Odum and Johnson, *Negro Workaday Songs*; Odum, *Man's Quest for Social Guidance*.

3. Simpson, *Fifty Years of the Southern Sociological Society*, 1–17. Odum established a graduate program in sociology in 1920; others followed at Vanderbilt University (1924), University of Virginia (1925), North Carolina State University (1926), Duke University (1928), and Louisiana State University (1932). The Southern Sociological Society was formed in 1935. Ibid., 3.

4. Laura Spelman Rockefeller Memorial, *Report for 1924* (New York: Laura Spelman Rockefeller Memorial, 1925), 11, and *Report for 1925* (New York: Laura Spelman Rockefeller Memorial, 1926), 8. "Memorial Policy in Social Sciences," Oct. 1922, 3, 5–7, 10, box 63, LSRM, RAC. Beardsley Ruml to Abraham Flexner, Jan. 9, 1925, ibid. Memorandum of interview between Sydnor Walker, Leonard Outhwaite, and Harry Woodburn Chase, March 8, 1927, box 74, ibid. The LSRM funded the creation of other institutes at Columbia University (1925), the University of Virginia (1926), Stanford University (1927), and the University of Texas (1927). On the LSRM and Ruml, see. Stanfield, *Philanthropy and Jim Crow*, 61–96.

5. Howard W. Odum to Ruml, Sept. 29, 1926, box 62, LSRM, RAC; Odum to Ruml, Jan. 7, 1927, ibid.; Memorandum of interview between Sydnor Walker, Leonard Outhwaite, Howard Odum and Jesse Steiner, March 8, 1927, box 74, ibid. For other examples of Odum's efforts to please the LSRM, see memorandums and correspondence between Odum, Ruml, and Outhwaite in box 74, ibid., and box 1, Odum Papers, SHC. Howard W. Odum to Thomas Jesse Jones, Feb. 21, 1927, box 9, ibid.; George Foster Peabody to Odum, March 6, 1927, ibid. See also. Johnson and Johnson, *Research in Service to Society*, 26, 29–55. On Odum's impact at UNC, see Grantham, "Regional Imagination," 8–9, 14–17.

6. Odum to Ruml, June 15, 1927, box 10, Odum papers, SHC. Toward the end of 1927, Odum's brother was seriously ill, and his father was nearly killed by a cow. On Odum's anxiety, see his correspondence with Jesse F. Steiner and his publishers. For example, Odum to Steiner, June 24 (twice), 1927, ibid.; Odum to D. L. Chambers, Oct. 31, 1927, box 11, ibid.; C. A. Madison to

Odum, Nov. 25, 1927, box 11, ibid. Gatewood, "Embattled Scholar," 375–92. Singal, *War Within*, 115–52.

7. Odum to Lawrence K. Frank, Jan. 29, 1927, box 74, LSRM, RAC. Odum to Steiner, April 4, 1927, box 10, Odum Papers, SHC; Odum to Will W. Alexander, June 15, 1927, ibid.

8. Leonard Outhwaite to Odum, Feb. 18, 1925, box 1, ibid.; Odum to Outhwaite, Feb. 24, 1925, ibid.; "Memorandum Concerning Studies of the American Negro," April 1, 1925, ibid.; Odum to Outhwaite, April 21, 1925, ibid.; Odum to Beardsley Ruml, April 29, 1925, ibid.; Odum to Outhwaite, May 12, 1925, ibid.

9. Odum to Thomas Jackson Woofter, Jr., Dec. 1, 1920, Woofter folder, box 17, Odum Papers, SHC. Will Alexander to Thomas Jesse Jones, Feb 24, 1927, box 27, PSF, SC. Clark Foreman to Alexander, Oct 1, 1927, ibid. Alexander to Isaac Fisher, Oct. 12, 1927, box 1, Isaac Fisher Papers, TUA. The Rosenwald Fund gave the CIC new money in 1928. Ellis, "Commission on Interracial Cooperation," 42. Dykeman and Stokely, *Seeds of Southern Change*, 162–63. Odum and Alexander knew each other from their war work for the Red Cross's southern division and the YMCA's War Work Council.

10. Odum to Will W. Alexander, Jan. 11, 12, 1927, box 9, Odum Papers, SHC; Alexander to Odum, Jan. 14, 1927, ibid.; Odum to Woofter (twice), Jan. 11, 1927, Woofter folder, box 29, ibid.; T. J. Woofter, Sr., to Odum, Jan. 14, 1927, ibid.; Odum to T. J. Woofter, Sr., Jan. 17, 1927, ibid. Alexander interview, 1952, CUCOHC, p. 223. On Outhwaite, see Stanfield, *Philanthropy and Jim Crow*, 71–77.

11. Odum to T. J. Woofter Sr., Jan. 17, 1927, Woofter folder, box 29, Odum Papers, SHC; Odum to Woofter, Jan. 17, 1927, ibid. Odum, memorandum for board, n.d., box 9, ibid.; Odum to Beardsley Ruml, March 22, 1927, ibid.; Odum to Sydnor Walker, March 24, 1927, ibid. Odum edited Walker's Columbia PhD dissertation, which was published by the UNC press. On Walker, see Amy E. Wells, "Considering Her Influence: Sydnor H. Walker and Rockefeller Support for Social Work, Social Scientists, and Universities in the South," in Walton, *Women and Philanthropy in Education*, 127–47.

12. Ruml to Chase, March 30, 1927, box 74, LSRM, RAC. Odum to Thomas Jesse Jones, Feb. 21, 1927, box 9, Odum Papers, SHC; George Foster Peabody to Odum, March 16, 1927, ibid.; Odum to Ruml, March 25, 1927, ibid.; Odum to Moore C. Tussey, March 25, 1927, ibid.; "Appropriations for Social Science and Social Technology up to December 1, 1927," box 63, ibid.; Odum to Woofter, March 22, 1927, Woofter folder, box 29, ibid. LSRM, *Report for 1927 and 1928* (New York: Laura Spelman Rockefeller Memorial, 1929), 9.

13. Odum to Henry Wisansky, Nov. 14, 1927, box 27, PSF, SC. On later racial and ethnic studies of the IRSS, see Johnson and Johnson, *Research in Service to Society*, 138–51. Frissell, "Farmer and Cooperation," 171. Frissell ran a farm at Burkeville, Va., after graduating from Yale University in 1908. He resigned from the IRSS in July 1928 to join the U.S. Department of Agriculture and later directed the Tri-State Tobacco Growers Association (Virginia, North and South Carolina). During the New Deal, he directed the U.S. Soil Survey and edited U.S. Soil Conservation Service publications. Obituary of Sydney D. Frissell, *Newport News Daily Press*, Jan. 19, 1966, 3, 10.

14. Odum to Richard H. Thornton, March 25, 1927, box 9, Odum Papers, SHC; Odum to Moore C. Tussey, March 25, 1927, ibid.; Odum to Harry Woodburn Chase, May 16, 1927, box 10, ibid.

15. *Atlanta Constitution*, June 26, 1924, 12; ibid., Sept. 28, 1924, D5.

16. Ibid. U.S. Federal Census, 1900, for Lee County, Ala., roll T623_25, 17A; U.S. Federal Census, 1910, for Birmingham, Ala. (Ward 16), roll T624_20, 19A. Student transcript, Ethel Ophelia Mays, Special Collections, Regenstein Library, University of Chicago. The city of Birmingham

annexed Ensley in 1910. Ethel Mays is not listed among graduates for this period in the *Corolla* (University of Alabama yearbook).

17. *Atlanta Constitution,* Sept. 15, 1920, 7; ibid., June 12, 1921, C5; ibid., Jan. 7, 1922, 9; ibid., March 29, 1922, 9; ibid., June 13, 1924, E5.

18. Ibid., June 26, 1924, 12. The Woofters lived in the Phelan Apartments, 790 Peachtree Street, built in 1915 as a modern development for middle-class professionals. Ethel Woofter sometimes hid the age gap between them. See passenger list of SS *Lafayette,* Aug. 20–28, 1937, New York Passenger Lists, Department of Labor, roll T715_6033, p38, where her date of birth is shown as June 8, 1893. The U.S. federal census gave it as June 1887 (see 1900 Census for Opelika, Ala., roll T623_25, p17A), and her Social Security Death Index record showed June 8, 1888.

19. Odum to Moore C. Tussey, March 25, 1927, box 9, Odum Papers, SHC; Woofter to Odum, April 11, 1927, Woofter folder, box 29, ibid.; Harry Woodburn Chase to Woofter, April 14, 1927, ibid.; Woofter to Chase, April 16, 1927, ibid.; Odum to Chase, May 16, 1927, box 10, ibid. US Federal Census, 1930, for Orange County, N.C., roll 1711, p17B.

20. Alexander to Odum, June 13, 1927, box 10, Odum Papers, SHC.

21. Odum to Alexander, June 15, 1927, ibid. Odum to Jesse Steiner, June 15, 1927, ibid.

22. Woofter, *Negro Migration,* 178.

23. *Danville Register,* June 16, 1927. The license was issued to the CIC office in Atlanta.

24. "Sociologist Gets in Bad at Danville," *Raleigh News and Observer,* June 17, 1927; "Erring Sociologist Is Freed from Prison," ibid., June 18, 1927. "Former Atlanta Author Arrested," *Atlanta Constitution,* June 17, 1927; "Woofter's Sentence Suspended by Court," ibid., June 18, 1927. The *Atlanta Constitution* at first reported that Woofter's jail sentence was 60 days. T. J. Woofter Sr. to Odum, June 17, 1927, Woofter folder, box 29, Odum Papers, SHC; Odum to T. J. Woofter Sr., n.d., ibid.; Woofter to Odum, June 18, 1927, ibid. Odum to Alexander, June 18, 1927, box 10, ibid.; Odum to Thomas Jesse Jones, June 20, 1927, ibid. Thomas Jesse Jones to Odum, June 28, 1927, box 10, ibid. *Athens Banner-Herald,* June 17, 1927, 3. T. J. Woofter Sr. to R. P. Brooks, June 18, 1927, Woofter folder, box 10, Robert Preston Brooks Papers, MS 1300, Hargrett Rare Book and Manuscript Library, University of Georgia Library, Athens (HRBML). T. J. Woofter Sr. described his son as "much mortified by his mishap" and remarked to Brooks on the gossip, "Such is Dame Rumor, but re-spell Dame." Alcohol law enforcement was difficult in Danville, one of the few Virginian cities to cast a "Wet" vote in the statewide prohibition referendum. *New York Times,* Sept. 23, 1914, 7.

25. Ashby, *Frank Porter Graham,* 65–66. Gatewood, "Embattled Scholar," 375–92.

26. Odum to Steiner, June 20, 1927, box 10, Odum papers, SHC

27. Odum to Alexander June 22, 1927, ibid.; Thomas Jesse Jones to John R. Mott, June 28, 1927, ibid.

28. Odum to Ruml, June 18, 1927, box 10, ibid.; Odum to Ruml, June 22, 1927, ibid. In her response to Odum's last letter, Sydnor Walker did not mention Woofter. Walker to Odum, June 28, 1927, box 74, LSRM, RAC; and Odum to Walker, June 29, 1927, ibid.

29. Odum to Woofter, June 18, 1927, Woofter folder, box 29, Odum papers, SHC.

30. Odum to Moore C. Tussey, June 22, 192, box 10, ibid. (Describing his meeting with T. J. Woofter Sr. to his publisher, Odum mentions only a discussion about textbooks, but they must have discussed Jack's predicament.) Odum to Alexander, June 22, 24, 1927, ibid.; Odum to Thomas Jesse Jones, June 24, 1927, ibid.; Thomas Elsa Jones to Woofter, June 30, 1927, ibid. T. J. Woofter Sr. to R. P. Brooks, June 18, 1927, Woofter folder, box 10, Robert Preston Brooks Papers, HRBML. Brooks had written Jack Woofter a sympathetic letter immediately after his arrest.

31. Stanfield, *Philanthropy and Jim Crow,* 87.

32. Thomas Jesse Jones to Odum, June 28, 1927, box 10, Odum Papers, SCH.

33. Alexander to Thomas Jesse Jones, June 30, 1927, box 11, ibid.

34. Johnson and Johnson, *Research in Service to Society,* 49–53.

35. Singal, *War Within,* 322; Sanders, *Howard Odum's Folklore Odyssey,* 127.

36. Guion Griffis Johnson interview, April 24, 1974 (G-0029-1), Southern Oral History Program Collection, http://docsouth.unc.edu/sohp/G-0029-1/G-0029-1.html. During G-0029-1, Johnson said, "I just blurt out everything."

37. Guion Griffis Johnson interview, May 28, 1974 (G-0029-3), Southern Oral History Program Collection, http://docsouth.unc.edu/sohp/G-0029-3/G-0029-3.xml.

38. Kiser et al. interview, April 26, 1973, and Dec. 15, 1976, 72, 103–104, PAA Oral History Project, vol. 1, "Presidents," no. 1, "From 1947 through 1960" (2005), http://geography.sdsu.edu /Research/Projects/PAA/paa.html. Woofter was PAA president in 1940–41.

39. Harriet Herring interview, Feb. 5, 1976 (G-0027), 65–72, Southern Oral History Program Collection, http://docsouth.unc.edu/sohp/G-0027/G-0027.html.

40. Odum to Thomas Jesse Jones, June 24, 1927, box 10, Odum Papers, SHC; see also Thomas Jesse Jones to Odum, June 28, 1927, ibid.; Thomas Jesse Jones to John R. Mott, June 28, 1927, ibid.; Thomas Jesse Jones to Odum, June 28, 1927, ibid.; T. E. Jones to Odum, June 28, 1927, ibid.; Alexander to Odum, June 30, 1927, box 11, ibid.; Odum to Thomas Elsa Jones, July 9, 1927, ibid.; Odum to Thomas Jesse Jones, July 9, 1927, ibid.

41. Jones, *Negro Education,* 2:483–85.

42. See Johnston, *Negro in the New World,* 386–420. Other St. Helena Island studies included Parsons, *Folk-Lore of the Sea Islands* and Ballanta, *St. Helena Island Spirituals.* Ballanta, from Sierra Leone, was commissioned to record traces of African dialect and song by the Penn School trustees. See also Cooley, *Homes of the Freed;* Robbins, "Rossa B. Cooley and Penn School," 43–51; Washington, "Education of Freedmen," 442–55; Hutchison, "Better Homes and Gullah," 102–18; and the SHC finding aid for the Penn School Papers, http://www.lib.unc.edu/mss/inv /htm/03615.html.

The Carnegie Foundation gave *Homes of the Freed* and Woofter's *The Basis of Racial Adjustment* to white colonial educators touring America in the 1920s. The Phelps-Stokes Fund bought 100 copies of Woofter's *Black Yeomanry,* on St. Helena, for "white educators" in the United States and abroad. See Anson Phelps Stokes, *Negro Status and Race Relations in the United States,* 172.

43. Outhwaite to Beardsley Ruml, March 29, 1927, box 101, LSRM, RAC. Woofter to Rossa B. Cooley, April 26, 1927, box 5, Penn School Papers, SHC; Woofter to Cooley, May 4, 1927, ibid. Odum to Woofter, May 6, May 7, May 23, 1927, Woofter folder, box 29, Odum Papers, SHC; Woofter to Odum, May 4, May 13, 1927, ibid.

44. Woofter to Cooley, May 4, 1927, box 5, Penn School Papers, SHC; Peabody to Woofter, May 16, 1927, ibid.; Francis R. Cope to Cooley, May 30, 1927, ibid.; L. Hollingsworth Wood to Cooley, May 31, 1927, ibid.; James E. Gregg to Cooley, May 31, 1927, ibid. Woofter to Odum, May 20, 1927, Woofter folder, box 29, Odum Papers, SHC.

45. Woofter to Cooley, Aug. 22, Sept. 30, 1927, box, Penn School Papers, SHC; Woofter to Peabody, Aug. 29, 1927, ibid. Odum to Alexander, Aug. 2, 5, 10, 1927, box 11, Odum Papers, SHC; Odum to Alexander, Sept. 13, 1927, ibid.; Odum to Alexander, Oct. 8, 1927, ibid.; Odum to D. L. Chambers, Oct. 17, 1927, ibid.; Odum to Chambers, Oct. 31, 1927, ibid. According to Stephen P. Turner, the Dartmouth meetings of the Social Science Research Council (SSRC) "provided a private forum within which issues could be debated and positions taken without these issues being used by the critics of quantitative social science to delegitimate the activity." Turner, "Does Funding Produce Its Effects?," 224. On the Dartmouth conferences, see also "Report of the Representatives on the Social Science Research Council," *American Economic Review* 17 (March 1927): 210.

46. Odum to D. L. Chambers, Oct. 31, box 11, Odum Papers, SHC; Odum to Ruml, Oct 21, 1927, ibid.; Odum to Walker, Oct. 25, 1927, ibid. Odum sought Woofter's opinion on *Rainbow*

Round My Shoulder as "a specialist in the Negro field." Odum to Chambers, Jan. 6, 1928, box 12, ibid. He also asked Woofter to read Thomas Jesse Jones's book, *Essentials of Civilization* (1929) for Henry Holt and Company, Odum's nonfiction publisher. See Odum to Richard H. Thornton, Jan. 2, Jan. 5, 1928, ibid.

47. Johnson and Johnson, *Research in Service to Society*, 38–43. On Odum, Chase, and protests about *Social Forces*, see Brazil, *Howard W. Odum*, 385–467.

48. Raushenbush, *Robert E. Park*, 88, 180.

49. Odum to H. W. Chase, July 22, 1927, box 11, Odum Papers, SHC.

50. Odum to Guion G. Johnson, May 25, 1927, box 2, Guion Johnson Papers, SHC. Woofter to Cooley, Sept. 30, 1927, box 5, Penn School Papers, SHC. Alexander to Odum, Nov. 7, 1927, box 11, Odum Papers, SHC. Odum to Ruml, Dec. 15, 1927, box 12, ibid. Guion Johnson interview, April 24, 1974, SHC.

51. "Saint Helena Island: A Study of Negro Culture and Social Development," 1927, box 5, Penn School Papers, SHC; "Negro Population of St. Helena, 1928," box 6, ibid.; M. McCulloch to Thomas Jesse Jones, Nov. 8, 1927, ibid.; McCulloch to Rosa Long, Nov. 8, 1927, ibid. Further raw data from the project is also filed. The SSRC awarded the project $1,000 more than the original bid, which was for $15,250. Odum to Thomas Jesse Jones, Dec. 19, 1927, box 12, Odum Papers, SHC.

52. "The Study of St. Helena Island: Preliminary confidential report for the Trustees of Penn School," 1928, box 6, Penn School Papers, SHC.

53. Ibid.

54. Conveyance from Ishmael Brown's heirs to T. J. Woofter, May 18, 1929, Beaufort County Deed Book, 235, South Carolina State Archives, Columbia, S.C. U.S. Federal Census, 1920, St. Helena, Beaufort County, roll T625_1686, 5B; U.S. Federal Census, 1930, St. Helena, Beaufort County, roll T2188, 4B. *New York Times*, April 29, 1945, R4. In 2009, plots like Woofter's along Edding Creek sold for up to $3 million.

55. Johnson, "The Isolated Negro Community of St. Helena Island," 1, 7, in box 74, Guy B. Johnson Papers, SHC.

56. Woofter to Thomas Jesse Jones, May 1, May 9, May 13, June 3, 1929, box 27, PSF, SC. Jones to Woofter, May 6, May 28, July 1, 1929, ibid.; Ethel Woofter to Jones, May 15, 1929, ibid.; Woofter to George Foster Peabody, May 1, 1929, ibid.; Peabody to Woofter, June 4, June 5, 1929, ibid.

57. Jones to Woofter, Sept. 16, Oct. 7, Dec. 31, 1929, Oct. 2, 1930, ibid. Woofter to Jones, Oct. 2, 1929; Jan. 2, Sept. 30, 1930, ibid.

58. Woofter, *Black Yeomanry*, 82–102. Census data for St. Helena, box 6, Penn School Papers, SHC. Kiser, *Sea Island to City*. Kiser completed his MA at Chapel Hill in 1927. *Sea Island to City* was part of a migration series produced in the Department of Sociology at Columbia, funded by the SSRC.

59. "Social Science Research Council, Hanover Conference," Aug. 1927, 52, box 66, LSRM, RAC. Peterson and Telford, "Results of Group and of Individual Tests," 115–44.

60. Woofter, "Difficulties in Measuring Racial Mental Traits," 415–18.

61. Thomas, "Black Intellectuals' Critique of Early Mental Testing," 258–92.

62. Woofter, *Black Yeomanry*, 13–47, 48–81; Guy B. Johnson, *Folk Culture on St. Helena Island*; Guion Griffis Johnson, *Social History of the Sea Islands*; Singal, *War Within*, 322–23. Research notes, correspondence, and draft chapters, box 110, Guion Johnson Papers, SHC. Reports and expenditures of Guion Johnson, Dec. 26–31, 1927, and May 13–18, 1928, ibid. Guion Griffis Johnson interview, April 24, 1974, SHC. Research materials collected by Guy Johnson for the St. Helena project are in boxes 74–76, Guy B. Johnson Papers, SHC. See also Guy B. Johnson to Ediphone Co., Norfolk, Va., Jan. 16, 1928, box 74, ibid. The UNC Press published other folklore studies, such as Newbell Niles Puckett's *Folk Beliefs of the Southern Negro* (1926), which gath-

ered 2,500 folk beliefs through four hundred informants and questionnaires sent to black colleges. Howard Odum had a longstanding interest in songs, having made cylinder recordings in Lafayette County, Miss., and Newton County, Ga., between 1905 and 1908. Steven Carl Tracy, "Introduction," in Odum, *Rainbow Round My Shoulder*, xi.

63. Woofter to Outhwaite, Dec. 13, 1927, box 74, LRSM, RAC; Woofter to Outhwaite, Jan 18, 1928, ibid.

64. Woofter to Frank M. Hohenberger, Nov. 6, Nov. 11, 1929, Hohenberger MSS and Photograph Collection, Lilly Library, Indiana University, Bloomington. Woofter, *Black Yeomanry*, 79. Coffin Point was named after a planter family that fled in 1861. *New York Times*, Jan. 10, 1933, 21.

65. Woofter, *Black Yeomanry*, 3–12. Woofter summed up the project's methodology:

> The general logic back of many of the conclusions follows these steps: (1) Here is a group of pure-blooded Negroes, hence next to nothing in their community life can be traced to biological relationship with the white people. (2) Here is a relatively isolated group whose earlier contacts with white culture were more frequent than the present contacts. (3) While physical isolation is pronounced, psychic contacts with white culture come through the classroom and community program of Penn School and its extension workers. Hence the adoption of modern white standards is due to this influence. (4) Other advances in culture in fields not touched by Penn School must be attributed largely to the Negroes themselves.

See ibid., 260.

66. Ibid., 243–45.

67. Ibid., 248–53.

68. Ibid., 266, 269, 270, 277, 280.

69. Ibid., 159–62, 168–69, 173–77, 181–84. There were 57 mostly "decrepit second-hand" cars on St. Helena, out of a total of 900 cars in Beaufort County. Most travel on St. Helena was by ox-cart on dirt roads. According to Heer, "The amount spent on maintenance of St. Helena's local roads is next to nothing. Yet of the eight school districts in the county, only two contribute more to the county's highway funds" (171). The basic facts about taxation of rural blacks were set out by Tipton Ray Snavely, the fourth Phelps-Stokes fellow at the University of Virginia. See Snavely, *Taxation of Negroes*.

70. Ibid., 180–81.

71. Warren A. Candler, "Our Common School and Our Common People," (1903), 9–10, cited in Fish, "Southern Methodism and Accommodation of the Negro," 205–206. On taxation and education, see also Harlan, *Separate and Unequal*, passim.

72. Woofter, *Black Yeomanry*, 187–204. Cooley and House, who ran the Penn School after the death of founder Laura Towne in 1901, both taught previously at Hampton Institute. Johnson, *Social History of the Sea Islands*, 211–12.

73. *Baltimore Afro-American*, Sept. 20, 1930, 45; ibid., Oct. 18, 1930, 6. Broderick, *W. E. B. Du Bois*, 126.

74. *Crisis* 37 (Nov. 1930): 378, 393.

75. Ibid., 393. Du Bois and Carter G. Woodson believed they were often refused funding because of their independence, race consciousness, and open disdain for trust officials. See Lewis, *W. E. B. Du Bois: 1919–1963*, 190–92, 423–37, 442–51.

76. Ibid., 443–44, cites several examples.

77. Du Bois, review of *The American Negro*, *Crisis* 35 (June 1928): 202, 211. Du Bois to Ira Reid, April 14, 1939, in Aptheker, *Correspondence of W. E. B. Du Bois*, 2:187–91.

78. Guy Johnson's views on Gullah provoked debate. See Johnson, "Gullah Dialect Revis-

ited," 417–24; Baird, "Guy B. Johnson Revisited," 425–35. Johnson said the St. Helena study led him to offer social anthropology at UNC in 1930. Johnson and Johnson, *Research in Service to Society,* 151.

79. Woodson, review of *Black Yeomanry,* 95–96

80. H. C. H., "A Community and a School," 430–33. Reid, review of *Black Yeomanry,* 342.

81. Redfield, review of *Black Yeomanry,* 829–31. *New York Herald Tribune,* Aug. 24, 1930, clipping, box 74, Guy B. Johnson Papers, SHC. Porterfield, review of *Black Yeomanry,* 627.

82. Research staff, publications, and projects of the IRSS in "IRSS Report to the President of the University, for 1927–1928," box 74, LSRM, RAC. Frank Porter Graham to Ruml, Nov. 28, 1928, ibid.; Howard Odum, "A Suggested Program of Cooperative Social Research under the Auspices of a Southern Regional Group and the Social Science Research Council," n.d., box 62, ibid.

83. Gordon, "Data and Not Trouble," 100, http://aapf.org/wp-content/uploads/2009/05/gordon-chapter-1-final.pdf. *Report of the National Research Council for the Year July 1, 1927–June 30, 1928,* 30–31.

84. Herskovits, "Race Relations in the United States, 1928," 1137.

85. Woofter, "Negro and the Farm Crisis," 615–21.

86. George E. Haynes to Thomas Jesse Jones, June 24, 1926, box 28, PSF, SC. *Washington Post,* Feb. 21, 1926, R10. Perkins, *Edwin Rogers Embree,* 76–77. Davis, *Clashing of the Soul,* 288–89. The original theme of the National Interracial Conference was the prosaic "How to Make Interracial Cooperation More Real." Mary van Kleeck, "Foreword," in Johnson et al., *Negro in American Civilization.* Stanfield, *Philanthropy and Jim Crow,* 74–75.

87. Will W. Alexander to Arnold B. Hall, March 26, 1927, box 66, LSRM, RAC.

88. Minutes of the Executive Committee, Nov. 30, 1927, box 28, PSF, SC. The original plan was to hold the conference in St. Louis, Mo. *Washington Post,* Dec. 17, 1928, 5. George E. Haynes, "Memorandum . . . for the Advisory Committee on Interracial relations of the Social Science Research Council, March 23, 1927," LSRM, RAC. Charles S. Johnson, "Memorandum on proposed field activity of the research committee . . . ," ibid. Johnson et al., *Negro in American Civilization,* vii–x.

89. Young, "Foreword," viii.

90. Locke, "Boxed Compass of Our Race Relations," 51–58.

91. *Washington Post,* Nov. 21, 1918, 4. Embree's abolitionist family and integrated hometown of Berea, Ky., made for an unusual southern upbringing. Perkins, *Edwin Rogers Embree,* 5–16, 82. Members and report, National Interracial Conference, Dec. 16–19, 1928, from NUL Papers, LC, http://lcweb2.10c.gov/ammem/coolhtml/coolhome.html.

92. Ibid. Other bodies present included the American Medical Association, the American Federation of Labor, and the Harmon Foundation. Frank Porter Graham's interest in race began at W. D. Weatherford's conferences at Asheville. As president of the North Carolina Conference for Social Service, he called for extra state spending on young black people. As president of UNC in the 1930s and a U.S. senator in the 1940s, his liberalism caused controversy. Ashby, *Frank Porter Graham,* 20, 68–69, 154–68, 258–71, 306–12.

93. Mary E. McDowell, "Summary of the Session on Recreation and Housing," in members and report, National Interracial Conference, Dec. 16–19, 1928, 23–24. Locke, "Boxed Compass of Our Race Relations," 57. Woofter, "Negro Migration to Cities."

94. Locke, "Summary of the Session on Race Relations," in members and report, National Interracial Conference, Dec. 16–19, 1928, 11–12.

95. Clark Foreman, "Summary of the Session on Citizenship," 17 members and report, National Interracial Conference, Dec. 16–19, 1928, 17.

96. Locke, "Boxed Compass of Our Race Relations," 55, 58.

97. Charles S. Johnson, note in *American Journal of Sociology* 34 (March 1929): 902–903.

98. White, "Solving America's Race Problem," 42. The *Nation* itself called the conference a "milestone in the progress of the human race." Ibid., 31. See also *New York Times,* Dec. 18, 1928, 26; ibid., Dec. 28, 1928, 12. Mary van Kleeck to Du Bois, Feb. 6, 1929, in W. E. B. Du Bois Papers, UMAL.

99. Gordon, "Data and Not Trouble," 51–58.

100. Gershenhorn, *Melville Herskovits and the Racial Politics of Knowledge,* 103, 142–43. Peterson later served on the Southern Regional Committee of the SSRC.

101. Arthur F. Raper, memorandum on T. J. Woofter Jr., Feb. 27, 1976, part 1, Arthur Franklin Raper Papers, SHC. Raper recalled that during his PhD defense, Woofter helped him by deflecting colleagues' racist questions. Woofter, "Race in Politics: An Opportunity for Original Research," 435–38. In this article (437), Woofter concluded: "Thus not only the future of the Negro in South, but also the future policies of democracy toward minority groups are involved in the questions which arise from the political aspects of race relations." See also Woofter, *Plight of Cigarette Tobacco;* Woofter, "Race Relations," 1039–44; Woofter, "What Is the Negro Rate of Increase?," 461–62; Woofter, "Interpolation for Populations Whose Rate of Increase Is Declining," 180–82; Woofter and Webb, "A Reclassification of Urban-Rural Population," 348–51; Woofter, "Common Errors in Sampling," 521–25; Woofter, "Difficulties in Measuring Racial Mental Traits," 415–18.

102. Lisio, *Hoover, Blacks, and Lily-Whites,* 246–48, 346n2. T. J. Woofter, "A Study of the Economic Status of the Negro," June 1930, file 377, series I, frames 253–375, microfilm reel 19, CIC Papers, AUC. See also, *New York Times,* Oct. 20, 1930, 21, and "Economic Status of the Negro," 847–51.

103. *Crisis* 38 (Feb. 1931): 41.

104. Du Bois, "Woofterism," 81–83. Du Bois's view of T. Arnold Hill stemmed from the latter's Vocational Opportunity Campaign in 1930 and his Woofterish article, "Negroes in Southern Industry," *Annals of the American Academy of Political and Social Science* 153 (Jan. 1931): 170–81. Leading black communist Harry Haywood regarded Hoover Commission connections between Woofter, Rosenwald, and "Negro reformists" like Hill as evidence that "Jim Crow nationalism [was] building up a sort of segregated group economy among the Negro masses in the cities, with the Negro bourgeoisie as intermediaries between the Negro masses and the ruling imperialist bourgeoisie." Haywood, "Crisis of the Jim-Crow Nationalism of the Negro Bourgeoisie," 330–38. In the *New York Herald Tribune,* labor journalist Benjamin Stolberg charged Charles S. Johnson with similarly flawed work, calling *The Negro in American Civilization,* "the most competent example of a certain type of very bad book. It deals with one of our major social issues exhaustively, very ably in its way, with a great air of scrupulous objectivity and 'scientific' modesty, without ever indicating or implying the reason for the problem. This book is, in fact, not a book at all. It is an amazingly skillfully edited collection of mimeographs, pamphlets, paper studies from many hands, rewritten, reshuffled, cut with a canny eye to avoid all controversy, excised of all meaning, expurgated of all views, Bowdlerized of the faintest trace of opinion or conclusion, as though a social outlook were almost an indecent thing in social research." Stolberg, review of *The Negro in American Civilization,* 313. Black economist Abram Harris Jr. told Stolberg he criticized Johnson to his face for "the mere presentation of facts. . . . I also asked if he did not think that the man who actually perceived certain valid conclusions in his facts and refused to draw them was not only dishonest but an intellectual hypocrite. Of course he said no." Harris to Stolberg, Nov. 12, 1930, cited in Darity, "Soundings and Silences on Race and Social Change," 244.

105. Woofter, *Southern Race Progress,* 118.

106. Lewis, *W. E. B. Du Bois, 1919–1963,* 426–34. Walter A. Jackson, *Gunnar Myrdal and America's Conscience,* 25–26. W. E. B. Du Bois to Alice Werner, Nov. 17, 1925, W. E. B. Du Bois Papers, UMAL. Du Bois to James Hardy Dillard, Nov. 30, 1931, ibid. Du Bois, "Memorandum to

the Conference on the Advisability of Publishing a Negro Encyclopedia," n.d., ibid. Robert R. Moton later told Du Bois, "Dr Jones never approved of the proposition even from the very beginning." Moton to Du Bois, Sept. 29, 1933, ibid. Board of trustees minutes, Nov. 18, 1931, box 2, PSF, SC; editorial conference minutes, Nov. 7, 1931, box 40, ibid.; editorial conference minutes, Jan. 9, 1932, box 39, ibid.; Robert T. Crane to Anson Phelps Stokes, Dec. 4, 1931, box 40, ibid.; Anson Phelps Stokes to Du Bois, April 10, 1938, box 39, ibid.; Jackson Davis to Anson Phelps Stokes, May 20, 1941, box 39, ibid.; Charles Dollard to Anson Phelps Stokes, June 12, 1941, box 40, ibid. *Washington Post,* May 29, 1932, M5.

107. Woodson, review of *Black Yeomanry,* 95–96. On Woodson's own encyclopedia project, see Goggin, *Carter G. Woodson,* 128–34.

108. Carter G. Woodson, "Too Much Foresight," *New York Age,* June 25, 1932, clipping, box 23, PSF, SC.

109. Woofter, "The Status of Racial and Ethnic Groups," 1:553–601; Woofter, *Races and Ethnic Groups in American Life.* See also Tobin, "Studying Society," 537–65; Lisio, *Hoover, Blacks, and Lily-Whites,* 280, 355n9; Karl, "Presidential Planning and Social Science Research," 345–409. Edward Eyre Hunt to Howard Odum, July 28, 1932, Odum folder, box 21, Edward Eyre Hunt Collection, Hoover Institution Archives, Stanford, Calif.; Odum to Hunt, Aug. 4, 1932, ibid. McKee, *Sociology and the Race Problem,* 131. Rees, *Shades of Difference,* 91–92. *Recent Social Trends* complemented *Recent Economic Changes in the United States* (1929), commissioned by Hoover as secretary of commerce in 1927.

110. Woofter included another chapter on "Health" by Hugh P. Brinton, a recent UNC doctoral student, and a section on the non-English press by *Russkoye Slovo* editor Mark Villchur. See Woofter, *Races and Ethnic Groups in American Life,* 192–203, 214–30. In *Social Forces,* Czech immigrant Joseph Roucek wished Woofter had included more black and immigrant opinion. See Roucek, Review of *Races and Ethnic Groups in American Life,* 304–305.

111. Jones, *Essentials of Civilization,* 20.

112. Woofter, *Races and Ethnic Groups in American Life,* 232–33.

113. Ibid., 241.

114. Howard Odum to Arthur E. Morgan, June 19, 1933, "Tennessee River Valley Project: Morgan A. E." folder, box 40, Odum Papers, SHC, UNC. Woofter, "Tennessee Basin," 809–17; Woofter, "Tennessee Valley Regional Plan," 329–38; Woofter, "Subregions of the Southeast," 43–50. Woofter to James D. Hoskins, Oct 1, 1933, Papers of the Presidents, Special Collections Library, University of Tennessee, Knoxville. See also Woofter correspondence, "The Tennessee Valley Study 1933–1934," box 41, Odum Papers, SHC.

115. Woofter to Odum, April 5, 1935, folder W-General, box 42, Odum Papers, SHC. See Hall, "Women Writers, the 'Southern Front,' and the Dialectical Imagination," 3–38.

116. Winston, "Thomas Jackson Woofter, 1893–1972," 6.

117. Correspondence and memorandums between Woofter, Myrdal, et al., 1939–1940, in General Correspondence and Memoranda, microfiche 26, Carnegie-Myrdal Study of the Negro in America Research Memoranda Collection, 1935–1948, SC. See this volume's bibliography for work published by Woofter after leaving Chapel Hill.

118. Jonathan Daniels, "Introduction," to Woofter, *Southern Race Progress,* v–vi. McGuinn, review of *Southern Race Progress,* 98–102. M. C. H., "More Illumination for Understanding the Processes of Integration" (review of *Southern Race Progress*), 315.

Conclusion

1. Woofter, *Southern Race Progress,* 1.

2. Ibid., 24. Sosna acknowledged the dilemma of the outspoken white person: "Southern

liberals who unequivocally opposed Jim Crow often found themselves either in exile from their native region, or if they remained in the South, ineffective and ostracized." He concluded that after 1920 "the primary question facing southern liberals was how far they would, or could, go." See Sosna, *In Search of the Silent South,* 172, 203–206.

3. Woofter, *Southern Race Progress,* 171–72.

4. Ibid, 172.

5. Dillard and Morse cited in Tindall, *Emergence of the New South,* 176, 183.

6. Fairclough, *Race and Democracy,* 41.

7. James O. Dobson, "Account of the Discussion," in *Christian Mission in the Light of Race Conflict,* 4:229–31.

8. Ibid., 227–29. Dobson was the missionary secretary of the Student Christian Movement. Davis, *A Clashing of the Soul,* 290–92.

9. W. S. Turner, "Negro and the Changing South," 115–19. Contrastingly, Turner was skeptical about the "New Negro": "Living in steam-heated flats and strutting Seventh Avenue cannot convert black peasants into modern men within a single year." See Turner, "Has the Negro Arrived?," 479–82.

10. Ellis, "Commission on Interracial Cooperation," 380. Ellis claims (preface) that the CIC "played a vital role in preparing the middle and upper-class whites to accept the later civil rights movement."

11. Hall, "Women Writers, the 'Southern Front,' and the Dialectical Imagination," 3–38. Gilmore states, "An Anti-Fascist Left moved the U.S. South from the status quo of interracial cooperation to more radical political action in the late 1930s." Gilmore, *Defying Dixie,* 246.

12. Woofter, "Race in Politics," 435–38.

13. Smith to Mozell Hill, March 11, 1957, in Gladney, *How Am I to Be Heard?* 209.

14. Hall, "The Long Civil Rights Movement and the Political Uses of the Past," 1263. Hall criticized a tendency to limit the civil rights movement conceptually to "a single halcyon decade" and called for acknowledgement of "a more robust, more progressive, and truer story— the story of a 'long civil rights movement' that took root in the liberal and radical milieu of the late 1930s." She added, "A national movement with a vital southern wing, civil rights unionism was not just a precursor of the modern civil rights movement. It was its first decisive phase." Ibid., 1234, 1235, 1245. Nikhil Pal Singh also writes of "the long civil rights era . . . bracketed by Roosevelt's New Deal and Johnson's Great Society." See *Black Is a Country,* 6. See also Michael Ezra's introduction to *Civil Rights Movement,* xi–xviii. My own view was influenced by Steven F. Lawson's plenary lecture, "The Long Origins of the Short Civil Rights Movement," at the 2010 conference of the Scottish Association for the Study of America, in Edinburgh.

15. See, for example, Randall L. Patton, "The Popular Front Alternative: Clark H. Foreman and the Southern Conference on Human Welfare, 1938–1948," in Inscoe, *Georgia in Black and White,* 225–45.

16. Olive Stone interview, Aug. 13, 1975, G-0059-4, Southern Oral History Program Collection, SHC, http://docsouth.unc.edu/sohp/G-0059-4/G-0059-4.html.

17. Dailey et al., *Jumpin' Jim Crow,* 4.

18. Stanfield, *Philanthropy and Jim Crow,* 186–92.

19. Howard Odum to Will Alexander, Oct. 8, 1927, box 11, Odum Papers, SHC. At Odum's request, Woofter read and commented on Raper's draft report on lynching. Odum to Woofter, Aug. 4, 1931, "W-General" folder, box 37, ibid. Raper, *Tragedy of Lynching,* 30–31. If the IRSS had published John R. Steelman's PhD dissertation in 1928, it would have served the same purpose as *The Tragedy of Lynching.* Stuart Tolnay and E. M. Beck, "Rethinking the Role of Racial Violence in the Great Migration," in Harrison, *Black Exodus,* 20–35. Tolnay and Beck, *A Festival of Violence,* 218–19. While at UNC in the early 1930s, Woofter was listed by the CIC as "Research Adviser." The CIC publication *A Sane Approach to the Race Problem* (1930) named him as one

of its top seven people, along with the president, William C. Jackson, the chairman, Robert B. Eleazer, and the cofounders, Richard H. King, Robert Moton, and Will Alexander, and Jessie Daniel Ames. Alexander to Southern Commission on the Study of Lynching, Oct. 2, 1930, box 9, Moton Papers, LC.

20. Bryan, *These Few Also Paid a Price*, 80–88, 114–18. Timothy B. Tyson, "Dynamite and the 'Silent South': A Story from the Second Reconstruction in South Carolina," in Dailey et al., *Jumpin' Jim Crow*, 275–97.

21. Biles, *South and the New Deal*, 150. Woofter, *Southern Race Progress*, 174. Matthews, "Virginius Dabney, John Temple Graves, and What Happened to Southern Liberalism," 405–20.

22. T. J. Woofter to editor, *Winston Salem Journal*, Aug. 17, 1957, copied to *Greensboro News* and *Charlotte News*, enc. with Woofter to Gordon Blackwell, Aug. 19, 1957, in "Woofter, T. J." folder, box 3, Gordon Williams Blackwell Papers, Jackson Library, University of North Carolina, Greensboro (UNC-G). He referred to Edwin A. Alderman (president of UNC, 1896–1900), Charles B. Aycock (governor of North Carolina, 1901–1905), Walter Hines Page (diplomat and author of *The Southerner* [1909]), and James Y. Joyner (North Carolina's superintendent of public instruction, 1902–19).

23. Gordon B. Hancock, "Redeeming the South," *Norfolk Journal and Guide*, Feb. 2, 1929, clipping, box 1, Gordon B. Hancock Papers, Rubenstein Rare Book and Manuscript Library (RRBML), Duke University, Durham, N.C.

24. Gordon B. Hancock, "The New Interracialism," unidentified clipping, Sept. 18, 1943, "Miscellany" folder, box 2, Hancock Papers, RRBML. Hancock, "The Tragedy of Interracial Understanding," unidentified clipping (from Hancock's column, "Behind the Lines," in 114 publications), ca. 1960, "Clippings/Writings. Race Relations" folder, box 1, ibid. The Phoenix Riot also affected Morehouse College president Benjamin Mays; one of his early memories was of riders who lynched a dozen black people in Greenwood County. Mays, *Born to Rebel*, 1.

25. See Lewinson, *Race, Class, and Party*, 218–19. Ortiz, *Emancipation Betrayed*, 171–228. Kimberley Johnson, *Reforming Jim Crow*, 193–203.

26. *Atlanta Constitution*, Dec. 28, 1926, 1; ibid., Dec. 29, 1926, 3; ibid., Dec. 30, 1926, 1; ibid., Dec. 31, 1926, 2; ibid., Jan. 2, 1927, 1; ibid., Feb. 25, 1927, 1; ibid., March 15, 1927, 1. *Sarasota Herald*, Dec. 29, 1926, 1, 2. *Los Angeles Times*, Dec. 29, 1926, 2. *Chicago Tribune*, Dec. 29, 1926, 16. *New York Times*, Dec. 29, 1926, 2. "Lynching: In Toombs," *Time Magazine*, Jan. 10, 1927, http://www.time.com/time/magazine/article/0,9171,881578,00.html.

27. "Lynching in America: Statistics, Information, Images," http://www.law.umkc.edu/faculty/projects/ftrials/shipp/lynchstats.html.

Brundage, *Lynching in the New South*, 242. See also Klarman, *From Jim Crow to Civil Rights*, 118–20.

28. Ellis, "Commission on Interracial Cooperation," preface. According to Myrdal, the CIC "rendered interracial work socially respectable in the conservative South." *American Dilemma*, 847. Chappell puts it thus: "The white southerners who dissented from the racial status quo in the 1950s did not just pop up out of nowhere." *Inside Agitators*, 3.

29. Selig, *Americans All*, 182.

30. Mary van Kleeck, "Foreword," in Charles S. Johnson, *Negro in American Civilization*, xi.

31. For a comparable, but contrasting, perspective, in which the NAACP and black witnesses are given the key roles, see Williams, *They Left Great Marks on Me*, 206–24.

Bibliography

Manuscript and Archive Collections

Auburn Avenue Research Library of African American Culture and History, Atlanta, Ga.
  Atlanta University Collection
Center for Oral History, Columbia University, New York
  Oral History Interview with Will Winton Alexander, 1952
David M. Rubenstein Rare Book and Manuscript Library, Duke University, Durham, N.C.
  Gordon B. Hancock Papers
  Negro Pamphlets, 1920–1929
  Negro Pamphlets, 1930–1939
Hargrett Rare Book and Manuscript Library, University of Georgia, Athens
  Robert Preston Brooks Papers
Hoover Institution Archives, Stanford, Calif.
  Edward Eyre Hunt Collection
J. Y. Joyner Library, East Carolina University, Greeneville, N.C.
  Junius D. Grimes Papers
Jackson Library, University of North Carolina, Greensboro
  Gordon Williams Blackwell Papers
John C. Hodges Library, Special Collections, University of Tennessee, Knoxville, Tenn.
  Papers of the Presidents
Library of Congress, Manuscript Division, Washington, D.C.
  R. R. Moton Papers, in Moton Family Papers
  Papers of Leonard Porter Ayres
  Papers of the National Association for the Advancement of Colored People
Lilly Library, University of Indiana, Bloomington
  Hohenberger MSS and Photograph Collection
Milbank Memorial Library, Special Collections
National Archives, College Park, Md.
  Records of the Office of Education (Record Group 12)
  Records of Statistical Division, Adjutant General's Department, G1, GHQ, AEF (Record Group 120)
  Records of the Adjutant General's Office, (Record Group 407)
National Personnel Records Center, St. Louis, Mo.
  Civilian Personnel Records
Regenstein Library, University of Chicago
  Special Collections
Robert W. Woodruff Library, Atlanta University Center, Atlanta, Ga.
  Papers of the Commission on Interracial Cooperation, 1919–1944 (microfilmed by Microfilming Corporation of America, 1984)
Rockefeller Archive Center, Sleepy Hollow, N.Y.

General Education Board Records
    Laura Spelman Rockefeller Memorial Collection
Schomburg Center for Research in Black Culture, New York Public Library
    Carnegie-Myrdal Study of the Negro in America, Research Memoranda Collection
    Papers of the Phelps-Stokes Fund
South Carolina State Archives, Columbia, S.C.
    Beaufort County Deed Book, 1929
Southern Historical Collection, Wilson Library, University of North Carolina, Chapel Hill
    Guion Johnson Papers
    Guy B. Johnson Papers
    Howard W. Odum Papers
    Penn School Papers
    Arthur Franklin Raper Papers
Teachers College, Columbia University, New York
    Papers of Thomas Jesse Jones
Tuskegee University Archives, Tuskegee, Ala.
    Isaac Fisher Papers
    Moton Collection

Online Archive Collections

Ancestry.com
    U.S. Federal Census Records
    World War I Draft Registration Records
Digital Library of Georgia
    Minutes of the Athens Woman's Club, 1899–1911, 1912–1920, http://dlg.galileo.usg
    .edu/athenswomansclub/
    Reed, Thomas Walter, *History of the University of Georgia*, ca. 1949, http://dlg
    .galileo.usg.edu/reed/
Population Association of America Oral History Project, http://geography.sdsu.edu
    /Research/Projects/PAA/oralhistory/PAA_Presidents_1947-60.pdf
    Interviews with Clyde V. Kiser et al., April 26, 1973; Dec. 15, 1976
University of Georgia Libraries
    Transcript of the Minutes of the University of Georgia Board of Trustees, 1786–
    1932, http://www.libs.uga.edu/hargrett/archives/trustees/index.html
University of Massachusetts Libraries, Amherst, http://credo.library.umass.edu/
    W. E. B. Du Bois Papers (MS 312)
University of North Carolina, Southern Oral History Program Collection
    Electronic editions from the UNC-Chapel Hill digital library, Documenting the
    American South, http://docsouth.unc.edu/
    Interview with Clark Foreman, Nov. 16, 1974 (B-0003)
    Interview with Harriet Herring, Feb. 5, 1976 (G-0027)
    Interviews with Guion Griffis Johnson, May 28, 1974 (G-0029-3); Aug. 19, 1974
    (G-0029-1)
    Interview with Guy B. Johnson, Dec. 16, 1974 (B-0006)

Interview with Broadus Mitchell, Aug. 14, Aug. 15, 1977 (B-0024)
Interview with Olive Stone, Aug. 13, 1975 (G-0059-4)
University of Virginia, Albert & Shirley Small Special Collections Library, http://www
.lib.virginia.edu/small/collections/jdavis/
Jackson Davis Collection of African American Educational Photographs

Newspapers and Periodicals

Atlanta Constitution
Baltimore Afro-American
Chicago Tribune
Christian Science Monitor
Cleveland Advocate
Crisis
Daily Mirror, London
Danville Register
Fort Worth Sentinel
Indianapolis Freeman
Nation
Newport News Daily Press
New York Times
Raleigh News & Observer
Time
Washington Post

Published Works

"African Education Commission. *Education in Africa.* New York: Phelps-Stokes Fund, 1922.
———. *Education in East Africa.* New York: Phelps-Stokes Fund, 1925.
Aiken, Charles S. *The Cotton Plantation South since the Civil War.* Baltimore: Johns
Hopkins University Press, 1998.
———. *William Faulkner and the Southern Landscape.* Athens: University of Georgia
Press, 2009.
Alderman, E. A., and Joel Chandler Harris, eds. *Library of Southern Literature.* Part 15.
Whitefish, Mont.: Kessinger, 2005; first pub. 1907.
Aldrich, Mark. "Progressive Economics and Scientific Racism: Walter Wilcox and Black
Americans, 1895–1910." *Phylon* 40 (Spring 1979): 1–14.
Alexander, Robert J. "Negro Business in Atlanta." *Southern Economic Journal* 17 (April
1951): 454–55.
Alexander, Will W. "The Negro in the New South." *Annals of the American Academy of
Political and Social Science* 140 (Nov. 1928): 145–52.
———. "Southern White Schools Study Race Questions." *Journal of Negro Education* 2
(Spring 1933): 139–46.
———. "A Usable Piece of Community Machinery." *Journal of Social Forces* 1 (Nov. 1922):
41–42.

American Civil Liberties Union. *Black Justice*. New York: ACLU, 1931.

Anderson, Eric, and Alfred A. Moss Jr. *Dangerous Donations: Northern Philanthropy and Southern Education, 1902–1930.* Columbia: University of Missouri Press, 1999.

Anderson, James D. *The Education of Blacks in the South, 1860–1935.* Chapel Hill: University of North Carolina Press, 1988.

———. "Northern Foundations and the Shaping of Southern Black Rural Education, 1902–1935." *History of Education Quarterly* 18 (Winter 1978): 371–96.

———. "On the Meaning of Reform: African-American Education in the Twentieth Century South." In *The American South in the Twentieth Century,* ed. Craig S. Pascoe et al., 263–84. Athens: University of Georgia Press, 2005.

"An Adventure in Good Will." *Outlook* 139 (Feb. 18, 1925): 254–55.

An Appeal to the Christian People of the South. N.p., 1920.

Appiah, Kwame Anthony, and Henry Lewis Gates Jr. "Introduction to the First Edition" (1999). In *Africana: The Encyclopedia of the African and African American Experience.* 2nd ed. http://www.oxfordaasc.com/public/books/t0002/t0002_intro_1st.jsp.

Aptheker, Herbert, ed. *The Correspondence of W. E. B. Du Bois.* Vol. 1: *Selections, 1877–1934.* Amherst: University of Massachusetts Press, 1973.

———, ed. *The Correspondence of W. E. B. Du Bois.* Vol. 2: *Selections, 1934–1944.* Amherst: University of Massachusetts Press, 1976.

———. *A Documentary History of the Negro People in the United States.* Vol. 2. New York: Citadel Press, 1968.

Arnold, Edwin T. *"What Virtue There Is in Fire": Cultural Memory and the Lynching of Sam Hose.* Athens: University of Georgia Press, 2009.

Ashby, Warren. *Frank Porter Graham: A Southern Liberal.* Winston-Salem: John F. Blair, 1980.

Attwell, Ernest T. "Recreation for Colored America." *American City Magazine* 35 (Aug. 1926): 162–65.

Ayers, Edward L. *The Promise of the New South: Life after Reconstruction.* New York: Oxford University Press, 2007.

Badger, Anthony J. *Prosperity Road: The New Deal, Tobacco, and North Carolina.* Chapel Hill: University of North Carolina Press, 1980.

Bagnall, R. W. Review of *Negro Problems in Cities,* by T. J. Woofter Jr. *Nation* 126 (April 25, 1928): 491.

Bailey, Hugh C. *Liberalism in the New South: Southern Social Reformers and the Progressive Movement.* Coral Gables, Fla.: University of Miami Press, 1969.

Bailey, Thomas Pearce. *Race Orthodoxy in the South, and Other Aspects of the Negro Question.* New York: Neale, 1914.

Baker, Bruce E. *This Mob Will Surely Take My Life: Lynching in the Carolinas, 1871–1947.* London: Continuum, 2008.

Baker, Paul E. *Negro-White Adjustment: An Investigation and Analysis of Methods in the Interracial Movement in the United States.* New York: Association Press, 1934.

Baird, Keith E. "Guy B. Johnson Revisited: Another Look at Gullah." *Journal of Black Studies* 10 (June 1980): 425–35.

Ballanta, N. G. J. *St. Helena Island Spirituals.* New York: G. Schrimer, 1925.

Barker, Colin, et al., eds. *Leadership and Social Movements.* Manchester: Manchester University Press, 2001.

Bassett, John Spencer. "Stirring Up the Fires of Race Antipathy." *South Atlantic Quarterly* 2 (Oct. 1903): 297–305.

Bauman, Mark K. "Race and Mastery: The Debate of 1903." In *From the Old South to the New: Essays on the Transitional South,* ed. Walter J. Fraser and Winfred B. Moore, 181–94. Westport: Greenwood Press, 1981.

Bauman, Mark K., and Beverley Kalin, eds. *The Quiet Voices: Southern Rabbis and Black Civil Rights, 1880s to 1990s.* Tuscaloosa: University of Alabama Press, 1997.

Beale, Howard K. *Are American Teachers Free? An Analysis of Restraints upon the Freedom of Teaching in American Schools.* New York: Charles Scribner's Sons, 1936.

Berman, Edward. "American Influence on African Education: The Role of the Phelps-Stokes Fund's Education Commissions." *Comparative Education Review* 15 (June 1971): 132–45.

Bernard, L. L. "The Southern Sociological Congress." *American Journal of Sociology* 19 (July 1913): 91–93.

Berry, Mary Frances. "Repression of Blacks in the South 1890–1945: Enforcing the System of Segregation." In *The Age of Segregation: Race Relations in the South, 1890–1945,* ed. Robert Haws, 29–43. Jackson: University of Mississippi Press, 1978.

Biles, Roger. *The South and the New Deal.* Lexington: University of Kentucky Press, 1994.

Blackburn, Burr. "A Forward Move in Georgia." *Journal of Social Forces* 1 (March 1923): 261–64.

Blackwell, Gordon W. "Rural Relief in the South: FERA's Problem in Eastern North Carolina." *Law and Contemporary Problems* 1 (June 1934): 390–97.

Boas, Franz. *The Mind of Primitive Man.* New York: Macmillan, 1911.

Bogardus, Emory S. "Social Distance and Its Origins." *Journal of Applied Sociology* 9 (Jan.–Feb. 1925): 216–26.

Bohannon, Keith S. "'These Few Gray-Haired, Battle-Scarred Veterans': Confederate Army Reunions in Georgia, 1885–95." In *The Myth of the Lost Cause and Civil War History,* ed. Gary W. Gallagher and Alan T. Nolan, 89–109. Bloomington: Indiana University Press, 2000.

Bond, Horace Mann. *Negro Education in Alabama: A Study in Cotton and Steel.* Tuscaloosa: University of Alabama Press, 1994; first pub. 1939.

———. "Self-Respect as a Factor in Racial Advancement." *Annals of the American Academy of Political and Social Science* 140 (Nov. 1928): 21–25.

Boswell, Angela, and Judith N. McArthur, eds. *Women Shaping the South: Creating and Confronting Change.* Columbia: University of Missouri Press, 2006.

Brazil, Wayne D. *Howard W. Odum: The Building Years, 1884–1930.* New York: Garland, 1988.

Breen, William J. "Foundations, Statistics, and State-Building: Leonard P. Ayres, the Russell Sage Foundation, and U. S. Government Statistics in the First World War." *Business History Review* 68 (Winter 1994): 451–82.

Brewer, William M. Review of *Southern Race Progress,* by Thomas J. Woofter. *Journal of Negro History* 43 (April 1958): 161–63.

Bristow, Nancy K. *Making Men Moral: Social Engineering during the Great War.* New York: New York University Press, 1996.

Broderick, Francis L. *W. E. B. Du Bois: Negro Leader in a Time of Crisis.* Stanford: Stanford University Press, 1959.

Brooks, Clayton McClure. "Unlikely Allies: Southern Women, Interracial Cooperation, and the Making of Segregation in Virginia, 1910–1920." In *Women Shaping the South: Creating and Confronting Change*, ed. Angela Boswell and Judith N. McArthur, 120–52. Columbia: University of Missouri Press, 2006.

Brooks, Robert Preston. *Georgia Studies*. Athens: University of Georgia Press, 1952.

Brough, Charles H. "Work of the Commission of Southern Universities on the Race Question." *Annals of the American Academy of Political and Social Science* 49 (Sept. 1913): 47–57.

Brown, Mary Jane. *Eradicating This Evil: Women and the American Anti-Lynching Campaign, 1892–1940*. New York: Garland, 2000.

Brundage, W. Fitzhugh, ed. *Booker T. Washington and Black Progress: Up from Slavery 100 Years Later*. Gainesville: University of Florida Press, 2003.

———. *Lynching in the New South: Georgia and Virginia, 1880–1930*. Urbana: University of Illinois Press, 1993.

———, ed. *Under Sentence of Death: Lynching in the South*. Chapel Hill: University of North Carolina Press, 1997.

Bryan, G. McLeod. *These Few Also Paid a Price: Southern Whites Who Fought for Civil Rights*. Macon, Ga.: Mercer University Press, 2001.

Bulmer, Martin. "The Social Survey Movement and Early Twentieth-Century Sociological Methodology." In *Pittsburgh Surveyed: Social Science and Social Reform in the Early Twentieth Century*, ed. Maureen W. Greenwald and Margo Anderson, 15–34. Pittsburgh: University of Pittsburgh Press, 1996.

Burgess, Ernest W. "Residential Segregation in American Cities." *American Academy of Political and Social Science* 140 (Nov. 1928): 105–15.

Burns, Adam. "Without Due Process: Albert E. Pillsbury and the Hoar Anti-Lynching Bill." *American Nineteenth Century History* 11 (June 2010): 233–52.

Caccamo, Rita. *Back to Middletown: Three Generations of Sociological Reflections*. Palto Alto, Calif.: Stanford University Press, 2000.

Calverton, V. F. "The New Negro." *Current History* 33 (Feb. 1926): 694–98.

Camic, Charles, and Yu Xie. "The Statistical Turn in American Social Science: Columbia University, 1890 to 1915." *American Sociological Review* 59 (Oct. 1994): 773–805.

Carlton, David L., and Peter A. Coclanis, eds. *Confronting Southern Poverty in the Great Depression: "The Report on Economic Conditions of the South."* Boston: Bedford/St. Martin's, 1996.

Chaddock, R. E. *Principles and Methods of Statistics*. Boston: Houghton Mifflin, 1925.

Chappell, David L. *Inside Agitators: White Southerners in the Civil Rights Movement*. Baltimore: Johns Hopkins University Press, 1994.

———. *A Stone of Hope: Prophetic Religion and the Death of Jim Crow*. Chapel Hill: University of North Carolina Press, 2004.

Chirhart, Ann Short. *Torches of Light: Georgia Teachers and the Coming of the Modern South*. Athens: University of Georgia Press, 2005.

The Christian Mission in the Light of Race Conflict: Report of the Jerusalem Meeting of the International Missionary Council, March 24th–April 8th, 1928. Vol. 4. London: Oxford University Press, 1928.

Clayton, Bruce. *The Savage Ideal: Intolerance and Intellectual Leadership in the South, 1890–1914*. Baltimore: Johns Hopkins University Press, 1972.

———. *W. J. Cash: A Life*. Baton Rouge: Louisiana State University Press, 1991.

"Col. Lawton on Mob Action." *Journal of Social Forces* 1 (Sept. 1923): 589–90.

Commission on Interracial Cooperation. *Southern Women and Race Cooperation.* Atlanta: CIC, 1921.

———. *A Sane Approach to the Race Problem: Justice and Goodwill between the Races through Conference and Cooperation.* New York: CIC, 1930.

———. *Southern Leaders Impeach Judge Lynch.* Atlanta: CIC, ca. 1931.

"Constructive Measure Recommended by Southern White Women." *Southern Workman* 50 (Jan. 1921): 35–37.

Cooley, Rossa B. *Homes of the Freed.* New York: New Republic, 1926.

Correia, Stephen T. "For Their Own Good: An Historical Analysis of the Educational Thought of Thomas Jesse Jones." PhD diss., Pennsylvania State University, 1993.

———. "Thomas Jesse Jones–Doing God's Work and the 1916 Report." In *The Social Studies in Secondary Education: A Reprint of the Seminal 1916 Report with Annotations and Commentaries,* ed. Murry R. Nelson, 98–124. Bloomington: ERIC-CRESS, 1994.

Crowe, Charles. "Racial Violence and Social Reform—Origins of the Atlanta Riot of 1906." *Journal of Negro History* 53 (July 1968): 234–56.

Cuff, Robert D. "Creating Central Control Systems: Edwin F. Gay and the Central Bureau of Planning and Statistics, 1917–1919." *Business History Review* 63 (Autumn 1989): 588–613.

Dailey, Jane Elizabeth, et al., eds. *Jumpin' Jim Crow: Southern Politics from Civil War to Civil Rights.* Princeton, N.J.: Princeton University Press, 2000.

Daniel, Pete. "Black Power in the 1920s: The Case of the Tuskegee Veterans' Hospital." *Journal of Southern History* 36 (Aug. 1970): 368–88.

———. *The Shadow of Slavery: Peonage in the South, 1901–1969.* Urbana: University of Illinois Press, 1972.

Daniel, Walter Green. "Current Trends and Events of National Importance in Negro Education." *Journal of Negro Education* 5 (April 1936): 300–309.

Darity, William, Jr. "Soundings and Silences on Race and Social Change: Abram Harris, Jr. in the Great Depression." In *A Different Vision: African American Economic Thought,* vol. 1, ed. Thomas D. Boston, 230–49. London: Routledge, 1997.

Davis, Leroy. *A Clashing of the Soul: John Hope and the Dilemma of African American Leadership and Black Higher Education in the Early Twentieth Century.* Athens: University of Georgia Press, 1998.

Davis, Matthew D. "Stimulation, Sustenance, Subversion: The General Education Board and Southern US Public Education." *Journal of Educational Administration and History* 38 (Dec. 2006): 313–22.

Degler, Carl N. *The Other South: Southern Dissenters in the Nineteenth Century.* New York: Harper & Row, 1974.

Dennis, Michael. "The Illusion of Relevance: Southern Progressives and American Higher Education." *Journal of the Historical Society* 8 (June 2008): 229–71.

———. *Lessons in Progress: State Universities and Progressivism in the New South, 1880–1920.* Urbana: University of Illinois Press, 2001.

———. "Schooling along the Color Line: Progressives and the Education of Blacks in the New South." *Journal of Negro Education* 67 (Spring 1998): 142–56.

———. "The Skillful Use of Higher Education to Protect White Supremacy." *Journal of Blacks in Higher Education* 32 (Summer 2001): 115–23.

Dinnerstein, Leonard. *The Leo Frank Case*. Rev. ed. Athens: University of Georgia Press, 2008.

Dittmer, John. *Black Georgia in the Progressive Era, 1900–1920*. Urbana: University of Illinois Press, 1980.

Donald, Henderson H. *The Negro Migration of 1916–1918*. Washington, D.C.: Association for the Study of Negro Life and History, 1921.

Donohue, John J., III, et al. "The Schooling of Southern Blacks: The Roles of Legal Activism and Private Philanthropy, 1910–1960." *Quarterly Journal of Economics* 117 (Feb. 2002): 225–68.

Dowd, Jerome. *The Negro in American Society*. New York: Century, 1926.

Dowden-White, Priscilla A. "To See Past the Differences to the Fundamentals: Racial Coalition within the League of Women Voters of St. Louis, 1920–1946." In *Women Shaping the South: Creating and Confronting Change*, ed. Angela Boswell and Judith N. McArthur, 174–203. Columbia: University of Missouri Press, 2006.

Dray, Philip. *At the Hands of Persons Unknown: The Lynching of Black America*. New York: Modern Library, 2003.

Droba, Daniel D. "Education and Negro Attitudes." *Sociology and Social Research* 17 (Nov.–Dec. 1932): 137–41.

Du Bois, W. E. B. *The College-Bred Negro*. Atlanta: Atlanta University Press, 1900.

———. "Education." *Crisis* 10 (July 1915): 136.

———. "Education in Africa." *Crisis* 32 (June 1926): 86–89.

———. "Georgia: Invisible Empire State." *Nation* 120 (Jan. 21, 1925): 63–67.

———. "Inter-Racial Comity." *Crisis* 22 (May 1921): 6–7

———. "Mixed Schools." *Crisis* 22 (Aug. 1921): 150–51.

———. "N.R.A. and Appointments."*Crisis* 40 (Oct. 1933): 237.

———. "Negro Education." *Crisis* 15 (Feb. 1918): 173–78.

———. "The Newer South." *Crisis* 31 (Feb. 1926): 163–65.

———. *The Negroes of Farmville, Virginia*. Washington, D.C.: U.S. Department of Labor, 1898.

———. *The Philadelphia Negro: A Social Study*. Philadelphia: University of Pennsylvania Press, 1899.

———. "Robert R. Moton." *Crisis* 18 (May 1919): 9–10.

———. Review of *What the Negro Thinks*, by Robert R. Moton. *Crisis* 36 (June 1929): 196.

———. "The Social Equality of Whites and Blacks." *Crisis* 21 (Nov. 1920): 16.

———. "Thomas Jesse Jones." *Crisis* 22 (Oct. 1921): 252–56.

———. "The Training of Negroes for Social Power." *Outlook* 75 (Oct. 17, 1903): 409–14.

———. "The Upbuilding of Black Durham." *World's Work* 23 (Jan. 1912): 334–38.

———. "Woofterism." *Crisis* 39 (March 1931): 81–83.

Du Bois, W. E. B., and Augustus G. Dill, eds. *The College-Bred Negro American*. Atlanta: Atlanta University Press, 1910.

Dunbar, Alice Moore, ed. *Masterpieces of Negro Eloquence: The Best Speeches Delivered by the Negro from the Days of Slavery to the Present Time*. New York: G. K. Hall, 1997; first pub. 1914.

Duncan, Hannibal Gerald. *The Changing Race Relationship in the Border and Northern States*. Lancaster, Pa.: Intelligence Printing, 1922.

"The Dyer Bill." *Crisis* 23 (Jan. 1922): 114.

Dykeman, Wilma. *Prophet of Plenty: The First Ninety Years of W. D. Weatherford.* Knox-ville: University of Tennessee Press, 1966.

Dykeman, Wilma, and James Stokely. *Seeds of Southern Change: The Life of Will Alexander.* Chicago: University of Chicago Press, 1960.

Eagles, Charles W. *Jonathan Daniels and Race Relations: The Evolution of a Southern Liberal.* Knoxville: University of Tennessee Press, 1982.

"Economic Status of the Negro." *Monthly Labor Review* 32 (April 1931): 847–51.

Educational Survey of Jones County, Georgia. Compiled by M. L. Duggan. Atlanta: Georgia Department of Education, 1918.

Educational Survey of Tift County, Georgia. Compiled by M. L. Duggan. Atlanta: Georgia Department of Education, 1918.

Egerton, John. *Speak Now against the Day: The Generation before the Civil Rights Move-ment in the South.* Chapel Hill: University of North Carolina Press, 1994.

Eleazer, Robert B. *An Adventure in Faith: A Brief Story of the Interracial Movement in the South.* Atlanta: Commission on Interracial Cooperation, 1929.

———. *An Adventure in Good Will: The Interracial Commission, It's [sic] Origin and Work.* N.p., n.d.

———. *America's Tenth Man: A Brief Survey of the Negro's Part in American History.* At-lanta: Commission on Interracial Cooperation, 1931.

———. "Broadcasting Good Will: The Press Service of the Commission on Interracial Cooperation." *Southern Workman* 60 (July 1931): 302–307.

———. "A Constructive Force in Race Relations." *Southern Workman* 53 (Oct. 1924): 442–44.

Ellis, Ann Wells. "The Commission on Interracial Cooperation, 1919–1944: Its Activities and Results." PhD diss., Georgia State University, 1975.

———. "A Crusade against 'Wretched Attitudes': The Commission on Interracial Coop-eration's Activities in Atlanta." *Atlanta Historical Journal* 23 (Spring 1973): 21–44.

Ellis, Mark. *Race, War, and Surveillance: African Americans and the United States Gov-ernment during World War I.* Bloomington: University of Indiana Press, 2001.

Ellison, Ralph. *Shadow and Act.* New York: Vintage, 1972.

Evans, Maurice S. "International Conference on the Negro." *Journal of the Royal African Society* 11 (July 1912): 416–29.

Ezra, Michael, ed. *Civil Rights Movement: People and Perspectives.* Santa Barbara, Calif.: ABC-CLIO, 2009.

Fairclough, Adam. "'Being in the Field of Education and also Being a Negro . . . Seems . . . Tragic': Black Teachers in the Jim Crow South." *Journal of American History* 87 (June 2000): 65–91.

———. *A Class of Their Own: Black Teachers in the Segregated South.* Cambridge, Mass.: Harvard University Press, 2007.

———. *Race and Democracy: The Civil Rights Struggle in Louisiana, 1915–1972.* 2nd ed. Athens: University of Georgia Press, 2008.

———. "Tuskegee's Robert R. Moton and the Travails of the Early Black College Presi-dent." *Journal of Blacks in Higher Education* 31 (Spring 2001): 94–105.

"Federal Power to End Lynching?" *Survey* 51 (Nov. 15, 1923): 232–33.

Feldman, Glenn, ed. *The Disfranchisement Myth: Poor Whites and Suffrage Restriction in Alabama.* Athens: University of Georgia Press, 2004.

———. *Reading Southern History: Essays on Interpreters and Interpretations.* Tuscaloosa: University of Alabama Press, 2001.

Ferrell, Claudine L. *Nightmare and Dream: Antilynching in Congress, 1917–1922.* New York: Garland, 1986.

Fish, John O. "Southern Methodism and Accommodation of the Negro, 1902–1915." *Journal of Negro History* 55 (July 1970): 200–214.

Fisher, Donald, and Theresa R. Richardson, eds. *The Development of the Social Sciences in the United States and Canada: The Role of Philanthropy.* New York: Ablex, 1999.

Fisher, Isaac. "Multiplying Dollars for Negro Education." *Journal of Social Forces* 1 (Jan. 1923): 149–53.

Fitzpatrick, Vincent. *Gerald W. Johnson: From Southern Liberal to National Conscience.* Baton Rouge: Louisiana State University Press, 2002.

Five Letters of the University Commission on Southern Race Questions. Charlottesville, Va.: Michie, 1927.

Foley, Barbara. "Jean Toomer's Sparta." *American Literature* 67 (Dec. 1995): 747–75.

Fraser, Walter J., and Winfred B. Moore, eds. *From the Old South to the New: Essays on the Transitional South.* Westport: Greenwood Press, 1981.

Frazier, Edward Franklin. "Is the Negro Family a Unique Sociological Unit?" *Opportunity* 5 (June 1927): 165–68.

———. "The Negro and Non-Resistance." *Crisis* 27 (March 1924): 213–14.

———. "The Negro Family." *Annals of the American Academy of Political and Social Science* 130 (Nov. 1928): 21–25.

———. "The Pathology of Race Prejudice." *Forum* 78 (June 1927): 856–62.

———. Review of *The Basis of Racial Adjustment*, by T. J. Woofter Jr. *Social Forces* 4 (Dec. 1925): 442–44.

———. Review of *Negro Problems in Cities*, by T. J. Woofter Jr. *American Journal of Sociology* 34 (Jan. 1928): 737–38.

———. "Social Work in Race Relations." *Crisis* 27 (April 1924): 252–54.

———. "Social Equality and the Negro." *Opportunity* 3 (June 1925): 165–68.

———. "Three Scourges of the Negro Family." *Opportunity* 4 (July 1926): 210–11, 234.

———. "Training Colored Social Workers in the South." *Social Forces* 1 (May 1923): 445–46.

Fredrickson, George M. *The Black Image in the White Mind: The Debate on Afro-American Character and Destiny, 1817–1914.* New York: Harper & Row, 1971.

———. *The Black Image in the White Mind: The Debate on Afro-American Character and Destiny, 1817–1914.* Middletown: Wesleyan University Press, 1987.

Friedman, Lawrence J. "The Search for Docility: Racial Thought in the White South, 1861–1917." *Phylon* 31 (3rd Qtr. 1970): 313–23.

Friedman, Lawrence J., and Mark D. McGarvie, eds. *Charity, Philanthropy, and Civility in American History.* Cambridge: Cambridge University Press, 2003.

Frissell, Sydney D. "The Farmer and Cooperation." *Social Forces* 7 (Sept. 1928): 171.

Fry, Charles Luther. "The Negro in the United States: A Statistical Statement." *American Academy of Political and Social Science* 140 (Nov. 1928): 26–35.

Frystak, Shannon Lee. *Our Minds on Our Freedom: Women and the Struggle for Black Equality in Louisiana, 1924–1967.* Baton Rouge: Louisiana State University Press, 2009.

Gasman, Marybeth. "W. E. B. Du Bois and Charles S. Johnson: Differing Views on the

Role of Philanthropy in Higher Education." *History of Education Quarterly* 42 (Winter 2002): 493–516.

Gatewood, Willard B. "Embattled Scholar: Howard W. Odum and the Fundamentalists, 1925–1927." *Journal of Southern History.* 31 (Nov. 1965): 375–92.

"Georgia Declares War on Peonage." *Literary Digest* 69 (May 14, 1921): 17–18.

"Georgia Women Inaugurate Important Health Work." *Journal of Social Forces* 3 (March 1925): 494.

"Georgia's Body-Blow at Mob Murder." *Literary Digest* 91 (Dec. 4, 1926): 10.

"Georgia's Death Farm." *Literary Digest* 69 (April 16, 1921): 13–14.

"Georgia's Indictment." *Survey* 46 (May 7, 1921): 183, 190.

Gershenhorn, Jerry. *Melville Herskovits and the Racial Politics of Knowledge.* Lincoln: University of Nebraska Press, 2004.

Gerster, Patrick, and Nicholas Cords, eds. *Myth and Southern History. Vol. 2: The New South.* Urbana: University of Illinois Press, 1989.

Giddings, Franklin H. *The Elements of Sociology.* New York: Macmillan, 1918.

———. *Scientific Study of Human Society.* New York: Macmillan, 1924.

———. "Social Self Control." *Political Science Quarterly* 24 (Dec. 1909): 569–88.

———. *Studies in the Theory of Human Society.* New York: Macmillan, 1922.

Giddings, Paula J. *Ida: A Sword among Lions.* New York: Amistad, 2008.

Gilmore, Glenda Elizabeth. *Defying Dixie: The Radical Roots of Civil Rights, 1919–1950.* New York: Norton, 2008.

———. *Gender and Jim Crow: Women and the Politics of White Supremacy in North Carolina, 1896–1920.* Chapel Hill: University of North Carolina Press, 1996.

Gilpin, Patrick J., and Marybeth Gasman. *Charles S. Johnson: Leadership beyond the Veil in the Age of Jim Crow.* Albany: SUNY Press, 2003.

Ginzburg, Ralph. *100 Years of Lynchings.* New York: Lancer, 1962.

Gladney, Margaret Rose, ed. *How Am I to Be Heard? Letters of Lillian Smith.* Chapel Hill: University of North Carolina Press, 1993.

Godshalk, David Fort. *Veiled Visions: The 1906 Atlanta Race Riot and the Reshaping of American Race Relations.* Chapel Hill: University of North Carolina Press, 2005.

Goggin, Jacqueline Anne. *Carter G. Woodson: A Life in Black History.* Baton Rouge: Louisiana State University Press, 1997.

Goodstein, Anita Shafer. "A Rare Alliance: African American and White Women in the Tennessee Elections of 1919 and 1920." *Journal of Southern History* 64 (May 1998): 219–46.

Gordon, Leah. "'Data and Not Trouble': The Rockefeller Foundation and the Social Science of Race Relations, 1926–1963" (2009). http://aapf.org/wp-content/uploads/2009/05/gordon-chapter-1-final.pdf.

Gossett, Thomas F. *Race: The History of an Idea in America.* New ed. New York: Oxford University Press, 1997.

"Governor Dorsey Stirs Up Georgia." *Literary Digest* 69 (June 4, 1921): 19.

Graham, Stephen. *Children of the Slaves.* London: Macmillan, 1920.

Grant, Donald L. *The Way It Was in the South: The Black Experience in Georgia.* Athens: University of Georgia Press, 1993.

Grantham, Dewey W. *Hoke Smith and the Politics of the New South.* Baton Rouge: Louisiana State University Press, 1967.

———. "The Regional Imagination: Social Scientists and the American South." *Journal of Southern History* 34 (Feb. 1968): 3–32.

———. *The South in Modern America: A Region At Odds*. New York: HarperCollins, 1994.

Greenwood, Janette Thomas. *Bittersweet Legacy: The Black and White "Better Classes" in Charlotte, 1850–1910*. Chapel Hill: University of North Carolina Press, 1994.

"Growing Sentiment against Mob Action." *Journal of Social Forces* 1 (Sept. 1923): 589.

Gruening, Ernest, ed. *These United States*. 2nd series. New York: Boni & Liveright, 1924.

Gudza, Henry P. "Labor Department's First Program to Assist Black Workers." *Monthly Labor Review* 105 (June 1982): 39–44.

Guterl, Matthew Pratt. *The Color of Race in America, 1900–1940*. Cambridge, Mass.: Harvard University Press, 2001.

H. C. H. [Helen C. Harris]. "A Community and a School." *Journal of Negro Education* 1 (Oct. 1932): 430–33.

H. J. S. [Herbert J. Seligmann]. Review of *Negro Migration*. *Freeman* 3 (April 20, 1921): 141–42.

Hahn, Steven. *A Nation under Our Feet: Black Political Struggles in the Rural South from Slavery to the Great Migration*. Cambridge, Mass.: Harvard University Press, 2003.

Hale, Grace Elizabeth. *Making Whiteness: The Culture of Segregation in the South, 1890–1940*. New York: Pantheon, 1998.

Hall, Jacquelyn Dowd. "Broadus Mitchell: Economic Historian of the South." In *Reading Southern History: Essays on Interpreters and Interpretations*, ed. Glenn Feldman, 25–31. Tuscaloosa: University of Alabama Press, 2001.

———. "The Long Civil Rights Movement and the Political Uses of the Past." *Journal of American History* 91 (March 2005): 1233–63.

———. *Revolt against Chivalry: Jessie Daniel Ames and the Women's Campaign against Lynching*. Rev. ed. New York: Columbia University Press, 1993.

———."Women Writers, the 'Southern Front,' and the Dialectical Imagination." *Journal of Southern History* 69 (Feb. 2003): 3–38.

———. "'You Must Remember This': Autobiography as Social Critique." *Journal of American History* 85 (Sept. 1998): 439–65.

Hall, Randal L. *William Louis Poteat: A Leader of the Progressive Era South*. Lexington: University of Kentucky Press, 2000.

Hammond, Lily Hardy. *In Black and White: An Interpretation of the South*. Ed. Elna C. Green. Athens: University of Georgia Press, 2008; first pub. 1914.

———. *Southern Women and Racial Adjustment*. Lynchburg, Va.: J. P. Bell, 1917.

Hankins, Frank H. *The Racial Basis of Civilization: A Critique of the Nordic Doctrine*. New York: A. A. Knopf, 1926.

Hargis, Peggy G. "Beyond the Marginality Thesis: The Acquisition and Loss of Land by African Americans in Georgia, 1880–1930." *Agricultural History* 72 (Spring 1998): 241–62.

Harlan, Louis R. *Separate and Unequal: Public School Campaigns and Racism in the Southern Seaboard States, 1901–1915*. Chapel Hill: University of North Carolina Press, 1958.

Harris, Abram L. "Economic Foundations of American Race Division." *Social Forces* 5 (March 1927): 468–78.

Harris, Carl V. *Political Power in Birmingham, 1874–1921.* Knoxville: University of Tennessee Press, 1977.

———. "Stability and Change in Discrimination against Black Public Schools: Birmingham, Alabama, 1871–1931." *Journal of Southern History* 51 (Aug. 1985): 375–416.

Harris, J. William. *Deep Souths: Delta, Piedmont, and Sea Island Society.* Baltimore: Johns Hopkins University Press, 2001.

Harris, Joel Chandler. *Life of Henry W. Grady, Including His Writings and Speeches.* Rahway, N.J.: W. L. Mershon, 1890.

Harrison, Alferdteen, ed. *Black Exodus: The Great Migration from the American South.* Jackson: University of Mississippi Press, 1991.

Harvey, Paul. *Freedom's Coming: Religious Culture and the Shaping of the South from the Civil War through the Civil Rights Era.* Chapel Hill: University of North Carolina Press, 2005.

Haygood, Atticus G. *Our Brother in Black: His Freedom and His Future.* New York: Phillips & Hunt, 1881.

Haywood, Harry. "The Crisis of the Jim-Crow Nationalism of the Negro Bourgeoisie." *Communist* 10 (April 1931): 330–38.

Henderson, Alexa Benson. "Heman E. Perry and Black Enterprise in Atlanta, 1908–1925." *Business History Review* 61 (Summer 1987): 216–42.

Herskovits, Melville J. *The American Negro.* New York: Alfred A. Knopf, 1928.

———. "Race Relations in the United States, 1928." *American Journal of Sociology* 34 (May 1929): 1129–39.

———. Review of *Negro Problems in Cities,* by T. J. Woofter Jr. *Journal of the American Statistical Association* 23 (Sept. 1928): 352–54.

Higginbotham, Evelyn Brooks. *Righteous Discontent: The Women's Movement in the Black Baptist Church, 1880–1920* Cambridge, Mass.: Harvard University Press, 1993.

Higgs, Robert. "Accumulation of Property by Southern Blacks before World War I." *American Economic Review* 72 (Sept. 1982): 725–37.

Hill, Robert A., ed. *The Marcus Garvey and Universal Negro Improvement Association Papers.* Vol. 5. Berkeley: University of California Press, 1986.

Hill, Walter B. "Negro Education in the South." *Annals of the American Academy of Political and Social Science* 22 (Sept. 1903): 76–85.

———. "A Rural Survey of Clarke County, Georgia, with Special Reference to the Negroes." *Bulletin of the University of Georgia.* 15, no. 3 (March 1915).

Hine, Darlene Clark. "Carter G. Woodson, White Philanthropy, and Negro Historiography." *History Teacher* 19 (May 1986): 405–25.

Historical Statistics of the United States. Vol. 1. Washington, D.C.: U.S. Government Printing Office, 1975.

Holloway, Jonathan Scott. *Confronting the Veil: Abram Harris Jr., E. Franklin Frazier, and Ralph Bunche, 1919–1941.* Chapel Hill: University of North Carolina Press, 2002.

Hovenkamp, Howard. "Social Science and Segregation before *Brown.*" *Duke Law Journal* 1985 (June–Sept. 1985): 624–72.

Hubbard, Kate. "Are There Any Blind Black Babies?" *Survey* 52 (April 15, 1924): 92–94.

Huelfer, Evan Andrew. *The "Casualty Issue" in American Military Practice.* New York: Greenwood, 2003.

Hutchison, Janet. "Better Homes and Gullah." *Agricultural History* 67 (Spring 1993): 102–18.

Inscoe, John C., ed. *Georgia in Black and White: Explorations in the Race Relations of a Southern State, 1865–1950.* Athens: University of Georgia Press, 1994.

"Inter-Racial Activities in the South." *Crisis* 21 (April 1921): 249–50.

"Inter-Racial Commission in Annual Meeting Emphasizes Anti-Lynching Crusade." *Journal of Social Forces* 3 (May 1925): 712–13.

"Inter-racial Committees." *Southern Workman* 49 (Jan. 1920): 4–5.

Jackson, John P., Jr. *Social Scientists for Social Justice: Making the Case against Segregation.* New York: New York University Press, 2001.

Jackson, Kenneth T. *The Ku Klux Klan in the City, 1915–1930.* New York: Oxford University Press, 1967.

Jackson, Walter A.. "Gunnar Myrdal and American Racial Liberalism." PhD diss., Harvard University, 1983.

———. *Gunnar Myrdal and America's Conscience: Social Engineering and Racial Liberalism, 1938–1987.* Chapel Hill: University of North Carolina Press, 1990.

James, Felix."Robert Russa Moton and the Whispering Gallery after World War I." *Journal of Negro History* 62 (July 1977): 235–42

Janken, Kenneth Robert. *White: The Biography of Walter White, Mr. NAACP.* New York: New Press, 2003.

John F. Slater Fund, *Proceedings and Reports for Year Ending September 30, 1919.* New York: 1919.

Johnson, Charles S., et al. *The Negro in American Civilization: A Study of Negro Life and Race Relations in the Light of Social Research.* London: Constable, 1931.

Johnson, Donald. "W. E. B. Du Bois, Thomas Jesse Jones and the Struggle for Social Education, 1900–1930." *Journal of Negro History* 85 (Summer 2000): 71–95

Johnson, Guion Griffis. *A Social History of the Sea Islands with Special Reference to St. Helena Island, South Carolina.* Chapel Hill: University of North Carolina Press, 1930.

Johnson, Guy B. *Folk Culture on St. Helena Island, South Carolina.* Chapel Hill: University of North Carolina Press, 1929.

———. "The Gullah Dialect Revisited: A Note on Linguistic Acculturation." *Journal of Black Studies* 10 (June 1980): 417–24.

———. "The Isolated Negro Community of St. Helena Island, South Carolina." *Bulletin of the Society for Social Research,* Jan. 1937, 1, 7.

———. "The Negro Migration and Its Consequences." *Journal of Social Forces* 2 (March 1924): 404–408.

———. "Recent Literature on the Negro." *Journal of Social Forces* 3 (Jan. 1925): 316–17.

———. "A Sociological Interpretation of the New Ku Klux Movement." *Journal of Social Forces* 1 (May 1923): 440–45.

Johnson, Guy B., and Guion G. Johnson. *Research in Service to Society: The First Fifty Years of the Institute for Research in Social Science at the University of North Carolina.* Chapel Hill: University of North Carolina Press, 1980.

Johnson, James Weldon. "Lynching–America's National Disgrace." *Current History* 19 (Jan. 1924): 596–601.

Johnson, Joan Marie. "The Shape of the Movement to Come: Women, Religion, Episcopalians, and the Interracial Movement in 1920s South Carolina." In *Warm Ashes:*

Issues in Southern History at the Dawn of the Twenty-First Century, ed. Winfred B. Moore Jr. et al., 201–23. Columbia: University of South Carolina Press, 2003.

Johnson, Kimberley. *Reforming Jim Crow: Southern Politics and State in the Age before Brown.* New York: Oxford University Press, 2010.

Johnston, Harry. *The Negro in the New World.* London: Methuen, 1910.

Jones, M. Ashby. "The Approach to the South's Race Question." *Journal of Social Forces* 1 (Nov. 1922): 40–41.

Jones, Thomas Jesse. "The Alley Homes of Washington." *Survey* 28 (Oct. 19, 1912): 67–69.

———. *Educational Adaptations: Report of Ten Years' Work of the Phelps-Stokes Fund, 1910–1920.* New York: Phelps Stokes Fund, 1920.

———. *Essentials of Civilization: A Study in Social Values.* New York: Henry Holt, 1929.

———. *Four Essentials of Education.* New York: Charles Scribner's Sons, 1926.

———, ed. *Negro Education: A Study of the Private and Higher Schools for Colored People in the United States.* 2 vols. Bureau of Education, Department of Interior, Bulletins no. 38 and 39. Washington, D.C.: U.S. Government Printing Office, 1917.

———. "Negro Population in the United States." *Annals of the American Academy of Political and Social Science* 49 (Sept. 1913): 1–9.

———. *Negroes and the Census of 1910.* Hampton, Va.: Hampton Institute Press, 1912.

———. *Social Studies in the Hampton Curriculum.* Hampton, Va.: Hampton Institute Press, 1908.

———. *The Sociology of a New York City Block.* New York: Columbia University Press, 1904.

Jordan, Harvie. "Cotton in the Southern Agricultural Economy." *Annals of the American Academy of Political and Social Science* 35 (Jan. 1910): 1–7.

Joshi, S. T., ed. *Documents of American Prejudice.* New York: Basic Books, 1999.

Judson, Sarah Mercer. "Solving the Girl Problem: Race, Womanhood, and Leisure in Atlanta during World War I." In *Women Shaping the South: Creating and Confronting Change,* ed. Angela Boswell and Judith N. McArthur, 152–73. Columbia: University of Missouri Press, 2006.

Karl, Barry D. "Presidential Planning and Social Science Research: Mr. Hoover's Experts." *Perspectives in American History* 3 (1969): 345–409.

Karl, Barry D., and Stanley N. Katz. "The American Private Philanthropic Foundation and the Public Sphere, 1890–1930." *Minerva* 19 (Summer 1981): 236–70.

Katz, Michael B., and Thomas J. Sugrue, eds. *W. E. B. Du Bois, Race, and the City.* Philadelphia: University of Pennsylvania Press, 1998.

Kelsey, Carl. Review of *Negro Migration.* by T. J. Woofter Jr. *Annals of the American Academy of Political and Social Science* 94 (March 1921): 216.

Kennedy, Louise V. *The Negro Peasant Turns Cityward.* New York: Columbia University Press, 1930.

Kennedy, Thomas C. "The Last Days at Southland." *Southern Friend* 8 (Spring 1986): 1–19.

———. "Southland College: The Society of Friends and Black Education in Arkansas." *Arkansas Historical Quarterly* 42 (Autumn 1983): 207–24.

Kerlin, Robert T. *The Voice of the Negro, 1919.* New York: E. P. Dutton, 1920.

"The Kerlin Case." *Southern Workman* 50 (Dec. 1921): 529–32.

Kesler, J. L. "In Justice to Waco." *Nation* 103 (Dec. 28, 1916): 609.

Kettleborough, Charles. "Amendments to State Constitutions, 1919–1921." *American Political Science Review* 16 (May 1922): 245–76.

Killian, Lewis M. *White Southerners.* New York: Random House, 1970.

Kincheloe, Samuel C. Review of *Negro Problems in Cities,* by T. J. Woofter Jr. *Journal of Religion* 9 (Jan. 1929): 150–51.

King, Kenneth James. *Pan-Africanism and Education: A Study of Race, Philanthropy and Education in the Southern States of America and East Africa.* Oxford: Clarendon Press, 1971.

Kirby, Jack Temple. *Darkness at the Dawning: Race and Reform in the Progressive South.* Philadelphia: J. B. Lippincott, 1972.

Kiser, Clyde Vernon. *Sea Island to City: A Study of St. Helena Islanders in Harlem and Other Urban Centers.* New York: Columbia University Press, 1932.

Klarman, Michael J. *From Jim Crow to Civil Rights: The Supreme Court and the Struggle for Racial Equality.* New York: Oxford University Press, 2004.

Kneebone, John T. *Southern Liberal Journalists and the Issue of Race, 1920–1944.* Chapel Hill: University of North Carolina Press, 1985.

Kuhn, Clifford M., et al., *Living Atlanta: An Oral History of the City, 1914–1948.* Athens: University of Georgia Press, 1990.

Kyriakoudes, Louis M. "Southern Black Rural-Urban Migration in the Era of the Great Migration: Nashville and Middle Tennessee, 1890–1930." *Agricultural History* 72 (Spring 1998): 341–51.

Lane, Russell A. "The Legal Trend toward Increased Provisions for Negro Education in the United States between 1920 and 1930." *Journal of Negro Education* 1 (Oct. 1932): 396–99.

Lange, Werner J. "W. E. B. Du Bois and the First Scientific Study of Afro-America." *Phylon* 44 (1983): 135–46.

Lasker, Bruno. *Race Attitudes in Children.* New York: Henry Holt, 1929.

Laura Spelman Rockefeller Memorial. *Report for 1924; Report for 1925; Report for 1927 and 1928.* New York: 1925, 1926, & 1929.

Leidholdt, Alexander S. *Editor for Justice: The Life of Louis I. Jaffe.* Baton Rouge: Louisiana State University Press, 2002.

Leloudis, James L. *Schooling in the New South: Pedagogy, Self, and Society in North Carolina, 1880–1920.* Chapel Hill: University of North Carolina Press, 1999.

Levy, Eugene. *James Weldon Johnson: Black Leader, Black Voice.* Chicago: University of Chicago Press, 1973.

Lewinson, Paul. *Race, Class, and Party: A History of Negro Suffrage and White Politics in the South.* New York: Oxford University Press, 1932.

Lewis, David Levering. *W. E. B. Du Bois: Biography of a Race, 1868–1919.* New York: Henry Holt, 1993.

———. *W. E. B. Du Bois: The Fight for Equality and the American Century, 1919–1963.* New York: Henry Holt, 2000.

Link, Arthur S., and Rembert W. Patrick, eds. *Writing Southern History: Essays in Historiography in Honor of Fletcher M. Green.* Baton Rouge: Louisiana State University Press, 1965.

Link, William A. *The Paradox of Southern Progressivism, 1880–1930.* Chapel Hill: University of North Carolina Press, 1992.

Lisio, Donald J. *Hoover, Blacks, and Lily-Whites: A Study of Southern Strategies.* Chapel Hill: University of North Carolina Press, 1985.

Locke, Alain. "The Boxed Compass of Our Race Relations. North and South: The Washington Conference on the American Negro." *Southern Workman* 58 (Jan. 1929): 51–58.

———, ed. *The New Negro.* New York: Boni, 1925.

Logan, Rayford W. "Educational Segregation in the North." *Journal of Negro Education* 2 (Jan. 1933): 65–67.

Loveland, Anne C. *Lillian Smith: A Southerner Confronting the South.* Baton Rouge: Louisiana State University Press, 1986.

Lowry, Mark, II. "Population and Race in Mississippi, 1940–1960." *Annals of the Association of American Geographers* 61 (Sept. 1971): 576–88.

Luker, Ralph E. *The Social Gospel in Black and White: American Racial Reform, 1885–1912.* Chapel Hill: University of North Carolina Press, 1991.

"Lynching Decreasing." *Literary Digest* 90 (July 24, 1926): 30.

M. C. H. "More Illumination for Understanding the Processes of Integration" (review of *Southern Race Progress*). *Phylon* 18 (3rd Qtr. 1957): 315.

MacLean, Nancy. *Behind the Mask of Chivalry: The Making of the Second Ku Klux Klan.* New York: Oxford University Press, 1994.

Margo, Robert. "Teacher Salaries in Black and White: The South in 1910." *Explorations in Economic History* 21 (July 1984): 306–26.

Martin, George Madden. "Race Cooperation." *McClure's Magazine,*54 (Oct. 1922): 9–20.

Martin, Robert F. *Howard Kester and the Struggle for Social Justice in the South, 1904–77.* Charlottesville: University Press of Virginia, 1991.

Matthews, John Michael. "The Georgia 'Race Strike' of 1909." *Journal of Southern History* 40 (Nov. 1974): 613–30.

———. "Virginius Dabney, John Temple Graves, and What Happened to Southern Liberalism." *Mississippi Quarterly* 45 (Fall 1992): 405–20.

Mays, Benjamin E. *Born to Rebel: An Autobiography.* Athens: University of Georgia Press, 1987.

Mazzari, Louis. *Southern Modernist: Arthur Raper from the New Deal to the Cold War.* Baton Rouge: Louisiana State University Press, 2006.

McCluskey, Audrey Thomas, and Elaine M. Smith, eds. *Mary McLeod Bethune: Building a Better World, Essays and Selected Documents.* Bloomington: Indiana University Press, 1999.

McCulloch, J. E., ed. *"Distinguished Service" Citizenship.* Nashville: Southern Sociological Conference, 1919.

McDonough, Julia Anne. "Men and Women of Good Will: A History of the Commission on Interracial Cooperation and the Southern Regional Council, 1919–1954." PhD diss., University of Virginia, 1993.

McFarland, David D. "Adding Machines and Logarithms: Franklin H. Giddings and Computation for the Exact Science of Sociology." *Social Science Computer Review* 22 (May 2004): 249–55.

McGill, Ralph. *The South and the Southerner.* Boston: Little, Brown, 1964.

McGuinn, Henry J. Review of *Southern Race Progress*. *Millbank Memorial Fund Quarterly* 36 (Jan. 1958): 98–102.

McKee, James B. *Sociology and the Race Problem: The Failure of a Perspective.* Urbana: University of Illinois Press, 1993.

McMillen, Neil R. *Dark Journey: Black Mississippians in the Age of Jim Crow.* Urbana: University of Illinois Press, 1990.

Meyer, Stephen Grant. *As Long as They Don't Move Next Door: Segregation and Racial Conflict in American Neighborhoods.* Lanham, Md: Rowman and Littlefield, 2000.

Mikkelsen, Vincent. "Coming from Battle to Face a War: The Lynching of Black Soldiers in the World War I Era." PhD diss., Florida State University, 2007.

Miles, R. W. "The North Carolina Inter-Racial Committee." *Journal of Social Forces* 1 (Jan. 1923): 154–55.

———. "The South Carolina Inter-Racial Committee." *Journal of Social Forces* 1 (Jan. 1923): 155.

———. "The Virginia Inter-Racial Committee." *Journal of Social Forces* 1 (Jan. 1923): 153–54.

Miller, E. E. "What Southerners Think of the Dyer Bill." *Outlook* 132 (Dec. 6, 1922): 598–99.

Miller, Glenn T. *Piety and Profession: American Protestant Theological Education, 1870–1970.* Grand Rapids: Wm. B. Eerdmans, 2007.

Miller, Kelly. "The Harvest of Race Prejudice." *Survey Graphic* 6 (March 1925): 682–83, 711.

———. "The Negro as a Workingman." *American Mercury* 6 (Nov. 1925): 310–13.

———. *Race Adjustment: Essays on the Negro in America.* New York: Neale, 1908.

———. Review of *Negro Migration,* by T. J. Woofter Jr. *American Journal of Sociology* 27 (Sept. 1921): 256–58.

Miller, Zane L. Review of *Negro Problems in Cities,* by T. J. Woofter Jr. *American Journal of Sociology* 76 (May 1971): 1157–59.

Milton, George Fort. "The Impeachment of Judge Lynch." *Virginia Quarterly Review* 8 (April 1932): 247–56.

Minutes of the University Commission on Southern Race Questions. N.p., ca. 1918.

Mitchell, Broadus. Review of *Negro Education. Sewanee Review* 26 (April 1918): 246–48.

Mitchell, Samuel C. "The Nationalization of Southern Sentiment." *South Atlantic Quarterly* 7 (April 1908): 107–13.

Mjagkij, Nina. *Light in the Darkness: African Americans and the YMCA, 1852–1946.* Lexington: University of Kentucky Press, 1994.

———, ed. *Organizing Black America: An Encyclopedia of African American Associations.* New York: Garland, 2001.

"Mob Violence a Federal Offense." *Outlook* 130 (Feb. 22, 1922): 285–86.

Morse, Josiah. "The University Commission on Southern Race Questions." *South Atlantic Quarterly* 19 (Oct. 1920): 302–10.

Montgomery, Rebecca S. *The Politics of Education in the New South: Women and Reform in Georgia, 1890–1930.* Baton Rouge: Louisiana State University Press, 2006.

Moton, Robert Russa. "The South and the Lynching Evil." *South Atlantic Quarterly* 18 (July 1919): 191–96.

———. *What the Negro Thinks.* London: Student Christian Movement, 1929.

Muntz, E. E. *Race Contact.* New York: Century, 1927.

———. Review of *Negro Problems in Cities,* by T. J. Woofter Jr. *Journal of Educational Sociology* 4 (Oct. 1930): 115–17.

Murphy, Edgar Gardner. *The Basis of Ascendancy.* New York: Longmans, Green, 1909.

———. *Problems of the Present South*. London: Macmillan, 1904.

Myrdal, Gunnar. *An American Dilemma: The Negro Problem and American Democracy*. New York: Harper & Brothers, 1944.

Myers, Martha. *Race, Labor, and Punishment in the New South*. Columbus: Ohio State University Press, 1998.

National Association for the Advancement of Colored People. *Burning at Stake in the United States*. New York: 1919; reprinted, Baltimore: 1986.

———. *Eleventh Annual Report*. New York: 1921.

National Interracial Conference. *Toward Interracial Cooperation: What Was Said at the First National Interracial Conference*. New York: Federal Council of Churches, 1926.

Negro Housing: Report of the Committee on Negro Housing of the President's Conference on Home Building and Home Ownership. Ed. John M. Cries and James Ford. Washington, D.C.: National Capital Press, 1932.

Negro Migration in 1916–17. Ed. James H. Dillard. Division of Negro Economics, Department of Labor special bulletin. Washington, D.C.: U.S. Government Printing Office, 1919.

Negro Population in the United States, 1790–1915. Bureau of the Census. Washington, D.C.: U.S. Government Printing Office, 1919.

"The Negro's Status Declared by the President." *Literary Digest* 71 (Nov. 19, 1921): 7–9.

Newbold, N. C. "Common Schools for Negroes in the South." *Annals of the American Academy of Political and Social Science* 140 (Nov. 1928): 209–23.

Newby, I. A. *Jim Crow's Defense: Anti-Negro Thought in America, 1900–1930*. Baton Rouge: University of Louisiana Press, 1965.

Newman, Harvey K., and Glenda Crunk. "Religious Leaders in the Aftermath of Atlanta's 1906 Race Riot." *Georgia Historical Quarterly* 92 (Winter 2008): 460–85.

Ng, Kenneth. "Wealth Redistribution, Race, and Southern Public Schools, 1880–1910." *Education Policy Analysis Archives* 9 (May 13, 2001). http://epaa.asu.edu/ojs/article /viewFile/345/471.

Northen, William J., ed. *Men of Mark in Georgia*. Atlanta: A. B. Caldwell, 1910.

O'Brien, Thomas V. "Perils of Accommodation: The Case of Joseph W. Holley." *American Educational Research Journal* 44 (Dec. 2007): 806–52.

Odum, Howard W. *American Sociology: The Story of Sociology in the United States through 1950*. New York: Longmans, Green, 1951.

———. "Fundamental Principles Underlying Inter-Racial Cooperation." *Journal of Social Forces* 1 (March 1923): 282–85.

———. *Man's Quest for Social Guidance*. New York: Henry Holt, 1927.

———. "Negro Children in the Public Schools of Philadelphia." *Annals of the American Academy of Political and Social Science* 49 (Sept. 1913): 186–208.

———. *Rainbow Round My Shoulder: The Blue Trail of Black Ulysses*. Bloomington: Indiana University Press, 2006; first pub. 1928.

———, ed. *Southern Pioneers in Social Interpretation*. Chapel Hill: University of North Carolina Press, 1925.

Odum, Howard W., and D. W. Willard, *State Systems of Public Welfare*. Chapel Hill: University of North Carolina Press, 1925.

Odum, Howard W., and Guy B. Johnson, *The Negro and His Songs: A Study of the Typical Negro Songs of the South*. Chapel Hill: University of North Carolina Press, 1925.

———. *Negro Workaday Songs*. Chapel Hill: University of North Carolina Press, 1926.

Oney, Steve. *And the Dead Shall Rise: The Murder of Mary Phagan and the Lynching of Leo Frank*. New York: Vintage, 2004.

Ortiz, Paul. *Emancipation Betrayed: The Hidden History of Black Organizing and White Violence in Florida from Reconstruction to the Bloody Election of 1920*. Berkeley: University of California Press, 2005.

Ovington, Mary White. "Revisiting the South: Changes in Twenty-One Years." *Crisis* 34 (April 1927): 42–43, 60–61.

Palmer, Dewey H. "Moving North: Migration of Negroes During World War I." *Phylon* 28 (1st Qtr. 1967): 52–62.

Palmer, Niall. *The Twenties in America: Politics and History*. Edinburgh: University of Edinburgh Press, 2006.

Park, Robert E. "The Bases of Race Prejudice." *Annals of the American Academy of Political and Social Science* 140 (Nov. 1928): 11–20.

———. "The Concept of Social Distance." *Journal of Applied Sociology* 8 (July–Aug. 1924): 339–44.

Park, Robert E., and Ernest W. Burgess. *Introduction to the Science of Sociology*. Chicago: University of Chicago Press, 1921.

Parsons, Elsie Clews. *Folk-Lore of the Sea Islands, South Carolina*. Cambridge, Mass.: American Folk-Lore Society, 1923.

Patler, Nicholas. *Jim Crow and the Wilson Administration: Protesting Federal Segregation in the Early Twentieth Century*. Boulder: University of Colorado Press, 2007.

Pascoe, Craig S., et al., eds. *The American South in the Twentieth Century*. Athens: University of Georgia Press, 2005.

Pearson, C. Chilton. "Race Relations in North Carolina: A Field Study of Moderate Opinion." *South Atlantic Quarterly* 23 (Jan. 1924): 1–9.

Perkins, Alfred. *Edwin Rogers Embree: The Julius Rosenwald Fund, Foundation Philanthropy, and American Race Relations*. Bloomington: Indiana University Press, 2011.

Peterson, Joseph, and C. W. Telford. "Results of Group and of Individual Tests Applied to the Practically Pure-Blood Negro Children on St. Helena Island." *Journal of Comparative Psychology* 11 (Dec. 1930): 115–44.

Peterson, Patti McGill. "Colonialism and Education: The Case of the Afro-American." *Comparative Education Review* 15 (June 1971): 146–57.

Phelps Stokes, Anson. *Negro Status and Race Relations in the United States, 1911–1946*. New York: Phelps-Stokes Fund, 1948.

Phelps-Stokes Fund. *Education for Life: Phelps-Stokes Fund and Thomas Jesse Jones. A Twenty-Fifth Anniversary, 1913–1937*. New York: ca. 1937.

Phillips, C. H. *From the Farm to the Bishopric: An Autobiography*. Nashville, Tenn.: Parthenon Press, 1932.

Pickens, William. *The New Negro: His Political, Civil and Mental Status and Related Essays*. New York: Neale, 1916.

Pilkington, Charles Kirk. "The Trials of Brotherhood: The Founding of the Commission on Interracial Cooperation." *Georgia Historical Quarterly* 69 (Spring 1985): 55–80.

Pilz, Jeffrey J. "The Beginnings of Organized Play for Black America: E. T. Attwell and the PRAA." *Journal of Negro History* 70 (Summer–Autumn 1985): 59–72.

Pitts, Timothy J. "Hugh M. Dorsey and 'The Negro in Georgia.'" *Georgia Historical Quarterly* 89 (Summer 2005): 185–212.

Platt, Anthony M. *E. Franklin Frazier Reconsidered.* New Brunswick: Rutgers University Press, 1991.

Platt, Anthony, and Susan Chandler. "Constant Struggle: E. Franklin Frazier and Black Social Work in the 1920s." *Social Work* 33 (July–Aug. 1988): 293–97.

Platt, Jennifer. *A History of Sociological Research Methods in America, 1920–1960.* Cambridge: Cambridge University Press, 1996.

Porterfield, A. W. Review of *Black Yeomanry,* by T. J. Woofter Jr. *Outlook* 155 (Aug. 20, 1930): 627.

Proceedings of the Eleventh Meeting of the Governors of the States of the Union Held at Salt Lake City, Utah, August 18–21, 1919. N.p, n.d.

Rabinowitz, Howard N. *Race Relations in the Urban South, 1865–1890.* New York: Oxford University Press, 1978.

Rable, George C. "The South and the Politics of Antilynching Legislation, 1920–1940." *Journal of Southern History* 51 (May 1985): 201–20.

Raper, Arthur. *The Tragedy of Lynching.* Chapel Hill: University of North Carolina Press, 1933.

Raushenbush, Winifred. *Robert E. Park: Biography of a Sociologist.* Durham, N.C.: Duke University Press, 1979.

Redfield, Robert. Review of *Black Yeomanry,* by Henry [*sic*] Woofter Jr. *Journal of American Sociology* 26 (March 1931): 829–31.

Reed, Ruth. *Negro Illegitimacy in New York City.* New York: Columbia University Press, 1926.

Rees, Richard W. *Shades of Difference: A History of Ethnicity in America.* Lanham, Md.: Rowman and Littlefield, 2007.

Reid, Ira De A. "Mirrors of Harlem–Investigations and Problems of America's Largest Colored Community." *Social Forces* 5 (June 1927): 628–34.

———. Review of *Negro Problems in Cities,* by T. J. Woofter Jr. *Opportunity* 6 (Sept. 1928): 277.

———. Review of *Black Yeomanry,* by T. J. Woofter Jr. *Opportunity* 8 (Nov. 1930): 342.

Report of the National Research Council for the Year July 1, 1927– June 30, 1928. Washington, D.C.: U.S. Government Printing Office, 1929.

Reuter, Edward B. *The American Race Problem, A Study of the Negro.* New York: Thomas Y. Crowell, 1927.

Rice, Arnold S. *The Ku Klux Klan in Politics.* Washington, D.C.: Public Affairs Press, 1962.

Robbins, Gerald. "Rossa B. Cooley and Penn School: Social Dynamo in a Rural Negro Subculture, 1901–1930." *Journal of Negro Education* 33 (Winter 1964): 43–51.

Robbins, Richard. *Sidelines Activist: Charles S. Johnson and the Struggle for Civil Rights.* Jackson: University Press of Mississippi, 1996.

"Robert Thomas Kerlin." *Journal of Negro History* 35 (April 1950): 230–32.

Robertson, Nancy Marie. *Christian Sisterhood, Race Relations, and the YWCA, 1906–46.* Urbana: University of Illinois Press, 2007.

Roediger, David R. *Working toward Whiteness: How America's Immigrants Became White.* New York: Basic Books, 2005.

Rolinson, Mary G. *Grassroots Garveyism: The Universal Negro Improvement Association in the Rural South, 1920–1927.* Chapel Hill: University of North Carolina Press, 2007.

Ross, Edward A. "The Causes of Race Superiority." *Annals of the American Academy of Political and Social Science* 18 (July 1901): 67–89.

Ross, Frank A. Review of *The Basis of Racial Adjustment*, by T. J. Woofter Jr. *Political Science Quarterly* 40 (Dec. 1925): 638–39.

Ross, Mary. "Where Lynching Is a Habit." *Survey* 49 (Feb. 15, 1923): 626–27.

Roucek, Joseph S. Review of *Races and Ethnic Groups in American Life*, by T. J. Woofter Jr. *Social Forces* 12 (Dec. 1933): 304–305.

Ryan, Garry D. "Disposition of AEF Records of World War I." *Military Affairs* 30 (Winter 1966–1967): 212–19.

Saint-Arnaud, Pierre, and Peter Feldstein. *African-American Pioneers of Sociology: A Critical History.* Toronto: University of Toronto Press, 2009.

Salmond, John A. *Miss Lucy of the CIO: The Life and Times of Lucy Randolph Mason.* Athens: University of Georgia Press, 1988.

———. *A Southern Rebel: The Life and Times of Aubrey Willis Williams, 1890–1965.* Chapel Hill: University of North Carolina Press, 1983.

Sanders, Lynn Moss. *Howard Odum's Folklore Odyssey: Transformation to Tolerance through African American Folk Studies.* Athens: University of Georgia Press, 2003.

Scally, Sister Anthony. "Phelps-Stokes Confidential Memorandum for the Trustees of the Phelps-Stokes Fund Regarding Dr. Carter G. Woodson's Attacks on Dr. Thomas Jesse Jones." *Journal of Negro History* 76 (Winter–Autumn 1991): 48–60.

Schultz, Mark. "Dream Realized? African American Landownership in Central Georgia between Reconstruction and World War Two." *Agricultural History* 72 (Spring 1998): 298–312.

Scott, Ann Firor. "After Suffrage: Southern Women in the 1920s." *Journal of Southern History* 30 (Aug. 1964): 298–318.

Scott, Emmett J. *The American Negro in the World War.* Chicago: Homewood Press, 1919.

———. *Negro Migration during the War.* New York: Oxford University Press, 1920.

Sealander, Judith. *Private Wealth and Public Life: Foundation Philanthropy and the Reshaping of American Social Policy from the Progressive Era to the New Deal.* Baltimore: Johns Hopkins University Press, 1997.

Selig, Diana. *Americans All: The Cultural Gifts Movement.* Cambridge, Mass.: Harvard University Press, 2008.

Seligmann, Herbert J. *The Negro Faces America.* New York: Harper, 1920.

Shapiro, Herbert. *White Violence and Black Response: From Reconstruction to Montgomery.* Amherst: University of Massachusetts Press, 1988.

Shenk, Gerald E. "Race, Manhood, and Manpower: Mobilizing Rural Georgia for World War I." *Georgia Historical Quarterly* 81 (Fall 1997): 622–62.

Sherman, Richard B. *The Republican Party and Black America: From McKinley to Hoover, 1896–1933.* Charlottesville: University of Virginia Press, 1973.

Shivers, Lyda Gordon. "Twentieth Century South-wide Civic and Lay Organizations for Human Welfare." In *The Walter Jackson Essays in Social Sciences,* ed. Vera Largent, 185–208. Greensboro: University of North Carolina, Woman's College, 1942.

Shofner, Jerrell H. "Judge Herbert Rider and the Lynching at Labelle." *Florida Historical Quarterly* 59 (Jan. 1981): 292–306.

———. "Postscript to the Martin Tabert Case: Peonage as Usual in the Florida Turpentine Camps." *Florida Historical Quarterly* 60 (oct. 1981): 161–73.

Shufeldt, R. W. *America's Greatest Problem: The Negro*. Philadelphia: F. A. Davis, 1915.

Simms, Ruthanna M. "Four Days at Southland Institute." *American Friend* (March 3, 1921): 165–66.

Simpson, Ida Harper. *Fifty Years of the Southern Sociological Society: Change and Continuity in a Professional Society*. Athens: University of Georgia Press, 1988.

Sims, F. W. "School Statistics from Mississippi." *Bulletin of Atlanta University* 163 (April 1906): 4.

Singal, Daniel J. *The War Within: From Victorian to Modernist Thought in the South, 1919–1945*. Chapel Hill: University of North Carolina Press, 1982.

Singh, Nikhil Pal. *Black Is a Country: Race and the Unfinished Struggle for Democracy*. Cambridge, Mass.: Harvard University Press, 2004.

Sledd, Andrew. "The Negro: Another View." *Atlantic Monthly* 90 (July 1902): 65–73.

Smith, Bolton. "The Negro in War-Time." *Public* 21 (Aug. 31, 1918): 1110–113.

Smith, J. Douglas. *Managing White Supremacy: Race, Politics, and Supremacy in Jim Crow Virginia*. Chapel Hill: University of North Carolina Press, 2002.

Smith, Mark M. *How Race Is Made: Slavery, Segregation, and the Senses*. Chapel Hill: University of North Carolina Press, 2006.

Smith, Patricia E. "Rhoda Kaufman: A Southern Progressive's Career, 1913–1956." *Atlanta Historical Bulletin* 18 (Spring–Summer 1973): 43–50.

Smith, S. L. *Builders of Goodwill: The Story of the State Agents of Negro Education in the South, 1910 to 1950*. Nashville: Tennessee Book Company, 1950.

Smith, William Benjamin. *The Color Line: A Brief in Behalf of the Unborn*. New York: McClure, 1905.

Snavely, Tipton Ray. *The Taxation of Negroes in Virginia*. Charlottesville: University of Virginia Press, 1916.

Sosna, Morton. *In Search of the Silent South: Southern Liberals and the Race Issue*. New York: Columbia University Press, 1977.

Soule, Sarah A. "Populism and Black Lynching in Georgia, 1890–1900." *Social Forces* 71 (Dec. 1992): 431–49.

Southern Commission on the Study of Lynching. *Lynchings and What They Mean*. Atlanta: 1931.

"Southern Press on the Georgia Lynching." *Literary Digest* 31 (July 15, 1905): 71–72.

"The South's Fight against Mob Murders." *Literary Digest* 84 (Jan. 17, 1925): 30–31.

Stanfield, John H. *Philanthropy and Jim Crow in American Social Science*. New York: Greenwood, 1985.

———. "The 'Negro Problem' within and beyond the Institutional Nexus of Pre–World War I Sociology." *Phylon* 43 (3rd Qtr. 1982): 187–201.

———. "Northern Money and Southern Bogus Elitism: Rockefeller Foundations and the Commission on Interracial Cooperation Movement, 1919–1929." *Journal of Ethnic Studies* 15 (Summer 1987): 1–22.

A Statement from Governor Hugh M. Dorsey as to the Negro in Georgia, April 22, 1921. N.p.

Steelman, John R. "A Study of Mob Action in the South." PhD diss., University of North Carolina, 1928.

Steffes, Tracy L. "Solving the 'Rural School Problem': New State Aid, Standards, and Supervision of Local Schools, 1900–1933." *History of Education Quarterly* 48 (May 2008): 181–220.

Stein, Judith. *The World of Marcus Garvey: Race and Class in Modern Society.* Baton Rouge: Louisiana State University Press, 1986.

Stewart, James B. "George Edmund Haynes and the Office of Negro Economics." In *A Different Vision: African American Economic Thought,* vol. 1, ed. Thomas D. Boston, 213–29. London: Routledge, 1997.

Stockley, Grif. *Blood in Their Eyes: The Elaine Race Massacres of 1919.* Fayetteville: University of Arkansas Press, 2001.

Stolberg, Benjamin. Review of *The Negro in American Civilization,* reprinted in *Crisis* 37 (Sept. 1930): 313.

Streitmatter, Rodger. "Defying the Klan: Three 1920s Newspapers Challenge the Most Powerful Nativist Movement in American History" (April 1996). http://list.msu.edu/cgi-bin/wa?A0=AEJMC.

Sullivan, Patricia. *Days of Hope: Race and Democracy in the New Deal Era.* Chapel Hill: University of North Carolina Press, 1996.

———. *Lift Every Voice: The NAACP and the Making of the Civil Rights Movement.* New York: New Press, 2009.

Taeuber, Karl E., and Alma F. Taeuber. *Negroes in Cities: Residential Segregation and Neighborhood Change.* Chicago: Aldine, 1965.

Talbot, Edith Armstrong. "Inter-Racial Co-Operation in South Commission's Aim." *Christian Science Monitor,* Aug. 1, 1922, 3.

Teel, Leonard Ray. *Ralph Emerson McGill: Voice of the Southern Conscience.* Knoxville: University of Tennessee Press, 2001.

Thomas, Jesse O. *My Story in Black and White.* New York: Exposition Press, 1967.

Thomas, Victor P. "Mr. B. T. Washington in Louisiana." *Crisis* 10 (July 1915): 144–46.

Thomas, William B. "Black Intellectuals' Critique of Early Mental Testing: A Little-Known Saga of the 1920s." *American Journal of Education* 90 (May 1982): 258–92.

———. "Howard W. Odum's Social Theories in Transition, 1910–1930." *American Sociologist* 16 (Feb. 1981): 25–34.

Thornbrough, Emma Lou. "Segregation in Indiana during the Klan Era of the 1920s." *Mississippi Valley Historical Review* 47 (March 1961): 594–618.

Thuesen, Sarah C. "The General Education Board and the Racial Leadership of Black Education in the South, 1920–1960." (2001). http://rockarch.org/publications/resrep/thuesen.pdf.

Tindall, George B. *The Emergence of the New South, 1913–1945.* Baton Rouge: Louisiana State University Press, 1967.

———. "Southern Negroes since Reconstruction: Dissolving the Static Image." In *Writing Southern History: Essays in Historiography in Honor of Fletcher M. Green,* ed. Arthur S. Link and Rembert W. Patrick, 337–61. Baton Rouge: Louisiana State University Press, 1965.

Tobin, William A. "Studying Society: The Making of *Recent Social Trends in the United States, 1929–1933.*" *Theory and Society* 24 (Aug. 1955): 537–65.

Tolnay, Stewart E., and E. M. Beck, "Racial Violence and Black Migration in the American South, 1910–1930." *American Sociological Review* 57 (Feb. 1992): 103–16.

———. *A Festival of Violence: An Analysis of Southern Lynchings, 1882–1930.* Urbana: University of Illinois Press, 1995.

Toppin, Edgar A. "Walter White and the Atlanta NAACP's Fight for Equal Schools, 1916–1917." *History of Education Quarterly* 7 (Spring 1967): 3–21.

Trawick, A. M. "The Good and Bad of Race Prejudice." *Methodist Quarterly Review* 74 (April 1925): 243–58.

Trotter, Joe W., and Earl Lewis, eds. *African Americans in the Industrial Age: A Documentary History, 1915–1945*. Boston: Northeastern University Press, 1996.

Turner, Stephen P. "Does Funding Produce Its Effects? The Rockefeller Case." In *The Development of the Social Sciences in the United States and Canada: The Role of Philanthropy*, ed. Donald Fisher and Theresa R. Richardson, 213–26. New York: Ablex, 1999.

Turner, W. S. "Has the Negro Arrived?" *Social Forces* 5 (March 1927): 479–82.

———. "The Negro and the Changing South." *Social Forces* 7 (Sept. 1928): 115–19.

Waldrep, Christopher, ed. *Lynching in America: A History in Documents*. New York: New York University Press, 2006.

———.*The Many Faces of Judge Lynch: Extralegal Violence and Punishment in America*. New York: Palgrave Macmillan, 2002.

Walton, Andrea, ed. *Women and Philanthropy in Education*. Bloomington: University of Indiana Press, 2005.

The War with Germany: A Statistical Summary. Compiled by Leonard P. Ayres. Washington, D.C.: U.S. Government Printing Office, 1919.

Ware, Edward T. "Higher Education of Negroes in the United States." *Annals of the American Academy of Political and Social Science* 49 (Sept. 1913): 209–18.

Warnock, Henry Y. "Andrew Sledd, Southern Methodists, and the Negro: A Case History." *Journal of Southern History* 31 (Aug. 1965): 251–71.

Washington, Booker T. *The Booker T. Washington Papers*. Ed. Louis R. Harlan and Raymond W. Smock. Vol. 8, 1904–1906; vol. 12, 1912–1914; vol. 13, 1914–1915. Urbana: University of Illinois Press, 1979–1984.

———. *My Larger Education: Being Chapters from My Experience*. Garden City, N.J.: Doubleday, Page, 1911.

———, ed. *Tuskegee and Its People: Their Ideals and Achievements*. New York: D. Appleton, 1905.

Washington, Delo E. "Education of Freedmen and the Role of Self-Help in a Sea Island Setting, 1862–1982." *Agricultural History* 58 (July 1984): 442–55.

Watkins, William H. *The White Architects of Black Education: Ideology, and Power in America, 1865–1954*. New York: Teachers College Press, 2001.

Weatherford, W. D. "The Amazing Progress of the Negro Race." *Methodist Quarterly Review* 62 (July 1913): 510–20.

———, ed. *Interracial Cooperation: A Study of the Various Agencies Working in the Field of Social Welfare*. Nashville: Interracial Committee of the War Work Council of the YMCA, ca. 1920.

———. *The Negro from Africa to America*. New York: George H. Doran, 1924.

———. *Negro Life in the South*. Nashville: YMCA Press, 1910.

———. *Present Forces in the Uplift of the Negro*. Nashville: YMCA Press, 1913.

Webster, David S. "The Bureau of Education's Suppressed Rating of Colleges, 1911–1912." *History of Education Quarterly* 24 (Winter 1984): 499–511.

Wells-Barnett, Ida B. *Lynch Law in Georgia*. Chicago: Chicago Colored Citizens, 1899.

Wheeler, Elizabeth L. "Isaac Fisher: The Frustrations of a Negro Educator at Branch Normal College, 1902–1911." *Arkansas Historical Quarterly* 41 (Spring 1982): 3–50.

White, Ronald C., Jr. *Liberty and Justice for All: Racial Reform and the Social Gospel (1877–1925).* San Francisco: Harper & Row, 1990.

White, Ronald C., Jr., and C. Howard Hopkins. *The Social Gospel: Religion and Reform in Changing America.* Philadelphia: Temple University Press, 1976.

White, Walter. "Solving America's Race Problem." *Nation* 128 (Jan. 9, 1929): 42–43.

——. "The Work of a Mob." *Crisis* 16 (Sept. 1918): 221–23.

Whiting, Theodore E., and T. J. Woofter, Jr. *Summary of Relief and Federal Work Program Statistics, 1933–1940.* Washington, D.C.: U.S. Government Printing Office, 1941.

Wiese, Andrew. "Blacks in the Suburban and Rural Fringe." In *Historical Roots of the Urban Crisis: African Americans in the Industrial City, 1900–1950,* ed. Henry Louis Taylor, Jr., and Walter Hill, 145–173. New York: Garland, 2000.

"William Taylor Burwell Williams." *Crisis* 41 (July 1934): 202.

Williams, Kidada E. *They Left Great Marks on Me: African American Testimonies of Racial Violence from Emancipation to World War I.* New York: New York University Press, 2012.

Williams, W. T. B. *Report on Negro Universities and Colleges.* [Baltimore?]: Trustees of the John F. Slater Fund, 1922.

——. *Report on Negro Universities in the South.* New Orleans: Tulane University Press, 1913.

——. "The South's Changing Attitude toward Negro Education." *Southern Workman* 54 (Sept. 1925): 398–400.

Williamson, Joel. *Crucible of Race: Black-White Relations in the American South since Emancipation.* New York: Oxford University Press, 1984.

——. *A Rage for Order: Black/White Relations in the American South since Emancipation.* New York: Oxford University Press, 1986.

Wilson, Francille Rusan. *The Segregated Scholars: Black Social Scientists and the Creation of Black Labor Studies, 1890–1950.* Charlottesville: University of Virginia Press, 2006.

Winston, Ellen. "Thomas Jackson Woofter, 1893–1972." *Footnotes* 1 (Jan. 1973): 6.

Wolff, Megan J. "The Myth of the Actuary: Life Insurance and Frederick L. Hoffman's *Race Traits and Tendencies of the American Negro.*" *Public Health Reports* 121 (Jan.–Feb. 2006): 84–91.

Wolters, Raymond. *Du Bois and His Rivals.* Columbia: University of Missouri Press, 2003.

Woodson, Carter G. Review of *Basis of Racial Adjustment. Social Forces* 4 (Dec. 1925): 442.

——. *A Century of Negro Migration.* Washington, D.C.: Association for the Study of Negro Life and History, 1918

——. *The Mis-Education of the Negro.* Washington, D.C.: Associated Publishers, 1933.

——. *The Negro in Our History.* Washington, D.C.: Associated Publishers, 1928; first pub. 1922.

——. Review of *Black Yeomanry: Life on St. Helena Island. Journal of Negro History* 16 (Jan. 1931): 95–96.

——. Review of *Negro Problems in Cities. Journal of Negro History* 13 (July 1928): 395–96.

——. "Thomas Jesse Jones." *Journal of Negro History* 35 (Jan. 1950): 107–109.

Woofter, Thomas Jackson, Jr. "Agencies for Inter-Racial Cooperation in the United States." In *The Christian Mission in the Light of Race Conflict: Report of the Jerusalem Meeting of the International Missionary Council, March 24th–April 8th, 1928* 4 (1928): 23–92.

————. *The Basis of Racial Adjustment*. New York: Ginn, 1925.

————. *Black Yeomanry: Life on St. Helena Island*. New York: Henry Holt, 1930.

————. "Children and Family Income." *Social Security Bulletin* 8 (Jan. 1945): 1–6.

————. "Children and Family Security." *Social Security Bulletin* 8 (March 1945): 5–10.

————. "Common Errors in Sampling." *Social Forces* 11 (May 1933): 521–25.

————. "Completed Generation Reproduction Rates." *Human Biology* 19 (Sept. 1947): 133–53.

————. "Difficulties in Measuring Racial Mental Traits." *Social Forces* 13 (March 1935): 415–18.

————. "Factors Sustaining the Birth Rate." *American Sociological Review* 14 (June 1949): 357–66.

————. "The Future Working Population." *Rural Sociology* 4 (Sept. 1939): 275–82.

————. "Georgia's Choice–Ignorance or Progress." *Home, School and Community*, (June 1925): 12–24. Reprinted in *Georgia's Educational Crisis*. Georgia Citizen's Education Movement, n.p., n.d.

————. "The Growing South." *Social Forces* 19 (March 1941): 346–51.

————. "Interpolation for Populations Whose Rate of Increase Is Declining." *Journal of the American Statistical Association* 27 (June 1932): 180–82.

————. "A Method of Analysis of Family Composition and Income." *Journal of the American Statistical Association* 39 (Dec. 1944): 488–96.

————. "Migration in the Southeast." *Demography* 4 (1967): 532–52.

————. "The Negro and Agricultural Policy, Parts A-B." Prepared for Carnegie-Myrdal Study of the Negro in America, 1940.

————. "The Negro and Industrial Peace." *Survey* 45 (Dec. 18, 1920): 420–21.

————. "The Negro and the Farm Crisis." *Social Forces* 6 (June 1928): 615–21.

————. "Negro Migration." *Missionary Voice* 11 (March 1921): 88.

————. *Negro Migration: Changes in Rural Organization and Population of the Cotton Belt*. New York: W. D. Gray, 1920.

————. "Negro Migration to Cities." *Survey* 59 (Feb. 15, 1928): 647–49.

————. "The Negro on a Strike." *Social Forces* 2 (Nov. 1923): 84–88.

————. *Negro Problems in Cities*. New York: Doubleday, Doran, 1928.

————. "The Negroes of Athens, Georgia." *Bulletin of the University of Georgia* 14, no. 4 (Dec. 1913).

————. *The Plight of Cigarette Tobacco*. Chapel Hill: University of North Carolina Press, 1931.

————. "Preliminary Population Estimates Based on Ration Book Applications." *Journal of the American Statistical Association* 37 (Dec. 1942): 437–40.

————. *Progress in Race Relations in Georgia: Report of the Secretary of the Georgia Committee on Race Relations for 1922*. Atlanta: Commission on Interracial Cooperation, 1922.

————. "Race in Politics: An Opportunity for Original Research." *Social Forces* 7 (March 1929): 435–38.

————. "Race Relations." *American Journal of Sociology* 36 (May 1931): 1039–44.

————. *Races and Ethnic Groups in American Life*. New York: McGraw-Hill, 1933.

————. "The Relation of the Net Reproduction Rate to Other Fertility Measures." *Journal of the American Statistical Association* 44 (Dec. 1949): 501–17.

————. Review of John Daniels, *In Freedom's Birthplace: A Study of Boston Negroes*. *Political Science Quarterly* 32 (Sept. 1917): 494–95.

———. "Rural Relief and the Back-to-the-Farm Movement." *Social Forces* 14 (March 1936): 382–88.

———. "Saving the Lives of Good Neighbors." *American Sociological Review* 12 (Aug. 1947): 420–23.

———. "Segregation–Voluntary and Involuntary." *Crisis,* 64 (March 1957): 133–38, 190.

———. "Size of Family in Relation to Family Income and Age of Family Head." *American Sociological Review* 9 (Dec. 1944): 678–84.

———. "Southern Backfires against Lynch Law." *Survey* 51 (Oct. 15, 1923): 99–100.

———. "Southern Children and Family Security." *Social Forces* 23 (March 1945): 366–75.

———. "Southern Population and Social Planning." *Social Forces* 14 (Oct. 1935): 16–22.

———. *Southern Population and Social Planning.* Chapel Hill: University of North Carolina Press, 1936.

———. *Southern Race Progress: The Wavering Color Line.* Washington, D.C.: Public Affairs Press, 1957.

———. "A Square Deal for Negroes at the American Rolling Mill Company's Plant in Middletown, Ohio." *Southern Workman* 50 (May 1921): 209–16.

———. "The Status of Racial and Ethnic Groups." In *Recent Social Trends in the United States,* vol. 1, ed. William F. Ogburn et al., 553–601. New York: McGraw-Hill, 1933.

———. "A Study of the Economic Status of the Negro." Prepared for Rosenwald Fund, 1930.

———. "The Subregions of the Southeast." *Social Forces* 13 (Oct. 1934): 43–50.

———. "The Teaching of Sociology in the South." *Social Forces* 4 (Sept. 1925): 71–72.

———. "The Tennessee Basin." *American Journal of Sociology* 39 (May 1934): 809–17.

———. "The Tennessee Valley Regional Plan." *Social Forces* 12 (March 1934): 329–38.

———. "Travel Also Broadens Social Issues." *Nation's Business,* April 29, 1941, 20–22, 114–17.

———. "Trends in Rural and Urban Fertility Rates." *Rural Sociology* 13 (March 1948): 3–9.

———. "What Is the Negro Rate of Increase?" *Journal of the American Statistical Association* 26 (Dec. 1931): 461–62.

———. "Will Defense End Unemployment?" *Harper's Magazine,* May 1941, 625–30.

Woofter, Thomas Jackson, Jr., and E. A. Fisher. *The Plantation South Today.* Washington, D.C.: U.S. Government Printing Office, 1940.

Woofter, Thomas Jackson, Jr., and Isaac Fisher, eds. *Cooperation in Southern Communities: Suggested Activities for County and City Inter-racial Committees.* Atlanta: Commission on Interracial Cooperation, 1921.

Woofter, Thomas Jackson, Jr., and Madge Headley Priest. *Negro Housing in Philadelphia.* Philadelphia: Philadelphia Housing Association, 1927.

Woofter, Thomas Jackson, Jr., and Oscar T. Richter. "El Porvenir de la Emigracion en los Estados Unidos de Nordamerica." *Revista Mexicana de Sociologia* 2 (3rd Qtr. 1940): 21–32.

Woofter, Thomas Jackson, Jr., and Edith Webb. "A Reclassification of Urban-Rural Population." *Social Forces* 11 (March 1933): 348–51.

Woofter, Thomas Jackson, Jr., and Theodore E. Whiting. "Households and Persons Receiving Relief or Assistance." *Journal of the American Statistical Association* 33 (June 1938): 363–72.

———. *Households and Persons Receiving Relief or Assistance.* New York: Joint Committee on Relief Statistics of the American Public Welfare Association and the American Statistical Association, 1938.

Woofter, Thomas Jackson, Jr., and Ellen Winston. *Seven Lean Years.* Chapel Hill: University of North Carolina Press, 1939.

Woofter, Thomas Jackson, Jr., et al. *Landlord and Tenant on the Cotton Plantation.* Washington, D.C.: WPA, Division of Social Research, 1936.

———. *The Plantation South, 1934–1937.* New York: Da Capo Press, 1971; first pub. 1940.

Woofter, Thomas Jackson, Sr. "Studies in Citizenship." *University of Georgia Bulletin* 23, no. 1 (1922).

———. *Teaching in Rural Schools.* Boston: Houghton Mifflin, 1917.

Work, Monroe N., ed. *The Negro Year Book: An Annual Encyclopedia of the Negro, 1931–1932.* Tuskegee, Ala.: Tuskegee Institute Press, 1931.

———. "The Race Problem in Cross Section: The Negro in 1923." *Journal of Social Forces* 2 (Jan. 1924): 245–52.

"Would the Dyer Bill Halt Lynching?" *Literary Digest* 73 (June 10, 1922): 14.

Woyshner, Christine. "'No Unfavorable Comments from Any Quarter': Teaching Black History to White Students in the American South, 1928–1943." *Teachers College Record* 114 (2012). http://www.tcreord.org.

Wright, Gavin. *Old South, New South: Revolutions in the Southern Economy since the Civil War.* New York: Basic Books, 1986.

Wright, George C. *Life behind a Veil: Blacks in Louisville, Kentucky, 1865–1930.* Baton Rouge: Louisiana State University Press, 1985.

Wynes, Charles E., ed. *Forgotten Voices: Dissenting Southerners in an Age of Conformity.* Baton Rouge: Louisiana State University Press, 1967.

Yellin, Eric S. "The (White) Search for (Black) Order: The Phelps-Stokes Fund's First Twenty Years, 1911–1931." *Historian* 65 (Jan. 2002): 319–52.

Young, Donald. "Foreword." *Annals of the American Academy of Political and Social Science* 140 (Nov. 1928): vii–viii.

Young, P. B. "Contribution of the Press in the Adjustment of Race Relations." *Southern Workman* 57 (April 1928): 147–54.

Zangrando, Robert L. *The NAACP Crusade against Lynching, 1909–1950.* Philadelphia: Temple University Press, 1980.

Index

Abbott, Grace, 223

Addams, Jane, 223

Adjutant General's Office (AGO), 66–67

African Americans: and education, 10, 31–33, 34–35, 37–61, 77–79, 154–55, 184–86; and migration, 63–66, 68–72, 81, 115, 122, 130, 133, 138, 144; and segregation, 6, 8, 10, 20, 52, 57, 64, 83, 101, 102, 105, 128, 131, 147–49, 155, 164–65, 170, 172, 176–77, 185–86, 217, 225, 260n61, 274n32 (*see also* Commission on Interracial Cooperation (CIC); interracial cooperation movement); and taxation, 9–10, 28, 32, 52, 74, 106–107, 120, 154, 163, 188, 209, 212, 215–18; and violence (*see* lynching)

African Methodist Episcopal Zion (A.M.E.Z.) Church, 131, 174

Alderman, Edwin A., 21, 153, 239

Alexander, Hooper, 120, 122

Alexander, Will W., 2, 5, 9, 11, 18, 79, 117, 123, 126, 168, 241, 246n18, 264n28, 271n81, 272n1, 277n9, 286n19; and antilynching legislation, 112, 127; and CIC, 80–112, 136, 140, 143–46, 153, 193, 197, 230; and "Encyclopedia of the Negro," 228; and first National Interracial Conference, 174–79; on Foreman, 180; on Frazier, 171–72, 178–79; historians on, 13–15; and International Missionary Council, 190, 233; on interracial cooperation, 233; and Jack Woofter's career, 197, 199–200, 202–204, 208, 236, 238; and New Deal agencies, 235; Ovington on, 271n81; on radicalism, 88; on research on race, 153–57, 179–80, 181, 237, 273n3; and second National Interracial Conference, 222–23; on segregation, 148, 150, 232; on shortcomings of white ministers, 193; and Social Science Research Council, 181; on southern sheriffs, 193–94; younger liberals on, 236

Allied Supreme War Council, 67

American Association for the Advancement of Science, 43

American Expeditionary Force (AEF), 66–67

American Federation of Labor, 226, 282n92

American Missionary Association, 10, 75

American School, Chicago, 17

American University, D.C., 62

Ames, Jessie Daniel, 2, 117, 235, 242, 286n19

Anderson, Mary, 223

Anna T. Jeanes Foundation, 21, 23, 31, 32, 33, 64, 75, 84, 164

Armstrong, Samuel Chapman, 36

Arthur, George R.: and YMCA, 224

Associated Negro Press, 174

Association for the Study of Negro Life and History (ASNLH), 55, 198, 224

Association of Negro Industrial and Secondary Schools (ANISS), 46–48

Association of Southern Women for the Prevention of Lynching, 117, 242

Athens, Ga., 17, 31, 44, 66, 68, 74, 120, 131; black education in, 45; Jack Woofter's study of black life in, 23–27, 38, 40, 41, 44, 64, 71, 74, 180; lynchings near, 114, 120, 180; Woofter's own life in, 18–21, 113–15, 165–66

Athens Banner-Herald, 201

Athens Colored High School, 45

Athens Woman's Club, 18

Atkins, Charlie, lynching of, 128, 265n53

Atlanta Constitution, 30, 86, 122, 167, 201; on Dorsey, 122; on Ethel Woofter, 198–99; on Jack Woofter, 73, 167; and interracial cooperation, 136; on lynching, 123, 125–27, 130, 264n43

Atlanta Plan of Inter-Racial Cooperation, 92

Atlanta School of Social Work, 171, 177, 272n96, 272n2

Atlanta University, 7, 23, 41, 134, 254n56

Aycock, Charles B., 239

Ayres, Leonard Porter, 66–67, 77, 255n13

Bailey, Thomas Pearce, 21

Baldwin, William H., Jr., 31, 32

Ballanta, N. G. J., 279n42

Baltimore Afro-American: on Jack Woofter, 167, 217; on lynching, 123; on "Woofterism," 226

Barrow, David Crenshaw, 2, 19, 23, 31; and *Cooperation in Southern Communities,* 107; on Jack Woofter, 23; and *Negroes of Athens, Georgia,* 249n32

Barrow County, Ga., 139, 144

317

MARK ELLIS is senior lecturer in history at the University of Strathclyde, Glasgow, Scotland, and author of *Race, War, and Surveillance: African Americans and the United States Government during World War I* (IUP, 2001).